# THE PUBLIC SCHOOLS

# THE
# PUBLIC
# SCHOOLS

*Susan Fuhrman*

*Marvin Lazerson*

EDITORS

**OXFORD**
UNIVERSITY PRESS

# OXFORD

UNIVERSITY PRESS

Oxford University Press, Inc., publishes works that further
Oxford University's objective of excellence
in research, scholarship, and education.

Oxford   New York
Auckland   Cape Town   Dar es Salaam   Hong Kong   Karachi
Kuala Lumpur   Madrid   Melbourne   Mexico City   Nairobi
New Delhi   Shanghai   Taipei   Toronto
With offices in
Argentina   Austria   Brazil   Chile   Czech Republic   France   Greece
Guatemala   Hungary   Italy   Japan   Poland   Portugal   Singapore
South Korea   Switzerland   Thailand   Turkey   Ukraine   Vietnam

Copyright © 2005 by Oxford University Press, Inc.

Published by Oxford University Press, Inc.
198 Madison Avenue, New York, New York, 10016
http://www.oup.com/us

Oxford is a registered trademark of Oxford University Press

Library of Congress Cataloging-in-Publication Data
The public schools / Susan Fuhrman, Marvin Lazerson, editors
p. cm. — (Institutions of American democracy series)
ISBN-13: 978-0-19-517030-6 (alk. paper)
ISBN-10: 0-19-517030-X (alk. paper)
1. Public schools—Social aspects—United States.   2. Democracy—United States.
I. Furhman, Susan.   II. Lazerson, Marvin.   III. Series.
LC191.4.P83   2005
371.01′0973—dc22        2004029862

Book design by Joan Greenfield
Copyedited by Melissa A. Dobson

Printed in the United States of America
on acid-free paper

# CONTENTS

## SECTION III:
## CITIZEN PARTICIPATION AND CIVIC ENGAGEMENT

## SECTION IV:
## VISIONS AND POSSIBILITIES

# DIRECTORY OF CONTRIBUTORS

Susan Fuhrman (Editor) [Introduction]

*George and Diane Weiss Professor of Education, University of Pennsylvania;*
*Dean, Graduate School of Education, University of Pennsylvania;*
*Founder and Director, Consortium for Policy Research in Education*

Dr. Fuhrman is the coeditor of the recent book, *Redesigning Accountability Systems for Education*. Dr. Fuhrman is a counselor to the Shanghai Municipal Education Commission, a former officer of the American Educational Research Association, and a member of the Board of Trustees of the Carnegie Foundation for the Advancement of Teaching and the Fund for New Jersey. She has published widely and serves on the editorial boards of *Educational Evaluation and Policy Analysis* and *Education Policy*.

Marvin Lazerson (Editor) [Introduction]

*Howard P. and Judith R. Berkowitz Professor of Education, Graduate School of Education,*
*University of Pennsylvania*

Dr. Lazerson is a distinguished historian and a recipient of the Spencer Foundation Mentoring Award. His numerous publications include articles in *The Chronicle of Higher Education* and *The Annals of the American Academy of Political and Social Science*. His most recent book, coauthored with W. Norton Grubb, is *The Education Gospel: The Economic Power of Schooling*, published by Harvard University Press.

Thomas Corcoran [The Governance of Public Education]

*Co-Director and Senior Investigator, Consortium for Policy Research in Education*

Mr. Corcoran is the principal investigator of the evaluation of the America's Choice secondary school design and an analyst of state teacher policy for Carnegie Corporation of New York. He has been a consultant to school districts, foundations, and other organizations concerned with public education issues. He is a member of the MacArthur Foundation's network on at-risk children, the National Research Council's Committee on Inquiry in Science Education, the Annenberg Institute's district task force, and the Research Committee of the International Baccalaureate Organization. Mr. Corcoran has authored and coauthored publications on working conditions in schools, instructional support systems, professional development, and the use of evidence in decision-making.

## Paul R. Dimond [SCHOOL CHOICE AND THE DEMOCRATICE IDEAL OF FREE COMMON SCHOOLS]

*Senior Counsel, Miller, Canfield, Paddock, and Stone, P.L.C.*

Paul Dimond, a lawyer in private practice, serves as board chair, trustee, or adviser for numerous corporations, foundations, and public charities, several public charter schools, and the Michigan Governor's Council of Economic Advisers. A graduate of Amherst College and the University of Michigan Law School, he is the author of several books, including *Beyond Busing*, which describes the major Supreme Court race cases of the 1970's and was honored by the American Political Science with its Ralph J. Bunche book of the year in 1986.

## Richard F. Elmore [AGENCY, RECIPROCITY, AND ACCOUNTABILITY IN DEMOCRATIC EDUCATION]

*Gregory R. Anrig Professor of Educational Leadership, Graduate School of Education, Harvard University*

Dr. Elmore's publications include *Restructuring in the Classroom: Teaching, Learning, and School Organization* and *Who Chooses, Who Loses? Culture, Institutions, and the Unequal Effects of School Choice*. His most recent book, *School Reform from the Inside Out: Policy, Practice, and Performance* was published by Harvard Education Press. He is a senior research fellow with the Consortium for Policy Research in Education and teaches regularly in programs for public sector executives. Dr. Elmore has served in positions with the Department of Health, Education, and Welfare, the U.S. Office of Education, and other government advisory positions at the city, state, and national levels.

## Bruce Fuller [SCHOOLING CITIZENS FOR EVOLVING DEMOCRACIES]

*Professor of Education and Public Policy, Graduate School of Education, University of California, Berkeley*

Trained in political sociology, Dr. Fuller worked for a state legislature, governor, and the World Bank before returning to the university. His books include *Inside Charter Schools: The Paradox of Radical Decentralization*, *Government Confronts Culture*, and *Through My Own Eyes: Single Mothers and the Cultures of Poverty*. Dr. Fuller codirects Policy Analysis for California Education.

## William A. Galston [THE POLITICS OF POLARIZATION: EDUCATION DEBATES IN THE UNITED STATES]

*Saul I. Stern Professor of Civic Engagement, School of Public Policy, University of Maryland;*
*Interim Dean, School of Public Policy, University of Maryland;*
*Director, Institute for Philosophy and Public Policy, University of Maryland;*
*Director, Center for Information and Research on Civic Learning and Engagement*

Dr. Galston is a founding member of the National Campaign to Prevent Teen Pregnancy and serves as chair of the Campaign's Task Force on Religion and Public Values. Dr.

Galston served as deputy assistant to the president for domestic policy during the first Clinton Administration, as director of economic and social programs at the Roosevelt Center for American Policy Studies, as a senior adviser to Albert Gore during his campaigns for the presidency in 1988 and 2000, and as executive director of the National Commission on Civic Renewal. Dr. Galston's books include *Liberal Purposes, Liberal Pluralism*, and most recently, *The Practice of Liberal Pluralism*.

Margaret Goertz [THE GOVERNANCE OF PUBLIC EDUCATION]
*Professor of Education, Graduate School of Education University of Pennsylvania;*
*Co-Director, Consortium for Policy Research in Education*

Dr. Goertz's writings have been published by the Council for Basic Education and in the National Society for the Study of Education yearbook. She is past president of the American Education Finance Association and was a member of the Advisory Council on Education Statistics of the U.S. Department of Education. Dr. Goertz co-edited *Education Politics for the New Century: The Twentieth Anniversary Yearbook of the Politics of Education Association* and recently contributed to *From the Capitol to the Classroom: Standards-Based Reform in the States* and *Redesigning Accountability Systems for Education.*

Amy Gutmann [AFTERWORD: DEMOCRATIC DISAGREEMENT AND CIVIC EDUCATION]
*President, University of Pennsylvania; Founding Director, University Center for Human Values,*
*Princeton University*

Amy Gutmann is President of the University of Pennsylvania, where she is Professor of Politics with secondary appointments in the Department of Philosophy, the Annenberg School of Communication, and the Graduate School of Education. She is also Laurance S. Rockefeller University Professor Emeritus of Princeton University where she was provost, dean of the faculty, and founding director of the University Center of Human Values. Her books include *Identity in Democracy; Democratic Education; Color Conscious:The Political Morality of Race* (coauthored with K. Anthony Appiah); and *Democracy and Disagreement*, and *Why Deliberative Democracy?* (both coauthored with Dennis Thompson). She has published over 100 articles and essays in democratic theory, education, and the ethics of public life. In 2003, Gutmann was awarded Harvard University's Centennial Medal for "graduate alumni who have made exceptional contributions to society." She has been elected a fellow of the American Academy of Arts and Sciences, a fellow of the National Academy of Education, and a W. E. B. Du Bois Fellow of the American Academy of Political and Social Science.

Matthew Hartley [THE ELUSIVE IDEAL: CIVIC LEARNING AND HIGHER EDUCATION]
*Assistant Professor of Education, Graduate School of Education, University of Pennsylvania*

Dr. Hartley studies organizational change at colleges and universities. A book based on his dissertation research, *A Call To Purpose:Mission-Centered Change at Three Liberal Arts Colleges*, was published in 2002. Dr. Hartley's recent work examines the institutionalization of civic engagement efforts and he has coauthored book chapters with Ira Harkavy and Lee Benson in the forthcoming edited volumes, *Higher Education for the Public Good: Emerging Voices from a National Movement and Looking In, Teaching Out: Critical Issues and Directions in Service-Learning.*

Jennifer Hochschild [Demographic Change and Democractic Education]

*Henry LaBarre Jayne Professor of Government and Professor of African-American Studies,*
*Harvard University*

Dr. Hochschild's books include *Facing Up to the American Dream: Race, Class, and the Soul of the Nation* (Princeton University Press), *The New American Dilemma: Liberal Democracy and School Desegregation* (Yale University Press), and *What's Fair? American Beliefs about Distributive Justice* (Harvard University Press). She is a fellow of the American Academy of Arts and Sciences and founding editor of *Perspectives on Politics*. Dr. Hochschild has also been a fellow at the Center for Advanced Study in the Behavioral Sciences and vice president of the American Political Science Association. In addition, she has served as a consultant or expert witness in several school desegregation cases. Dr. Hochschild's most recent book, coauthored with Nathan Scovronick, is *The American Dream and the Public Schools* published by Oxford University Press.

Elizabeth L. Hollander [The Elusive Ideal: Civic Learning and Higher Education]

*Executive Director, Campus Compact*

Ms. Hollander directs an organization serving over 900 college and university presidents and their faculty and staff in their efforts to educate the next generation of active citizens. She is a fellow of the National Academy of Public Administration and serves on the board of the National Civic League and a number of advisory boards including the *Journal of College and Character*, and the Center for Information and Research on Civic Learning and Engagement at the University of Maryland. Ms. Hollander is past president of the Government Assistance Program in Illinois and past director of planning for the city of Chicago.

Michael C. Johanek [The State of Civic Education: Preparing Citizens in an Era of Accountability]

*Executive Director for K-12 Professional Development, The College Board*

Dr. Johanek manages programs supporting over 300,000 high school teachers, college faculty, coordinators, and administrators. A former high school teacher, his publications include *A Faithful Mirror: Reflections on the College Board and Education in America* (ed.); "Accounting for Citizenship" (with John Puckett); "Race, Gender and Ethnicity in the United States History Survey"; "Private Citizenship and School Choice"; "The Evolution of College Entrance Examinations" (with Donald Stewart); and "School-College Connections: Deweyan Waste, Limited Pipelines, and Intellectual Vitality" (with Donald Stewart). Dr. Johanek is coauthoring a book on the history of community-centered schooling, and occasionally teaches adjunct in the History of Education Program, New York University. He serves as Co-PI and advisor in several NSF-funded professional development research projects, on the National Education Advisory Board for the French & Indian War 250th, and on the OAH-Advanced Placement Joint Advisory Board on Teaching the U.S. History Survey. He recently served on the Alumni Council at Teachers College, Columbia University, and on the Board of Trustees of *The Concord Review*.

Susan Moore Johnson [Working in Schools]

*Carl H. Pforzheimer, Jr. Professor of Teaching and Learning, Graduate School of Education,*
*Harvard University*

A former high school teacher and administrator, Dr. Johnson studies teacher policy, school organization, and educational leadership. She directs The Project on the Next

Generation of Teachers, a multiyear research study examining how best to recruit, support, and retain a strong teaching force in the next decade. Dr. Johnson's publications include *Teachers at Work: Achieving Success in Our Schools, Teachers Unions in Schools*, and *Finders and Keepers: Helping New Teachers Survive and Thrive in Our Schools.* She is past academic dean of the Harvard Graduate School of Education and a member of the Board of Directors of the National Academy of Education.

## John Merrow [YOUTH, MEDIA, AND CITIZENSHIP]

*Host and Executive Producer, "The Merrow Report";*
*President, Learning Matters Incorporated*

Dr. Merrow reports on education for "The NewsHour" with Jim Lehrer. His most recent documentary for PBS, "Degrees of Mediocrity," examined the state of American higher education. He coedited a companion book of essays titled, *Degrees of Mediocrity*, which was published in June 2005. Earlier in his career, he produced and hosted the NPR radio documentaries "Options in Education" and the PBS series "Your Children, Our Children." Dr. Merrow has also been education correspondent for the "The MacNeil/Lehrer NewsHour," a columnist for *Children*, and a commentator on several NPR shows including "All Things Considered." Dr. Merrow, the author of *Choosing Excellence*, received the George Foster Peabody Award in 2001.

## John Puckett [THE STATE OF CIVIC EDUCATION: PREPARING CITIZENS IN AN ERA OF ACCOUNTABILITY]

*Associate Professor, Graduate School of Education, University of Pennsylvania;*
*Associate Dean, Graduate School of Education, University of Pennsylvania*

John Puckett is Associate Professor at the University of Pennsylvania Graduate School of Education. He is the author of *Foxfire Reconsidered: A Twenty-Year Experiment in Progressive Education.* Dr. Puckett has been a National Academy of Education/Spencer Foundation Postdoctoral Fellow and a Fulbright Scholar to Germany. His research interests include American education reform, urban community schools, and university-community relations. He is currently coauthoring a book on the history of America's community schools.

## Wendy D. Puriefoy [THE EDUCATION OF DEMOCRATIC CITIZENS: CITIZEN MOBILIZATION AND PUBLIC EDUCATION]

*President, Public Education Network (PEN)*

Ms. Puriefoy, former executive vice president and chief operating officer of The Boston Foundation—one of the nation's largest, most influential community foundations—is a nationally recognized expert on issues of school reform and civil society. She has been a leading force for systemic reform in school finance and governance, curriculum and assessment, parental involvement, school libraries, and school health services. Under her leadership, PEN has grown into a national network of local education funds reaching 11.5 million children nationwide.

## Arun Rasiah [SCHOOLING CITIZENS FOR EVOLVING DEMOCRACIES]

Arun Rasiah is a doctoral candidate in education at the University of California, Berkeley. His dissertation examines Islamic education and literacy learning in Muslim communities of the United States.

Julie A. Reuben [PATRIOTIC PURPOSES: PUBLIC SCHOOLS AND THE EDUCATION OF CITIZENS]

*Professor of Education, Graduate School of Education, Harvard University*

Julie A. Reuben is a professor at the Harvard Graduate School of Education. She is the author of *The Making of the Modern University: Intellectual Transformation and the Marginalization of Morality* (1996). She has written several articles on campus activism and its impact on higher education and is currently writing a book entitled *Campus Unrest: Politics and American Higher Education in the 1960s.*

Nathan Scovronick [DEMOGRAPHIC CHANGE AND DEMOCRATIC EDUCATION]

*Director, Undergraduate Program, Woodrow Wilson School of Public and International Affairs, Princeton University*

In addition to directing the Undergraduate Program, Dr. Scovronick teaches courses in education policy, as well as in management and leadership, at the Woodrow Wilson School. He has served as Executive Director of the Treasury Department of the State of New Jersey and has held several policy positions with the New Jersey Legislature, including its education committees. Among his publications is *The American Dream and the Public Schools*, which he coauthored with Jennifer Hochschild.

Katherine Simon [CLASSROOM DELIBERATIONS]

*Co-Executive Director, Coalition of Essential Schools (CES)*

A former high school English and drama teacher, Dr. Simon has taught novice teachers in the Stanford University Teacher Education Program, and now leads CES, a national school-reform organization. She is the author of Moral Questions in the Classroom: How to Get Kids to Think Deeply About Real Life and Their School Work, which won the AERA award for outstanding book in curriculum for 2001-2002. She is co-author of Teaching as Inquiry: Asking Hard Questions to Improve Practice and Student Achievement, Teachers College Press (2004).

Clarence N. Stone [CIVIC CAPACITY: WHAT, WHY, AND FROM WHENCE]

*Research Professor, Public Policy and Political Science, George Washington University;*
*Professor Emeritus, Department of Government and Politics, University of Maryland, College Park*

Dr. Stone has authored and edited numerous books, including *Changing Urban Education*. His most recent book is the coauthored volume, *Building Civic Capacity: The Politics of Reforming Urban Schools*, winner of the best book award of the Urban Politics Section of the American Political Science Association. Dr. Stone has a continuing interest in the politics of social reform.

# GENERAL INTRODUCTION:

## THE PUBLIC SCHOOLS AS AN INSTITUTION
## OF AMERICAN CONSTITUTIONAL DEMOCRACY

*Jaroslav Pelikan*

T HERE IS NO REFERENCE TO SCHOOLS IN THE CONSTITU-
tion of the United States, and yet education has made possible both its
original composition and its ongoing implementation. The absence of
explicit language about schools, in the original document as well as in any of its
amendments (so far, at least), has not prevented education from becoming, over
the years, both a major constitutional issue in its own right and the primary
occasion for democratic debate over and judicial interpretation of the
Constitution's provisions, and for legislative action at the local, state, and federal
levels. Two of the most persistent and intractable problems in American society,
and therefore in the application of the Constitution to its changing realities, are
(to put them in their constitutional context): the tension between the establishment clause and the free exercise clause of the First Amendment of the Bill of
Rights as this amendment defines the relation between government and organized religion; and the guarantee of the right to vote and of equal protection
under the law for all citizens regardless of "race, color, or previous condition of
servitude" as this is set down in the Fourteenth and Fifteenth Amendments.

Balancing the requirement that "Congress shall make no law respecting an
establishment of religion" against the no-less-binding stipulation "or prohibiting
the free exercise thereof" has proved to be a difficult assignment in many areas of
political life. The employment of clergy as chaplains in the armed forces—wearing military uniforms, carrying military rank, and receiving a salary from the federal government—has seemed to many to privilege the free exercise clause at the
expense of the establishment clause. Governmental restriction on the distribution of religious tracts, whether, under the First Amendment, it is seen as pertain-
ing to the freedom of the press or to the freedom of religion,[1] can be construed

as honoring the establishment clause at the risk of jeopardizing the free exercise clause. But in both legislation and litigation, the most bitterly contested venue for disputes about what is commonly, if rather loosely, identified as "the separation of church and state" has been the schools. When champions of public education as the primary democratic institution for the Americanization of immigrants sought to limit parochial schools as a danger to the creation of a unified social ethos, the Supreme Court affirmed the authority of the family, not the state, with respect to the education of children.[2] The permissibility of providing publicly supported buses to transport children to parochial schools as well as public schools was the provocation for one of the most important Supreme Court decisions about the establishment clause.[3] And when supporters of schools as shapers of moral character required the reading of the Bible as part of the school day, the Court declared that such reading, "even without comment, possesses a devotional and religious character and constitutes in effect a religious observance" and forbade it.[4] Controversy over the recitation of the pledge of allegiance in the classroom has concentrated on the relatively recent (1954) addition of the words "under God" to the phrase "one nation indivisible," as a violation of the civil rights of any schoolchildren who may not share the theistic assumption being affirmed by those two words.

Similarly, the ever so gradual implementation of the three amendments that were enacted after the Civil War to root out the vestiges of slavery has been a program on many fronts. Application of the antidiscriminatory provisions not only to elections but to primaries, especially where these have been tantamount to election, has tested the authority of the Fourteenth and Fifteenth Amendments.[5] Equality of access to employment, and equity in compensation for employment, continues to be a major assignment for the courts and governmental agencies.[6] But the most dramatic—and arguably the most momentous—cases advancing the cause of civil rights have been those dealing with the schools. The well intentioned and superficially attractive formula of "separate but equal" as applied to school segregation turned out to be—if not juridically and politically, then educationally—the ultimate oxymoron.[7] The most important legal step forward in civil rights since the Emancipation Proclamation and the Fourteenth Amendment, whose fiftieth anniversary coincided with the preparation of this volume, dealt not with jobs or with the ballot box (vital though both of these undoubtedly were and remain), but with the schools.[8]

The applications of the fundamental principles of American constitutional democracy to the schools have all been assertions of the power of the federal judiciary over educational laws and institutions at the state and local level. For until the separation of the Department of Education from the Department of Health, Education, and Welfare in 1979 there was a bipartisan consensus that the role of the federal government in education was a highly limited one; and even after such visible enhancements of that role, the consensus still dominates educational philosophy and policy, as is made evident in Thomas Corcoran and Margaret Goertz's contribution to this volume, "The Governance of Public Education." It would be a mistake, and one which the language of the debates over the politics of public education in the national media could easily lead an unsuspecting reader to make, to conclude from the involvement of the Supreme Court, the Congress, and the executive branch that the center of gravity in public education, as in many other aspects of American national life such as taxes, has gradually shifted from the state and local levels to the federal and national level. Rather, "where the rubber meets the road," as the colloquial expression puts it with characteristic pungency and relevance, the mysterious process between child and teacher remains a prime documentation of the frequently quoted maxim of the former House Speaker Thomas P. ("Tip") O'Neill that "all politics is local"—and, one could add, so is public education.

That maxim is a pithy summary of what has long been a defining characteristic of American democracy, as its prime observer and interpreter, Alexis de Tocqueville, pointed out when he stated: "There is nothing centralized or hierarchic in the constitution of American administrative power." Coincidentally, though anything but incidentally, Tocqueville likewise observed, as part of his inquiry into the exceptionalism of American democracy: "It is the provisions for public education which, from the very first, throw into the clearest relief the originality of American civilization."[9] In America, he noted, the very concept of a "peasant" was unknown, at least partly because of these "provisions for public education." When Tocqueville published his first volume, in 1835, the worldwide dominance of American higher education, on which such astute observers as Derek Bok and the late Ernest Boyer have commented, still lay a century or more away in the distant future, so that he was right in observing that "primary education is within reach of all; higher education is hardly available to anybody"; and his necessarily brief excursus on "Education of Girls in the United States"[10] identified an agenda item for the twentieth and even the twenty-first century. But in the succession of continuing efforts by scholars, thinkers, and politicians to define American exceptionalism, and to identify "the originality of American civilization," from "the frontier thesis" of Frederick Jackson Turner to "the city on a hill" of Ronald Reagan, Tocqueville's "provisions for public education" do indeed still "throw it into the highest relief." For example, a close reading will show that Goethe's celebrated apostrophe of 1827, beginning "Amerika, du hast es besser / Als unser Kontinent, das alte," ("America, it is better for you than it is for our old continent") is primarily a celebration of American education for its freedom from the superstition and dead traditionalism of Europe, and therefore for the opportunity it provides to its children to exercise their literary and artistic imagination without hindrance.[11]

A measure of the centrality of education in democratic America is the frequency with which it has become not only a theme but a controlling metaphor.

Thus one of the seminal autobiographies in American literature, linking the world of the founders and framers through one of their scions with the emerging (and bewildering) new world of pluralism and diversity, is *The Education of Henry Adams,* originally published in 1918. The author's schooling, with its strengths and weaknesses, serves almost as a parable for nineteenth-century American society, especially when this text is put alongside Adams's other classic work, *Mont-Saint-Michel and Chartres* (1904), in which the figure of the Virgin Mary appears as the symbol for a thirteenth century in which pluralism and diversity were held under control by a unifying vision.[12] This use of education and school to characterize an entire culture cannot but remind us of ancient Greece. Werner Jaeger has defined "the unique position of Hellenism in the history of education" by the term *paideia,* which is, both in etymological derivation and in content, closely related to the English word *pedagogy,* and means education or culture or civilization or worldview (or all of the above); therefore "the German word Bildung clearly indicates the essence of education in the Greek, the Platonic sense."[13] One of the heroes of Jaeger's three-volume *Paideia* is Pericles, who in his most famous oration—in which an American reader is bound to hear anticipations of Abraham Lincoln's Gettysburg Address[14]—celebrated what must by analogy be seen as the quest for the exceptionalism of Athenian democracy when he called Athens "the school of Hellas."[15] Therefore Donald Kagan has rightly devoted an entire chapter of his life of Pericles to his standing as educator, specifically to the design and layout of the Parthenon as a teaching force.[16]

There is good reason for us to link the founders and framers of American constitutional democracy with education and the schools. One by one, the biographies of each of them trace the ways in which their early schooling and the continuing education that came out of it shaped the democratic ideals and institutions for which their memory is still cherished, and it was as true for them that democracy served education as that education served democracy. So central were research and teaching and "the erudition of the world" that Thomas Jefferson could even exalt them above "the commonplace drudgery of governing a single state, a work which may be executed by men of an ordinary stature, such as are always and every where to be found."[17] For in a real sense constitutional democracy depends on the process described by John Puckett and Michael Johanek in this volume as "civic education," because it is in the schools that the capacity to participate meaningfully and critically in the democratic process is communicated. Democracy is distinguished from demagogy by a responsible use of thought and language and the ability to state the case for an idea—and, conversely, on the ability to recognize when these are being perverted. Those correlative abilities, however, are not innate, but require training and cultivation. Similarly, the "civic capacity" of which Clarence Stone speaks herein requires analytical skills and continuing reflection, which presuppose an understanding of "education" that is not confined to the schoolroom or to the schooling years, but is marked by a lifelong habitude or mindset.

Ultimately, then, the schools can be an institution of democracy only if they define themselves also in moral terms. The realities of cultural and religious pluralism as reflected in the demographics of American elementary and secondary schools in the twenty-first century—a cluster of topics tellingly set forth here by Jennifer Hochschild and Nathan Scovronick—represent a challenge not only politically, but philosophically. As the often fatuous contemporary public discussion of "values" demonstrates, and as all the hot-button issues of contemporary public discourse prove, in what Laurence H. Tribe has called "the clash of absolutes,"[18] there is no philosophical and political need more urgent than finding a way to ground moral beliefs (whatever their metaphysical presuppositions may be for one or another individual person or community of faith) in a shared concern and a mutual respect. When the population of the nation or of a single community, of an entire school or of a single class, includes not only believers of many kinds but also nonbelievers of many kinds, is it possible to define moral imperatives that do not depend on the authority of any alleged divine revelation but are valid in and of themselves, "within the limits of reason alone," as Immanuel Kant posed the question? Significantly, the most ambitious philosophical effort to answer this question for the mission of American education came, whatever one's judgment of its metaphysics or its pedagogics may be, from John Dewey, who had initially defined his philosophical position via a dissertation on Kant, and who entitled his philosophical consideration of the question *A Common Faith* (1934). Here he sought to find a modern equivalent of what the framers and founders of American constitutional democracy had meant by "natural law."[19]

The founders and framers of American constitutional democracy also embody one of the central paradoxes (or mysteries) of schools as an institution of American democracy: that a system of education explicitly committed to the common education of the many has nevertheless had the capacity to raise up in each generation those relatively few who have demonstrated the capacity of leadership. The French lycée, the English "public school," and the German gymnasium have traditionally been elitist institutions where the future leaders of the nation were prepared: the saying attributed to the Duke of Wellington, that "the battle of Waterloo was won on the playing fields of Eton," could, without difficulty and with only a slight change of names, apply to schools in France and Germany. The ideal of the "public school" system of the United States—regardless of what the reality may be at one or another time or place—has held that in a democratic society, as distinguished from an aristocratic or oligarchic one, the best way to raise up a leadership cadre in each generational cohort is to begin with the shared experience and the shared curriculum of the institution that we used to call "the common school." Often unremarked upon in that ideal were the obstacles that the system often placed in the path of the gifted and talented, as well as the recognition that as leadership in many fields of endeavor has become increasingly specialized, it is increasingly not the primary or the secondary school but the later stages of education—not even the college but the graduate and the professional school—that prepare the gifted and talented for their eventual leadership roles.

For as John Dewey constantly pointed out in his writings about education, most effectively in the classic *School and Society* (1899), it is precisely the concrete participation in the schoolroom community that is the training ground of democracy, and therefore of leadership in a democracy as well. Not only is character shaped by the dynamics of this interaction; but both the image of the self and the understanding of how a society functions come out of the give-and-take and the compromise that neither family nor church nor neighborhood can provide as lavishly as does the American classroom, with its Tower of Babel of many voices, languages, cultures, and belief systems. For the classroom is, on the one hand, not democratic but hierarchical: "A ship is not a parliament," the sailors of the old British Navy used to say, and not everything can be put to a vote. But on the other hand, when the atmosphere it fosters is a healthy one, the school is a democratizing institution. Being one book in a five-volume set bearing the title *Institutions of American Democracy,* therefore, this text deals with the public schools as one of those institutions, and documents how indispensable they are to the successful achievement of true democracy. Yet in a special way, much of the material in this volume could conceivably appear in one or another of the other four, because the topic of each one bears a particular relation to the educational enterprise.

When Article 1, Section 8 of the Constitution sets out in detail the many areas of national life over which "the Congress shall have Power," including the power "to promote the Progress of Science and useful Arts" and "to make all Laws which shall be necessary and proper," this seems to imply that the members of the Congress ought to meet not only the minimum requirements of age set forth in Section 2 for the House of Representatives and in Section 3 for the Senate, but a minimum requirement of knowledge and competence, if not of formal education. The range of those powers, moreover, suggests that it would be best if the educational and professional preparation of the members covered all of the various areas of national life specified in Sections 7 and 8, with no single educational background predominating, not even the study of the law. The evolution of the committee system in the two houses of Congress, and perhaps above all the increasing professionalization and specialization of congressional staffs, would seem to imply that the schools of the several states at all levels must take responsibility for shaping a cohort in each succeeding generation to whom such great responsibilities can be entrusted.

The list of the powers of the president, in whom "the executive Powers shall be vested" according to Article II, is much less detailed than that for the

Congress, and the qualifications for the office set down in Section 1 of Article II do not include a minimum educational requirement. Nevertheless, not only a foreign observer like Tocqueville, but any thoughtful citizen and voter, must ponder how potential candidates for this office have prepared themselves for it. This preparation includes, though it is not confined to, their formal schooling and formation of character. From the very first, and with an exponential increase throughout the twentieth century, the president's "Power, by and with the Advice and Consent of the Senate, to make Treaties," which is conferred in Article II, Section 2, makes it obligatory, for example, that the president demonstrate the geographical and historical learning that underlie such treaties, in addition to the diplomatic skills needed to negotiate them. Ever since King Philip of Macedon, "looking upon the instruction and tuition of his youth to be of greater difficulty and importance than to be wholly trusted to the ordinary masters in music and poetry and the common school subjects," turned over the education of the young Alexander (soon to be Alexander the Great) to the tutelage of Aristotle[20]—and long before that—the education of a chief executive has been a challenging assignment, even when, as in Alexander's case, it was obvious all along just who that chief executive was to be. A democracy, where the chief executive is to be voted on and elected, makes that challenge far more complex and profound.

Of the three branches of government itemized by the Constitution, it is "the judicial Power of the United States ... vested in one supreme Court, and in such inferior Courts as the Congress may from time to time ordain and establish" (Article III, Section 1) that has the most obvious connection to education. Students and observers of the courts often debate the effects, beneficial or deleterious, of what Richard A. Posner, himself both an academic and a judge, has identified as "the increased academification" of the study and interpretation of the law.[21] But before and behind the particular education of judges and lawyers in professional schools of law, the process of "general education" during the sixteen or so years leading up to law school is of vital importance. So much of the work of judges depends on parsing sentences, whether of statutes or of the Constitution, that without the elements of English grammar, syntax, and vocabulary, as these are (or are not) taught in the common schools, the judicial system would face the danger of a breakdown both in functioning and in credibility.

Not a fourth branch of government, but often called (already, according to Thomas Carlyle, by Edmund Burke) "the fourth estate,"[22] the press, broadly viewed, is an educational force whose interaction with the schools is at least as influential as is its interaction with government. It must be acknowledged that at the state and local level, the coverage of public education in the press, apart from the annual deadlock over school budgets and the repeated controversy about new construction, is often inadequate at best. Yet in many respects the schools can be said to be successful as an institution of American constitutional democracy to the extent that they prepare and equip their students for an ongoing critical engagement with the press and the media as agencies of continuing civic education. Indeed, such a formulation of this interaction makes it sound as though the press and media take over after the schools have done their job, when every statistical survey makes it clear that in the life of the students, the schools and the media, above all television, are running along on parallel tracks—sometimes competitive with each other, sometimes oblivious of each other. There is a frequently voiced concern, and one that is addressed in the accompanying volume on the press, that entertainment value has trumped educational responsibility in the mission statement of the media. The success or failure of the public schools as an institution of American constitutional democracy depends in considerable measure on this subtle interrelation with the press and media.

Having had the opportunity in two monographs of 1983 and 1992 to reflect at some length about the college and the university,[23] but not about the public schools, and being obliged (for the sake of truth in packaging) to admit to having spent only three years as a pupil in such a school, I have cherished this opportunity of carrying on my private education in public by participating in the work of this commission. The thoughtful volume that is a result of that work is sure to help define the issues not only of elementary and secondary education, but of the genius of American constitutional democracy, both for those who have a direct stake in the schools (as do we all) and for those who are concerned (as all of us had better be) about the health and welfare of democratic institutions everywhere.

## Notes

1. *Lovell v. City of Griffin,* 303 U.S. 444 (1938).
2. *Pierce v. Society of Sisters,* 268 U.S. 510 (1925).
3. *Everson v. Board of Education of Ewing Township,* 330 U.S. 1 (1947).
4. *Abington School District v. Schempp,* 374 U.S. 203 (1963).
5. *Nixon v. Herndon,* 273 U.S. 536 (1927).
6. *Griggs v. Duke Power Co.,* 401 U.S. 424 (1971).
7. *Plessy v. Ferguson,* 163 U.S. 537 (1896).
8. *Brown v. Board of Education,* 347 U.S. 483 (1954).
9. Alexis de Tocqueville, *Democracy in America,* edited by J. P. Mayer and Max Lerner, translated by George Lawrence (New York: Harper and Row, 1966), 65, 38.
10. Ibid, 48, 565–67.
11. Johann Wolfgang von Goethe, "Den Vereinigten Staaten," in *Goethes Werke: Festausgabe* (Leipzig: Bibliographisches Institut, 1926), vol. 2, 416.
12. J. C. Levenson, *The Mind and Art of Henry Adams* (Stanford, Calif.: Stanford University Press, 1968).
13. Werner Jaeger, *Paideia: the Ideals of Greek Culture,* translated by Gilbert Highet, 2nd ed. (New York: Oxford University Press, 1943), vol. 1, xxii–xxiii.

14. See Garry Wills, *Lincoln at Gettysburg: The Words that Remade America* (New York: Simon and Schuster, 1992).
15. Thucydides, *The Peloponnesian War,* vol 2, 41.
16. Donald Kagan, *Pericles of Athens and the Birth of Democracy* (New York: Free Press, 1991), 151–71.
17. Quoted in Edmund S. Morgan, *Benjamin Franklin* (New Haven, Conn.: Yale University Press, 2002), 27.
18. Laurence H. Tribe, *Abortion: The Clash of Absolutes,* 2nd ed. (New York: Norton, 1992).
19. See Charles Grove Haines, *The Revival of Natural Law Concepts* (Cambridge, Mass.: Harvard University Press, 1930); Benjamin F. Wright, *American Interpretations of Natural Law: A Study in the History of Political Thought* (Cambridge, Mass.: Harvard University Press, 1931).
20. Plutarch, "Alexander," in *The Lives of the Noble Grecians and Romans,* translated by John Dryden.
21. Richard A. Posner, in *The Unpredictable Constitution,* edited by Norman Dorsen (New York: New York University Press, 2002), 219.
22. *Oxford English Dictionary,* s.v. "Press."
23. Jaroslav Pelikan, *Scholarship and Its Survival: Questions on the Idea of Graduate Education* (Princeton, N.J.: Carnegie Foundation for the Advancement of Teaching, 1983); *The Idea of the University: A Reexamination* (New Haven, Conn.: Yale University Press, 1992).

# INTRODUCTION

*Susan Fuhrman and Marvin Lazerson*

THE UNITED STATES' FAITH IN PUBLIC SCHOOLING HAS HIS-torically known no bounds. Universal common schools were, in Horace Mann's nineteenth-century phrase, "the great equalizer," "the balance wheel of the social machinery" that would bring together children of varied backgrounds, teaching them literacy, moral values, and the patriotism necessary for informed citizenship. More so than any other nation, the United States has expanded educational opportunities to more people for longer periods of time, from elementary school through high school and on to college. Indeed, so powerful has the faith in schooling been that it is inconceivable to talk about American democracy without reference to universal public education.

At the beginning of the twenty-first century the promise of public education has come under question. While complaints about schooling's quality and calls for educational reform have historically always been part of the educational landscape, they have recently taken on a new edge. Efforts to improve the public schools now exist alongside doubts as to whether public education in its current form can be salvaged. If these doubts were to prove justified, what would become of the once strong link between public education and democratic citizenship?

Americans both agree upon and are divided in their view of the public schools. As a working paper by Patrick Jamieson for the Annenberg Public Policy Center at the University of Pennsylvania finds, there is an extraordinary consensus about the goals of schooling.[1] At proportions that range from 80 to 99 percent, Americans believe that schools should teach reading, writing, and arithmetic and computer literacy, teach the difference between right and wrong and such values as freedom and democracy, foster active citizenship, and prepare students for future careers. Eighty-five percent believe that students, in order to graduate from high school, should be required to show that they understand the common history and ideas that bind Americans together.

And yet there are also sharp disagreements over what public education is accomplishing. Almost half of those surveyed do not think that the schools are doing a good job of preparing citizens. Much of the public has ceased to believe that the current organization of public schooling works, and they are prepared to support increased choice in schooling through the use of tax dollars to pay for tuition at private or religious schools. The public is sufficiently disturbed to favor greater accountability, including requiring standardized tests in order for students to graduate and to assure that teachers are doing their jobs.

These findings suggest that Americans continue to place enormous expectations on the schools—to teach literacy skills and knowledge that prepares students for their economic, civic, and ethical responsibilities—and simultaneously have tremendous doubts that the public schools, as they currently exist, can accomplish these tasks. What Americans want from their schools mirrors their expectations of what it means to be a citizen in the American democracy.

The struggle to create public schools that measure up to the expectations that Americans have for their schools, and to do so in the context of preparation for informed and active citizenship, is the subject of this volume. Each chapter gives voice to the ways America's schools are linked to the preparation of citizens. They suggest the vitality of debate, the depth of concerns and disagreements, and the possibilities of improvement. They provide data and evidence on a range of activities and viewpoints that encompass the relationship between education and citizenship in the United States.

## Historical Trajectories

The belief that public schooling and citizenship are inextricably linked has been one of the United States' abiding themes. As John Merrow writes in this volume, "Deep democratic principles, particularly the belief that individuals, given the proper tools, will take on the responsibility of democratic citizenship, have been the bedrock of American education for over two centuries." Even before the United States existed, schooling's moral importance to social stability and economic prosperity was embedded in legislation. In the famous words of the Massachusetts Bay Colony's school law of 1647, "It being one chief project of that old Deluder, Satan, to keep men from the knowledge of the Scriptures," every township should appoint an individual to teach children to read and write. With the creation of the United States, following the American Revolution, every new state asserted in its constitution that public schools were essential to the republic.

In the nineteenth century, as the common-school movement flourished, education's importance to democratic citizenship grew. The curriculum took as its primary responsibilities the teaching of moral values and literacy and numerical skills, under the assumption that the nation would thrive to the degree that its citizens were literate, ethical, and patriotic. These were the essential conditions of a prosperous and strong country, and they depended upon the widespread availability of public education—in the nineteenth century, elementary schools; in the twentieth century, secondary schools; and in the last half of the twentieth century into the present, postsecondary education.

The association of citizenship and public education has always been complicated by controversy over who should be a citizen. In the nineteenth century, women were frequently viewed as daughters and mothers of citizens, and thus entitled to an education similar to men, but they did not attain full citizenship nationally until the twentieth century. African Americans, before 1860 overwhelmingly slaves, struggled for the rights of citizenship and for the right to be educated. With slavery extinguished, they fought for equal access to schools. The twentieth-century civil rights movement was formed around the right to adequate public education. For Native Americans, public schooling was often offered as both an opportunity and an attack on native cultures. For other groups—Hispanics, European immigrants—schooling meant becoming an American. Whatever the controversies, however, the essays in this book make abundantly clear that, in Julie Reuben's words, "The history of citizenship in the United States has been closely intertwined with the history of education. Americans have looked to schools to foster individuals' identification with the nation. They have expected schools to prepare future citizens, nurturing in children loyalty and common values and forging from them a strong national character."

Connecting public education to citizenship required widespread access to schools, whether elementary and high schools in thousands of school districts, evening citizenship classes for adults, or more colleges per population than any other nation in the world. But if access to schooling has historically been the highest priority, the content of education—schooling's curriculum—was a close second. What should young people learn on the path to democratic citizenship? And how should it be taught? Initially the curriculum consisted of reading, writing, and arithmetic, taught in the context of moral values. In the second half of the nineteenth century, American history became important, so much so that states soon made completion of the course a requirement for high school graduation. Early in the twentieth century, a new dimension was introduced into the curriculum—preparation for employment. While the public schools had always made one's economic role an important part of citizenship education, historically they had implemented this goal through a curriculum that emphasized literacy and moral values such as hard work and individual responsibility. Very little in the way of direct job training was undertaken. With the development of vocational education, however, young people were to be prepared for specific jobs.

Preparation for citizenship through schooling has thus combined efforts to expand access—reflecting the goal of inclusion—with a curriculum differentiated by projected economic roles. Nowhere was this more evident than in the comprehensive public high school, a uniquely American invention. Throughout the twentieth century, all young people could attend the public high school in their neighborhood—and increasingly states required that they remain in secondary school until age sixteen—while much of their actual education took place in differentiated classrooms: academic tracks for those preparing for college, vocational tracks for those who would seek jobs after graduation, and a general track that seemed to have little purpose beyond keeping youth in school. The very success of the comprehensive public high school ultimately became a source of contention. Whereas the responsibilities of citizenship seemed to require a common education, the differentiated curriculum suggested that preparation for citizenship could be distinguished by future occupations and by levels of academic learning. The comprehensive high school could thus offer algebra and geometry alongside "business math" and arithmetic for everyday use.

After the mid-twentieth century, Americans became divided over what citizenship required. During the 1950s, anticommunist fervor led to intense concerns about the nature of civic education, as well as to worries about whether communist sympathizers were teaching in the schools. National defense competition engendered by the cold war took concrete shape with the launching of the Soviet satellite *Sputnik 1* in 1957, which accelerated efforts in the United States to increase academic standards, especially in the sciences, mathematics, and foreign languages. In the aftermath of the Supreme Court's 1954 *Brown v. Board of Education* decision declaring unconstitutional state-mandated racially segregated public schools, the nation's focus shifted toward issues of equality; debates about public education became less about preparing the academically most talented, and more about providing equal educational opportunity to all.

In the last decades of the twentieth century, education in the United States faced a new controversy—whether the schools were teaching students a sufficiently high level of knowledge and skills to enable them to be effective and productive citizens in a globally competitive world. The debate was spurred largely by a heightened sensitivity to international economic competition during the 1970s and 1980s, when the American economy seemed to be slipping behind that of other industrialized countries. Criticism was leveled at what looked like a corrupt bargain, documented in *The Shopping Mall High School* (1985): All children would attend school, but except for the few in advanced programs, expectations for learning were low.[2]

## Defining—and Assuring—Quality

A recession and fears of foreign economic competition in the 1970s and early 1980s led to concern about the quality of American schooling. Were we failing to keep up with bullish Asian and European economies because our schools were insufficiently preparing the workforce? In 1983 the Reagan administration, which had previously sought to distance itself from education policy, even proposing the abolition of the new Department of Education, released *A Nation at Risk: The Imperative for Educational Reform,* which turned out to be one of the most important federal education efforts in American history. In stirring language, the report cited many indicators of education system failure, ranging from poor showings on national tests and international comparisons to the need for businesses to provide remedial education to high school and college graduates. It called for shoring up educational standards for students, by raising graduation requirements and increasing testing, and for teachers, by toughening teacher education requirements and certification standards.

Interestingly, although the context was the relationship between education and economic preparedness, the report also made citizenship a central theme. One of its most sensational metaphors likened the seriousness of "the rising tide of mediocrity" overtaking America's schools to an invasion by an unfriendly power, suggesting that improving educational quality was a patriotic necessity. Further, the report explicitly linked education for democracy to educational quality. *A Nation at Risk* acknowledged that education is the source of shared values essential to democracy, but asserted that values are not enough for democracy to function well; expert skills are also needed: "For our country to function, citizens must be able to reach some common understandings on complex issues, often on short notice and on the basis of conflicting or incomplete evidence."[3]

*A Nation at Risk* unleashed a more than two-decades-long upsurge in attention to educational quality. Education boosters in the Reagan administration used the bully pulpit to press states to raise standards. State after state, some starting even earlier than the report's release but reacting to the same concerns, fashioned omnibus reform packages, increasing course requirements for graduation, instituting more student assessment, specifying specific courses deemed important, lengthening the school day or year, and stiffening certification requirements and requirements for teacher relicensure.

These new policies were more restrictive of local prerogative than past state policies, which mostly concerned minimum inputs for districts, such as the requirement to employ certified teachers. Although many districts rose to the challenge, with some designing even higher standards policies than their states required, the initial "excellence" reforms, as these post–*A Nation at Risk* reforms were called, came to be seen as "top down," and were charged with inhibiting local creativity. A countermovement, called the "restructuring" movement, which focused on giving individual schools more autonomy, encouraging parent and community participation on school councils, and making more space for teacher decision-making in school schedules, developed. Like the "excellence" movement, the justification focused on quality. Many business elites and policy proponents argued that results were better assured when schools were given freedom to make their own decisions, mirroring the trend toward flatter management and greater flexibility for line workers then popular in the business sector. But many educational proponents argued for school-based decision making on democratic grounds, urging that increased community-member and teacher participation in decisions would not only empower those actors but also contribute to school policies more responsive to local needs.

Neither the "excellence" nor the "restructuring" reforms produced the results their supporters desired. Student performance remained basically flat. The top-down state reform policies were accused of leading to superficial change. Although districts complied, for example, by adding more mathematics courses, many made changes that were less than meaningful; for example, by putting new titles on remedial math courses and counting them toward the new requirements. The "bottom up" school-based reforms often failed to focus on instruction; new, more democratic school-councils often focused on tangential issues, such as hallway traffic patterns, rather than on the complex task of improving teaching and learning. Frustration with the failure to make more progress led to a third reform movement.

In the late 1980s a few leading states decided to go beyond requiring more courses and began to develop substantive standards for student learning. They used these expectations for what students should know and be able to do in different subjects—content and performance standards—as anchors to which policies on textbook adoption, student assessment, and teacher certification could be tied. Not coincidentally, this approach was common in many of the other nations that were outscoring the United States on international assessments.

So began the "standards" reform movement, which in many ways was able to bring the excellence and restructuring movements together and hence was sometimes called a "third wave" of reform. While top-down actors—state policymakers—would explicate standards, or expectations for student learning, and hold schools accountable for achieving them, bottom-up actors—teachers and local educators—would have great authority in restructuring their own processes.

By the early years of the twenty-first century, all states were engaged in the standards movement, and the federal government had reoriented its policies for disadvantaged and special-needs children to promote standards-based education. In fact, the federal reauthorization of the Elementary and Secondary Education Act, the No Child Left Behind Act (NCLB) of 2001, specified that, as a condition for receiving Title I aid for disadvantaged students, states would test all children in grades three through eight on their standards every year and once in high school, bring all children to proficiency on these measures by 2014, and intervene in (or even close) schools that failed to make adequate progress toward this goal in individual subjects and for specific subgroups of students. NCLB's focus on testing and accountability for student performance both accelerated and reflected a similar trend in the states. While originally much focus was given to how to set standards and on how to reach consensus about what knowledge should be valued, more recently the standards movement has come to focus on

testing. And as testing has become more prominent and widespread, early experiments with sophisticated, performance-based assessments have given way to
broader use of commercial tests that focus more on lower-level skills and are less
able to reflect the more challenging conceptions of knowledge that original
standards designers had in mind.[4]

Despite the emphasis on assessment and the fact that current tests assess only
a small portion of standards, the question of what should be in the standards
remains a salient one, especially in the case of civics. As John Puckett and Michael
Johanek attest in this volume, different views of American democratic traditions
are represented in major controversies over standards in civics and history. To
what extent should history standards focus on the United States' progress and
stress patriotism and loyalty or, alternatively, encourage study of problematic
aspects of American history? How much should the standards emphasize mastery
of factual content as opposed to analytic and critical skills?

At about the same time as the standards movement was developing, some
bottom-up advocates argued that the restructuring movement's primary weakness was a failure to go far enough in granting schools autonomy. If schools were
truly freed from regulations, it was argued, they could better design programs to
meet the needs of their students and to innovate and develop creative solutions
to meeting accountability expectations. Thus was born the charter school movement, characterized by legislation in many states to encourage groups of teachers, parents, and citizens to start new innovative schools or to convert existing
schools to freer status. Some market advocates went even further, experimenting
with private and public voucher systems that supported student choice of private
as well as public charter schools. As Paul Dimond points out in this volume, the
issue of citizens' rights to choose schools, in addition to questions about the
extent to which the common public school is necessary for shared values, is fundamental to democracy.

The relationship of public schools to democracy has held a central place in
the history of the United States. The authors in this volume address that ongoing
relationship in diverse ways. But they also reveal a set of crosscutting themes and
challenges that suggest the complexity of what it means to educate for democratic citizenship.

## Themes and Challenges

The United States is unique in its embrace of the link between public
schooling and democracy. The notion that schools must be "public" to be democratic is an alien idea in places such as the Netherlands, Australia, the United
Kingdom, and the many other countries that provide public funds for private
schooling. The definition of "public" is a subject of debate. Proponents of vouchers, for example, argue that the public benefit of schooling is the key concept, so

if private schools serve a public purpose, that of educating citizens, they are by definition public. Does our rhetoric about public schooling describe how we think about schools and democracy? What does "public" mean and how necessary is "public" to democracy?

Second, is there something "democratic" about how Americans choose to govern their schools? Many arguments supporting local control of education rest on the closeness of schools to citizens and the importance of schooling as an issue around which citizens have the opportunity to express themselves. Advocates of community engagement in schools extend this view: the more the public is involved in local schools, the more education will express community values. But the governance of education is shifting, with more authority going to state and local governments. At the local level, mayors are taking control from separately elected school boards. Does this make schooling less democratic? And what precisely ought to be the relationships between schools and various levels of governance?

Third, what does "citizenship" mean? How do schools educate for citizenship when we differ over who is a citizen? In a companion book to this volume, Patricia A. Graham describes the historical expectations of schooling for citizenship, from assimilation to adjustment to access to achievement.[5] These expectations have always been contested, and they remain so today. What commonalties make us citizens of one country? What is the nature of our differences? Is citizenship defined by engagement in the political process? If so, does educating for citizenship involve encouraging activism, something that may go beyond traditional education approaches?

Fourth, education is both a public good with a collective economic and civic benefit and a private good with benefits to individuals whose future earnings depend on the quality of their education. Are the individual goals of schooling with respect to getting ahead in the race for economic achievement in conflict with the ethical values of shared participation and engagement in civic cooperation? How might these multiple and potentially conflicting goals be balanced?

Fifth, Americans seem to be more preoccupied with citizen and community involvement, with mobilizing citizens to be active in social issues, than other countries. Americans have historically expressed this preoccupation with unprecedented commitments to voluntarism, a willingness to become engaged as individuals in social activities, a characteristic noted almost two hundred years ago by Alexis de Tocqueville. Does this emphasis on direct citizen activism signify a lack of faith in representative democracy for the expression of citizen concerns? Why is citizen mobilization so important to us? And what are the consequences of this mobilization for our schools?

Sixth, what type of curriculum is most important for civic education and how should it be taught? There is both an intentional curriculum, around which arguments over content flow, and a "hidden" curriculum, through which students are given messages about how active they can be, how much power they can exercise in their schools, and how teachers are valued as citizens of schools. Do students need to exercise a sense of agency in order for them to be good citizens? Is it the school's responsibility to make sure that students are recipients of knowledge so that they can use that knowledge to be citizens? Can one teach in ways that enable students to think of themselves as involved citizens even as they attend school?

Seventh, Americans have made equality of educational opportunity central to the expansion of schooling. But economic differences among families play a substantial role in shaping how well children do in school. Economic differences among communities and states play a role in how much money is provided to schools. Differences in how money is spent within school districts and among schools shape the educational programs available to students. Americans have repeatedly attempted to adjust and limit fiscal inequalities, with mixed results. What policies are necessary to give all students a chance at high levels of educational achievement?

Eighth, and finally, to what extent are the concepts of "education for democracy" and "democratic education" related? Can we educate students for democratic citizenship in schools that are not democratically governed or internally democratic? Are schools even fundamental for the functioning of a democracy, when so many other institutions and social conditions—family life, peer groups, politics, television and computers, labor markets, levels of wealth—shape behavior? To what extent are Americans making a mistake by insisting that schools bear the burden of assuring that democracy functions well?

The chapters in this book address these questions. The topics range from broad historical and theoretical analyses to policy recommendations and pragmatic suggestions on how to improve the quality of teaching or to engage citizens in the potential of public education. Some essays focus on describing the landscape, how the questions emerged, and review the evidence on the consequences of our decisions. Others pose potential answers to the dilemmas of education for democracy. Within the diversity of approaches and topics a common theme is the belief that public education both reflects and shapes our understanding of ourselves and of our aspirations as a nation. Whatever the future shape of public schooling, Americans are likely to insist that education be about citizenship.

## Plan of the Book

We have organized this volume to illuminate the themes and challenges discussed above. In the first section, "Education and Democracy: American Schooling in Context," the chapters provide a frame of reference—the historical context for schooling in the United States, the way schools are governed, how arguments about schooling get framed, and the contrasts between the United States and other nations in the organization of schooling.

Julie Reuben begins this section with "Patriotic Purposes: Public Schools and the Education of Citizens," by tracing the relationship between education and citizenship. Reuben takes us back to the beginnings of American democracy, analyzing the period from the 1790s to the 1820s, when the founding fathers were implementing the structure and building the citizenship of the newly formed country. At a time when most people wanted to keep government small, Thomas Jefferson and other proponents of public education had difficulty gaining support for a public schooling system. In the mid-nineteenth century as British influence slowly receded and patriotic principles figured more heavily in the public mindset, common schools became more prevalent in much of the United States, except in the South, set apart by the institution of slavery. Reuben next focuses on industrialization and urbanization at the turn of the century, which created a need for educating the masses of new immigrants. Education played a dual purpose during this time period, both to Americanize young immigrants and to segregate and separate them into different groups. The two World Wars, the cold war, the civil rights movement, and globalization have all contributed to focusing educational goals on equality and individual gain versus civic and democratic responsibility. As the definition of citizenship changed so did the needs of education, according to Reuben, who recommends that civic purposes and education continue to be linked in order to further American democracy.

Next, Thomas Corcoran and Margaret Goertz, in "The Governance of Public Education," review the current multilevel governance structure of public education. This chapter starts with an outline of what the public wants from education and then describes the historical and current governance structures at local, state, and federal levels. The authors explain that since the 1950s and 1960s, authority and policymaking has moved more from the local level to federal and state governments, driven by the need to improve equity across school districts and by the accountability/standards movement. They then point out the inherent tension in this governance system, where national and local interests, along with individual attainment and the public good, compete. The chapter demonstrates how these conflicts lead to differences over issues concerning funding, curriculum, and access, and how expansion of involvement at the parent and school level is now being offered as a solution to these issues.

In chapter 3, "The Politics of Polarization: Education Debates in the United States," William Galston explores the politicization of education issues. Generally, these political divisions are related to the tension created between individual choice and equality (delivered by the government). To unpack the multiple and complex political issues surrounding public education, Galston examines this topic from various perspectives, such as conflict over the purposes of education, the influence of ideology, and the role of partisanship and organized interests. Galston notes that, unlike in many other nations, especially in Europe, the divisions in the United States over education have multiple dimensions, which can lead to a lack of focus in the policies that are developed and implemented. He closes the chapter with the observation that such deep divisions on education policy will continue to exist in the United States as long as Americans strive toward social equality yet manifest such dramatic disparities in individual wealth and power.

The final chapter in section 1, "Schooling Citizens for Evolving Democracies," by Bruce Fuller and Arun Rasiah, assesses democracy and education in other countries. Clearly the United States is not the only nation with democratic governance of schooling, yet the arrangements for education vary significantly across nations. Fuller and Rasiah seek to understand whether schools create democratic citizens, by looking at practices in other nations. They provide an in-depth analysis of two countries: South Africa, which, postapartheid, sought to include many new citizens in its school system, and Turkey, which is in the process of balancing multiple cultures in both the government and schools. They conclude the chapter with some lessons that can be imported to the United States from other nations, especially around balancing individual needs and pluralistic ideals. They assert that studying the systems from other nations allows us to see that what students learn about citizenship and democratic participation stem directly from the placement of the school in the nation's political economy.

The second section of the volume, "Teaching, Learning, and Working," turns the focus inside schools to examine questions of democracy. In "Classroom Deliberations," Katherine Simon argues for the importance of "democratic deliberation" in the classroom as the foundation for informed citizenship. In democratic deliberation, the student discusses opposing viewpoints, gathers evidence to defend his or her arguments, formulates an opinion, and reflects on the deliberative process. Simon acknowledges that although conducting classroom discourse in such a manner can provide many advantages, including producing a more informed voter and an independent critical thinker, there are opponents of and challenges to such an approach. For example, it is sometimes difficult to facilitate or grade discussions if there is no "right" or "wrong" answer. Simon addresses these concerns and provides real-life examples and strategies to implement deliberation in the classroom.

Michael Johanek and John Puckett continue the theme of preparing individuals for citizenship, in "The State of Civic Education: Preparing Citizens in an Era of Accountability." They first discuss how well the American educational system prepares its citizens for civic participation. They then investigate the intentional activities planned by schools that prepare students for citizenship, the nation's and students' desired outcomes for citizenship participation, and plans for changing the outcomes of civic education in schools. They conclude that such efforts develop personally responsible citizens but that they fall short of helping students become "participatory" or "public work" citizens. The chapter closes with a recommendation for more schools to make an institutional commitment to civic participation in order to produce more civic-minded individuals.

Susan Moore Johnson examines the extent to which schools are democratic places in which to work. "Working in Schools" contemplates two opposing sides to a teacher's role in the classroom: Do they determine what gets taught or are they told what to teach? Although neither extreme is preferable, Johnson argues that the difference between teacher control and public control has direct implications for democratic education. She begins with an outline of the factors, such as low pay, short-term work, public funding, challenging work conditions, and school organizational structures, among others, that explain why teachers are often placed in a subordinate position. However, unionization of teachers has led to better pay, and teachers' roles have been enhanced through greater professionalization, the provision of advanced certification, career ladders, and decentralizing school governance. In the end, Johnson argues that teachers who have a voice in instructional practices demonstrate democratic participation to students firsthand.

In the final chapter of section 2, John Merrow examines the educative influence of various media and their relationship to democracy, particularly as they are used within schools. "Youth, Media, and Citizenship" points out that the media—television, computers, the Internet, and other technologies—are now a part of the daily lives of children. With such powerful media at their disposal, Merrow contends that schools are not using these resources appropriately to create informed citizenry, primarily because of current curricular and instructional constraints. The chapter contains examples of how schools have utilized media in creative ways, but Merrow contends that not all schools have the resources to do so, and some have allowed corporate advertising in their schools in order to procure appropriate technology. The promise of media as a source of positive learning thus remains unfulfilled.

Section 3, "Citizen Participation and Civic Engagement," turns to citizens outside the schools, those who govern, support, and fund public education. In "Civic Capacity: What, Why, and from Whence," Clarence Stone considers public education, especially where public schools are struggling, as an opportunity for broad-based community engagement, as opposed to either national intervention or narrow efforts by school governance officials. He illustrates his point by presenting four cases—Kent County, Maryland; El Paso, Texas; Boston, Massachusetts; and Philadelphia, Pennsylvania—as examples of such involvement at the community level. Stone concludes from these examples that successful civic capacity requires shared definitions of a problem, cross-sector mobilization, appropriate resources, and a detailed plan; ultimately, shaping new relationships, not just utilizing existing ones, is what defines civic capacity.

What if such civic capacity is lacking? Wendy Puriefoy argues that citizens must mobilize around schooling if improvements are to be achieved. In "Citizen Mobilization and Public Education," Puriefoy begins with an examination of the need for, history of, and influence of public engagement. There are different levels of public engagement—information dissemination, involvement, collaboration, constituency building, and citizen mobilization, which is designed for comprehensive change to the system itself. To be successful, the mobilization must be intentional, systemic, and sustainable. Puriefoy's belief is that school reform demands a citizen-mobilization effort. She asserts that citizen mobilization can seek to guarantee quality public education for everyone, in addition to securing public education as a fundamental institution of democracy.

Citizens pledged to supporting public schools are products not only of the public schools but of postsecondary institutions. Is higher education faring any better than K–12 education in preparing good citizens? In "The Elusive Ideal: Civic Learning and Higher Education," Matthew Hartley and Elizabeth Hollander point out that higher education institutions are not structured appropriately, lack the cultural norms, answer to too many external constituents, and do not have sufficiently unified missions to allow for promoting broad-based change. As a result, civic participation at the institutional level and among students is often marginalized. However, Hartley and Hollander note that since the 1980s there has been an increase in efforts to boost civic and community engagement in and across campuses. Examples are service learning, community service, democratic participation, and other activities. The authors believe that civic engagement can be directly incorporated into institutional missions.

Section 4, "Visions and Possibilities," presents particular points of view with respect to enhancing democracy in public schooling. "Agency, Reciprocity, and Accountability in Democratic Education," by Richard Elmore, argues that accountability—or holding schools responsible to public authorities for performance—is, under certain conditions, compatible with democracy, even though many opponents argue that the emphasis on accountability diminishes learning and the capability of educators to teach. At each level of the school system—from the classroom to the school to the governance structure—accountability works when actively engaged participants get the support they need. When there is reciprocity, as well as an acceptance of responsibility by students and teachers, accountability follows and models democratic principles.

Jennifer Hochschild and Nathan Scovronick take a look at the demographic profile of the nation and its impact on education in "Demographic Change and Democratic Education." They contend that the nation will need particular policy approaches, such as bilingual education and equity in public education, to assure that democracy accommodates the coming changes in demography. The changing demography of U.S. citizens to an older white population combined with a young immigrant population will create a huge generational and cultural gap in the country, which will have direct impact on education policy. California and Texas, which faced some of these changes first, initially turned to restrictive and arguably discriminatory policies instigated by the citizens in power. Hochschild and Scovronick argue that, eventually, political recalibration occurred in these states, and that the nation must proactively consider policies that help more people achieve the American dream rather than restrict their progress.

One educational policy approach that proponents argue is key to democracy is the ability of parents to choose schools for their children. Paul Dimond addresses this issue in "School Choice and the Democratic Ideal of Free Common Schools." Dimond opens the chapter with a description of how changing demographics have affected how parents choose where their children go to school. He contends that a system that makes a family's place of residence the determining factor in children's educational opportunities is not an equitable means of providing public education. Dimond outlines a methodology to create a "social market" of schools, and ends the chapter by examining how such a market fits under democratic ideals and traditions.

The volume ends with an afterword by Amy Gutmann on the broad nature of democratic education. "Democratic Disagreement and Civic Education" focuses on the three ways in which democracies deal with disagreement: procedurally, constitutionally and deliberatively. To support, protect, and participate in these mechanisms, citizens must possess certain skills and virtues such as tolerance, civility, judgment, and respect for others. Gutmann argues that educating children to develop such skills and values, to have the capacity to become citizens, is a central role of public schools in a democracy. We agree.

## Notes

1. Patrick Jamieson, *My Schools Are Better Than Yours? A Look at U.S. K–12 Public Schools through the Eyes of People in General, Parents, Teachers, and Administrators* (Philadelphia: Annenberg Public Policy Center, forthcoming).
2. Arthur G. Powell, Eleanor E. Farrar, and David K. Cohen, *The Shopping Mall High School: Winners and Losers in the Educational Marketplace* (Boston: Houghton Mifflin, 1985).
3. National Commission on Excellence in Education, *A Nation at Risk: The Imperative for Educational Reform,* available at U.S. Department of Education Web site, www.ed.gov/pubs/NatAtRisk/risk.html.
4. See Robert Rothman, "Benchmarking and Alignment of State Standards and Assessments," in *Redesigning Accountability Systems for Education,* edited by Susan H. Fuhrman and Richard F. Elmore (New York: Teachers College Press, 2004), 96–114.
5. Patricia A. Graham, *The Promise of Virtue and Knowledge: American Education in the Twentieth Century* (New York: Oxford University Press, forthcoming).

# EDUCATION AND DEMOCRACY: AMERICAN SCHOOLING IN CONTEXT

# 1

# PATRIOTIC PURPOSES: PUBLIC SCHOOLS AND THE EDUCATION OF CITIZENS

*Julie A. Reuben*

THE UNITED STATES, AS ONE OF THE FIRST NATIONS consciously "created," has sustained an enduring obsession with issues of national identity. On the one hand, Americans have continually analyzed and asserted the nation's distinctive character and unique mission. On the other, they have questioned and recast the boundaries of inclusion and the meanings of citizenship. Citizenship determines membership in the nation and the relationship between individuals and government. In the eighteenth century, when the United States was established, citizens were largely assumed to be adult white men who owned property. Over time, excluded groups challenged this restrictive definition, expanding citizenship to include anyone born within the United States or having completed the process of naturalization. This expansion, accomplished often through bitter struggle, accompanied many changes in the meaning of citizenship—changes having to do with the characteristics of a "good" American, tensions between individual rights and communal norms, the relative position of minority groups within society, and the scope of government and its responsiveness to citizens' needs.

The history of citizenship in the United States has been closely intertwined with the history of education. Americans have looked to schools to foster individuals' identification with the nation. They have expected schools to prepare future citizens, nurturing in children loyalty and common values and forging from them a strong national character. Thus, as key aspects of citizenship have been defined and redefined, expectations of schools have changed as well. The expansion of public education reflected changing notions about the proper scope of government and its role in the socialization of youth. The changing population of schools—what groups were included in schools and how they were treated there—has closely tracked the relative status of groups within the nation. Political values dominant at various periods in the country's history have strongly influenced what children learn about their country and their own role in its future. Educators, by embracing the expectation that one of school's primary responsibilities is the preparation of future citizens, have ensured that schools have both reflected and helped shape the ongoing debates about the boundaries and meanings of citizenship.

## Thwarted Plans: 1790s–1820s

After winning independence from England, American leaders turned their attention to building the nation. Founders looked in two main directions to accomplish this task—well-formed structures of government and the character of the citizenry. The search for the first led to the ratification of the U.S. Constitution. The second spurred leaders to propose plans for public education. Benjamin Rush, Noah Webster, Thomas Jefferson, and others argued that the new nation needed to expand and reform schools in order to ensure the virtue of its citizens. These individuals sought to enlarge government involvement in education, fashioning schools and curricula that directly embodied their ideal. Although their plans foundered on sharp disagreements over what citizenship meant, their ideas charted a moderate course between egalitarian and elitist conceptions of political rights and the role of the state in the socialization of youth.

Revolutionary leaders' ideas about citizenship derived from their knowledge of classical history and English commonwealth writers. From these sources, American leaders learned that republics could survive only if they possessed a virtuous citizenry, actively engaged in public affairs and willing to place the common good ahead of self-interest. Republican theorists maintained that such participation required a high level of moral development, a level that was perhaps beyond the capacity of the average person. Classical republicanism cast doubt on the possibility that citizenship could be widespread; it assumed that material independence and intelligence developed through careful education were preconditions for the moral rectitude essential for this status. The Revolution, however, unleashed more-egalitarian sentiments, opening the possibility that citizenship in the new nation might be more inclusive. The Constitution, with the notion of popular sovereignty enshrined in its preamble, supported this possibility but remained largely silent on matters of citizenship. The nation was formed without specifically defining the requirements for or rights of citizenship.

As unsettled questions about citizenship bubbled up in public debates, leaders focused greater attention on the role of education. Education offered a potential antidote to the problems associated with expanding boundaries of citizenship; it presented both a way to strengthen a governing elite and to prepare the wider population for the responsibilities of representative government. To fulfill these duties, however, schooling would have to be transformed. During the colonial period, home and church provided the bulk of children's education. Nonetheless, many children studied for a period of time in some sort of school. They might have learned to read in dame schools, or attended a town school or a subscription school or, if poor, an urban charity school. Some boys learned skilled crafts in apprenticeships, and a small minority prepared for one of the nine colonial colleges in grammar schools or with private tutors. These nine colleges, the best-established educational institutions at the time, served only a small portion of the population. Formal educational opportunities were sporadic and depended largely on local circumstances and familial values and resources.

For leaders who believed that education could play an important role in securing the political stability of the nation, this haphazard array of schools proved worrisome. They proposed government support of new public educational institutions specifically designed to prepare individuals to take on their political responsibilities in the new nation. These proposals aimed to temper the egalitarianism that was threatening republican notions of good government. Suggestions ranged from Benjamin Rush's proposal to create a national university to Noah Webster's search for a common school curriculum that would be explicitly crafted to the political needs of the new republic.

Thomas Jefferson developed the most comprehensive scheme for the expansion of schooling in the early national period. He sponsored legislation in Virginia to create a pyramidal structure of public education, made up of common schools for young children, grammar schools for more advanced students, and a college. The common schools would be funded on a local "ward" level and free to all white children; the grammar schools and college would charge tuition, but a small number of poor boys who demonstrated exceptional intelligence and character would be selected to attend at public expense. Jefferson's common schools would offer a basic curriculum of a few years' length, ensuring that the populace as a whole had the minimum intellectual skills needed to be self-sufficient and develop an upright and steady character. Grammar schools and the college were designed for the preparation of future leaders. The grammar schools would provide a fairly traditional education based in classical languages and texts. The college's curriculum would be expanded beyond the classics to include modern and professional subjects.

Jefferson's educational ideas sought a compromise between republicanism's traditional distrust of the masses and the egalitarian principles that were gaining popularity in North America. Jefferson argued that talented youth could be found among the poor, and if separated from their families and educated properly, they could become patriotic and valuable leaders. However, he assumed that the grammar schools and college would primarily serve the sons of an already established elite, and that one of the primary benefits of common schools would be to teach citizens to willingly defer to their natural betters. He also doubted that all people had the capacity to be citizens of the republic. Like most white Americans at the time, he did not think that African Americans and Native Americans could join the body politic, and he was skeptical of some his contemporaries' optimistic beliefs about the power of the American environment and institutions to assimilate all Europeans, questioning whether all groups had characteristics needed to become virtuous citizens. While he supported expanding political rights beyond the hereditary elite, he believed that this required the state to take a more active role in preparing citizens of the new republic.

Although leaders launched vigorous campaigns on behalf of their plans for educational reforms, they could not muster enough support in Congress or state legislatures to build a system of public education before the 1830s. A few states did pass provisions for public support for local schools. Massachusetts required towns with over fifty families to provide elementary schools, and those with over two hundred to provide a grammar school. The state, however, did not provide any funds for these schools, nor did it vigorously enforce the requirement for grammar schools. In 1795 the state of New York appropriated funds to pay for up to half of the cost of local schools, encouraging towns to create schools. When the costs outstripped the amount designated, however, the state legislature refused to raise additional funds through new taxation. Connecticut offered more generous support, creating a large school fund from the sale of its western territory. While these advances confirmed the principle of government support for education, they did not fulfill the hopes or soothe the fears of the revolutionary generation.

Attempts to give the state a more intensive role in socializing citizens were held up by unsettled disputes about the nature of citizenship in the new nation. One of the key debates involved the question of how extensive popular involvement in government would be. Revolutionary rhetoric raised the hope, among some Americans, of expanded political equality. This issue surfaced most directly in the debates about whether voting would be understood as a right of citizens or whether it would be viewed as a privilege, restricted to those with sufficient property to be deemed trustworthy. If property restrictions on voting were to be removed or greatly liberalized, as had been done in some states after the Revolution, then educating all citizens was an urgent public concern. Ensuring that common laborers had the education needed to select (and defer to) appropriate leaders was among the most prominent arguments in favor of free public schools. However, if voting was restricted to men with economic means, then the argument for widespread public education was less compelling; in this case, educational reform would best focus on higher education.

Several other unsettled questions inhibited the progress of public education. In this period, Americans understood citizenship education in primarily moral terms—future citizens needed to be honest, loyal, hardworking, trustworthy, and selfless. However, moral education had always been closely associated with reli-

4

gion, and many people distrusted the idea that "Christian" virtues could be inculcated in a secular setting. In addition, there was little agreement about how intensively government should be involved in citizens' lives. Plans for a system of public schools rested on support for an active government, centralized at the state or national level. In the early national period, there was simply not enough support for this kind of government, either materially or philosophically, to sustain a comprehensive system of public education.

While plans for public schools languished, opportunities for formal schooling expanded. For children, access to schooling still depended largely on geography and family resources. In the North, a growing number of district schools, funded by a combination of parental fees and public funds, educated rural children for at least a few months each year. In other regions, itinerant teachers offered instruction. In cities, churches sponsored a growing number of charity schools for poor children, and families with means could send their children to a variety of day schools. The most impressive expansion occurred at advanced levels, as the number of academies and colleges proliferated. The term "academy" encompassed a wide range of schools, from boarding schools preparing the sons of the urban elite for college to venture schools with a single teacher instructing future clerks in penmanship and accounting. Because of the flexibility of its form, academies became sources of educational innovation in this period, offering courses in "modern" subjects not well represented in traditional grammar schools and colleges, and practical skills formally taught through apprenticeship, as well as serving individuals, such as girls, who previously did not have access to advanced institutions.

Although by contemporary standards these were private institutions—funded largely through tuition and outside the direct sponsorship and supervision of the state—they embraced public purposes, particularly the preparation of citizens. At the elementary level, this focused on morality and basic intellectual skills. Since many district schools relied on whatever books children found in their home, there was not yet a large market for American texts, and schoolchildren learned little explicit information about government and American political ideology. Academies' public service was also largely indirect, accomplished through the diffusion of useful knowledge, rather than direct attention to social, economic, and political questions. Colleges made explicit claims about their relevance in the new nation. Republican ideology relied heavily on the classical texts and history, so the college curriculum was easily adapted to political purposes. In addition, colleges put greater emphasis on moral philosophy, expanding the subject to include both political philosophy and discussions of contemporary social issues. This pattern of semipublic institutions accommodated the current debates about citizenship—it allowed for a continued role for churches in education; it limited the direct role of government in people's lives; and it skirted questions about who needed to be prepared for participation in public affairs.

5

## Partial Successes: 1830s–1870s

Beginning in the 1830s, the prospects for public education began to improve as strong movements for common schools developed throughout the country. Over the next few decades, these movements would achieve important legislative victories in all regions except the South. These victories, though, would produce their own conflicts. By the 1870s, the push for the expansion of educational rights faltered as it ran up against another unsettled question about citizenship—the extent of ethnic and racial inclusion.

Over the first half of the nineteenth century, the association of citizenship with political rights became stronger. Suffrage restrictions based on property ownership or taxation level came under sharp attack. The people, not property, critics argued, should form the basis of the nation. In response, most states revised their constitutions, revoking economic restrictions and making voting a right of citizenship. The growth of political parties during the first half of the nineteenth century enhanced the value of voting. Parties mobilized new voters, and offered, through newspapers, clubs, parades, and other activities, an outlet for political activism. Voting became the primary form of political participation and the defining feature of citizenship.

The expansion of suffrage coincided, not surprisingly, with renewed concerns about the education of citizens. The success of government, after all, depended on the quality of elected officials, which in turn depended on the good judgment of the mass of voters. At the same time, industrialization and the expansion of a market economy fueled disturbing social conflict. The "common" citizen no longer fit the image of the simple and hardworking farmer who could be trusted to share the values and defer to the leadership of his more prosperous neighbors. Advocates of public schools took advantage of the anxiety caused by social change. They maintained that a "common" school, educating the children of poor and rich together, would prevent divisions among the classes from hardening. They brought out old arguments about the necessity of a virtuous citizenry, and said existing schools, with their short terms, haphazard curriculum, and local variation, were simply unable to meet this need. Only publicly financed, free schools open to all children could ensure that future citizens would responsibly exercise their rights as American citizens.

In addition, a new pattern for the role of religion in public life aided the cause of public education. Leaders of Protestant denominations began to cooperate with one another to spread the influence of Protestant Christianity. Ministers from various denominations joined together to sponsor prayer meetings, and these meetings grew into a series of powerful revivals that swept through different regions of the nation. These joint endeavors expanded to incorporate various causes, from antiprostitution campaigns to prison reform. From these activities, a new form of religious establishment emerged—a wide network of churches and voluntary societies dedicated to infusing all public institutions with Protestant values. This model promised that public schools could indeed be Christian even though there was no state-supported church. It also mobilized powerful allies in the cause of public education—ministers. In numerous communities, Protestant clergy took up the cause of public education, viewing it as an essential piece of their larger battle for the moral regeneration of the nation.

Still, questions about the extent and nature of state intervention in citizens' lives remained unsettled in this period, and continued to fuel resistance to common-school reform. In many communities, opponents fought reformers' plans to consolidate small district schools into a uniform system. The level of central state control divided the Democratic and Whig plans for public education. But despite this ongoing dispute, the populist rhetoric of common-school reforms appealed to enough people to overcome the distrust of state intervention everywhere but in the South. In the 1840s and 1850s state legislatures established tax-supported free primary schools, consolidated district schools, expanded school terms, and created state superintendents of education. While the authority of the new state offices of education varied considerably, state superintendents generally gathered statistics about school attendance, encouraged the creation of graded classrooms, expanded training for teachers, and advocated greater consistency in the curriculum.

Common schools, like earlier schools for children, emphasized morality and basic academic skills such as reading, writing, and arithmetic. The school curriculum expanded only gradually in the nineteenth century: geography instruction became widespread by the 1830s, but American history was not well established in the schools until the 1860s. Common-school reformers promised to prepare citizens by inculcating Christian virtues, and personal discipline was imparted through Bible reading and prayers. Pedagogical practices aimed to teach children the value of hard work and the importance of self-restraint. Students were expected to memorize texts and recite them in unison and individually. Teachers punished mistakes with a lash, or other public forms of humiliation, such as dunce caps and standing or squatting for long periods of time in front of the class, blurring the distinction between academics and morality.

While school subjects had not changed dramatically, students in this period were exposed to more patriotic ideology than their predecessors had been. In the 1830s, as public school systems began to expand, textbooks written by American authors displaced British counterparts. These books, although avoiding topics that might provoke partisan conflict, embedded political concepts in general school subjects. Noah Webster's now ubiquitous spellers taught students words such as "democracy," "senate," and "tyrant," and encouraged them to memorize sentences extolling the glory of the United States and the importance of love of country. Popular readers such as the McGuffey series included biographical sketches of American heroes like George Washington and Benjamin Franklin, and other selections emphasizing nationalistic themes. Readings proclaimed the republic as the highest form of government, and depicted the Constitution as the wisest document written by men. Children learned that liberty was their most cherished possession and their birthright as Americans.

Geography texts reinforced the lessons of spellers and readers. These books characterized nations by their political and social institutions and the traits of their people, which in turn were explained by race. Books assumed that whites were superior to other races, and presented Africans as degraded and Native Americans as noble but cruel and backward. Whites were divided into different racial groups, corresponding roughly to national divisions. Differences among whites also reflected common prejudices. Students learned, for example, that Germans were industrious, honest, and thrifty, but that the Irish were morally depraved and, therefore, poor. Catholic countries were consistently depicted in more negative terms than Protestant ones. In the comparison of nations, the United States clearly triumphed. Americans, schoolchildren learned, were the freest, best educated, and most prosperous people in the world. This exposure to nationalist rhetoric, along with prayers, Bible reading, and especially personal discipline, was supposed to ensure that all children would grow up to become good citizens.

Girls were included in the new common schools despite being denied the important badge of citizenship, the right to vote. According to classical republicanism, women could not be citizens because they were not "independent"— their interests were inevitably intertwined with those of fathers and husbands who supported them. As this notion of independence was challenged and states abolished property restrictions on voting, these arguments against women's citizenship lost some of their power. But instead of extending voting rights to women, an ideology about women's special citizenship status developed. This ideology, known as "republican motherhood," maintained that women exercised their citizenship in distinct ways, through the education of their children and their moral influence over their husbands. Women were given a special role in the maintenance of the republic as its moral conscience, and they exercised this influence first and foremost at home, but also in public, through membership in reform societies, church activities, and as teachers. Republican motherhood clearly justified girls' inclusion in common schools, despite the fact that they were not being educated as future voters.

Efforts to establish public schools in all states of the nation were stymied in the South. There, sparse population settlement, particularly severe economic downturns in the late 1830s and 1840s, and political domination by large slaveholders, who had no interest in the education of white laborers and who feared the education of blacks, inhibited the development of public school systems. By the 1850s, common schooling had become associated with the North and with abolitionism. As a result, southern resistance to public schools hardened, and became associated with regional pride and the defense of slavery.

In addition, public school supporters met new challenges as the boundaries of American identity were tested in the middle decades of the nineteenth century. One of the aims of common schools was to create cultural unity, reducing ethnic, class, and regional distinctiveness. Schools were expected to assimilate the children of the steady stream of European immigrants who were welcomed to the United States in the early decades of the century. A huge wave of Irish Catholic immigrants in the 1840s and 1850s tested this inclusive attitude. As the numbers of Catholics increased in cities, church leaders began to try to get public schools to be more accommodating to Catholic children. They protested daily readings from the King James Bible, the recitation of Protestant prayers, and the anti-Catholic language in school texts. Public school leaders, sharing the prevalent distrust of Catholicism and believing that immigrants needed to conform to the values taught in school, not vice versa, generally refused these requests. Some efforts were made to accommodate Catholic concerns. In 1870, with Catholic schools enrolling twelve thousand students, compared with nineteen thousand in the public schools, Cincinnati school officials negotiated a plan to absorb the Catholic schools into the public school system in exchange for dropping Bible reading and Protestant prayers and hymns from the school routine. The plan, however, provoked public protest, which politicians in Ohio quickly exploited, triggering national hysteria about Catholic conspiracies and godless schools. In 1884 the American bishops declared "every Catholic child in a Catholic school" as a goal of the church.

Race presented another challenge to the ideal of common schools. In the first half of the nineteenth century, African Americans were largely considered to be outside the body politic and their children were generally excluded from public schools. In some cities, churches created charity schools for black children, providing an opportunity for free schooling. Some of these were later incorporated into segregated public school systems in northern cities. As the abolitionist movement grew in strength, black and white activists tried to challenge these practices and establish blacks' rights as American citizens. On a national level, these efforts were thwarted by the Supreme Court, which decided in the 1857 *Dred Scott* case that free blacks were not U.S. citizens. Activists continued to push on local and state levels. For example, in 1850 Sarah C. Roberts, with the abolitionist Charles Sumner as her lawyer, brought the Boston schools to court for forbidding her to attend a white public school near her home. Although she lost this case, in 1855 the Massachusetts legislature mandated that public schools in the state racially integrate. In most places, however, popular racial prejudice presented an insurmountable barrier to such change.

The Union victory in the Civil War offered new hope for both public education and racial justice. The Republican Party, after the demise of the Whigs, had become the chief political proponent of expanding and centralizing public education. Republican Party leaders saw Reconstruction as an opportunity to make public schools a national institution, and they made the creation of public education systems a prerequisite for reestablishment of state governments and sponsored legislation for federal aid to public schools. They hoped this would be the first step in establishing national standards for public education.

Republicans were divided about how to best advance the cause of black education. The principle of racial inclusion and equality seemed to demand integrated schools, but rival Democrats exploited the electorate's fear of racial integration. As a consequence, legislation for federal funding for education languished. Democrats took control of state governments in the South, and in some cases dismantled the public schools built during Reconstruction. Support for the expansion of public education stalled on the threat of inclusiveness. Now that African Americans and Catholics were citizens, would they demand admittance to public schools on equal terms? Was it perhaps time to reconsider the ideal of a common school that would educate all of the nation's citizens together? Proponents of public education were forced to address these questions as they faced the new century.

## Expansion and Differentiation: 1880s–1920s

In the late nineteenth and early twentieth centuries, public schooling expanded tremendously, incorporating groups that had been previously excluded and extending beyond primary school into secondary education. This expansion, however, did not follow the ideal of the common school—educating all children together in the same way. Instead, educators developed a model of differentiated schooling. Although the idea for differentiated education was developed from pedagogical theories that stressed the importance of adapting teaching to each child's particular learning patterns, its application in this period emphasized group rather than individual differences and the organization of schools rather than classroom practices. The growth of public schooling in this period refers not only to the enrollment of a larger portion of the nation's children but to the influence that schools sought to exert in their lives. Progressive Era educators believed that government should take a more active role in securing citizens' welfare. This view animated their own programs for school reform, and became one of the primary messages communicated to children in new civics curricula.

The United States experienced intense change and instability in the decades surrounding the turn of the twentieth century. Industrialization spurred massive migration within the country as people moved from rural areas to cities, and immigration, as people moved to the United States from other regions of the world. Labor strife increased and cities mushroomed in size, straining housing, transportation, and other resources. Political scandals shocked the nation, which was still trying to rebuild after the crises of war and disunion. Elite reformers responded to this instability by targeting "dangerous classes" and trying to contain their influence within the nation. To improve the quality of government, reformers proposed restricting suffrage to those who would exercise it "responsibly." They advocated a number of measures, most notably literacy tests, poll taxes, and ballot reforms, to restrict suffrage. African Americans in the South, who were essentially disenfranchised by the 1890s, suffered the most from these measures. However, northern states adopted a parallel set of reforms, aimed at immigrants and the poor. In addition, reformers proposed measures that strengthened the state's ability to control disruptive people, such as the development of professional police forces, the expansion of prisons and psychiatric hospitals, programs for juvenile offenders, and public health measures. Reformers, recognizing that these were essentially negative policies limited to restraining problematic groups, also sought positive interventions that would transform people so that they no longer posed a threat. They believed that schools, if redesigned for these purposes, could be one of the most effective instruments for individual and social transformation.

One important change in educational policy was a greater degree of state coercion. Although some states had adopted compulsory education laws in the middle of the century, none enforced them. Americans distrusted such intrusive governmental authority, and middle-class families who used public schools had little interest in mixing poor and immigrant youth in their children's classrooms. But toward the end of the century, truancy began to receive a great deal of public attention. Magazines and newspapers raised fears about the dangers of idle youth on city streets, and the need for outside intervention in these children's lives. More states passed compulsory education laws, and cities moved to enforce them by creating special truant schools.

Truant schools did not become a major feature of American education, but the ideas that informed their creation—that schooling should be more intensive, differentiated, and inclusive—came to define Progressive educational reform. Progressive reformers proposed that schools build kindergartens and playgrounds, offer hot lunches and physical examinations. They encouraged pedagogical and curriculum reforms that would engage children by building on their existing interests and relating what they learned in school to their world outside. Progressives argued that children who had previously been excluded from schools, either by parental choice, community prejudice, or because they were considered unteachable, be given an education suited to their individual needs and future station in life.

The comprehensive high school epitomized this expansive vision for public schools. In the early twentieth century, public high schools grew rapidly, drawing in a much larger percentage of youth than had previously attended secondary schools. Progressive educators wanted these students to enter schools that were "comprehensive" in three ways: first, all youth would be enrolled; second, they would address the "whole" student, attending to their personal, social, academic, and vocational development; and third, they would serve students from varied backgrounds and with a wide range of plans for the future. To meet these aims, educators expanded the high school curriculum, adding vocational training, courses dealing with life concerns such as health and interpersonal relations, and "tracks" for academic subjects, which would tailor instruction to students' ability levels and future interests. Comprehensive high schools created gendered programs, such as home economics and secretarial courses for girls, and shop for boys. They marked out separate course sequences for students preparing for college and those who planned to go directly into the workforce. They hired guidance counselors to help students navigate these choices by determining students' "aptitude" for particular subjects and careers. Educators also introduced extracurricular activities, such as athletics, social clubs, and student government, to increase students' engagement in school. These programs, educators hoped, would turn high schools into effective institutions for the socialization of youth.

This desire to make schooling a more significant intervention in students' lives also directed the development of new forms of citizenship education. In the late nineteenth century, educators responded to political scandals by calling for more explicit training for citizenship. This led to the establishment of American history as a standard school subject and to the spread of short courses in civil government during the senior year of high school. American history textbooks emphasized the development of a single unified nation and, like the readers popular earlier in the century, provided sketches of the lives of national heroes to inspire patriotism and provide moral exemplars for students. In the early twentieth century these books gave way to ones written by professional historians. Although still designed to instill patriotism, these newer books downplayed the role of individual heroes and emphasized the development of political, economic, and social institutions. Civil government courses generally focused on the U.S. Constitution and taught students basic facts about the organization of government.

Despite these additions to the curriculum, Progressive Era reformers remained dissatisfied with citizenship education. They argued that civil government, coming at the end of high school, reached too few students, too late in life. They called for a "new civics" that built on students' experiences and engaged them through active learning, whose linchpin was "community civics," a course for students at the end of elementary school. Community civics involved a range of activities, including discussions that incorporated students' personal experiences, class visits by police and firemen, field trips, and student studies of local agencies and "community surveys." It would be supplemented by a new course for the end of high school, Problems of Democracy.

The aim of these innovations was to stimulate students' interest by relating civics instruction to their lives and to allow students to learn by doing. This reflected the influence of Progressive philosopher John Dewey, who argued that schooling should build on students' interests and experiences and give them practice operating in a democratic community. In addition to these pedagogical innovations, the new civics shifted attention away from the structure of government to its functions and services, emphasizing local rather than national and state needs and seeking to help students understand their relations to others. The community civics course was organized around the concept of "community welfare." According to this concept, communities existed to secure individual and group "welfare." "Welfare" consisted of a number of needs, such as health, recreation, and education. A good portion of a class in community civics was devoted to studying how government helped citizens meet their basic needs.

Advocates of community civics wanted students, even children in elementary school, to think of themselves as citizens. But students' relationship to government was analogous to the relationship to their parents. The new citizenship educators were particularly concerned that students acknowledge government officials' expert knowledge. This attitude reflected the professional interests of social scientists who were among the most active supporters of the new civics curriculum and who presented themselves as the experts qualified to determine public policy. Proponents of the new civics envisioned limited citizen involvement in determining public policy in favor of professional guidance.

By de-emphasizing voting and extending citizenship to children, the new civics courses claimed to define citizenship in terms "broader" than politics. The broad definition of citizenship articulated in the community civics curriculum was part of a larger effort to alter the relation of individuals to government, and expand the sphere of the state. Educators who designed community civics thought that older political ideals that emphasized minimal government and maximum individual liberty and initiative were not well suited to industrial, urban society. One of the goals of community civics was to wean students from individualistic philosophies and develop support for government activism. In order to build a more powerful and effective national government, advocates of community civics programs believed that the United States must first moderate its guarantees of individual rights. The vision of citizenship communicated in the new curriculum, therefore, complemented educators' own efforts to make public schools a more powerful counterweight to the influence of families and neighborhoods.

Progressive Era educators saw inclusive public schools as essential in a democratic polity that included immigrants and their children. They envisioned schools as helping different groups assimilate into American culture and society, and perhaps even enriching it by incorporating elements from their own cultures. These educators drew on a long tradition that viewed American identity as a distinct amalgam of European cultures transformed by unprecedented opportunity and equality. They maintained that changing social conditions, particularly industrialization and urbanization, transformed the process of assimilation (hence necessitating the intervention of intensive schooling); but they remained optimistic that this older process of "Americanization" could continue forever. For this group, the main imperative was getting immigrant children into public schools and keeping them enrolled so that they could be quickly and thoroughly transformed into Americans.

Many educators, however, did not trust the natural power of assimilation. They drew on developments in biology and anthropology to argue that there was a biologically determined racial hierarchy, descending from the intellectually and morally superior northern Europeans down through eastern and southern Europeans, Asians, Native Americans, and Africans. They believed that the strength of the United States rested on the predominance of northern European "blood" in the population, and the survival and adaptation of values and institutions from northern European nations in North America. They argued that schools needed special programs suited to the limited abilities of inferior groups. This entailed the creation of academic and nonacademic tracks in schools. The nonacademic tracks included "remedial" behavioral education to try to inculcate the personal discipline and respect for authority that were naturally weak. These tracks led to vocational programs, the worst of which "prepared" students for low-skill jobs by emphasizing orderly behavior, the best of which provided concrete training for skilled industrial and commercial jobs. While biological determinism never completely eclipsed more optimistic views about assimilation, the hysteria surrounding World War I amplified the influence and popular appeal of this position.

Some textbooks taught these racist theories and expressed support for policies such as immigration restriction and eugenics. Catholic schools, which grew quickly in the early twentieth century, often used their own editions of American history books so that they could shield their students from anti-immigrant and anti-Catholic sentiments expressed in books prepared for public schools. Despite this religious and ethnic prejudice, most European immigrants sent their children to regular public schools, and some of them thrived in those contexts. Nonwhite groups, considered by many educators dangerously "degraded," faced more hostile circumstances, including physical separation. Education practice varied considerably (depending to a large degree on local conditions), but generally segregation followed "color" lines with African Americans, Native Americans, Asian immigrants, and Mexican immigrants consigned to segregated schools in some regions of the country.

In the South, racial segregation became a condition for the development of public schools. Immediately following emancipation, blacks formed schools to educate themselves for freedom. Southern whites responded to these schools in the same way as they did the suggestion of integrated public education—with violent opposition—because both were predicated on the association of educa-tion with political inclusion and equality. But powerful northern white philan-thropists argued that schooling did not need to serve such purposes and advocated the creation of separate black schools aimed at adjusting black youth to their subservient place within the new southern economy. Proponents of black schools had to convince white southerners that freed slaves were more of a threat without education than with it. They maintained that black schools, if appropriately designed, could strengthen the existing social order in the South. African Americans struggled to use education for their own empowerment, but they had to do so within a system designed for the opposite purpose.

African Americans fared marginally better in northern schools. In the 1870s and 1880s, most states outside the South ended legal school segregation. However, states did not aggressively enforce these changes on the local level. Even in places where schools were racially integrated, black children suffered discrimination. Despite widespread poverty, black families were deeply commit-ted to the education of their children, sending them to school in large numbers and keeping them enrolled for a relatively long time. However, black children were frequently held back in grades, placed into nonacademic tracks, and deemed uneducable. A disproportionately small number were admitted into high schools. They were assigned history textbooks that portrayed slavery sympathet-ically and questioned the wisdom of Reconstruction acts that granted African Americans' full citizenship. Racism permeated the school curriculum, and until the 1960s, educators generally ignored African Americans' efforts to correct this bias and introduce more accurate course materials.

At the beginning of the twentieth century, African Americans clearly had greater access to schools than they had in the previous century. However, this inclusion did not signal equal membership in the body politic. Instead it reflected changes in the predominant cultural constructs of citizenship. These changes de-emphasized individual political rights and liberty, and instead pro-moted a vision of a complex, interdependent society in which individuals and groups played different roles, and government distributed services and promoted order and stability. Progressives maintained that differentiated education pro-vided appropriate opportunities for all to develop their own capacities and con-tribute to society based on those capacities, and was, therefore, better than the old common school education that excluded children not suited for the single academic regime.

## Conflicts and Crises: 1930s to the Present

As a larger portion of American children spent a longer period of their lives in public schools, the stakes over controlling the influence of schools on individuals and society increased. Consequently, despite various attempts to insulate schools from politics, the period since the 1920s has been marked by repeated and intense educational "wars." These battles focused both on the content of curriculum, particularly in subjects such as American history and social studies in which notions of citizenship were explicitly taught, and on the conduct of schools, especially the ways in which schools distributed opportunity in society and mediated the relation between individuals and government. The overall direction of educational reform in this period has been away from the differentiated inclusion of the turn of the century toward more egalitarian inclusion. This change paralleled broader efforts to eradicate differential status within citizenship and ensure all Americans equal political and social rights. Ironically, the push for equality has engendered such strife that many Americans have begun to abandon the ideal of schools as broad socializing institutions, and adopted a more limited, instrumental view of the purpose of public education.

While not a novel phenomenon, controversies over textbooks and curriculum reached a new intensity in the 1920s. One of the first national campaigns attacking school texts centered on American history books written by professional historians based in the new research universities. These books downplayed traditional patriotic themes and hero worship in favor of institutional analyses that aligned history with the new social sciences. Culturally conservative patriotic societies, disturbed by the secular scientific outlook of the experts who wrote the books, wanted children to learn a traditional narrative of American distinctiveness and triumph. On the other hand, immigrant organizations wanted texts that presented more positive accounts of their own ethnic groups, and in some cases, more sympathetic views of immigrants and cultural diversity generally.

The fight for textbooks more sympathetic to ethnic groups was part of a larger movement to confront discrimination within the United States. In the 1930s challenges to prejudice against Catholics and Jews began to make headway in American society and schools. Social scientists, led by the anthropologist Franz Boas, rejected theories of biologically based racial differences and developed new ideas about cultural pluralism. The intercultural education movement encouraged knowledge of and respect for cultural diversity among American schoolchildren. Schools also adopted voluntary pullout religious instruction for Protestant, Catholic, and Jewish children. These programs helped to undermine the presumption that the United States was a Protestant nation, and popularize the idea that the country's values were rooted in a broad Judeo-Christian heritage. Religious and ethnic tolerance was furthered during World War II. European fascism heightened Americans' awareness of the problems facing minorities and cast doubts on the moral standing of racist ideologies. In addition, various ethnic groups used their service in war to demonstrate their patriotism and lay claim to full inclusion in American society. American history textbooks reflected the success of these campaigns—anti-Catholic views became much less common, the contributions of ethnic groups were extolled, and schoolchildren learned to celebrate America as a nation of immigrants. Blacks used a strategy similar to European immigrant groups to advance their status within American society and schools, but with much less immediate success.

Civics curriculum in the 1930s built on the community civics model. Harold Rugg, a faculty member at Columbia University's Teachers College, wrote the most popular social studies texts. Rugg subscribed to the ideal of a strong government, securing citizens' basic welfare. This notion of government, of course, coincided with Franklin Roosevelt's New Deal policies, policies Rugg warmly praised. Rugg's texts were, however, much more attentive to inequality than Progressive Era civic programs. He rejected images of the United States as a classless society with easy economic mobility, and presented American history as a series of struggles of the poor against the rich for social justice. Although Rugg's books sold quickly, they were too controversial for some school districts, which dropped the social studies curriculum in favor of a traditional sequence of ancient, medieval, and modern history, and at the end of the decade, their sales plummeted.

Controversies over curriculum were part of larger political battles involving education. During the Depression, educators, led by the National Education Association (NEA), lobbied for federal aid to schools. Several New Deal programs helped schools and teachers and/or had educational components. These programs, though defined as relief measures, bypassed existing educational authorities and professional organizations. They also did not begin to meet the full needs of financially strapped public schools or offset the tremendous inequities in resources that had developed as a result of the tradition of local financing of public schools. Arguing that federal aid was the only effective way to address unequal school funding, the NEA helped engineer the introduction of several bills for federal aid to schools. This proposed legislation excited a great deal of opposition, much of it from groups already mobilized against the growing scope of the federal government, and dedicated to the maintenance of local control over schools. These groups argued that federal funding would inevitably lead to the federal government dictating the content and conduct of schools, taking away authority from families and communities. In addition, longtime tensions over religion and race worked to defeat proposed legislation. Catholic organizations wanted parochial schools to qualify for funding, but professional educators opposed this provision. The National Association for the Advancement of Colored People (NAACP) demanded that new funds be split proportionately between black and white schools, which in turn triggered southern resistance. These divisions created insurmountable barriers for supporters of federal funding.

During World War II, questions about school funding moved off the agenda as did public disputes over the political content of schoolbooks. The tone of civics instruction altered significantly as social studies educators united behind the idea that schools should serve the needs of home front morale. Educators argued that the most important goal of civics was to ensure that all children understand the value of the "democratic way of life" and be willing to do their part to defend it. Schoolchildren were encouraged to contribute to the war effort by selling war bonds, collecting scrap materials, and taking more responsibility at home. Teachers encouraged patriotism through flag salutes and pledges, patriotic songs, plays and pageants, posters, and the celebration of national heroes. In this context, the Progressive Era idea of government as the guarantor of citizens' basic welfare gave way to an emphasis on individual rights and citizens' reciprocal responsibilities to their government. Social studies educators also encouraged teachers to prepare students for the postwar period by introducing the ideals of world citizenship and emphasizing tolerance.

Peace, however, quickly gave way to the cold war, which provided a particularly fertile ground for attacks on schools, textbooks, and teachers. The cold war mobilized and gave legitimacy to groups arguing that public schools were not only failing to prepare good citizens, they were undermining the nation by planting seeds of subversion in American youth. Numerous conservative organizations criticized books that discussed social class, described poverty, or included positive accounts of governmental activism. Between 1958 and 1962, over a third of state legislatures sponsored inquiries on the appropriateness of texts. Publishers responded by dropping or revising controversial texts. Individual teachers also came under attack as localities, states, and the federal government sponsored investigations of suspected "subversives." The House Un-American Activities Committee (HUAC) targeted teachers in the early 1950s. Teachers who refused to cooperate with HUAC or state investigating committees often lost their jobs. An estimated six hundred teachers were fired for political reasons in this period, and many more censored themselves out of fear of reprisals.

The strains of the Depression and war produced serious problems for American public schools. Low teacher salaries and the availability of better-paying jobs created a severe teacher shortage. Years of neglect left school buildings dilapidated and overcrowded. Budget cuts gutted elements of Progressive reform such as social services, project learning, and extracurricular programs. These problems, along with hysteria about political subversion, focused public attention on education. Several critical books and reports, such as Arthur Bestor's *Educational Wastelands: The Retreat from Learning in Our Public Schools* (1953) and Albert Lynd's *Quackery in the Public Schools* (1953), blamed Progressive reformers for undermining the academic rigor of the curriculum, encouraging unsound pedagogy, and introducing expensive "frills" into public schools. In public debates, legitimate critiques about the limits of Progressive education became confused with attacks on Progressive politics, further undermining the authority of educational leaders and increasing repression within schools. This negative attention, though, also mobilized people to "fix" schools. In many communities, citizens' committees were formed to look at local schools and raise funds for them. On a national level, cold war fears that low-quality education was hurting the United States in its competition with the Soviet Union led to the passage of the National Defense Education Act (1958), breaking the logjam on federal funding for public education.

The red scare initially hurt movements for racial equality, as opponents branded activists "communists" or "communist dupes." But black activists and their white allies continued to fight for equal citizenship and used the cold war rhetoric of freedom to advance their cause by arguing that racial injustice under-mined the United States' credibility in the worldwide struggle against commu-nism. Black activists achieved a major breakthrough in 1954, when the Supreme Court ruled in *Brown v. Board of Education* that racially segregated schools were unconstitutional, but for decades, state and local governments devised ways to thwart large-scale integration. By the late 1960s, federal legislation, along with many court cases and local protests, forced southern communities to finally dis-mantle racially segregated school systems. Outside the South, however, little progress was made toward school integration. Large numbers of whites responded to urban desegregation plans by fleeing to suburbs or private schools. In the 1974 case *Milliken v. Bradley*, the Supreme Court severely limited the use of urban-suburban cross-district busing, thus making it nearly impossible for schools to overcome the effects of residential segregation. By the 1990s, residen-tial segregation would begin to reverse racial mixing in southern schools as well.

For most black activists, desegregation was not an end in itself, but a means to a larger goal, full and equal inclusion. They thus sought other changes in schools, such as access to higher academic tracks, an end to excessive disci-pline, greater respect for their families and culture, and more employment and leadership opportunities in schools. In the context of the civil rights move-ment, the treatment of race in American history courses became an explosive issue. Blacks demanded that schoolbooks include their history, as they under-stood it, not as a justification for white supremacy. This, however, did not fit with the prevailing norms of textbooks, which avoided negative depictions of the country and emphasized freedom as the predominant value of the nation. Attempts to introduce textbooks with more critical accounts of race in the nation's history provoked counterattacks from patriotic organizations. The fights over American history and other textbooks became fiercer as other polit-ical movements emerged in the late 1960s. Feminists, Native Americans, Latinos, and Asian Americans all saw schools and their curriculum as impor-tant turf in the struggle for equal citizenship.

In addition to demanding curricular changes, activists pushed the federal government to intervene in public schools to address inequities. These efforts helped support the passage of several landmark educational laws, including the Elementary and Secondary Education Act (ESEA), which provided federal aid to schools educating poor children, the Higher Education Act, which extended federal financial aid programs, the Bilingual Education Act, establishing special programs for children who did not speak English, and Title IX, requiring equity for girls and boys. These laws established new levels of federal involvement in public education and a strong commitment to the ideal of equality.

By the mid-1970s, these social movements peaked and began to recede from the center of national politics. The corresponding battles over schooling lost some of their intensity, but were not resolved. Indeed, they would be refought in different guises, such as the controversy over the National History Standards, during the last decades of the twentieth century.

The federal government funded a group of scholars, led by historian Gary Nash of UCLA, to develop guidelines for the teaching of American history. The day before the group's report was released, Lynne Cheney, former head of the National Endowment for the Humanities, published an editorial in the *Wall Street Journal* blasting the group for ignoring major historical figures in the name of multiculturalism. This led to a protracted battle over the standards, which largely undermined efforts to develop consensus regarding history instruction.

In this relative calm, a new and disturbing stance was evident—cynicism about the public purposes of schooling. This cynicism, which mirrored broader developments in American culture, manifested itself in a number of ways. Tax revolts, such as Proposition 13 in California, reversed positive trends in school financing, and signaled a new unwillingness to provide financial support for public schools. This made efforts to equalize resources for schools more difficult. Civics lost its secure place in the school curriculum as educators became uncertain about its efficacy and its proper content. Some of the activists who had been fighting for inclusive education shifted their attention to the education of their own groups. The rhetoric about the purposes of education shifted from citizenship to economics. Individuals were encouraged to pursue education in order to get better jobs and make more money. The nation's interest in education became framed around economic growth and competitiveness. For example, the well-publicized 1983 report criticizing the quality of American schools, *A Nation at Risk: The Imperative for Educational Reform*, highlighted the threat of industrial decline, not ignorant voters. In the 1990s business leaders led efforts to improve the quality of schools, because they (and by extension, the nation) needed more skilled employees. This launched the standards movement, which was supported both as a way to improve the quality of the labor force and a mechanism for overcoming inequities in the quality of students' education. At the same time, various educational policies sought to improve education by offering alternatives to public schools. Charter schools and vouchers, for example, assumed that individual choice and market mechanisms would produce better schools than public agencies. The explosive growth of homeschooling represented the most extreme example of the privatization of education, in which each family decides the educational aims of their own children, and the government's interest in socializing children for the public good is negated.

## Conclusion

While private interests continue to dominate contemporary discussions about the benefits of education, there is evidence of a resurgent concern about civics (see Puckett and Johanek in this volume). Since the early 1990s several foundations, including the Council for the Advancement of Citizenship, have initiated programs related to citizenship education. The federal government has also taken a more active role in encouraging new programs. In 2003 the Senate passed by unanimous consent the American History and Civics Education Act, and President Bush hosted "We the People," A White House Forum on American History, Civics, and Service. As in the past, these efforts are caught in the crossfire of larger disputes over the meaning of citizenship in the United States. Once again, basic questions are being reconsidered: How inclusive should American society be? What values define a common American culture? How can individual rights be reconciled with community norms? How should authority be shared within a democracy? It is tempting for educators to retreat from these explosive issues in order to protect schools from political controversy. But the history of public schools indicates that a rigid separation of education and politics is impossible. Education remains a key means of "enacting" ideals of citizenship—communicating and debating changing values, translating ideas into expectations for behavior, and expressing beliefs in institutional forms. Civic purposes are deeply ingrained in the history of American education, and cannot be abandoned.

## Bibliography

Adams, David Wallace. *Education for Extinction: American Indians and the Boarding School Experience, 1875–1928*. Lawrence: University Press of Kansas, 1995.

Anderson, James D. *The Education of Blacks in the South, 1860–1935*. Chapel Hill: University of North Carolina Press, 1988.

Angus, David L., and Jeffrey E. Mirel. *The Failed Promise of the American High School, 1890–1995*. New York: Teachers College Press, 1999.

Bailyn, Bernard. *The Ideological Origins of the American Revolution*. Cambridge, Mass.: Belknap Press of Harvard University Press, 1967.

Beadie, Nancy, and Kim Tolley, eds. *Chartered Schools: Two Hundred Years of Independent Academies in the United States, 1727–1925*. New York: Routledge Falmer, 2002.

Cremin, Lawrence A. *American Education: The Colonial Experience, 1607–1783*. New York: Harper and Row, 1970.

Cremin, Lawrence A. *American Education: The National Experience, 1783–1876*. New York: Harper and Row, 1980.

Elson, Ruth Miller. *Guardians of Tradition: American Schoolbooks of the Nineteenth Century.* Lincoln: University of Nebraska Press, 1964.

Fehrenbacher, Don E. *The Dred Scott Case: Its Significance in American Law and Politics.* Oxford, U.K., and New York: Oxford University Press, 1978.

Field, Sherry L. "Citizens for a 'New World Order': A Historical Perspective of Citizenship Education in the United States." In *Citizenship, Education and the Modern State,* edited by Kerry Kennedy. London and Washington, D.C.: Falmer, 1997.

Foster, Stuart J. *Red Alert!: Educators Confront the Red Scare in American Public Schools, 1947–1954.* New York: P. Lang, 2000.

Gaustad, Edwin S. *Proclaim Liberty throughout All the Land: A History of Church and State in America.* Oxford, U.K., and New York: Oxford University Press, 2003.

Gordon, David T. *A Nation Reformed?: American Education 20 Years after A Nation at Risk.* Cambridge, Mass.: Harvard Education Press, 2003.

Gonzalez, Gilbert G. *Chicano Education in the Era of Segregation.* Philadelphia: Balch Institute Press, 1990.

Gorn, Elliott J. Introduction to *The McGuffey Readers: Selections from the 1879 Edition.* Boston: Bedford, 1998.

Graham, Hugh Davis. *The Uncertain Triumph: Federal Education Policy in the Kennedy and Johnson Years.* Chapel Hill: University of North Carolina Press, 1984.

Grossman, James R. *Land of Hope: Chicago, Black Southerners, and the Great Migration.* Chicago: University of Chicago Press, 1989.

Hellebrand, Harold. *The Unfinished Revolution: Education and Politics in the Thought of Thomas Jefferson.* Newark: University of Delaware Press, 1990.

Hertzberg, Hazel W. *Social Studies Reform, 1880–1980.* Boulder, Colo.: Social Science Education Consortium, 1981.

Higham, John. *Strangers in the Land: Patterns of American Nativism, 1860–1925.* New York: Atheneum, 1963.

Johnson, Paul E. *A Shopkeeper's Millennium: Society and Revivals in Rochester, New York, 1815–1837.* New York: Hill and Wang, 1978.

Kaestle, Carl F. *Pillars of the Republic: Common Schools and American Society, 1780–1860.* New York: Hill and Wang, 1983.

Kammen, Michael. *A Machine That Would Go of Itself: The Constitution in American Culture.* New York: Knopf, 1986.

Kerber, Linda K. *No Constitutional Right to Be Ladies: Women and the Obligations of Citizenship.* New York: Hill and Wang, 1998.

Keyssar, Alexander. *The Right to Vote: The Contested History of Democracy in the United States.* New York: Basic, 2000.

Krug, Edward A. *The Shaping of the American High School.* New York: Harper and Row, 1964.

Margo, Robert A. *Race and Schooling in the South, 1880–1950: An Economic History.* Chicago: University of Chicago Press, 1990.

McAfee, Ward M. *Religion, Race, and Reconstruction: The Public School in the Politics of the 1870s.* Albany: State University of New York Press, 1998.

McGreevy, John T. *Catholicism and American Freedom: A History.* New York: Norton, 2003.

Meyer, D. H. *The Instructed Conscience; The Shaping of the American National Ethic.* Philadelphia: University of Pennsylvania Press, 1972.

Monaghan, E. Jennifer. *A Common Heritage: Noah Webster's Blue-back Speller.* Hamden, Conn.: Archon, 1983.

Montalto, Nicholas V. *A History of the Intercultural Education Movement, 1924–1941.* New York: Garland, 1982.

Moreau, Joseph. *Schoolbook Nation: Conflicts over American History Textbooks from the Civil War to the Present.* Ann Arbor: University of Michigan Press, 2003.

Nash, Gary B., Charlotte Crabtree, and Ross E. Dunn. *History on Trial: Culture Wars and the Teaching of the Past.* New York: Knopf, 1997.

Patterson, James T. *Brown v. Board of Education: A Civil Rights Milestone and Its Troubled Legacy.* Oxford, U.K., and New York: Oxford University Press, 2001.

Pangle, Lorraine Smith, and Thomas J. Pangle. *The Learning of Liberty: The Educational Ideas of the American Founders.* Lawrence: University of Kansas Press, 1993.

Perlmann, Joel. *Ethnic Differences: Schooling and Social Structure among the Irish, Italians, Jews, and Blacks in an American City, 1880–1935.* Cambridge, U.K., and New York: Cambridge University Press, 1988.

Polenberg, Richard. *One Nation Divisible: Class, Race, and Ethnicity in the United States since 1938.* New York: Viking Press, 1980.

Raftery, Judith Rosenberg. *Land of Fair Promise: Politics and Reform in Los Angeles Schools, 1885–1941.* Stanford, Calif.: Stanford University Press, 1992.

Ross, Dorothy. *The Origins of American Social Science.* Cambridge, U.K., and New York: Cambridge University Press, 1991.

Rudolph, Frederick, ed. *Essays on Education in the Early Republic.* Cambridge, Mass.: Belknap Press of Harvard University Press, 1965.

Schulman, Bruce J. *The Seventies: The Great Shift in American Culture, Society, and Politics.* New York: Free Press, 2001.

Smith, Gilbert E. *The Limits of Reform: Politics and Federal Aid to Education, 1937–1950.* New York: Garland Publishers, 1982.

Stocking, George W., Jr. *Race, Culture, and Evolution: Essays in the History of Anthropology.* Chicago: University of Chicago Press, 1982.

Takaki, Ronald. *Strangers from a Different Shore: A History of Asian Americans.* Rev. ed. Boston: Little Brown, 1998.

Tuttle, William M., Jr. *Daddy's Gone to War: The Second World War in the Lives of America's Children.* New York: Oxford University Press, 1993.

Tyack, David, and Elisabeth Hansot. *Learning Together: A History of Coeducation in American Schools.* New Haven, Conn.: Yale University Press, 1990.

Tyack, David, Robert Lowe, and Elisabeth Hansot. *Public Schools in Hard Times: The Great Depression and Recent Years.* Cambridge, Mass.: Harvard University Press, 1984.

Tyack, David B. *The One Best System: A History of American Urban Education.* Cambridge, Mass.: Harvard University Press, 1974.

Van Nuys, Frank. *Americanizing the West: Race, Immigrants, and Citizenship, 1890–1930.* Lawrence: University Press of Kansas, 2002.

Vinovskis, Maris. *The Origins of Public High Schools: A Reexamination of the Beverly High School Controversy.* Madison: University of Wisconsin Press, 1985.

Walsh, Julie M. *The Intellectual Origins of Mass Parties and Mass Schools in the Jacksonian Period: Creating a Conformed Citizenry.* New York: Garland, 1998.

Winterer, Caroline. *The Culture of Classicism: Ancient Greece and Rome in American Intellectual Life, 1780–1910.* Baltimore: Johns Hopkins University Press, 2002.

Wood, Gordon S. *The Creation of the American Republic, 1776–1787.* Chapel Hill: University of North Carolina Press, 1969.

Zilversmit, Arthur. *Changing Schools: Progressive Education Theory and Practice, 1930–1960.* Chicago: University of Chicago Press, 1993.

Zimmerman, Jonathan. *Whose America?: Culture Wars in the Public Schools.* Cambridge, Mass.: Harvard University Press, 2002.

# 2

## THE GOVERNANCE OF
## PUBLIC EDUCATION

### *Thomas Corcoran and Margaret Goertz*

THE RESPONSIBILITY FOR K–12 EDUCATION IN THE United States is spread across multiple levels of government and administrative units. Forty-seven million students attend 93,000 public schools located in nearly 15,000 school districts, in 50 states and the District of Columbia. Another 5.2 million students are enrolled in 27,000 private schools that are subject, in varying degrees, to state and federal laws and regulations. Nearly 700,000 students are enrolled in charter schools and at least another 850,000 are homeschooled. This complex and fragmented system is a legacy of the deep-seated fear of centralized authority that shaped the nation's founders' views of government, the content of the U.S. Constitution, and the design and evolution of the federal system.[1]

The founding fathers viewed the education of all citizens (however narrowly defined at the time) as essential to sustaining a representative form of government. Thomas Jefferson, for example, advocated the creation of free "common schools" that would teach young children the moral values and basic skills needed to be economically self-sufficient and virtuous citizens. The education of civic leaders, however, would be more extensive and reserved mainly for sons of the elite (see Reuben in this volume). While education was considered a public good and a national interest, responsibility for the delivery of schooling was placed in the hands of the states, which then delegated it to local communities, reflecting the colonists' strong distrust of centralized authority. Education was also seen as a means for the pursuit of individual happiness and advancement. The idea of the self-made citizen who seeks advancement through education, as embodied in Horatio Alger's popular nineteenth-century stories for children, is central to the nation's ideology of individualism and has deep roots in American culture. Thus, inherent in the education governance structure are tensions between national and local interests in education, and between education as a means to advance the public good and as a vehicle to further individual success. These tensions have been reflected historically in decisions concerning who gets educated and with what level of resources (equal educational opportunity), what students should learn (control over curriculum), and where they are educated and how (compulsory attendance and assignment to schools and programs).

In this essay, we examine how the diverse system of public elementary and secondary schools is governed in the United States. The questions that concern us include how policy gets made in the multilayered and fragmented governance structure of American public education. What are the relationships among the levels of government and how are they changing? How are the interests of parents and citizens addressed and protected? How does this governance structure address the core tensions between collective and individual interests?

Describing and understanding the governance system requires an examination of the systemic relations among the public, the profession, and the polity. We are using Thomas F. Green's definition of the polity as the set of "institutional and social arrangements whereby power and authority are distributed, and within which debates on policy and procedure are carried on, and through which decisions are implemented and enforced."[2] It includes federal and state agencies and local boards of education. Here we focus on the public and the polity, leaving the role of the profession to be covered elsewhere in this book.

We begin with a discussion of what citizens want from the system of public education and how their interests have been represented in local education systems. We then examine how the nationalization of education issues has expanded the federal and state roles in education and created access to educational policymaking for new groups, such as racial/ethnic minorities, business, and the religious Right. We return to the local level to describe new governance structures that are emerging to provide greater power to parents and citizens and conclude with a discussion of challenges facing the governance of public education.

## What the Public Wants from Education

There is widespread support in the United States for the maintenance of a free system of public schools. The public is committed to public schools as institutions that bind society together. They want safe, orderly schools where all children learn at least basic skills and more if possible. Public support for the local public school has risen since the 1980s, and the vast majority of citizens want to fix what they see as an ailing institution rather than find an alternative system.[3] However, a growing minority of citizens seem to believe that changes in policy cannot revitalize the existing system. They look back on almost fifty years of investment in school reform and see little benefit. As a consequence, they are raising questions about the purposes of education, what is public about public education, the structure of the system, how authority is distributed within it, and the roles of the public and professionals in making decisions. In short, they are challenging the current polity of education. Some call for giving more power to parents through decentralization or school choice. Others call for increased central authority with national testing and stronger accountability. Opinions about education policy and interest in education as a public versus a private good vary along with personal stakes in schooling, philosophies about its purposes, cultural background, and political values.

One major fault line lies between parents of young or school-age children and those without children or whose children have completed their K–12 education. While citizens in all three categories should be concerned about the quality and costs of public schools, the nature of their interests, and the priority given to them, often differ. Parents of children under eighteen have a high stake in the quality of the schools because their children stand to gain economically and socially from access to a better education. However, they are more likely to be concerned about the quality of the schools their children attend than they are in the schools attended by other people's children. In a technologically advanced market economy, ensuring that one's children receive a more, and better, education than their peers is perceived to be an effective way of preparing them for the economic and social competition that they will face as adults. In the twentieth century, educational attainment became the equivalent of property for the middle class, as it was a tangible asset that could be passed on to children, enabling them to maintain or improve their family's social standing. Parents of school-age children, particularly those who are well-educated or affluent, seek the best possible schools for their children. Middle-income American families often select their places of residence in part based on the perceived quality of the local community's public schools, and typically they are willing to pay higher taxes if necessary to maintain or improve the quality of these schools. And they are likely to support efforts by local, state, or federal policymakers to raise school quality by adopting high standards and rigorous curriculum, lowering class sizes, improving the quality of teaching, recruiting better teachers, and expanding preschool education—as long as these actions do not negatively affect their own children's schools.[4]

In contrast, the interests and political positions of citizens who have no children enrolled in the public schools differ. This includes citizens who have no children, and those whose children attend private schools, are homeschooled, or have completed their public schooling. These groups may support their local schools because they believe in ideals of social justice, or because they feel that good education raises the quality of life in their communities or is good for the economy, or because of concern about local property values or their pensions. But these perceived benefits are indirect, long term, and uncertain, and may be less salient than the immediate effects of rising school taxes in their communities. As a consequence, those without children enrolled in the public schools tend to be more skeptical about investments in the schools, and they are likely to value home rule because it provides them with a reliable political check on increases in the costs of schooling, and hence their taxes.

The balance of political power between the parents of public school children and other citizens has shifted since the 1960s. In 1969, slightly less than half of all American households had children under eighteen, but by 2000, this proportion had dropped to about one-third of all households. During the same period, the number of non-family households (a person living alone or with someone who is not related) rose from 15 percent to 32 percent, and the number of senior citizen households increased from 17.5 percent to 21 percent.[5] As a result of these demographic changes, households without children in the public schools now outnumber those with enrolled children in most school districts. This change in the composition of local electorates poses serious problems for education policymakers. In many communities, school budgets must be approved by the local voters, and inflation, rising costs for special education and other mandated programs, and teacher salary scales linked to years of experience produce annual increases in these budgets. The turnout for these school elections—for board members and for school budgets—is generally much lower than for general elections, about 15 percent to 20 percent for school elections compared with 50 percent to 60 percent for general elections. So in most communities, parents are able to mobilize those who support public education and pass school budgets. In a typical year, only a small minority of school budgets are defeated. From time to time, particular issues, such as the adoption of controversial programs, misuse of funds, or excessive costs, rankle local electorates, and as the turnout at the polls increases, the chances of budgets being defeated increases. It is ironic that the operation of the public schools, viewed as a pillar of American democracy, is dependent in many communities on keeping participation in elections down.

A second source of conflict over education policy arises from differences in cultural values. The United States is a highly diverse society, but most citizens expect the public schools to teach all children a set of common values and prepare them for participation in a secular democracy while still protecting and respecting the diversity of their cultural backgrounds. In theory, the public schools provide the space in which children from diverse racial, ethnic, and religious heritages learn how to live together. In short, the schools are expected to pursue and promote the common good and provide the civic glue that holds this culturally diverse society together. However, the role of schools in socializing children has always been controversial. Throughout the history of public education, there have been clashes of cultural values. These have included struggles over curriculum, such as the continuing battle over teaching theories of evolution and creationism, struggles over the appropriateness and nature of sex education, and local debates over the selection of novels for language arts classes. Add to these the persistent political fights over language policies, religious expression, and student rights and discipline policies, and the contentious nature of education policy at all levels becomes apparent. Many parents with strong religious or ideological orientations have opted for private education or, more recently, home schooling, rather than expose their children to values that they find unacceptable. But even with these outlets for those who are unhappy with the public schools, the cultural conflicts continue.

At the local level, these cultural conflicts are exacerbated by the increasing diversity within communities. High mobility—over 40 million Americans move each year—immigration, and changing housing patterns are contributing to this increased diversity. In 1990 cities were largely populated by minorities, immigrants, and poor people; inner-ring suburbs were home to blue-collar whites and older people, and affluent whites lived in the outer-ring suburbs.[6] By 2000, poverty, race, and cultures were more diversely scattered through the metropolitan rings. Minority families have moved to the suburbs, and wealthy whites back to the inner city. As a consequence, middle-class white families find themselves in the same districts as poor and immigrant families, who may have quite different priorities and concerns, and whose children may have different needs.

Should pluralism and diversity be reflected in our arrangements for schooling? This is the fundamental issue for public education. Do we simply want schools to teach tolerance and respect for personal cultural differences, while socializing all children into a common secular culture? Or do we believe that schools can be segregated by culture and socialize children into different belief systems, while preserving a unified society? Where citizens stand on these questions depends in part on the importance they place on their own group's beliefs and values and the degree to which they perceive them to be different from those of the national, secular culture, in part on how much emphasis they place on individual freedom of belief and expression, and in part on how they perceive the public good. Arguments for a more diverse, pluralistic system of public schools range from the ideological (e.g., teaching Christian values) to the practical (overcoming obstacles to academic progress).

A third divide among Americans arises from different understandings of the meaning of equal opportunity. Since the 1950s, the federal and state governments, especially the courts, have actively sought to make the provision of public schooling more equitable. Actions to eliminate school segregation, protections for students with disabilities, and school finance reform are prime examples of these struggles to achieve greater equality of educational opportunity. While many believe that the current public school system continues to fall short of this ideal, social reformers have waged a struggle for nearly two hundred years to make the schools more equal, and they have made considerable progress.

However, the achievement gaps among white, African American, and Hispanic students remain large. Data from the National Assessment of Educational Progress, the federally funded system for monitoring student progress, show large and persistent gaps in achievement. And results from the Program for International Student Assessment (PISA) conducted in 2000 by the Organization for Economic Co-operation and Development show that the United States has among the largest disparities in achievement among the thirty-two participating nations.[7]

As a consequence, the goals of reformers have shifted from equalizing expenditures and access to services to ensuring that children at risk, meaning poor and minority children, receive an adequate education and that performance gaps are significantly reduced. "Adequacy" is often defined as the package of services that would result in children meeting academic standards and narrowing achievement gaps. While most citizens support the policy changes that have been made to advance equal opportunity and agree that the performance gaps are a serious problem, an overwhelming majority also believe that these gaps are a result of factors unrelated to the quality of the public schools, such as home and community environment, and lack of student interest and parental involvement. The public is split on whether schools should spend more money on at-risk children, and the majority do not seem to be convinced that the provision of equitable schooling will close achievement gaps and ensure social mobility and a fairer, more stable society.[8]

Americans hold conflicting and inconsistent views of equal opportunity. Many who voice support for equal spending also accept the proposition that local communities should be able to provide whatever amount and quality of education they can afford. They see differences in the quality of the schools across communities as natural and inevitable, consequences of a social sorting based on talent, work ethic, income, and commitment to education. Many, perhaps a majority, resist efforts to equalize expenditures across communities, viewing them as "leveling down" or as "intrusions in local control." Confronted with the differences in the quality of education between rich and poor communities, most Americans would probably argue that fairness does not demand that everyone receive the same education. Some might even say that people in poorer communities should work hard, save their money, and move to a community in which their children can attend better schools. Middle-class Americans seem to simultaneously embrace two opposing principles: all children should have equal opportunity for a good education and—through hard work—upward mobility and economic success, and families should be able to use their resources to secure educational advantages for their children.

There is a fundamental tension between the interests of the education polity and the interests of parents on this issue. The state may view advancement of equal educational opportunity as in its interest and as a fundamental duty, but parents are unlikely to see this as their ultimate goal. What they want is not for their children to have equal opportunity but to receive the best possible education and better outcomes than others. This can mean receiving better opportunities relative to other children. Many parents actively seek advantages for their children within their community schools by supporting policies such as tracking, gifted education, and specialized programs in academics, the arts, and athletics. The vast majority believe that there are innate differences in intelligence and other talents. They support the concept of providing special opportunities for high-achieving children, and, as any suburban school official can attest to, there is considerable pressure from parents to have their children placed in these special programs. The same phenomenon is seen in larger systems that operate magnet programs, innovative programs not generally available in local schools and that are intended to attract students from diverse racial backgrounds. In fact, one of the common justifications for the provision of magnet or selective programs in urban districts is keeping middle-class families in the system. These programs are often costly and benefit small numbers of students at the expense of the general student population. While these programs are often justified in terms of the public good, the trade-offs associated with allocating resources to support them are seldom discussed.

The tensions between private interests and the public good play out in the context of multiple layers of governance. Most obviously, they appear at the local level, where some fifteen thousand school districts are the dominant governance structure. They are affected by the federal government through funding, public policies, and regulatory mechanisms. And they are shaped by each state, especially as state governments have come to play a larger role in the oversight of local school districts.

## Local Control of Education

Constitutional authority for education resides in the states, a "reserved" power arising from the Tenth Amendment to the U.S. Constitution. States, in turn, decide how much authority to retain, and how much power to give to local education agencies (LEAs), schools, and parents. The extent of this delegation varies widely across the states, reflecting different political histories, traditions, and political cultures, but for the most part, until the 1960s both responsibility for and control of education rested firmly in the hands of local communities through their elected school boards and school administrators. State and federal governments had limited involvement in elementary and secondary education. Outside the major cities, school districts were generally small. In 1950 the average school district had only two school buildings and three hundred students, allowing the system to reflect the goals of the community and enabling direct communication between citizens, their schools, and their school boards.

The governance picture is much different today. The consolidation of school districts—from over eighty thousand in 1950 to about fifteen thousand in 1990—has resulted in larger and more bureaucratic entities with weaker connections to the local populace. Expanded control by states and the federal government, with policies increasingly aimed at influencing curriculum and instruction, has narrowed the locus of local decision-making. Yet even as the federal and state governments increase their roles in education policy, local control continues to predominate in the United States. Local school districts retain primary responsibility for curriculum and instruction, the hiring and assignment of teachers and principals, the funding of schools, and the operation and maintenance of school buildings. And states hold school districts accountable for implementing state and federal policies.

In most communities, elected school boards are the public's main vehicle for exercising democratic control. School board members are elected either at-large (representing the entire district) or from subdistricts, generally in nonpartisan elections that are held on a different day than municipal, state, or national contests. This structure is a legacy of the Progressive movement of the early twentieth century, when school reformers sought to isolate public education from the ward-based, partisan politics of the cities. While most school board elections are apolitical, with few contested seats, school boards in large districts (of twenty-five thousand students or more) generally have active interest groups, politically oriented candidates, and competitive elections.[9]

Some commentators question whether school boards are truly representative bodies if elections are noncompetitive and voter turnout is low. Others argue that low turnout is a sign of a community's satisfaction with its schools at a given point in time, and that when citizens become dissatisfied with the status quo, they will use the channel of elections to express their displeasure and, in time, to seat new school board members.[10] And voting represents only one form of citizen involvement in local schools. About half of registered voters reported that they are most likely to support their public schools by attending local school events, talking to friends and neighbors about education, following the activities of their school board, and/or signing a petition, and one-third of voters say that they raise money for local schools.[11]

The intent of the Progressive reformers was for school boards to serve primarily as legislative bodies, raising and allocating education revenues, setting education policy, passing regulations, appointing the chief administrative officer, and responding to constituent concerns. The appointed superintendent and central office staff, experts in education administration, would be responsible for implementing board policy. This distinction often breaks down in reality, however. School boards have executive, judicial, and policymaking roles. They approve expenditures and personnel appointments and hold hearings on matters such as student suspensions and expulsions.[12] Local education bureaucracies have grown larger and increasingly complex, particularly after the advent of federal and state programs for special-needs students. They have been criticized for being unresponsive to community needs and for being incapable of educating children.

These local education boards and bureaucracies are not always perceived to be "local" to parents whose children attend a neighborhood school. In many large school districts, the influence of parents, students, and local residents over the education of children is quite limited and they often feel disenfranchised and powerless. If they are dissatisfied, these groups can appeal to local school leaders, or to the bureaucratic hierarchy or to representatives of a larger, disinterested public, or they can protest to try to gain the support of the larger public. But at all levels, they are begging for relief. The polity does not provide an effective avenue for them to express their interests in their children's education.

Concern over this lack of responsiveness, as well as concerns about accountability and poor performance, has led some states and school districts to enact two types of governance change. The first kind of change expanded the authority of schools through local school councils and other forms of school-based management. This devolution served two purposes: to shift from centralized democratic control, exercised through a district board and central bureaucracy, to expanded local democratic control, exercised through a school council composed of parents, community members, and school staff;[13] and to give those who have primary responsibility for student learning—teachers—the flexibility to select and use instructional programs that they feel meet the needs of their students. The second governance change alters the nature of centralized democratic control, by moving the control of the school system from the school board to the mayor's office. The type and level of mayoral involvement in local school systems ranges from appointing a subset of school board members to appointing both the full board and the superintendent of schools. The specifics reflect each city's educational and political context and history. Although there is limited information on the impact of mayoral control, proponents of this approach argue that such control provides a single point of electoral accountability for education, improves the management of the school system, facilitates the integration of education with other children's services, and ultimately will improve educational quality and student performance.[14]

However, the most significant trend in local governance is the shifting of control over central decisions about education—standards, curriculum, resource allocation, qualifications of staff, and so on—to the state and federal governments. In the next two sections, we examine the growing role of the state and federal governments. Since recent actions of the federal government are reshaping the role of the states in education, we will discuss it first.

## The Federal Role in Education

The federal government is often called the "junior partner" in American education because it provides only a small amount of funding—less than 10 percent of what is spent on elementary and secondary education—and because it has limited control over the structure and content of education. For over two hundred years, however, the federal government has intervened when vital national interests were involved and states and local communities were either unwilling or unable to act. These national interests include supporting democracy by educating citizens in common schools; enhancing national productivity and providing for the defense of the country by building the technical skills of workers; and ensuring educational opportunity by protecting the rights and expanding the opportunities of students with special needs.[15] Today, the impact of the federal government far exceeds its fiscal contribution and legal responsibility. Its institutions—the courts, Congress, and the executive branch—have used multiple strategies to advance federal goals of equity, access, and quality education.

Until the 1950s, the federal government played a limited role in education. Congress encouraged the establishment of public schools and universities in new territories and states through land grants, and promoted vocational training of high school and college students through categorical grants to states. The national draft for World War I revealed an unexpectedly high illiteracy rate among young men, raising a general concern for the nation's educational standards and the adequacy of local resources to support education. From time to time, Congress debated whether the federal government should authorize general education aid to address the inequitable distribution of educational resources across states, but legislation was defeated for both philosophical and economic reasons. Opponents of federal aid argued successfully that education was rightfully a state and local responsibility and that federal funds would lead to federal control and regulation of education. Support for a larger federal role was also eroded by pressures on the federal budget after World War II. By 1950, federal aid represented only 3 percent of elementary and secondary education revenues.

The national discourse about the equality and quality of education and the federal role changed dramatically starting in 1954 when the U.S. Supreme Court declared that racially segregated schools were unconstitutional. Although education is not a fundamental right under the U.S. Constitution, the federal courts turned to the equal protection and due process clauses of the Constitution to give many categories of students—first racial and ethnic minority students, and then students with disabilities, English-language learners, and children of illegal aliens—more equal access to schooling and appropriate programs of education, and to provide them with procedural safeguards while they attend school. These civil rights and service mandates were subsequently embedded in federal legislation such as the Civil Rights Act of 1964, Section 504 of the Rehabilitation Act of 1973, and the Education for All Handicapped Children Act of 1975, and in other government regulations. The perceived threat to national security during the 1950s provided another justification for an expanded federal role in education. In response to warnings that the United States was falling behind in scientific fields, especially given Russian advances in space travel, Congress enacted the National Defense Education Act of 1958, the largest federal commitment to elementary and secondary education until the enactment of the Elementary and Secondary Education Act (ESEA) in 1965.

Equal educational opportunity for students with special needs expanded in the mid-1960s with the passage of the ESEA. While calls for increased federal aid to education had continued through the 1950s as local school districts faced booming enrollments and insufficient facilities, the politics of race (resistance to the court-ordered desegregation of schools) and religion (constitutional separation of church and state), as well as the continuing fear of federal control, limited new aid programs to those that addressed narrower issues, such as a shortage of scientifically trained personnel. The ESEA addressed these political issues by targeting federal aid on economically and educationally disadvantaged children, regardless of where they lived or attended school, and by leaving the design and content of programs to state and local decision-makers. Subsequent federal aid programs targeted assistance to students with disabilities, English-language learners, and other special-needs students. The federal government used fiscal and administrative requirements to ensure that recipients of its funds advanced the federal objectives of student equity, and subsequently of educational quality.

For the first twenty years of ESEA, for example, there were concerns that state and local policymakers did not embrace the federal equity agenda. Therefore, the federal government emphasized the use of targeting provisions and fiscal compliance audits to ensure that its funds were spent on poor students. Starting in the late 1980s, the federal focus began to shift from student access to additional services to the quality of the services provided, and from procedural accountability to educational accountability, bringing together the goals of equity and quality. The 1988 amendments to ESEA required states, for the first time, to set a minimum performance level for students receiving federal funds through Title I of ESEA, and to identify schools that did not show progress toward these goals. These provisions, however, applied only to Title I funded students. As discussed in greater detail below, the Improving America's Schools Act of 1994 (IASA) and its successor, the No Child Left Behind Act of 2001 (NCLB), used federal aid to promote educational quality by requiring states—all of which receive Title I funds—to adopt more rigorous academic standards, implement extensive testing aligned with these standards, accept greater accountability for the performance of all students, and ensure the placement of "highly qualified" teachers in all classrooms. These laws reconceptualized equity as ensuring all students access to a quality education program rather than to supplemental and often compensatory services. They shifted the focus of the federal government from students with special needs to all students, and involved the federal government in the provision of general education, until then the sole responsibility of state and local governments.

The national discourse in education has also been shaped by the deliberations and publications of federal commissions and speeches and other actions by
top officials, particularly the president and secretary of education. For example,
the release in 1983 of the National Commission on Excellence in Education's
report *A Nation at Risk: The Imperative for Educational Reform,* and the subsequent
response from the press, the business community, the public, and President
Ronald Reagan, are often cited as the impetus for the "education excellence"
movement in the United States. The report's findings that students were not prepared to meet the demands of a technological society or to maintain the United
States' international competitive position led states to create their own study
commissions and ultimately adopt many of the recommendations contained in it
and other national reports.[16] President George H.W. Bush's 1989 education summit with the nation's governors placed educational outcomes on the policy
agenda with the promulgation of six national education goals. Congress subsequently codified these goals and funded the development of the country's first
national academic standards. The administration of President George W. Bush
launched an extensive public relations campaign to build political support for
NCLB and used local media to hold states and districts accountable to the public for implementation of the law.

The expanded federal role during the second half of the twentieth century
was shaped, in part, by national movements, such as the civil rights movement. The
nationalization of education policy, in turn, created a new arena for other organized interests, such as business, political conservatives, and religious groups.[17] The
NCLB Act was the product of an unusual political coalition in the United States,
and one that could be created and sustained only at the national level. Groups that
in the past fought about whether there should be a federal role in education found
common ground in the NCLB legislation. The civil rights community viewed
accountability for "high standards for all children" as a way of ensuring that poor
children and children of color get access to a quality education. The business community viewed the law as a way of raising educational standards and holding educators accountable for improving student performance, and conservatives saw in
the law a mechanism for expanding parental choice and market-driven educational options. They all faced the challenge, however, of seeing the law implemented in the United States' highly decentralized educational system.

## The State Role in Education

In the United States, all state constitutions contain provisions requiring states to
create systems of free public schools, but until the mid-1960s, the state role in
education was largely limited to creating and funding local school districts, setting broad goals and general guidelines, and licensing teachers. Today, states play
a major role in the funding and regulation of education, and education has come

to dominate state policy agendas. Several forces led to this major expansion in state responsibilities: the explosion in federal education programs and mandates in the mid-1960s and 1970s; the provision of federal funds to support state administration of these programs and to strengthen the capacity of state education agencies; increases in state spending on education to address fiscal and programmatic inequities among school districts; and the national call for a renewed emphasis on academic excellence that emanated from *A Nation at Risk.*

States vary in the substance and scope of their education policies, but they all focus on five policy domains: curriculum and instruction, accountability and assessment, teacher preparation, governance, and finance. Since 1990, policies in these areas have been shaped by standards-based reform, a movement that has redefined both educational outcomes and accountability systems. Under the theory of standards-based reform, states establish challenging, rather than minimal, content and performance standards for all students. Then states give schools and school districts greater flexibility to design appropriate instructional programs in exchange for performance-based accountability. States monitor the results rather than the process of education; they hold schools accountable for student achievement rather than for compliance with rules and regulations.

States use a variety of measures to influence the content of school curriculum, but until the 1990s, most state activity focused on instructional time and/or required courses or credits. Nearly all states mandate the minimum number of days students must attend school (generally 180 days) and/or the minimum length of the school day, and set a minimum age when students must enter and may leave school. Forty-three states mandate the number and type of courses students must take to graduate from high school. Most of these states raised their course work standards in the wake of *A Nation at Risk,* but by 2002, only eighteen states required students to take four years of English and three years each of mathematics, science, and social studies as recommended by the National Commission on Excellence in Education. Only about one-third of the states require high school students to take specific courses, such as algebra, biology, or physical science.[18]

Course work and instructional time requirements provide little substantive guidance to local districts about developing appropriate curricula. In order to provide students with higher levels of academic content and critical thinking skills, many states have adopted content and student performance standards and state curriculum frameworks as the foundations of their education reform initiatives. The concept of standards-based reform emerged in the late 1980s and early 1990s through the work of a group of education leaders, governors, businesspeople, and researchers, and organizations such as the National Council of Teachers of Mathematics and the American Association for the Advancement of Science. These ideas initially received the support of President George H. W. Bush who, in the aftermath of the 1989 education summit, unsuccessfully proposed a system of voluntary national standards and tests. The Clinton administration subsequently took a "carrot and stick" approach to promote and support nascent state reform efforts. The Improving America's Schools Act of 1994 called for states to develop challenging standards in at least reading and mathematics, create high-quality assessments to measure performance against these standards, and have local districts identify low-performing schools for assistance. The Goals 2000 legislation and programs like the National Science Foundation's State and Urban Systemic Initiatives provided funds for states and localities to design the components of a standards-based system and to build the capacity of local districts to implement these reforms. The No Child Left Behind Act, enacted in the early days of George W. Bush's administration, continues the federal requirement that states enact standards-based policies.

By 2003, all but one state had developed content standards in reading and mathematics, and all but two in science and social studies as well.[19] States have not adopted common standards, however. Although many states have aligned their mathematics and science, and to a lesser extent their reading, standards to those developed by the professional organizations in these fields, states differ in the coverage, rigor, and prescriptiveness of their curriculum frameworks. In addition, while some states require local districts to adopt state frameworks and to write local curriculum guides to implement these objectives, curriculum frameworks in other states are only advisory. Some states have developed both professional and community consensus around the content of the standards. Other states have faced philosophical battles over what should be taught (e.g., evolution or social science content) and how (e.g., different approaches to teaching mathematics and reading). Although the federal government requires states to adopt standards in at least reading and mathematics, it does not review or approve the content of these standards. Federal law forbids its agencies from mandating, directing, or controlling the specific instructional content, curriculum, programs of instruction, or academic achievement standards and assessments of states, districts, or schools,[20] although it can and does use grants to support the adoption of instructional programs with a particular focus.

One way in which states hold schools and districts accountable for the adoption and implementation of state standards is through their state accountability and assessment systems. States have historically used accountability policies to monitor and regulate education in their communities. Traditionally, state accountability policies were designed to ensure a minimum level of education inputs, a minimum level of quality in these inputs, student access to educational programs and services, and the proper use of education resources, primarily through systems of auditing and compliance monitoring. In the 1970s states expanded their monitoring role to examine education outcomes through basic skills testing. In line with their adoption of standards-based education reforms, most states revamped their accountability systems in the 1990s to focus more heavily on student achievement and less on compliance with rules and regulations. Prior to the enactment of the NCLB Act, however, state accountability and assessment systems differed in a number of ways: who was held accountable (students, schools, and/or school districts), how performance was measured (e.g., the grades and subjects assessed), measures of progress and performance goals, and the consequences of not meeting state goals (ranging from public scrutiny to state takeover of schools).

In response to this variation, the NCLB Act standardized state accountability and assessment policies. By the 2005–2006 school year, states must test all students in grades three through eight and high school students at least once in reading and mathematics using assessments that are aligned with state standards. They must test students once per grade span in science by 2007–2008. As of 2003–2004, only twenty states had met this first requirement. States also must establish annual goals and objectives for student performance so that all students are proficient on state standards by 2014. States and school districts must report on the progress of districts, schools, and specific subgroups of students (racial/ethnic, impoverished, disabled, and limited-English-proficient) using a federally prescribed set of measures. Schools and school districts that receive Title I funds and that fail to meet annual goals for their students, and/or for any of the specified subgroups, are subject to an increasingly punitive set of sanctions, beginning with granting parents the right to choose another school and possibly culminating with school closure or state takeover. Each state's accountability and assessment plans must be approved by the federal government. While the government cannot dictate the form or content of a state assessment, it can judge whether assessments are aligned with state standards.

A growing number of state officials view the assessment and accountability provisions of the No Child Left Behind Act as inappropriate intrusions of the federal government into state and local functions. Two years after passage of the law, several state legislatures had passed resolutions challenging the law. Two states enacted laws prohibiting the use of nonfederal funds to implement the NCLB Act, but none, by 2004, had rejected the federal funds tied to the NCLB requirements. The chief state school officers of fourteen states asked for greater flexibility in how they measure student progress toward academic goals, but it was doubtful that Congress would make the requested changes to the law.[21]

A third responsibility of state governments is to establish minimum requirements for entrance into the teaching profession. States require that prospective teachers complete an approved teacher-education program and/or a prescribed course of study. Like high school course work demands, these requirements generally focus on the type rather than the content or quality of the courses taken. In 2002 only half of the states required teachers to major in the subject they planned to teach; another eleven states required prospective teachers to have either a major or minor in their teaching field. Most new teachers must also pass tests of basic skills (forty-one states), the subject-matter knowledge in their field of teaching (thirty states), and/or the professional knowledge of teaching (thirty-five states). While states select their own assessments and passing scores, thirty-one states in 2002 used the same commercially developed test of professional knowledge and/or subject-matter knowledge for teacher licensure.[22] Most states allowed individuals with a college degree to seek licensure through an "alternative route" by passing a subject-area test and, in some cases, completing a specified level of professional development. States also regulated the recertification of teachers, but generally limited their requirements to the successful completion of specified years of teaching and/or of additional education. Individual teachers, and sometimes their schools, usually determined the content of this training.

The federal government plays no direct role in the preparation of teachers, their licensure, or their ongoing professional development. Concerned with the perceived lack of teacher quality, however, the government added a provision to the Higher Education Act of 1998 that requires states to report the percentage of prospective teachers who pass state licensure examinations, by higher education institution. In addition, the NCLB Act requires states to establish criteria for a "highly qualified teacher" and ensure that every child is taught by individuals who are certified and have subject-matter expertise in the courses they teach. Meeting this requirement is a challenge in middle schools across the country, as most middle school teachers are certified in elementary education and not a subject area, and in rural and high-poverty urban high schools that face teacher shortages. In 2000, one-third of students in high-poverty high schools took at least one core academic course with a teacher who did not have an academic major or minor in that subject.[23]

Design of the local governance structure for public education is left up to the states. Local school districts are creations of state policy, which defines their boundaries, governance structures, and responsibilities. The standards-based reform movement, with its call for greater local flexibility in exchange for increased performance accountability, coupled with a growing political demand for the decentralization and deregulation of education, led many states to place more authority in the hands of schools and parents. For example, some states encourage or mandate the use of site-based management (SBM) or school-based planning activities. The Kentucky Education Reform Act requires all schools to establish school site councils and has shifted responsibility for curriculum, personnel, and finance from the local school board to these councils. In Illinois, the state passed the Chicago School Reform Act of 1988 requiring that city to reallocate the resources of the system to the school level and create local school councils with the responsibility of adopting a school plan, budgeting its funds, and hiring and firing its principal. A court-ordered school-finance law in New Jersey gave schools in urban districts extensive planning and fiscal powers. Most states require schools to develop annual plans, but limit their authority over budgets and personnel.

States also began experimenting with the deregulation of state education policy in the mid-1980s as a way of promoting school-based innovation and teacher professionalization. Initially, states permitted schools to seek waivers from regulation, but the early waiver programs were limited in their eligibility criteria and in the rules for which schools could seek exemptions.[24] The deregulation movement then evolved to the creation of charter schools and an expansion of parental choice options, discussed below.

At the same time that states are allocating greater authority to schools and parents, they have increased their oversight of low-performing schools and school districts, and expanded their powers to intervene in the operation of these entities. Twenty-four states have the power to take over a school district due to academic problems, and fifteen states have enacted policies to allow state takeovers of low-performing schools.[25] The level and type of state control in takeovers varies across states, however, and includes relieving local school boards of their duties, installing a state-appointed superintendent, and placing governance authority in the hands of a city's mayor. Under the NCLB Act, Title I–funded schools that fail to meet student performance goals for five consecutive years must be restructured, and this could lead to an increase in state takeovers.

Finally, state policymakers determine the financial structure of public K–12 education; that is, how revenues are raised and allocated across the school districts in their state. This has resulted in fifty separate state systems of funding education with considerable variation across the states in the average revenue behind each student and the sources of education revenue. In 2000–2001, school districts received, on average, 50 percent of their revenues from state aid, 43 percent from local sources, and 7 percent from federal sources. State support ranged from a low of 29 percent to a high of 71 percent across the United States, while reliance on local revenues ranged from a low of 15 percent to a high of 66 percent.[26] Spending can vary considerably within states, particularly those in which the majority of funds are raised locally, because the level of local education revenues available to schools is driven by the interaction of the wealth and tax effort of a community. This close relationship between wealth and revenues makes it possible for wealthy communities, which sometimes have ten times the per-pupil tax base as their neighbors, to raise substantially more money for education than poorer communities, even though both are applying the same education tax rate. Thus, in many states, poor school districts cannot generate sufficient revenue for an adequate education program or one that matches that of their more affluent neighbors.

Since the late 1960s, wealth-based disparities in educational spending have been the focus of school-finance litigation in most states. State courts have used their interpretation of the education clauses in their state constitution to define the scope and substance of states' responsibilities for education and the degree and type of equity and adequacy required of school funding systems. This judicial activism spurred states to restructure and expand their education funding systems in the 1970s and 1980s, leading states to increase their share of education funding to the current 50 percent. In states with court-ordered reform, inequities in education expenditures decreased, usually because states targeted additional state aid to the lowest-spending and/or lowest-wealth districts.[27] In the 1990s litigants and courts turned their attention to the adequacy of state funding systems. Courts began to define the states' obligations in terms of broad educational outcomes, and in some cases, in terms of the level of spending or kinds of inputs needed to prepare all students for higher education, skilled employment, and other aspects of adult life.

Although court decisions have forced legislatures to design more equitable funding systems, inequities persist. In thirty states, those districts serving the greatest number of students in poverty (one-quarter of districts) received at least $100 per pupil less than districts with the lowest poverty concentrations (one-quarter of districts), despite the greater level of student need. In ten states, the difference exceeded $800 per student. Similar funding inequities are observed when comparing districts with the highest and lowest minority enrollments in each state. Considerable spending disparities exist across states as well. In 2000–2001, the average per-pupil expenditure was $7,376, but ranged from a low of $4,674 in Utah to a high of $11,248 in New Jersey. Using a national database, researchers found that in 1992 variation across the states accounted for two-thirds of the total variance in per-pupil spending.[28] These intra- and interstate expenditure disparities raise the question of adequacy at a national level—what is the level of spending needed to bring all students to a proficient level of performance, as required under the No Child Left Behind Act?

Expansion of the state role in public education has been accompanied by an expansion of the number and types of citizens and organizations seeking to shape education policy decisions, transforming the political structure from a statewide monolith to a fragmented system of education politics. Until the late 1960s, state education policy was the province of broad-based education interest groups (state education departments, schools of education, school administrators, teachers' organizations) and a small number of legislators who specialized in education policy. The growth of collective bargaining for teachers, the civil rights movement, and the creation of interest groups organized around federal programs for special-needs students shattered the old consensus-building structures. State courts entered the fray in the 1970s with decisions that set new agendas for how states must fund their schools. Some governors emerged as leaders in school finance reform in their states, and their role expanded dramatically in the 1980s as they undertook education reforms in response to the challenges raised by *A Nation at Risk*. Business groups also emerged as powerful new voices in the

1980s as the focus of education policy shifted to quality and educational outcomes, and they have remained stalwart supporters of standards-based reforms. Religious groups and some groups of inner-city parents have coalesced in support of school-choice programs, particularly those that give parents vouchers for private schools. In a few states, where voters can enact fiscal and programmatic policy through ballot initiatives and referenda, vocal interests take their political agendas directly to the electorate, and in some instances, they have succeeded in imposing changes such as tax limitations and antibilingual education policies.

## An Evolving Governance System

In spite of increased state and federal activism, there continues to be strong public support for local control of schools. For many, local control remains the best way to protect community values and interests, and it provides a defense against unwanted government intrusion in the schools. Local control of public education continues to be revered, and even as Americans express increased concern about the performance of the public schools, there is a reluctance to enact reforms that would threaten this unique American institution. Even though polls indicate public majorities in support of national testing and a national curriculum, such reforms are unlikely to be enacted given the climate of strong support for local control of schools.[29]

Most Americans do not seem to consider their local boards of education to be a part of "government." To many, government consists of those distant bureaucrats in the state capital or in Washington who are viewed as inaccessible and unresponsive to citizens' concerns or needs. Since the vast majority of the nation's fifteen thousand school districts are small, and board members are known to the public and are not buffered by large bureaucracies, they do not seem to behave like "government." In large urban or county districts, of course, the relationships between boards and the public are more distant and much more bureaucratic. Nevertheless, most Americans appear to be satisfied with the multilevel governance structure, and when the existing balance of power among federal, state, and local authorities is threatened or altered, they tend to rise to its defense. After the No Child Left Behind Act was passed, a Gallup poll found that 49 percent of the respondents felt that the federal government was gaining too much influence (as opposed to 29 percent who felt that it had the right amount of influence), and a similar percentage felt that local boards of education had less influence than they should have.[30]

Nevertheless, the poor performance of public schools serving poor and minority children and stresses arising from demographic changes and related value conflicts are placing pressure on the traditional governance structure, and the cornerstone of the governance system, local control through boards of education, is being assaulted on two fronts. Earlier in this essay, we described the efforts of the federal and state governments to exercise more authority over public education and increase their oversight of the schools through stronger accountability systems. These actions from higher levels of government are reducing the freedom of action of local boards of education. In spite of the public's reverence for local control of schools, there is strong public support for state standards and majority support for state assessments. And the public seems willing to accept interference with local control in cases where performance is low and mismanagement and corruption are rampant. This is particularly the case with respect to urban school districts, especially those with large minority populations.

However, some citizens see these actions as futile, inadequate, and even threatening as they appear to recast a historic balance between collective interests and individual interests by imposing uniform standards or curricula reflecting particular values or by reducing individual choice. Increased nationalization of education policy threatens democratic localism and the pluralism that resulted from local control over education and the socialization of children. These citizens see the solution to improving public education as increasing parents' control over their children's education. In response, state legislatures have been creating new ways for citizens to pursue their educational preferences and interests. These efforts to empower parents generally take one of two forms: the creation of new structures for citizen representation, and the expansion of parents' capacity to exercise choice through vouchers, charter schools, or homeschooling. These actions also constrain and reduce the authority and reach of local boards of education.

## Expansion of Democratic Localism

A number of states—Kentucky, California, and Florida, for example—and many localities, such as Chicago, Denver, and Cincinnati, require schools to have councils composed of parents and teachers, and occasionally students. The powers of these councils vary from making policy to advising school administrators. Their composition also varies. Typically they include parents and teachers, and some include other community representatives. In 2001 over three-quarters of all elementary schools in the United States reported having at least an advisory body.[31] In general the influence of these bodies is limited to matters of parent involvement, special events, and fund-raising, but in some locales, such as Chicago and Kentucky, state legislators have granted these councils broad powers over school policies. The results of this experiment in democratic localism have been mixed.[32] Where the councils have real power, the members are typically elected by the parents whose children attend the school and by the staff of the school. As with school board elections, it has often proved difficult to get parents to participate in these councils. As a consequence, the councils often are not broadly representative of the communities served by their schools.

Granting school councils authority over curriculum also raises questions about the competence of citizens to make decisions affecting educational practice. Should decisions that require knowledge of the students' achievements, staff knowledge and skills, and understanding of cognitive development, learning theory, and standards be made by bodies with lay majorities? Do decisions about scope and sequence of the curriculum and instructional materials require specialized professional knowledge? These issues about the roles of lay policymakers and professional educators arise with school boards as well, but because school council members are so close to the teaching and learning process and often personally involved through their children, the issues take on a new saliency.

## Expanding Parental Choice

Choice is a highly popular concept in American culture. It is considered to be a manifestation of individual liberty and a reflection of the nation's diversity. Generally, it is considered to be a good thing, and something that should be limited only if there are overriding collective interests such as safety, health, protection of the environment, or national security. The preparation of children for participation in a democratic society and ensuring their acquisition of the core values and habits necessary for a diverse society to function have been viewed historically as a justification for limiting choice in public education. The common school has been viewed as a necessary mechanism for protecting the collective interest in developing and preserving a just and civil society. Nevertheless, many parents have been able to choose public schools for their children because they have the economic means to reside in communities that maintain good schools. Poorer families have had fewer choices, and ironically often live within large school districts that are run by unresponsive bureaucracies. Critics of public education contend that as a result many children are trapped in bad schools. There are differing views about how to provide choice and the range of choices that would be acceptable. The more radical reformers argue that the money supporting each child should go to the parents, who should decide where to spend it, giving them consumer power in the education marketplace. Some advocates would include private and religious schools as choices. This approach is referred to as vouchers. Less radical proposals to expand choice include controlled choice or public school choice and the creation of charter schools. All of these approaches break down the monopoly of the local school district and provide parents with alternatives to the assigned public school.

CHOICE AND VOUCHERS. Advocates of choice programs and vouchers contend that efforts to reform the current system have failed and that it is time to take a new approach. They argue that a market system would be more democratic than the current arrangements as it would provide real power for individual citizens and it would generate meaningful choices reflecting consumer preferences. Most important, they believe that market competition would lead to improved school performance, and that the market would be a more efficient mechanism for governing education than are representative bodies such as local boards or public bureaucracies. They emphasize individual goals and benefits and appear less concerned about the collective interests in education such as teaching democratic values, promoting equal opportunity, or developing tolerance and cross-group understanding and respect. Opponents fear that a market system would erode if not eliminate the common socialization experience provided by public education, resulting in a radical and dangerously divisive pluralism that would threaten social stability. They contend that the shared values that are the foundation of American democracy must be taught and that an institution dedicated to teaching them is essential.

While the advocates of choice agree about empowering consumers and the value of offering curricular options, they disagree about how much the government should regulate the market. Some voucher advocates want a virtual free market for education that would allow vouchers to be used at any school, regardless of its affiliation or ideology. In contrast, advocates of public choice programs argue that parents should be able to choose among educational options within a publicly regulated system of schools. They are prepared to accept considerable governmental regulation to ensure fairness of access in the system, teaching of a common core curriculum, and accountability.

Nearly all of the states have public school choice laws in addition to charter schools. These laws allow students to attend other public schools within their district (intradistrict choice) or in other districts (interdistrict choice), take courses in postsecondary institutions, or attend public or private specialized schools. In 1999, 25 percent of districts provided intradistrict choice; 14 percent of public school students (and nearly one-quarter of African-American students) exercised that choice option.[33] It is expected that public school choice options and attendance will increase with the implementation of NCLB as the law requires districts to provide choice to students who attend failing Title I schools.

While privately funded voucher programs serve students in a small number of districts, by 2003 only four states had enacted state-financed tuition or voucher programs that allow students to attend nonsectarian or religious schools of their choice. These programs are limited to students attending the states' lowest-performing schools and/or to students with special needs or from low-income families, and, in two states, to specific school districts. Advocates of voucher programs predict that more states will adopt voucher plans in the aftermath of the 2002 U.S. Supreme Court decision in *Zelman v. Simmons-Harris*. The Court found that the inclusion of private religious schools in choice plans did not violate the establishment clause of the U.S. Constitution, a clause that prohibits the government from passing laws respecting the establishment of religion.

Public support for vouchers is mixed. National polls show that in the early years of the twenty-first century about 40 percent to 45 percent of American citizens supported the use of public funds for private school choice. However, when asked whether they would prefer to spend money to improve the existing systems of public schools or give vouchers for attendance at private or parochial schools, about 70 percent of those polled indicated a preference for the former. Future voucher plans may also face constitutional challenges based on state constitutional provisions dealing with the separation of church and state.[34]

CHARTER SCHOOLS. A less radical and controversial approach to choice is the development of charter schools. Charter schools offer parents alternatives that operate within their state system of public schools under varying degrees of regulation and accountability. In the 1990s many states enacted legislation permitting the establishment of charter schools, and the number of new charters grew at more than a 10-percent rate in the late 1990s. By 2003, forty-one states had charter laws, and there were 2,800 charter schools serving almost 685,000 students.[35] Most of these schools are small, and are concentrated in a few states—Arizona, California, Florida, Michigan, and Texas.

Charter schools are public schools that operate under contract with designated sponsoring agencies (e.g., local school boards, universities, state boards of education) that specify the outcomes and how they will be measured and the nature and extent of the school's freedom from state and district regulation. However, the degree of autonomy granted charter schools by state legislatures varies widely across these states. A few states grant superwaivers to charter schools, limiting state regulation to health, safety, and civil rights issues, while charter schools in other states must specify what state and local rules they want waived or negotiate their powers with local districts. State policies also differ in the number of charters permitted, who qualifies as a chartering agency, how charter schools are funded, and the qualifications of charter school staff.

Charters serve as an option for many parents who are dissatisfied with traditional public schools. Many parents who choose charter schools are seeking different curriculum—either more traditional or more progressive—higher standards and levels of performance, or different values as reflected in tougher discipline, more attention to religion, or a stronger work ethic. Charters offer these parents a low-cost alternative to private schools. They may serve as a release valve for disaffection with public education and, in some communities, may reduce the pressure on the public schools for reform. Advocacy and support organizations have sprung up in the states permitting charters, and these groups lobby state and federal legislatures for expansion of charters, increased government aid, and reduced regulation. Although they have more organizational and programmatic flexibility, under NCLB, charter schools are subject to the same accountability measures as traditional public schools—student performance on a common core of state curriculum standards.

HOMESCHOOLING. Perhaps the ultimate expression of dissatisfaction with public education and with its governance structures is homeschooling. Parents who have concluded that they cannot obtain the education they wish for their children in the public schools and cannot achieve changes through the governance structure can choose to educate their children at home. State regulations about homeschooling vary widely. Nine states have no requirements and do not even ask parents to notify the public schools that they are educating children at home, and fifteen states require only notification. Eleven states have taken steps to regulate the quality of homeschooling by requiring testing or professional evaluation of children or setting curriculum standards. Estimates of the number of American children whose parents are educating them at home range from 850,000, or 1.7 percent of the total school population, to about 1.2 million, or 2.4 percent.[36] Numerous homeschooling associations have appeared and a small but growing industry of publishers and Web-based providers is serving the homeschool market.

## Recentralizing Local Control

Another trend in local school governance is worth noting here: a recentralization of authority over curriculum, instruction, and school budgets, particularly in school districts with low-performing schools. In Chicago, for example, a 1995 reform law strengthened the authority of the central office over the governance and performance of local schools, allowing the city to disband local school councils when warranted and to intervene in poorly performing schools. Other large school districts, such as New York City, have implemented district-wide reading and mathematics curricula to ensure that mobile students have access to the same educational programs, and to offset the uneven quality of school-based instructional programs. As the sanctions associated with the NCLB Act kick in, districts will be responsible for providing technical assistance to low-performing schools and, where necessary, reassigning staff and possibly restructuring and closing schools. A few urban districts have already assigned the management of low-performing schools to private contractors, nonprofit community organizations, and universities.

## Challenges Facing School Governance

Public education is facing a host of serious challenges. The most important of these is the performance problem. The public has been persuaded that significant sectors of public education are underperforming and that solving this problem is more a matter of mobilizing will and competence than providing additional resources or new knowledge. That is, the public has been led to believe that the education profession possesses the knowledge to do a better job, but incompetent, underproducing, or poorly led educators are not using it. This view has led, on the one hand, to the No Child Left Behind Act and the increase in federal and state authority, and on the other hand, to the creation of charter schools and increased political activism in support of vouchers. Will the actions taken by the federal and state governments to set standards and hold schools and educators more accountable for making improvements in performance prove effective? If not, what will be the implications for the governance system? Will failure to raise academic performance or to reduce gaps among population groups lead to increased government activism—perhaps even state or national curricula or national examinations—or to expanded experimentation with choice and vouchers and an even stronger emphasis on outcomes? Will some version of representative democracy continue to be the primary means of governing public education or will the market approaches proposed by voucher advocates prevail?

The jury is still out on whether the governance changes we have described—centralized standards-driven reforms, expanded democratic localism, and parental choice—have positive effects on educational outcomes. The research base is incomplete, and research findings are inconclusive. Studies of state-level standards-based reform policies have found that schools and school districts are paying attention to state standards, aligning curriculum, school improvement plans, local assessments, and professional development with state curricular frameworks and assessments. And states with strong accountability policies (those with significant consequences for students and schools) have shown larger score gains on the National Assessment of Educational Progress.[37] The effect of standards on the core technology of teaching seems to be more mixed, reflecting differences in teachers' understanding and acceptance of standards, and their willingness and ability to change instructional practices.[38] Structures that have expanded local participation in setting school policy have enabled some schools to create more democratic decision-making processes, while in other schools, the same structures have led to consolidation of power in the hands of the principals or little change in the distribution of authority within the building. Researchers have not found a direct relationship between more democratic decision-making and instructional change. Rather, schools with strong democratic practice were more likely to engage in restructuring practices that, in turn, often stimulated instructional innovation, but the extent of these changes has varied widely.[39] There is considerable agreement among researchers about the varied and modest effects of these school governance changes on teaching and learning.

In contrast, research on voucher programs has been highly charged, often contradictory, and based on small programs. To date, there is not good evidence to support the claims of either voucher advocates or their opponents. More research has been conducted on charter schools, but again the findings are inconsistent and so far the reported effects on student achievement, whether positive or negative, have been small.[40]

49

If representative forms of governance are to flourish in public education, reforms are needed to make them work more democratically, in particular to ensure that local boards and school councils have legitimacy with the publics they are intended to represent and serve. This may mean expanding the powers of school councils. It may mean moving school elections to the dates of general elections. These actions risk further politicization of school elections. But as the locus of decisions shifts from local boards to state and federal agencies and legislative bodies, education policy issues are already being treated in a partisan manner. Shifting the election dates may simply be a recognition that the era of nonpartisan governance of the schools has passed.

A related challenge is to more sharply define the decisions that should be the purview of lay boards or school staffs and those that should be made by individuals with professional expertise. As advances are made in cognitive science and stronger scientific evidence about program effects becomes available, it will be harder and harder to justify granting lay boards the kind of authority and discretion that they currently have over matters of curriculum and instruction. There also will be pressure to have government bureaucracies or professional organizations set parameters to guide and limit the kinds of decisions made by school teaching staffs. The current shift in federal policy toward requiring local districts to adopt reading curricula that are supported by scientific evidence represents a step in this direction. In the future, such requirements may become significant constraints on the decision-making authority of local boards and school councils.

The governance system also faces the challenge of finding a politically acceptable balance between the school's traditional emphasis on the development of individual talents and the achievement of more equitable results. Pursuit of more equitable outcomes will be politically acceptable as long as it does not entail any limitations on the resources or opportunities available to children from affluent families. As discussed earlier in this essay, considerable resource disparities remain both within and across states. The public is willing to invest more in the education of students in low-wealth communities, but only if they can be assured that education funds are spent efficiently, effectively, and without waste.[41] Efforts to reallocate in the name of equity, however, are likely to produce demands for changes in governance that shift the balance of power toward parents and away from public agencies.

Collective bargaining and the content of conventional labor agreements in education represent another challenge for the governance system. The scope of bargaining in many states results in important policy issues being resolved at the bargaining table rather than in public forums where citizens have a voice. The public is growing dissatisfied with labor agreements that do not reward performance. There is concern about the use of a uniform salary schedule that does not recognize differences in workload or levels of expertise and does not permit school districts to effectively bid for needed skills in the marketplace. And there is increasing awareness that seniority rights affect the allocation of teachers within districts, often resulting in the least experienced, least qualified teachers teaching the most vulnerable children. On the other hand, district leaders have shown little inclination to treat teachers as professionals, improve their working conditions, or to respect and use their expertise in shaping policies and programs. Such changes are needed to raise the status of the profession and to attract talented young people into teaching. Thus, it seems clear that teachers would be worse off both financially and professionally without strong unions.

A final challenge concerns the impact of the Internet and computer technology on families and schools. New technologies offer the possibilities of changing both the locus and character of learning. Children and parents now have access to powerful tools for finding information and communicating globally. These new tools make homeschooling easier. They also make it easier for parents to supplement traditional school instruction. New technologies allow parents and students to be less dependent on formal instruction in classrooms and on teachers. These technologies will make it easier for parents to monitor the performance of their children and their children's schools, easier for them to communicate with school authorities, and easier for them to find and assess options. Such changes are bound to have profound effects on the governance of the public schools.

## Conclusions

We have described a complex and evolving governance structure that faces serious challenges. While the public continues to express great confidence in the familiar aspects of this system—the local board of education and school district—this confidence may whither if the performance problems are not solved or if state and federal activism strip local authorities of any real power. Yet the very complexity of the governance system is an obstacle to implementing the kinds of reforms that might improve performance. As a consequence, state and federal authorities are expanding their reach and eroding the power of local boards of education. Conservatives offer the public market-based alternatives that promise to solve the performance problem, while enhancing the power of individual citizens and diminishing the power of local communities and educational bureaucracies at all levels. These options seem to be gaining favor with the public. Those who are responsible for the governance of public education may have only limited time to demonstrate that they can effectively address, and ameliorate, the problems of performance, quality, and equity that are undermining public support for a critical public institution—the common school.

## Notes

1. National Center for Education Statistics, *Digest of Education Statistics, 2002* (Washington, D.C., 2003), http://nces.ed.gov/programs/digest/d02/; Stacey Bielick, Kathryn Chandler, and Stephen P. Broughman, "Homeschooling in the United States: 1999," *Education Statistics Quarterly* 3, no. 3 (2001), http://nces.ed.gov/programs/quarterly/vol_3/3_3/q3-2.asp.
2. Thomas F. Green, "Schools and Communities: A Look Forward," *Harvard Education Review* 39, no. 2 (1969): 223.
3. Jean Johnson, *Assignment Incomplete: The Unfinished Business of Education Reform* (New York: Public Agenda, 1995); Lowell C. Rose and Alec M. Gallup, "The 33rd Annual Phi Delta Kappan/Gallup Poll of the Public's Attitudes toward the Public Schools," *Phi Delta Kappan* 83, no. 1 (2001): 41–58.
4. Lowell C. Rose and Alec M. Gallup, "The 35th Annual Phi Delta Kappan/Gallup Poll of the Public's Attitudes toward the Public Schools," *Phi Delta Kappan* 85, no. 1 (2003): 41–52.
5. Frank Hobbs and Nicole Stoops, *Demographic Trends in the 20th Century* (Washington, D.C.: U.S. Census Bureau, 2002), www.census.gov/prod/2002pubs/censr-4.pdf.
6. Harold L. Hodgkinson, *Leaving Too Many Children Behind: A Demographer's View on the Tragic Neglect of America's Youngest Children* (Washington, D.C.: Institute for Educational Leadership, 2003), www.iel.org.
7. Patricia L. Donahue, Mary C. Daane, and Wendy S. Grigg, *The Nation's Report Card: Reading Highlights 2003* (Washington, D.C.: National Center for Education Statistics, 2003); Organisation for Economic Co-operation and Development, *Reading for Change: Performance and Engagement across Countries* (Paris: OECD, 2002).
8. Jean Johnson and Ann Duffett, *Where We Are Now: 12 Things You Need to Know about Public Opinion and Public Schools* (New York: Public Agenda, 2003); Rose and Gallup, "The 35th Annual Phi Delta Kappan/Gallup Poll"; Rothstein, *Class and Schools*.
9. Frederick M. Hess, *School Boards at the Dawn of the 21st Century: Conditions and Challenges of District Governance* (Washington, D.C.: National School Boards Association, 2002), www.nsba.org.
10. Wirt and Kirst, *The Political Dynamics of American Education*.
11. Public Education Network and Education Week, *Learn. Vote. Act: The Public's Responsibility for Public Education*, www.publiceducation.org/portals/Learn_Vote_Act/default.asp.
12. Wirt and Kirst, *The Political Dynamics of American Education*.
13. Bryk et al., *Charting Chicago School Reform*.
14. Michael W. Kirst, *Mayoral Influence, New Regimes and Public School Governance* (Philadelphia: Consortium for Policy Research in Education, 2002), www.cpre.org.
15. John F. Jennings, "Title I: Its Legislative History and Its Promise," *Phi Delta Kappan* 81, no. 7 (2000): 516–522.
16. McDonnell and Fuhrman, "The Political Context of School Reform."
17. James G. Cibulka, "The Changing Role of Interest Groups in Education:

Nationalization and the New Politics of Education Productivity," *Educational Policy* 15, no. 1 (2001): 12–40.

18. Abigail Potts, Rolf K. Blank, and Andra Williams, *Key State Education Policies on PK–12 Education* (Washington, D.C.: Council of Chief State School Officers, 2002), www.ccsso.org/content/pdfs/KeyState2002.pdf.

19. *Education Week,* "Quality Counts 2004: Count Me In: Special Education in an Era of Standards," vol. 23, no. 17 (2004), www.edweek.org/sreports/qc04/.

20. Fuhrman, "The 10th Amendment: Standards, Testing, and Accountability."

21. Sam Dillon, "Utah House Rebukes Bush with Its Vote on School Law," *New York Times,* February 11, 2004, A16; Diana J. Schemo, "14 States Ask U.S. to Revise Some Education Law Rules," *New York Times,* March 25, 2004, A16.

22. Potts, Blank, and Williams, *Key State Education Policies on PK–12 Education.*

23. *Education Week,* Quality Counts 2003, "To Close the Gap, Quality Counts," analysis by Richard Ingersoll of the National Center for Education Statistics, Schools and Staffing Survey (1999–2000), vol. 22, no. 17 (2003), 14.

24. Fuhrman and Elmore, *Ruling Out Rules.*

25. Education Commission of the States, "State Takeovers and Reconstitutions," ECS policy brief (Denver, Colo., 2003), http://ecs.org/clearinghouse/13/59/1359.htm.

26. Frank Johnson, *Statistics in Brief: Revenues and Expenditures for Public Elementary and Secondary Education: School Year 2000–01* (Washington, D.C.: National Center for Education Statistics, 2003), http://nces.ed.gov.

27. See Evans, Murray, and Schwab, "The Impact of Court-Mandated School Finance Reform," and Goertz and Natriello, "Court-Mandated School Finance Reform: What Do the New Dollars Buy?"

28. Kevin Carey, *The Funding Gap: Low-Income and Minority Students Still Receive Fewer Dollars in Many States* (Washington, D.C.: Education Trust, 2003), www2. edtrust. org/NR/rdonlyres/EE004C0A-D7B8-40A6-8A03-1F26B8228502/0/funding2003. pdf; Frank Johnson, *Statistics in Brief: Revenues and Expenditures for Public Elementary and Secondary Education: School Year 2000–01*; Evans, Murray, and Schwab, "The Impact of Court-Mandated School Finance Reform."

29. See Lowell C. Rose and Alec M. Gallup, "The 34th Annual Phi Delta Kappan/Gallup Poll of the Public's Attitudes toward the Public Schools," *Phi Delta Kappan* 84, no. 1 (2002): 41–56; and Rose and Gallup, "The 35th Annual Phi Delta Kappan/Gallup Poll."

30. Rose and Gallup, "The 35th Annual Phi Delta Kappan/Gallup Poll."

31. National Center for Education Statistics, *Condition of Education 2002* (2002), http://nces.ed.gov.

32. See Bryk et al., *Charting Chicago School Reform;* and Malen, Ogawa, and Kranz, "What Do We Know about School-based Management? A Case Study of the Literature—A Call for Research."

33. Education Commission of the States, "School Choice: State Laws," *ECS State Notes,* ecs.org/clearinghouse/13/75/1375.htm; Kerry J. Gruber et al., *Schools and Staffing Survey, 1999–2000: Overview of the Data for Public, Private, Public Charter, and Bureau of Indian Affairs Elementary and Secondary Schools* (Washington, D.C.: National Center for Education Statistics, 2002), http://nces.ed.gov; and Stacey Bielick and

Christopher Chapman, *Trends in the Use of School Choice: 1993 to 1999* (Washington, D.C.: National Center for Education Statistics, 2003), http://nces.ed.gov.

34. Rose and Gallup, "The 34th Annual Phi Delta Kappan/Gallup Poll"; Van Geel, "Vouchers, the Supreme Court, and the Next Political Rounds."
35. U.S. Charter Schools, *National Statistics* (2004), www.uscharterschools.org.
36. Bielick, Chandler, and Broughman, *Homeschooling in the United States.*
37. Goertz, "Implementing Standards-based Reform: Challenges for State Policy"; Carnoy and Loeb, "Does External Accountability Affect Student Outcomes? A Cross-State Analysis."
38. See, for example, Corcoran and Christman, *The Limits and Contradictions of Systemic Reform*; Herman, "The Effects of Testing on Instruction"; and Wilson and Floden, "Hedging Bets: Standards-based Reform in Classrooms."
39. Bryk et al., *Charting Chicago School Reform*; J. L. David, "Educators and Parents as Partners in School Governance."
40. Miron and Nelson, "Student Achievement in Charter Schools: What We Know and Why We Know So Little."
41. Peter D. Hart, and Robert M. Teeter, *Equity and Adequacy: Americans Speak on Public School Funding* (Princeton, N.J.: Educational Testing Service, 2004).

## Bibliography

Bryk, Anthony S., et al. *Charting Chicago School Reform: Democratic Localism as a Lever for Change.* Boulder, Colo.: Westview, 1998.

Carnoy, Martin, and Susanna Loeb. "Does External Accountability Affect Student Outcomes? A Cross-State Analysis." In *Redesigning Accountability Systems for Education,* edited by Susan H. Fuhrman and Richard F. Elmore, pp. 189–219. New York: Teachers College Press, 2004.

Chubb, John E., and Terry M. Moe. *Politics, Markets, and America's Schools.* Washington, D.C.: Brookings Institution, 1990.

Corcoran, Tom, and Jolley B. Christman. *The Limits and Contradictions of Systemic Reform: The Philadelphia Story.* Philadelphia: Consortium for Policy Research in Education, 2002.

David, Jane L. "Educators and Parents as Partners in School Governance." In *All Children Can Learn: Lessons from the Kentucky Reform Experience,* edited by Roger S. Pankratz and Joseph M. Petrosko. San Francisco: Jossey-Bass, 2000.

Evans, William N., Sheila E. Murray, and Robert M. Schwab. "The Impact of Court-mandated School Finance Reform." In *Equity and Adequacy in Education Finance: Issues and Perspectives,* edited by Helen F. Ladd, Rosemary Chalk, and Janet S. Hansen, pp. 72–98. Washington, D.C.: National Academy Press, 1999.

Fuhrman, Susan H. "The 10th Amendment: Standards, Testing, and Accountability." In *Who's in Charge Here? The Tangled Web of School Governance,* edited by Noel Epstein. Washington, D.C.: Brookings Institution Press, 2004.

Fuhrman, Susan H., and Richard F. Elmore. "Governors and Education Policy in the 1990s." In *The Governance of Curriculum,* edited by Richard F. Elmore and Susan H. Fuhrman, pp. 56–74. Alexandria, Va.: Association for Supervision and Curriculum Development, 1994.

Fuhrman, Susan H., and Richard F. Elmore. *Ruling Out Rules: The Evolution of Deregulation in State Education Policy*. Philadelphia: Consortium for Policy Research in Education, 1995.

Goertz, Margaret E. "Implementing Standards-based Reform: Challenges for State Policy." In *Closing the Gap*, edited by Terri Duggan and Madelyn Holmes. Washington, D.C.: Council for Basic Education, 2000.

Goertz, Margaret E., and Gary Natriello. "Court-Mandated School Finance Reform: What Do the New Dollars Buy?" In *Equity and Adequacy in Education Finance: Issues and Perspectives*, edited by Helen F. Ladd, Rosemary Chalk, and Janet S. Hansen, pp. 99–135. Washington, D.C.: National Academy Press, 1999.

Green, Thomas F. *Education and Pluralism: Ideal and Reality*. Syracuse, N.Y.: Syracuse University School of Education, 1966.

Green, Thomas F. *Predicting the Behavior of the Educational System*. Syracuse, N.Y.: Syracuse University Press, 1980.

Herman, Joan L. "The Effects of Testing on Instruction." In *Redesigning Accountability Systems for Education*, edited by Susan H. Fuhrman and Richard F. Elmore, pp. 141–166. New York: Teachers College Press, 2004.

Hochschild, Jennifer L., and Nathan Scovronick. *The American Dream and the Public Schools*. New York: Oxford University Press, 2003.

Kannapel, Patricia J., Lola Aagaard, Pamelia Coe, and Cynthia A. Reeves. *Elementary Change: Moving toward Systemic School Reform in Rural Kentucky*. Charlestown, W.Va.: AEL, 2000.

Kirst, Michael W. *Mayoral Influence, New Regimes and Pubic School Governance*. Philadelphia: Consortium for Policy Research in Education, 2002.

Malen, Betty, Rodney T. Ogawa, and Jennifer Kranz. "What Do We Know about School-Based Management? A Case Study of the Literature. A Call for Research." In *Choice and Control in American Education*, vol. 2, *The Practice of Choice, Decentralization and School Restructuring*, edited by William H. Clune and John F. Witte. New York: Falmer, 1990.

McDonnell, Lorraine M., and Susan H. Fuhrman. "The Political Context of School Reform." In *The Fiscal, Legal and Political Aspects of State Reform of Elementary and Secondary Education*, edited by Van D. Mueller and Mary P. McKeown, pp. 43–64. Cambridge, Mass.: Ballinger, 1986.

Miron, Gary, and Christopher Nelson. "Student Achievement in Charter Schools: What We Know and Why We Know So Little." In *Taking Account of Charter Schools: What's Happened and What's Next?* edited by Katrina E. Bulkley and Priscilla Wohlstetter, pp. 161–175. New York: Teachers College Press, 2004.

Reese, William J. "Ways of Seeing the Common Good in Public Education: The Past Informing the Present." In *Reconstructing the Common Good in Education: Coping with Intractable American Dilemmas*, edited by Larry Cuban and Dorothy Shipps. Stanford, Calif.: Stanford University Press, 2000.

Rothstein, Richard. *Class and Schools: Using Social, Economic, and Educational Reform to Close the Black-White Achievement Gap*. New York: Teachers College Press, 2004.

Van Geel, Tyll. "Vouchers, the Supreme Court, and the Next Political Rounds." In *American Educational Governance on Trial: Change and Challenges*, edited by William L.

Boyd and D. Miretzky, pp. 136–154. Chicago: National Society for the Study of Education, 2003.

Wilson, Suzanne M., and Robert E. Floden. "Hedging Bets: Standards-based Reform in Classrooms." In *From the Capitol to the Classroom: Standards-Based Reform in the States,* edited by Susan H. Fuhrman. Chicago: National Society for the Study of Education, 2001.

Wirt, Frederick M., and Michael W. Kirst. *Schools in Conflict: The Politics of Education.* 2nd ed. Berkeley, Calif.: McCutchan, 1989.

Wirt, Frederick M., and Michael W. Kirst. *The Political Dynamics of American Education.* Berkeley, Calif.: McCutchan, 2001.

# 3

# THE POLITICS OF POLARIZATION: EDUCATION DEBATES IN THE UNITED STATES

*William A. Galston*

WHY IS IT THAT EDUCATION ISSUES IN THE UNITED States frequently become deeply politicized, and often polarized? At the most general level, the answer is clear: Education policy straddles the fault lines of the major divisions in U.S. politics and society, and it cannot avoid reflecting those divisions. Moreover, public education in the United States is bound to evoke passion because it is linked to virtually everything Americans care about, especially with respect to the nation's children.

The reasons for this are deeply rooted in American history and political culture. Judged against the citizens of other developed nations, Americans are unusually individualistic. They believe that people must be free to constitute their own lives and that they must take responsibility for the outcome of their choices. On the other hand, they believe that government should act to ensure basic opportunities for all individuals to develop and employ their talents. Educational opportunity is at the core of public responsibility thus understood; more so than for societies that construe public responsibility to include substantial equality of outcomes, regardless of the market's evaluation of individual talents.

Public education, in short, is close to the heart of Americans' understanding of democracy, and debates about education are bound to reflect competing and evolving conceptions of what democracy requires. Through much of the nineteenth century, for example, as immigration from Ireland and southern Europe surged, Americans debated the compatibility of Catholic doctrine and democratic institutions. A blend of democratic ideology and generic Protestantism became the informally established religion in public schools, exacerbating the exodus of Catholic students.

In the early decades of the twentieth century, a new question came to dominate public debate—the relation between mass industrialization and democracy. Progressives argued successfully for three educational responses to the challenge of the new political economy. First, public education needed to be removed from the baleful influence of local and ward politics; that is, it had to be centralized and professionalized. Second, public education had to transform the children of immigrant factory workers into individuals who considered themselves Americans, by intentionally fostering a common civic consciousness. Third, public education had to set aside the "old-fashioned" common education in the liberal arts in favor of a more practical curriculum that recognized the diversity of roles that public school graduates would play in the new industrial economy. To execute this strategy, Progressive educators and their allies in the business community transformed the organization of public schooling along industrial lines, creating a system of school districts with broad central powers over personnel and procurement that has persisted into the twenty-first century. (See Reuben in this volume.)

Since the 1970s, debates about American democracy have revolved around the norms of inclusion and equality, and public schools have once again been at the epicenter of these controversies. Successive waves of reform have pushed for full inclusion and equal treatment of African Americans, nonmajority cultures, women and girls, students with disabilities, and immigrants for whom English is a second language. From busing to funding equalization, multicultural curricula, and bilingual education, efforts to redefine democracy in more inclusive and egalitarian terms have generated new contestation over the relation between democracy and public education.

This is not to suggest that every educational controversy leaves the contestants at loggerheads. A reauthorization of the Elementary and Secondary Education Act of 1965, the No Child Left Behind Act of 2001, reflected an agreement that crossed lines of party and ideology. In return for promises of increased federal funding, many liberals acknowledged claims that existing policies were poorly serving low-income and minority students and accepted stringent new accountability standards for schools and students. For their part, conservatives accepted a strong federal role, which they had long resisted, in a policy arena that states and localities had long dominated. In the first few years after its enactment it was uncertain whether the new law as implemented would be able to address the concerns both of those who viewed the promise of equal opportunity through an egalitarian prism and those who interpreted it in more achievement-oriented, meritocratic terms.

The complexity of educational politics in the United States reflects both the multiple dimensions of conflict within which the U.S. system of public education is embedded and the contested character of democratic citizenship and democracy itself. For these reasons, among others, the politics of education is bound to be a large and unruly topic. This chapter discusses the politics of education under the following headings: first, conflict over the purposes of education; second, the influence of ideology; third, the role of partisanship and organized interests; fourth, the effects of tensions among different institutions in the U.S. governance system of federalism and separation of powers; fifth, the economic dimension of educational conflict; sixth, the pervasive consequences of racial conflict; and finally, ethnocultural issues stemming from the surge of immigration since 1965.

## The Purposes of Public Education

There is agreement at the most general level about the purposes of K–12 education in the United States. Schools are expected, first, to prepare students for economic life, by imparting basic knowledge and skills and (in many cases) readying them for postsecondary education and training. Second, schools are expected to help prepare students for social life, in which they will need to interact civilly and work cooperatively with many different kinds of people. Third, it is believed that schools should prepare students for democratic citizenship, by giving them the knowledge and skills that they will need to vote, serve on juries, evaluate the performance of elected leaders, and participate in neighborhood and community affairs. Finally, many (not all) believe that schools have a general cultural purpose, imparting to students a love of knowledge, learning, and artistic excellence. Even this bland and familiar enumeration points toward multiple sources of contestation. For example, during periods in which the meaning of American citizenship is in dispute, the parameters of civic education are anything but assured. Starting in the late 1960s and early 1970s, public schools began backing away from classroom-based civic education. Many teachers revolted against the traditional civics curriculum, which they came to regard as exclusionary, triumphalist, and mystifying. At the same time, many school administrators and boards worked to avoid classroom discussion of issues that political groups or even individual parents might find controversial. Starting in the 1990s, the pendulum began to swing back, partly in response to public concern about the increasing failure of young people to engage in the country's public life. The emerging consensus that the civic dimension of public education deserves more emphasis has yet to yield agreement on the conception of democratic citizenship to be promoted, however. Some advocates would focus on obedience to law, personal responsibility, and respect for the traditional institutions of representative democracy; others variously emphasize individual service, critical analysis, active participation, and common or "public" work.

Conflicts can also arise about the balance to be struck between or among different educational purposes. Consider, for example, the relation between knowledge and socialization. In 1893, responding to concerns about the disorganization of high school curricula, a prestigious commission of American educators dominated by college presidents released a report recommending that all students receive the fundamentals of a liberal education—English, history, foreign languages, the sciences, and mathematics. The "Committee of Ten," as it was known, based its recommendation on the belief that "such an education" best prepared students for meaningful, productive lives.

Faced with a rising tide of diverse high school students, many public education professionals objected to what they regarded as the dead hand of academic traditionalism. In 1918 the Commission on the Reorganization of Secondary Education issued a report titled *Cardinal Principles of Secondary Education*. Its basic principle was that "secondary education should be determined by the needs of the society to be served [and] the character of the individuals to be educated." On this basis, the commission argued for reorienting secondary education away from academics and toward what we would now call vocationalism and socialization. The main objectives of secondary education, the commission declared, were "1. Health. 2. Command of fundamental processes. 3. Worthy home-membership. 4. Vocation. 5. Citizenship. 6. Worthy use of leisure. 7. Ethical character." This report laid the foundation for dividing ("tracking") students into "academic," "general," and "vocational" tracks, and it reserved the rigorous academic curriculum for college-bound students. In Diane Ravitch's characterization, "The controlling principles in this readjustment were social utility and efficiency. Every subject was judged by whether it was immediately useful and whether it met the needs of students."[1] For more than a century, these dueling reports have defined a battlefront in the education wars. In the wake of the Soviet Union's successful launch, in 1957, of Sputnik I, the first artificial satellite, and the beginning of the space race, vocationalism in the United States gave way to a renewed emphasis on academic education. Starting in the late 1960s, the demands for "relevance" pushed the pendulum back toward meeting students' "needs," and helped justify diminishing the required core curriculum in favor of what has been called the "cafeteria-style" high school. After more than a decade of declining academic performance in the public schools, the National Commission on Excellence in Education published a report in 1983 titled *A Nation at Risk: The Imperative for Educational Reform,* which advocated a new required core curriculum, the building blocks of which bore a remarkable resemblance to the Committee of Ten's 1893 list. This report helped popularize the view that all students, whatever their aspirations, need a solid foundation in the academic basics, and launched a reform movement that is now enshrined in state-level curricular reform and in the precepts of the No Child Left Behind Act.

Each of the parties to this long-running dispute lays claim to the mantle of democratic legitimacy. Inspired by the Progressive Era educator John Dewey, the high school principals, academic administrators, and professors of education who rallied around the "Cardinal Principles" criticized the advocates of the Committee of Ten report as elitists out of touch with the changing needs of a modern democratic society. But the tracking system to which the Cardinal Principles gave rise could be, and ultimately was, criticized in turn as elitist and antidemocratic. The new core curriculum appealed to the norm of equal educational opportunity for all, a claim fortified by evidence that rigorous instruction in the basics yields gains in achievement, high school completion, and college attendance for low-income and minority students. Nonetheless, early results of testing suggest that as states implement achievement standards in core subjects as conditions for promotion and graduation, disproportionate numbers of these students will fail to clear the bar. If so, the country will face a choice between the democratic rhetoric of "No child left behind" and an educational reality that many will criticize as elitist, and the result may well be renewed calls for a more differentiated approach to public education, and another swing of the pendulum.

## *Ideology*

Disagreements over the purposes of public education are linked to, and reinforce, differences of ideological worldviews. Compared with many conservatives, liberals tend to think well of government and to be suspicious of the market. They are more confident that public purposes can be achieved through collective choice, crystallized in enforceable laws and regulations, rather than through individual choice, and they are more willing to restrict individual choice (through measures such as school busing) to attain important public goals (such as integration).

Liberals are also more likely to believe that resources are the key to solving public problems and that government should act to overcome inequalities of resources among groups and jurisdictions. For this reason, among others, liberals typically prefer to expand the authority of larger political units (regions, states, the federal government) that have the capacity to redistribute resources from better- to less-well-endowed localities. One consequence of their relentless push in this direction is that the states' share of overall funding for public education has risen by ten percentage points between 1970 and 2000. While the federal government's share during this period has barely budged, the pressure to increase the allocation is intensifying: federal funding for national mandates such as special education and testing and assessment regimes is likely to expand more rapidly than overall education spending during the first decade of the twenty-first century.

Ideology is also linked, sometimes in surprising ways, to conflicts over pedagogical aims and methods. Liberals tend to favor curricula and teaching styles that they see as "meeting the needs" of children and fostering creativity. Conservatives typically emphasize the "basics" and are willing to promote competence in essential skills through drills and rote learning that restrict the freedom of students and teachers alike. These differences can lead to bitter conflict, such as the long-running battle between those who believe that reading instruction should begin with drilling on the sounds of letters, letter groups, and syllables and those who advocate a less directive, more wholistic approach focused on words and context. Parallel differences over the use of authority to enforce discipline in classrooms and school facilities can lead to ideological conflict over policies such as suspension and expulsion, especially because these policies have what many liberals regard as a disproportional impact on minority groups.

Liberals are more likely than conservatives to embrace what Paul Hill, a specialist in education policy, has called a public education "ideology" that is "hostile to focused, distinctive schools." As Hill describes it, this ideology: favors the school as a common space in which people of unlike backgrounds gather; opposes schools that appeal to groups because of distinctive subject-matters, teaching methods, or value orientation; and stands against market values of competition and efficiency in the name of social values such as cooperation and equality.[2] This ideology reinforces opposition to choice, the exercise of which (opponents argue) tends to sort individuals into affinity groups, gives parents too much control over the content of their children's education, and imposes cognitive responsibilities on disadvantaged parents that they are poorly equipped to discharge.

At the far end of the public school ideology, we find systematic opposition to the very existence of nonpublic educational alternatives. The founding of the "common school" in the 1830s coincided with a wave of Catholic immigration. Many Protestants believed that Catholicism was incompatible with democracy and that a separate system of Catholic schools would become a hotbed of antidemocratic sentiments. After the Civil War, a majority of states adopted constitutional amendments prohibiting any use of public funds for private schools, and a parallel amendment to the U.S. Constitution was seriously considered. The years between 1875 and World War II were characterized by widespread hostility toward private elementary and secondary education, especially Catholic and German-language schools.

This sentiment reached a peak in the nativist reaction that followed World War I. The state of Nebraska prohibited all schools from conducting instruction in any modern language other than English, a direct assault on the minority German-speaking Lutheran immigrant population. Oregon went even farther, passing a ballot initiative requiring parents to send all children between the ages of eight and sixteen to public schools. This measure, which would have effectively abolished private and parochial schools, was spawned by an improbable coalition that included the Ku Klux Klan and egalitarian Progressives who wanted schools to promote civic unity. The Supreme Court struck down both these measures as violations of fundamental constitutional liberties, and nativism and anti-Catholicism gradually subsided.

Many liberals remain suspicious of faith-based schools. These schools are criticized for (among many alleged shortcomings) lacking diversity, allowing parents to indoctrinate their children at the expense of critical thinking, and failing to convey the essentials of shared citizenship. Some of these claims are open to empirical scrutiny (research has suggested that Catholic schools foster engaged citizens as least as effectively as do public schools), while others revolve around issues of principle and ideology. While few partisans approve of measures that would go as far as those of Nebraska and Oregon in the 1920s, many antagonists of private education seek to use government's regulatory authority to rein in what they see as the dangerous distinctiveness of faith-based schools. It is one of the many ironies of the contemporary debate that the flow of public funds to such institutions would expand opportunities for state regulation. As this realization has dawned on conservatives who have long advocated public support of faith-based activities, some have begun to rethink their position: public money with conditions that erode the autonomy and distinctiveness of private entities may be worse than no money at all.

Many contemporary ideological divisions in American politics are rooted in differing understandings of the appropriate relation between religion and public life. It is hardly possible to avoid confronting this question; as is well known, levels of religious faith and observance are far higher in the United States than in most other advanced industrialized societies. Many liberals see the faith-saturated character of American society as a threat to politics and to liberty itself, and they endorse the kind of strict separationism that the U.S. Supreme Court defined in the 1960s and 1970s. Many conservatives see religion as an essential asset for public life and have never accepted Court decisions outlawing administered prayers in public schools. They favor policies such as equal treatment for all groups, whether religious or not, in the provision of public funds for public purposes. Not surprisingly, most conservatives cheered, and liberals deplored, the 2002 Supreme Court decision in *Zelman v. Simmons-Harris* that publicly funded vouchers redeemable at private and parochial schools are consistent with the Constitution.

A different kind of religious choice in education arouses controversy that disrupts normal partisan affinities. Parents often raise faith-based objections to aspects of the public school curriculum and seek alternatives for their children within the public school framework. In a well-known case, a handful of Christian fundamentalist parents in Hawkins County, Tennessee, charged that textbooks selected by the school board conveyed teachings at variance with the moral code they sought to impart to their children. They requested that their children be allowed to use alternative textbooks and (if necessary) study the contested subjects outside the regular classroom. After early efforts by individual school administrators collapsed, a complex legal process ensued, culminating in a 1987 decision by the U.S. Sixth Circuit Court of Appeals, *Mozert v. Hawkins County,* in favor of the school board.

This case, and others like it, have created surprising new political alliances. While many religious conservatives support fundamentalists' appeals for accommodation, others do not. Writing for a Court majority in 1990, the conservative (and practicing Catholic) Justice Antonin Scalia charged that any society adopting an accommodationist approach would be "courting anarchy," a danger that increases "in direct proportion to the society's diversity of religious beliefs, and its determination to coerce or suppress none of them."[3] Many liberals who believe in public schools as a principal source of civic unity agree with Scalia, while other liberals who focus on the free expression of social diversity end up finding common cause with proaccommodation religious conservatives. One thing is clear: the appropriate stance toward religious and cultural diversity within the framework of constitutional and civic unity is an issue that will continue to roil U.S. education policy (and American politics).

## Partisanship and Organized Interests

The two major ideological dimensions discussed above—the role of government and the relation between religion and public life—shape the interest-group structure of the major American political parties. Republicans tend to attract groups favoring a modest role for government and a robust role for religion, including pro-market advocates and many (though not all) evangelical Christians. While these groups disagree on many cultural issues, they agree on the importance of school choice (among others). By contrast, Democrats attract groups favoring a robust role for government and a modest role for religion in public life. For obvious reasons, public-sector employees, including teachers' unions, form a key part of the party's base, as do secular voters, who constitute an expanding minority of the electorate and who tend to espouse strict separationism. These groups oppose school choice, at least to the extent that it threatens to erode the dominant role of public education and increase faith-based institutions' access to public funds.

Two other key features of contemporary American politics reflect the tendency toward intense polarization around education issues. As voting and other kinds of political participation have declined during the past generation, highly ideological and partisan voters have become a larger share of the active electorate since the 1960s. Increasingly, parties and candidates view politics not as persuasion but rather as the mobilization of already-committed voters. Mobilization requires focusing on, and intensifying, key differences between political adversaries. This discourages compromise and civility while rewarding extreme positions, passionately presented and intransigently defended.

In the late twentieth century, moreover, the major political parties began using decennial redistricting to protect incumbents by packing individual districts with large majorities from the incumbents' political parties—a process that tends to squeeze out competitive seats in the U.S. House of Representatives and in state legislatures. The number of truly competitive House seats fell to an all-time low of 15 (out of 435) in 2002, and only one incumbent was defeated for reelection. The consequence: fewer and fewer elected officials need to appeal across party lines; more and more can prevail by mobilizing their partisan and ideological base voters. This kind of politics increases the power of more extreme factions within each party while diminishing incentives to craft moderate positions.

Taken together, the interest-group structure of the parties, declining political participation by less-partisan voters, and the diminishing number of contested legislative races help explain why many education issues are debated with almost theological intensity. Consider one battle in the long-running war over school vouchers. Along with the head of the Washington, D.C., school board and the most powerful member of the city council, District of Columbia mayor Anthony Williams in 2003 came out in support of a modest program of federally funded vouchers for District students stuck in low-performing schools. After the mayor agreed to appear before a meeting of free-market-oriented state legislators, a leader of the outspokenly liberal People for the American Way sent the mayor a public letter accusing him of lending a "veneer of bipartisan respectability to a group whose goals are destructive to the public interest and the people you serve."[4]

There is more to democratic sentiment, however, than the foregoing catalog of ideological contestation would suggest. Many citizens believe that this hyper-partisan template distorts the real structure of public opinion, leaving much of the public unrepresented, and considerable evidence supports this belief. More Americans regard themselves as moderates than as liberals or conservatives; most are willing to deal with public education pragmatically rather than ideologically. From time to time, leaders are able to activate this latent coalition of the center against a party and interest-group structure that pushes toward extremes; the No Child Left Behind Act is in part an example of this possibility. But for the most part, experience confirms what theory predicts: in education as in other arenas, those who are most passionate, and whose interests are most directly affected, tend to dominate the policy process.

Indeed, the politics of education consists largely in the clash of organized interests. As illustrated in the Baltimore case study presented below, teachers' unions tend to be dominant actors, and little can be accomplished without their acquiescence. From time to time, other key actors emerge—business coalitions, reform groups led by parents, and local foundations, among others. And as political scientists have continually argued, entrepreneurial politicians can change the balance of power by expanding the sphere of conflict, typically from the local to the state level. Mayors who form alliances with state legislatures (or, in the case of Washington, D.C., with key congressional committees) can force through policy changes over local objections. On occasion, moreover, policies engineered at the state and federal levels can create the context for otherwise unattainable local changes.

## Interinstitutional Conflicts

The U.S. political system is deliberately engineered to prevent oppression by fostering conflict among different centers of institutional power. One axis of conflict is vertical—namely, tension among the different tiers of the federal system. Another is horizontal, stemming from struggles among different branches of government. To some extent, every public issue is bound to get embroiled in the complexities of interinstitutional conflict. But some issues are structured in a manner such that they are more likely than others to trigger intense competition, and education policy is one of them.

Consider the relation among the federal government, states, and localities. Until the 1960s, the federal government played a limited role in public education; the U.S. Constitution is virtually silent on the issue. (By contrast, state constitutions without exception specify education as one of the core responsibilities of government.) Since the 1960s, however, the federal role has expanded—to overcome segregation and discrimination, mitigate inequality, and most recently, to promote academic achievement for all students. But federal laws and regulations concerning public education have increased far more than has federal funding, leading to bitter complaints from states and localities about "unfunded mandates."

Special education is a classic example of this process at work. Inspired in part by the civil rights movement, advocates for handicapped and disabled children lobbied vigorously for instructional programs carefully tailored to each child's needs, conducted within the regular school environment to the maximum feasible extent. Their efforts culminated in 1975 with the passage of the Education for All Handicapped Children Act, which established a web of legally enforceable rights. It was clear from the outset that the per-student cost of this legislation would be high, and the federal government promised to provide 40 percent of the total. Policy has never matched the promise, however. As late as the mid-1990s, federal support for special education was still less than 10 percent of total costs, and it remained less than 20 percent in 2004. As a result, states and (especially) local governments have been forced to bear much of the burden, which has been considerable. When the needs of certain students covered by the law cannot be met within public schools, public authorities are often forced to place them in private schools, at a cost per student that can go as high as $50,000 each year. Not surprisingly, soaring costs for special education, now more than $40 billion per year, have absorbed a significant portion of total education funding increases, restricting the ability of localities to implement broadly popular programs such as reductions in class size.

In addition to these vertical relationships, special education also illustrates horizontal tensions among branches of government in implementing education policy. Special education is governed, not only by the Individuals with Disabilities Education Act (IDEA), the successor to the original 1975 legislation, but also by the Americans with Disabilities Act (ADA) and Section 504 of the Rehabilitation Act of 1973. Each of these laws establishes enforceable rights and prohibitions. For example, the Rehabilitation Act prohibits recipients of federal funds from discriminating on the basis of disability, while the ADA mandates the removal of many architectural barriers to the inclusion of individuals with disabilities. These statutes offer families with grievances against local school authorities ready access to the courts, which have not been shy about requiring expensive and complex remedies.

While civics textbooks dwell on the three constitutional branches of government, the reality is far more complex, as education policy clearly shows. For example, local school boards, which became the standard form of school governance during the Progressive Era and have dominated the landscape ever since, enjoy substantial independence from mayors (and often from city councils as well). This arrangement was intended to insulate educational professionals from the influence of local political machines, allowing decisions to be made on the basis of "neutral" expertise—what works best to educate children—as opposed to the distributive politics of graft, favoritism, and nepotism. While it substantially attained this objective in the early decades of the twentieth century, over time new organized interests learned how to use the autonomy of the schools to their advantage, and aspiring politicians used positions on the school board as springboards to higher elective office. It became apparent that the flip side of insulation from normal democratic politics was the dilution of democratic accountability.

When the underperformance of schools becomes a hot political issue, this institutional structure can generate epic battles. In 1995, frustrated by decades of decline, Chicago's mayor Richard Daley worked with the Illinois state legislature to seize control of the school system, installed his own management team, and took personal responsibility for the results. Other cities, Philadelphia among them, pursued a similar path.

Another example of controversial horizontal relations involves what might be called the "politics of place." While each local jurisdiction exercises substantial control over its own education system, some become dissatisfied with the consequences of jurisdictional boundaries and work to erode their significance. This often happened during school-integration controversies, when some localities tried to use the courts to bring surrounding jurisdictions under the aegis of a single "metropolitan" plan, triggering fervent controversy and ultimately a definitive Supreme Court decision. In an effort to remedy racial segregation in the overwhelming black Detroit school system, a lower court fashioned a remedy that mixed Detroit's children with those of the surrounding (mostly white) suburbs. But in *Milliken v. Bradley* (1974), the Supreme Court struck this remedy down, declaring that unless the suburban boards could be shown to have substantially contributed to racial segregation, they could not be forced to enroll students from other jurisdictions. No Child Left Behind has created a legal basis (and incentives) for parents of students in schools designated as low performing to pressure schools in surrounding districts to accept their children. Prior experiments with public school choice suggest that these parents will encounter resistance and controversy.

The politics of place can work in the opposite direction as well, when local jurisdictions seek to avoid amalgamation with others. In many rural areas, the local public schools are key symbols of community pride and identity. Since the end of World War II, however, two forces have combined to eliminate many of these schools. As the population of rural small towns has declined, so did the number of students in their schools, making it harder to maintain curricular diversity and separate classes for students of different ages. At the same time, many education experts argued that larger schools were pedagogically superior. The result was a consolidation movement that over the next half century dramatically reduced the number of rural schools while more than doubling the median size of their student bodies. Local communities vigorously resisted, but to little avail. Today, most rural schools are regional institutions that bring students together from multiple jurisdictions spread over a large geographical area.

## Economic Dimension of Educational Conflicts

Public education in the United States is a vast, costly, and valuable enterprise. There are more than ninety-two thousand public schools, located in roughly fifteen thousand separate school districts. More than forty-seven million students are enrolled in public K–12 classes, about 90 percent of total school-age children. The total amount required to educate these students each year now exceeds $400 billion (roughly 4 percent of GDP) and is rising relentlessly. Local districts pay about 44 percent of this total, financed mostly through property taxes. The states pay another 48 percent, a share that has risen by ten percentage points since the 1970s. (K–12 education now consumes about one-quarter of all state expenditures.) Despite increases since 1999, the federal government contributes only 8 percent of the total.

Localities' dependence on property taxes to fund education has a number of adverse consequences. This tax imposes a disproportionate burden on retirees, who typically own their homes debt-free but must live on fixed incomes, stiffening their resistance to spending increases for public education. When historically cyclical housing markets stagnate, local governments are hard-pressed to fill the fiscal gap. And most important, because property values per capita vary dramatically across jurisdictional lines, localities have vastly differing capacities to support local education. One study found that in Connecticut, the wealthiest town has fifteen times more property value per student than does the poorest town, forcing property-poor jurisdictions to tax themselves at a much higher rate to reach even minimal funding levels.[5]

As previously discussed, Americans now regard equality of educational opportunity as economically and morally essential. While equal opportunity does not require perfect equality of resources, clearly the kinds of inequalities found at the local level are incompatible with equal opportunity. Because of the federal government's limited fiscal role in education, the burden of compensating for local inequalities falls heavily on state governments. In most states, this responsibility pits wealthy suburbs against cash-strapped cities in an unending struggle. The politics of equalization is especially difficult in states such as Illinois, Michigan, and Pennsylvania with very large cities that require huge transfers and become focal points for suburban and rural resistance. (As shown in the next section, racial tensions exacerbate these political difficulties.)

States have gradually come to bear a larger share of total education costs, with significant fiscal consequences: If the state share of education costs had remained at the level of the early 1970s, states in the aggregate would be spending about $40 billion dollars less on education each year than they do today. These extra funds have helped reduce inequalities between richer and poorer areas. During periods of fiscal pressure, such as the severe downturn in revenues that began early in 2001, the politics of educational equalization becomes even more conflictual than usual, and many states have been forced to freeze or even cut funding for education.

In a labor-intensive sector such as education, large expenditures yield enormous numbers of jobs. About 7 million persons work part and full time for public education systems, more than half of all local employees. These jobs tend to be concentrated, moreover, in urban jurisdictions where traditional industrial sources of private sector employment have been declining for decades. As a result, public education is often among the largest employers, public or private, in urban areas. In Detroit, for example, the public school system is the single largest employer, far outpacing industrial giants such as General Motors and Chrysler. The picture is much the same in Baltimore, where the public school system offers three thousand more jobs than does the largest private employer. Although Los Angeles County has a more diverse economy than either Detroit or Baltimore, public schools are that jurisdiction's second largest employer. When Clarence Stone and his colleagues carried out their authoritative research on the politics of urban education reform, they did not find a city in which the schools ranked lower than fourth on the jobs list. This led them to characterize urban school systems as "employment regimes"—that is, as bundles of material benefits including jobs, contracts, and career ladders.[6]

The employment function of urban public education helps explain policies pursued by urban school administrators. In Washington, D.C., for example, very high per-pupil expenditures coexisted for years with shortages of basic classroom materials and a huge backlog of deferred maintenance. This stemmed in part from the systematic diversion of resources to sustain jobs, hundreds of which had never been authorized. Parents and school reformers struggled for years against administrative resistance to achieve a minimum level of budgetary transparency.

The central role schools play in maintaining urban employment also helps explain the ferocity of battles over proposals seen as threatening jobs. Even when jobs are available in today's economy, decent health and retirement benefits along with job security and opportunities for advancement are increasingly rare. As unionized industrial jobs have evaporated in urban areas, the schools have emerged as one of the few remaining sources of job stability. So initiatives such as outsourcing, private management, teacher testing, and expedited termination procedures, which are unwelcome in any school system, are anathema to urban professionals who see few alternatives to employment in the public schools.

In many ways, this conflict is but the latest chapter in a very old American story. Historically, public sector employment in urban areas has served as a key vehicle for upward mobility among immigrant groups. During the nineteenth century, Irish immigrants used their new political power to dominate city police and fire departments, and often used that power to procure construction contracts. Nepotism and political favoritism were rife in school systems as well. For middle-class reformers, these employment trends stood in opposition to "good government"—the dominance of disinterested leaders and neutral experts over policy and administration. Progressive Era reforms were designed to tip the balance away from the distributive politics of group mobility and toward the efficient achievement of essential public purposes.

Today, urban school systems play much the same economic role as did police and fire departments a century ago and have become sources of upward mobility for groups such as African Americans and Latinos. Once again, reformers focused on promoting public purposes—in today's context, raising overall academic achievement and closing the gap between whites and minorities—are pushing policy and institutional changes that threaten hard-won economic gains. And once again, the struggle between the politics of security and the politics of reform is central to conflicts over the future direction of education.

It would be wrong to suggest, however, that the conflict between class-based economic interests and educational policy is confined to urban areas. In the suburbs, there is a politics of homeownership that exerts a powerful, often distortive effect on educational policy. The basics are well known. Families choose suburban housing based on the perceived quality of the local schools. Good schools affect property values, and higher assessments in turn increase the tax base available for funding schools. With the value of what is for most families their single largest asset linked so closely to specific schools, parents fiercely resist changes in catchment area boundaries, even when clearly warranted by demographic changes or key educational goals.

## Racial Politics and School Reform: A Case Study

Race has been the single most divisive factor in American education policy. Since the 1950s, efforts to address the legacy of the United States' long history of discrimination against African Americans have sparked some of the most intense battles in American politics. The struggles over desegregation in the South, busing in the Northeast and Midwest, and decentralization in New York City are oft-told tales that need not be repeated here. The focus of this section is rather on the contemporary legacy of racial discrimination—in particular, on the travails of many urban school systems in which African American students now form the majority.

In the 1980s, concern about the overall performance of U.S. public schools sparked a new wave of education reform. While decades later this concern had not completely abated, the focus had shifted somewhat, to the "achievement gap" between white and minority students and to the steps required to narrow it. Key features of the No Child Left Behind Act of 2001 reflect this emphasis.

As measured by the National Assessment of Educational Progress (NAEP), the gap is wide indeed. The median African American (and Hispanic) twelfth-grader scores at roughly the level of the median white eighth-grader in most core academic subjects. Comparable gaps in SAT scores complicate college admissions and fuel the national debate over affirmative action. In some low-performing urban schools, fewer than half of entering ninth-graders march at high school graduation ceremonies four years later.

If the legacy of racial discrimination is at the core of urban educational ills, it also complicates the search for effective solutions. Moving beyond statistical aggregates, this section seeks to explore this legacy by means of a case study in the micropolitics of racial conflict.

Baltimore, Maryland, is in many ways a typical midsize American city. In the decades after the Civil War, Maryland instituted racial segregation, enforced through law and social mores. As late as 1955, nearly all commercial establishments in Baltimore treated black and white customers differently. African Americans faced widespread discrimination in Baltimore's private sector employment market and were systematically underrepresented in nearly every public agency. The one exception was the school system, where black teachers staffed the black-only schools required by law.

Along with many other cities outside the Deep South, Baltimore enjoyed a surge of black immigration in the decades after World War II. Between 1940 and 1970, Baltimore's African American population soared from 166,000 (19 percent of the total) to more than 420,000 (46 percent). During that same period, the white population fell from 693,000 to 480,000. During the next two decades, as the African American population stabilized, whites continued to leave the city, and by 1990 the white population had dropped to 288,000 (41 percent of the total).

The effects of this shift were even more dramatic in Baltimore's schools. In 1950 whites accounted for about 72 percent of all school-age children and 67 percent of students in city schools. By 1990, only 29 percent of school-age children were white, and the percentage of white students in Baltimore's schools was even lower—just 19 percent. According to Marion Orr in *Black Social Capital: The Politics of School Reform in Baltimore, 1986–1998* (1999), many African Americans viewed these changes as evidence that whites had simply abandoned the public schools.

This demographic earthquake occurred against the backdrop of an equally momentous transformation of Baltimore's economy. Between the Civil War and the 1950s, Baltimore had become a center of manufacturing, adding 103 new plants in the 1920s alone. World War II ratcheted up production and employment in sectors such as steel and shipbuilding. By 1950, the city could claim over 1,800 manufacturing establishments.

That proved to be the peak, however. Manufacturing in Baltimore slipped by 12 percent during the 1950s and more quickly thereafter. By 1990, only 844 manufacturing firms remained in the city. The decline in manufacturing employment was even steeper, from a peak of 127,000 in the early 1950s to only 44,000 in 1990.[7] The effects of this shift from manufacturing to white-collar jobs rippled through Baltimore's economic and social fabric. For the purposes of this discussion, three consequences are key. First, middle-class incomes were no longer available to workers lacking high school diplomas and, in many cases, advanced training and skills. Second, African Americans became increasingly dependent on public sector jobs to maintain a robust middle class. (The white-dominated business community's continued racial discrimination in hiring for better-paying jobs exacerbated the black concentration in the public sector.) And third, poverty increased among African Americans who could not attain jobs in the public sector. By 1990, more than one-sixth of all black families were living below the poverty line, three times the state average. The figure for children was much worse, with nearly one in three below the poverty line (versus a statewide average of one in ten). Most black children not officially in poverty were near-poor; about two-thirds qualified for free or reduced-cost lunch programs.

During the 1960s, these trends interacted with a newly vigorous civil rights movement to leverage rapid change in Baltimore's public sector. Both Republican and Democratic mayors adopted a policy of appointing roughly equal numbers of blacks and whites to municipal jobs. By the early 1970s,

African Americans filled nearly one-half of Baltimore's forty-one thousand public sector positions.

Nowhere did this process proceed faster, or farther, than in the city's schools. As the racial composition of the student body shifted, black leaders insisted that the percentage of employees at every level of this system follow suit. This is precisely what happened. By 1993, fully 70 percent of the principals and assistant principals were African American, versus only 20 percent in 1965. By the mid-1990s, African Americans constituted about 60 percent of the instructional staff, and 70 percent of the district's more than eleven thousand total jobs. As Orr puts it, the public school "had become the linchpin of Baltimore's black employment base" (p. 68).

Black employment in public schools was more than a statistical aggregate; it was a powerful social network. Many of the teachers and administrators had grown up together, gone to the same colleges and universities, and even pledged at the same fraternities and sororities. Senior teachers and administrators had joined the system at roughly the same time, and they had remained. By the early 1990s, 35 percent had served for twenty years or more. They tended to think alike, and they were intensely loyal both to the system and to one another. It is no exaggeration to say that they had a powerful sense of ownership, born of struggle, perseverance, and community pride.

In the wake of racially charged controversy over the firing of an African American superintendent, the then mayor William Donald Schaefer tacitly ceded administrative control over the school system to Baltimore's black community. At the same time, he used school jobs as a patronage system, rewarding supporters and punishing individuals who resisted his policies. And he viewed the schools through the lens of politics rather than pedagogy. The result, according to many observers including Orr, was that the "true function of public education, mastery of sufficient skills to assume the rights and responsibilities of citizenship, was lost" (p. 58).

Even under the most favorable circumstances, economic change in the black community would have challenged Baltimore's public schools to maintain high academic achievement. As we have seen, circumstances were far from ideal. Neither political nor school leaders were adequately focused on the schools' core academic mission. The near inevitable result: soaring dropout rates and plunging test scores. By the early 1980s, observers were using terms such as "failure" and "disaster" to characterize the system's performance.

Although the officials most directly responsible did not concentrate on academic performance, some outside the system did, and they began to agitate for change. One source of discontent was Baltimore's business community, which was under pressure to hire more graduates of the city's school system but was reluctant to do so because the postindustrial jobs needing to be filled required skills that the schools were not conveying to students.

Another important force for change was state government. During the four decades from the mid–1950s to the mid–1990s, state aid jumped from 25 percent of Baltimore's total school expenditures to 63 percent. Even this level of subsidy left spending per student in Baltimore well below the state average. Still, state aid required transfers from taxpayers in other jurisdictions that were large enough to stimulate political resistance. Not surprisingly, state legislators and officials began scrutinizing the management and performance of Baltimore's schools.

With this history as background, it can now be understood why a series of efforts in the 1980s and 1990s touched off such fierce battles. Starting in the early 1980s, Baltimore's then superintendent of schools, Alice Pinderhughes, threw her support behind a plan, eventually dubbed site-based management (SBM), to shift administrative and fiscal responsibility away from the central bureaucracy toward individual school principals. With the election of a young, reform-minded African American mayor, Kurt Schmoke, this proposal moved to the top of the agenda. Richard Hunter, his handpicked candidate for superintendent, indicated his full support for the idea.

Implementing the plan proved difficult, however. Community groups bitterly complained that they had been left out of the planning process. Central administrators were reluctant to yield authority to schools, and many principals were reluctant to accept it, arguing that functions such as facilities management were best left to central headquarters.

By 1989, Schmoke had begun to lose confidence in the new superintendent, whose support for SBM had wavered in the face of unexpectedly broad opposition. News reports and rumors suggested that the mayor was trying to engineer Hunter's resignation before the expiration of his three-year contract. At that point, leaders of the African American community intervened. The president of the Baltimore chapter of the National Association for the Advancement of Colored People urged the mayor to retain Hunter in the name of African American unity. A group of leading black ministers told the mayor that they objected to his public criticisms of a fellow black leader. The city's leading newspaper, the *Baltimore Sun*, reported that other prominent black leaders were complaining that the "white establishment" was out to get Hunter. After the school board voted not to renew the superintendent's contract, Mayor Schmoke tried to persuade Hunter's deputy, Edward Andrews, who was white, to take the job. Andrews refused, fearing that the appointment of a white superintendent would be politically untenable. When the mayor then approached another white candidate, leading black ministers advised him that the next superintendent would have to be black. In the thick of a tough reelection campaign, the mayor capitulated.

Another racially charged dispute involved the efforts of Baltimoreans United in Leadership Development (BUILD), a grassroots organization inspired by the American reformer Saul Alinsky, to pressure the Greater Baltimore Committee (GBC), the lead organization of the business community, into hiring more graduates of Baltimore's public schools. BUILD pressed for job guarantees, while the GBC resisted anything that smacked of quotas or curbed the authority of executives. One BUILD representative stated that "The GBC refused to hear us out. They didn't see it in their self-interest to help a school system where 80 percent of the students are black" (Orr, p. 128). BUILD threatened to retaliate by releasing statistics detailing the racial distribution of hiring by leading businesses, raising the specter of a public racial controversy that would impede the ability of political and corporate leaders to attract new businesses to Baltimore. After protracted negotiations, the parties agreed to a plan in which high school graduates with good GPAs and attendance records would be guaranteed multiple job interviews and given preferred positions in the hiring pool.

BUILD viewed this agreement as a reasonable first step but believed that movement toward a broader relationship with the business community would require active mayoral involvement. Under Mayor Schmoke, this occurred, but even the enlarged program yielded limited results. For example, barely one in ten of the nearly five thousand students in the 1987 graduating class met the threshold GPA and attendance requirements, and members of the GBC registered continuing dissatisfaction with the quality of even the high school graduates who managed to qualify for the employment program.

The program was also hobbled by the divergent objectives of its principal authors. The GBC saw it as a strategy for leveraging reform in the public schools, an objective that school leaders did not fully embrace. This fed the business community's doubts about the quality of the system's graduates. By contrast, the leaders of BUILD viewed the agreement as a way of extracting additional resources from local businesses and were disappointed by the meager results. For their part, black school administrators interpreted the business community's stance in racial terms, arguing that even when the schools sent their best graduates for interviews, middle managers regularly chose white suburban kids instead. At best, they believed, the business community was too distant from the reality of black Baltimore to get behind the program with the needed enthusiasm. Said one black school board member, "GBC does not live and breathe black life. These are black kids we are talking about" (Orr, p. 137).

This case study of Baltimore helps us understand what racially inflected controversy over urban school reform is actually about. Money, jobs, and power are at stake, of course. But the conflict goes deeper. It is about the pride African Americans gain from leading the school systems in which their children form the majority, and the sense of vulnerability they feel in the face of forces they suspect of trying to wrest control back from them. It is about a continuing fear of social exclusion, and of standards (however facially neutral), the application of which might exacerbate exclusion. It is about a sense of community that makes leaders hesitant to accept measures that might worsen the plight of their least-well-off members. It is about the intracommunal advantages that leaders who stand up to (white) outsiders can reap. And it is about the memory of the past, which shapes perceptions and interpretations in the present. As many other groups also show, the memory of oppression defines collective identities. For this reason, among others, outsiders who parachute into racially charged situations filled with good intentions but ignorant of communal and local history are virtually certain to come to grief.

## Ethnicity and Cultural Conflict: The Case of Bilingual Education

In the 1960s, it would have made sense to discuss majority/minority conflicts primarily in black/white terms. Restrictions on immigration put in place in the 1920s had reduced the percentage of foreign-born residents in the United States to an all-time low of less than 5 percent. In 1965, however, Congress all but eliminated these restraints and opened the immigration gates to previously underrepresented countries and regions. The result: the percentage of foreign-born residents has more than doubled and continues to rise, while the ethnic composition of the U.S. population has become much more diverse.

Nowhere have the effects been more dramatic than in the group of immigrants from Spanish-speaking Central and South America, labeled "Hispanics" by the U.S. Census Bureau. Sometime in the late 1990s, the number of school-age Hispanics exceeded the number of school-age African Americans for the first time. Early in the twenty-first century, Hispanics became the largest minority in the United States. If current patterns of immigration and reproduction continue, by 2050 they will constitute fully one-quarter of the U.S. population.

As Hispanic youngsters surged into the public schools, they became the heart of a new conflict over pedagogy and culture. On average, educational achievement among Hispanic students is low, and their dropout rate is very high. (Fewer than 60 percent complete high school.) Poverty and school quality help explain these results, of course, but there is a linguistic dimension as well. Hispanics constitute three-quarters of the 5 million students who speak English poorly or not at all. Both Congress and the courts have determined that this constitutes an important barrier to equal educational opportunity.

The question is how best to tear down this barrier. Some educators advocate an approach known as full (or structured) immersion, in which students are placed in an English-speaking setting and are encouraged to learn English as quickly as possible. Others support instruction in the student's language of origin as well as English ("bilingual education") for a "transitional" period that some believe should last as long as seven years. Scholars and evaluators are sharply divided over the comparative effectiveness of these approaches. A mounting body of evidence suggests, however, that poorly conceived bilingual programs can leave even high school graduates without an adequate working knowledge of English and can have negative effects on the earnings of adult Hispanics who participated in these programs.[8] Not surprisingly, many Hispanic parents have begun resisting traditional bilingual programs on the grounds that they amount to a separate and unequal education that threatens to leave their children at a permanent disadvantage. (In response, the No Child Left Behind Act gave parents greater power over the assignment of their children to bilingual education classes and mandates language proficiency testing of all English learners after three years of attending schools in the United States.)

There is an interest-group dimension to this conflict as well. Many bilingual-education teachers and teachers' aides have a large stake in the continued existence of substantial bilingual programs. Some of these individuals themselves have at best limited English proficiency; absent bilingual programs, they might well find themselves without employment in the public schools. As a result, they are well organized and highly vocal, and they have strong advocates throughout the educational system, including the U.S. Department of Education.

The debate goes beyond academic attainment and jobs. Antibilingual referenda in California, Arizona, and elsewhere have touched an anti-immigrant chord, one note of which is the fear that linguistic and cultural diversity are undermining national unity. Some advocates of bilingual education have added fuel to the fire by defending the program, not as a temporary transition to the mainstream, but as a permanent vehicle for cultural preservation. The point is to symbolize, and promote, the equal status of minority languages and cultures. Advocates of this "strong multiculturalism" support their position, not only with moral and constitutional claims, but also with arguments about the importance of cultural harmony between parents and children and the confusion that can result when children are uprooted from their culture of origin. Some connect strong multiculturalism to a critique of the majority U.S. culture as excessively competitive, individualistic, and individualist and as fostering disrespect for family and community ties.

There is a form of multiculturalism that enjoys widespread support in the United States, based on the idea that numerous groups have nourished U.S. institutions and culture in ways unrecognized in the pedagogies of the 1950s. This "liberal" multiculturalism argues against the legitimacy of many traditional hierarchies and for mutual respect among different traditions and ways of life. It advocates using school texts in many subjects to stress the contributions of women, African Americans, Native Americans, and many other groups. And it favors a less triumphalist approach to U.S. history, more open to the costs as well as the benefits of U.S. geographic and cultural expansion.

In the end, however, liberal multiculturalism does not deny—indeed, it affirms—the existence and importance of a shared citizenship based on common ideals and institutions. And it insists on the importance of public schools as the transmitters of this commonality to all, immigrants as well as native-born. This is the bright line in the conflict over language and culture that

77

has roiled U.S. education since the late 1960s. The Constitution protects the rights of dissenters to maintain their own schools, subject to reasonable regulation. But it is hard to imagine that taxpayers will knowingly subsidize pedagogies that directly challenge the foundations of the regime that nearly all cherish.

While strong multiculturalism has a base in the academy and has sparked a contentious debate, it is unlikely to gain a mass following. By and large, groups that voluntarily come to the United States are willing to accept their side of the bargain—the responsibility to master the basics of the majority language and culture. Indeed, most are eager to do so, rightly seeing linguistic and cultural competence as key to economic success, especially for their children. In light of this, it is not hard to predict that large numbers of Hispanic parents will use their new legal rights to opt out of bilingual education programs that do not teach their children how to read, write, and speak the English language.

## Conclusion

This forced march through the terrain of educational conflicts in the United States has not revealed any single dominant axis of division. In this respect, among others, the texture of U.S. controversies differs from that of many European nations, in which such motifs may be discerned. In France and Italy, the struggle between secular republican governments and the Catholic Church long configured the politics of education. In the Netherlands, the essential task was to work out an educational *modus vivendi* involving Catholics, Protestants, and public authorities. In the United Kingdom, partisans of meritocratic reform battled the defenders of traditional class privilege.

In the United States, by contrast, educational policy reflects innumerable institutional, economic, and cultural divisions. Demographic diversity, institutional complexity, and a distinctive tradition of local control combine to create a multiplicity of battles that do not coalesce into a single war. From time to time, a dominant theme emerges—the Progressive institutional reforms of the late nineteenth and early twentieth centuries, or the standards and assessments movement of the late twentieth and early twenty-first. But inevitably, these initiatives are refracted through the overlapping cleavages of U.S. society. A French minister once boasted that in any hour of any day, he knew exactly what every schoolchild in France was studying. It is hard to imagine anything more alien to the tradition of education in the United States.

That U.S. education policy lacks focus does not mean that it lacks intensity. As we have seen, disagreements over matters such as partisanship and ideology, resources and power, and race and culture can be bitter indeed—all the more so when differences of class and life-experience generate mutual incomprehension

78

and suspicion. As long as the United States is marked, on the one hand, by deeply held principles of social equality and fair opportunity and, on the other, by vast disparities of wealth, power, and status, the conflicts traced in this chapter are unlikely to abate.

## Notes

1. Ravitch, *The Schools We Deserve,* 73.
2. Paul Hill, "The Supply-Side of School Choice," in Sugarman and Kemerer, *School Choice,* p. 151.
3. *Employment Division v. Smith,* 888 (1990).
4. Letter from People for the American Way Foundation Ralph G. Neas to Washington D.C. Mayor Anthony Williams, July 29, 2003.
5. Hochschild and Scovronick, *The American Dream and the Public Schools,* 62.
6. Information on Detroit and other urban schools is from Stone et al., *Building Civic Capacity,* 137–138; for Baltimore, see Orr, *Black Social Capital,* 148–149; for Los Angeles County, see Hochschild and Scovronick, *The American Dream and the Public Schools,* 20.
7. Orr, *Black Social Capital,* 63–64; 69.
8. Hochschild and Scovronick, *The American Dream and the Public Schools,* 152–155.

## Bibliography

Bates, Stephen. *Battleground: One Mother's Crusade, the Religious Right, and the Struggle for Control of Our Classrooms.* New York: Poseidon, 1993.

Carnegie Corporation of New York and CIRCLE: Center for Information and Research on Civic Learning and Engagement. *The Civic Mission of Schools.* New York: Carnegie Corp., 2003.

Erie, Steven P. *Rainbow's End: Irish-Americans and the Dilemmas of Urban Machine Politics, 1840–1985.* Berkeley: University of California Press, 1988.

Galston, William A. *Liberal Pluralism: The Implications of Value Pluralism for Political Theory and Practice.* Cambridge, U.K., and New York: Cambridge University Press, 2002.

Henig, Jeffrey R., et al. *The Color of School Reform: Race, Politics, and the Challenge of Urban Education.* Princeton, N.J.: Princeton University Press, 1999.

Hochschild, Jennifer L., and Nathan Scovronick. *The American Dream and the Public Schools.* New York: Oxford University Press, 2003.

Orr, Marion. *Black Social Capital: The Politics of School Reform in Baltimore, 1986–1998.* Lawrence: University Press of Kansas, 1999.

Ravitch, Diane. *The Schools We Deserve: Reflections on the Educational Crises of Our Times.* New York: Basic, 1985.

Rich, Wilbur C. *Black Mayors and School Politics: The Failure of Reform in Detroit, Gary, and Newark.* New York: Garland, 1996.

Stone, Clarence N., et al. *Building Civic Capacity: The Politics of Reforming Urban Schools.* Lawrence: University Press of Kansas, 2001.

Sugarman, Stephen D., and Frank R. Kemerer, eds. *School Choice and Social Controversy: Policy, Politics, and Law.* Washington, D.C.: Brookings Institution Press, 1999.

# 4

## SCHOOLING CITIZENS
## FOR EVOLVING DEMOCRACIES

*Bruce Fuller and Arun Rasiah*

*The body-politic is formed by a voluntary association of individuals: It is a social compact, by which the whole people covenants with each citizen, and each citizen with the whole people . . . for the common good.*
—Massachusetts Constitution, Preamble
(authored by John Adams, 1780)

POLITICAL LEADERS AND EDUCATORS AROUND THE globe struggle to create the conditions under which children can truly grow up to become influential citizens with a meaningful stake in economic and civic life. This essential project to democratize society typically implicates the school, the premier institution within which young citizens are shaped and their covenant with civil society is formed. In the United States, the notion of education for democratic participation arose in the eighteenth century, when proponents of the modern neoclassical contract promised civil rights to individuals who agreed to pledge allegiance to and participate in a unified and secular society.

Other essays in this volume have put forward two crucial arenas in which the school institution attempts to advance democratic participation. First, public schools, under modern forms of statecraft, are *governed democratically,* presumably accountable to parents and voters through various mechanisms. These include popular election of school board members, accountability reforms advanced by elected legislators, and the positioning of schools in educational markets, unfettered by state bureaucracy, with the aim of shifting power to parents and local educators.

Second, governments and teachers sometimes encourage students to *participate actively* in classrooms or the community, even to *think critically* at times, resulting in more informed, even inspired, forms of civic participation. Still, it remains unclear whether democratic governance and pedagogies have made much headway within government-run schools in motivating democratic engagement and political hopefulness in the hearts and minds of students.

## *Internationalizing the Debates:*
## *School Governance, Pedagogies, and Institutional Roles*

This essay illuminates core reform ideas—surfacing across diverse nations—that aim to democratize education governance and social participation inside schools. We will examine how policy leaders in diverse societies think about change in these arenas and explore how the contemporary reform discourse is driven by deeper economic and cultural shifts occurring around the world. In the United States, reformers and scholars assume much about the democratic aims of education, at times criticizing how schools fall short of these ideals. By expanding the context beyond North America, the constitutive rules that constrain our policy debates recede; we move beyond our tacit conceptions of citizenship, the character of civil society, and how schools could more forcefully advance the democratic common good.

How policymakers and educators link the constructs of democratization and education, of course, varies around the globe, as our two country cases will illuminate. We begin the essay by briefly cataloging illustrative issues that give life and local context to these ideas. Making school systems "more democratic" often connotes widening access, inviting peripheral or low-status groups into formal school institutions. Indeed, schools largely provide the basic structural arrangements for getting ahead and attaining higher social status in a society. Other advocates argue that democratizing the institution means limiting the power of professional educators and shifting authority to parents. Still others rightfully worry about why so many youth, from various ethnic and social classes, feel alienated from schools and public institutions, which they see as uninspiring, limiting opportunity and putting forth a monochromatic form of culture and human expression. Indeed, John Adams's hopeful ideals of nurturing young citizens and stakeholders through public schooling quickly meet the realities of class inequalities, cultural dominance by particular groups, and governments that are not accustomed to thinking deeply about widening economic and political participation.

We have sorted contemporary cross-national controversies into two sections. First, we explore how diverse governments around the globe attempt to organize schooling and prepare citizens for civil society, including the pivotal issue of whether civic space is wide and inclusive or narrow and stratified among social classes. The state's organization of schooling necessarily leads to the question of who runs schools and who holds local educators accountable for results. Some Western governments' newfound faith in market forms of accountability is one manifestation that we consider. Second, we examine cross-national debates over the local social organization of schooling and classroom practice. This leads to the fundamental question of how government tries to raise and socialize children in particular ways—to serve individual and community interests. This initial survey of theory and policy mechanisms moves across topics and societies. We then dig deeper into two country cases—South Africa and Turkey—to bring these dynamics to life inside particular contexts.

Overall, we emphasize that what children learn about civic membership and participation and how it is taught—be it active or passive, inside one's school or community—is conditioned by the school's basic position and aims within the nation's political economy. When government aims to prepare children for a highly stratified labor and wage structure, certain institutional forms emerge. When government is committed to economic equity and cultural pluralism, other forms of schooling are crafted. These varieties in basic institutional structure and political ideals emerge as we move outside the U.S. context, removing our conceptual blinders. We close with lessons for North American policymakers, educators, and activists—especially those who struggle to advance democratic values through education and civic engagement.

## Schools and the Creation of Democratic Citizens: Variation across Nations

How individuals become engaged and economically secure citizens differs across democracies. Not all individuals will participate fully in civil society as citizens or workers, and schools play a pivotal role in "allocating" graduates into jobs and social roles. How the school is positioned in a society and which families gain access to particular schools help to legitimate the terms of civic membership and social power for different groups. For example, attendance at high-status high schools and elite private universities in the United States is far from evenly distributed across groups.

Certainly, individual effort and merit play a role in determining how children and youth move through stratified education systems. But institutional arrangements differ greatly across nations, providing wide or narrow points of access, typically starting with selective admission into secondary school. These institutional arrangements condition who moves to higher levels of education, and often the social relations that students encounter inside schools—rules and norms that encourage or limit participation, self-expression, and more complex forms of teaching and learning.

### School Organization and Social Stratification

The inclusiveness of school systems varies dramatically across societies, as seen in the basic contours of the education sector across three contrasting

TABLE 1

Three-Country Comparison of Educational Institutions

|  | | Great Britain | South Africa | Turkey |
|---|---|---|---|---|
| Public spending on education as percentage of GDP | | 4.5 | 5.5 | 3.5 |
| Enrollment rates for Secondary school (%) | | | | |
| Gross enrollment rates[a] | Females | 169 | 91 | 48 |
| | Males | 144 | 83 | 67 |
| Net enrollment rates[b] | Females | 95 | 60 | 57 |
| | Males | 93 | 54 | 74 |
| Gross enrollment rates for postgraduate institutions (%) | Females | 68 | 17 | 20 |
| | Males | 53 | 14 | 27 |

NOTE: Unless otherwise stated, all data are estimates for 2000. Data from Great Britain are for 1999.
[a]Gross enrollment rates use a constant age cohort as the denominator across all countries. This leads to an overstatement of enrollment rate for Britain. Data from Turkey are for 1999.
[b]Net enrollment rates use a country-specific age cohort for the denominator. This estimate for Turkey is unavailable.
SOURCE: UNESCO Institute for Statistics (2003).

nations. In Great Britain, public spending on education equaled 4.5 percent of the gross national product (GNP) in 1999, significantly below the industrialized-country average of 5.4 percent (Table 1). While strident debate has unfolded in post-apartheid South Africa over the level of educational investment, spending equaled 5.5 percent of GNP in that country, far above the developing-country average of 3.6 percent. This level approximates Turkey's level of spending on education, at 3.5 percent of GNP in 2000.

The capacity of school systems to provide enrollment opportunities also varies. In 2000, gross enrollment rates in secondary schools ranged from 48 percent of all girls in Turkey to almost 100 percent of girls in England. Just 20 percent of all females in the appropriate age cohort were enrolled in higher education in Turkey, compared with 17 percent in South Africa and 68 percent in England. A greater share of females participated in secondary and postsecondary schooling than males in England and South Africa, but not in Turkey, where male enrollment rates remained much higher.

The ways in which children are tracked into unequal futures vary across nations as well. Some see this as a functional attempt to efficiently sort youth into their eventual occupation; others argue that such tracking reproduces and legitimates social-class disparities. Few countries resemble the United States, where, increasingly, every child receives academic preparation to enter higher education. Indeed, in the United States, 42 percent of all eighteen-year-olds enter a four-year university and another 19 percent enter a two-year community college.[1]

Many democratic governments build school systems with narrow passageways into secondary school, unlike the more egalitarian secondary school system found in the United States. For example, Britain has built an inclusive system for children through age eleven, at which point almost all enter a comprehensive public secondary school. In 1998 Britain moved to standardize the curriculum around six core subjects for all students, leading to a general certificate at age sixteen. But then, entry into upper secondary schools becomes highly selective, based on competitive exams. In the American system, no selection mechanism operates formally until students complete secondary school at age eighteen.

Britain allocates a larger share of total education spending on secondary schools, relative to elementary schools, compared with the United States. Overall, Britain allows a smaller share of youth to move into senior secondary schools, higher up the education pyramid, then invests more in these advanced students, relative to the U.S. system, which is more inclusive and invests comparatively more in the elementary grades.[2] Even sharper differentiation of educational opportunities is apparent in other nations, including Germany, where nonacademic students turn down a separate, more vocational stream early in secondary school, and China, where highly selective and well-funded "key schools" select and richly serve the most promising students.

Turkey, located at the cusp of Western and Islamic traditions, offers a fascinating case of highly differentiated secondary schools that bestow a wide range of skills and social memberships upon young graduates. Only the first eight years of schooling are compulsory. Then, just under half the girls and two-thirds of the boys move into one of five types of academic, or four varieties of vocational, secondary school. On the academic side, students compete for admittance into elite math-science schools where Turkish is the language of instruction, elite Anatolian (general) high schools, or "foreign-language high schools," where the four-year instructional program can be in English or French. The losers in this competition go to three-year academic high schools, or one of four types of vocational school, which often are gender tracked. One track, enrolling 178,000 students in 2001, trains imams, Islamic prayer leaders.

These structural parameters of the education system are formed in response to, and then legitimate, how certain groups believe that children should be socialized, achieve, and get ahead. Of course, "public" institutions are shaped by dominant groups, defined by their social class and ethnic and gender characteristics. So the extent to which the school truly advances democratizing ideals is constrained by the extent to which a society's underlying political economy is committed to being inclusive and participatory.

## Governance, Finance, and Parental Choice

Pivotal debates over who "controls" public schools—especially the distribution of power between professional educators and parents—persist in many nations of the world. Pro-market advocates press to reduce the size and influence of government and, often, the authority of professionals, advocating parental choice and voucher forms of finance. Although an issue in the United States only since the late twentieth century, several countries have long aided sectarian schools within a decentralized governance structure. Over 14 percent of all students in New Zealand, for example, attend church-run schools at public expense. Research has detailed how such a market-oriented system tends to further stratify students and families.[3] Yet even social-democratic nations, such as Sweden, have long had decentralized governance and finance systems while policymakers continue to push hard to provide equitable levels of achievement. And South Africa, despite its painful history of racial and religious segregation, has implemented a pro–school choice governance arrangement, described below.[4]

Great Britain offers an intriguing theory-of-action by which government, since the prime ministership of Margaret Thatcher, has tried to widen civic participation through radical decentralization of school governance. Dating back to 1944, the British government has supported voluntary-aid schools, initially benefiting Anglican schools, which at the turn of the twenty-first century numbered more than five thousand. Resembling New Zealand's school finance system, the British mechanism offers capitation grants—fully portable, as public dollars follow students to parent-selected schools—to over two thousand Catholic, thirty-two Jewish, and most recently, five Islamic schools, all told serving about 1.7 million students. Prince Charles has vocally backed the spread of culturally diverse schools. Visiting an Islamic school in a district of London, he said, "You are ambassadors for a much misunderstood faith [with] much to tell people in a secular society like ours."[5]

Thatcher and Prime Minister Tony Blair after her advocated governance reforms that reduce the central state's authority, after setting uniform learning objectives, a national curriculum, and a nationwide testing program. Thatcher's government, from 1988 forward, broke the old system of assigning children to neighborhood schools, implementing a wide-open parental-choice scheme. The allocation of school resources, as well as local-school management, was decentralized. Parents or school principals can now break from their local education authority (LEA), for example, contracting with private firms for teacher training and other services. These mechanisms, according to the Thatcher government, empowered parents to select higher-quality schools and enabled local educators to shape their own workplaces, free of bureaucratic state controls.

Thatcher's supporters sparked a vociferous debate over the central inspectorate's role in implementing a new national curriculum, even attempting to mold pedagogical practices. School inspectors have fanned out from London since 1839; yet the new Office for Standards in Education (OFSTED) has been more aggressive in furthering the education ministry's preferred way of teaching, emphasizing didactics and discouraging constructivist pedagogy. This directly shapes the extent to which more-democratic social relations are modeled daily inside schools, both among teachers and with children. The centralized attempt to control classroom behavior abated only slightly under Blair's New Labor government, which mandated a "literacy hour" and then a "numeracy hour" in every British primary school. Whether this micromanagement of educators by central government, blended with parental choice locally, will yield learning gains or narrow achievement gaps remains unclear.[6]

What is notable about the evolving British case is government's decisive shift away from structuring children's time in ways that encourage active participation, beginning with the attack, under Thatcher, on progressive forms of pedagogy. On the other hand, pro–school choice advocates might argue that if parents prefer this form of pedagogy, they can select a school that emphasizes more democratic or constructivist forms of teaching.

### School Accountability and Democratic Participation

The ability of children to achieve and become efficacious citizens depends largely on schools' capacity to close learning gaps. When governments are frustrated with the pace of school improvement, accountability and governance reforms tend to be legislated at a more rapid clip. As we see in the British case, the distribution of authority and funding is linked to policy theories that aim to raise organizational effectiveness, even spark innovation, inside schools. Increasingly, political leaders no longer assume that more money alone will equalize children's achievement. The strength of public funding in creating incentives for local educators to improve thus has become a crucial question. Central governments continue to set uniform learning objectives and national curricula, support teachers, and distribute instructional materials. But governments are increasingly trying to target resources on specific interventions deemed promising by centralized policymakers, such as lowering class sizes, creating smaller schools, and aiding "low-performing" schools.

Indeed, the way in which incentives are structured and implemented locally, through participatory or bureaucratic means, to spur school gains, reflects the social relations and assumptions about human motivation that government ascribes to educators and students at the local level. For example, Edmonton, Canada, is gaining notoriety with the decision to allocate school funds directly to principals, based on enrollments and weighted in favor of students with particular learning needs, including those with limited English proficiency, reading problems, or disabilities. Public monies follow students to more popular and, it is hoped, more effective schools. The weighting of certain students creates incentives for schools to serve a mix of children and families. Principals and teachers benefit from having more discretionary resources at hand, presumably sparking more vibrant engagement in school-improvement efforts.[7] Again, we see financing policies blended with a theory about how to encourage social participation by local educators and parents, since those actors now control dollars and discretion locally. Charter schools—small publicly funded organizations that operate largely independent of state regulation—which have spread internationally, offer a similar experiment in decentralized finance and governance, spurred politically by a colorful array of teachers, activists, and parents who often seek greater civic participation.[8]

A persisting truism around the globe is that the effectiveness of schooling depends on the quality of a nation's teaching force. Yet surprisingly little is known about teacher labor markets and governments' ability to attract stronger teachers (see Johnson in this volume). Despite various attempts to improve classroom practices, little empirical understanding is available concerning what kinds of teacher recruitment and retention policies really work. We do know that starting salaries for, say, elementary school teachers, vary across nations: Japan pays only $22,670 for new teachers and Britain, $22,430, compared with $27,630 in the United States.[9] Given impressive levels of student learning in Japan, detailed in various studies and by the Organization for Economic Cooperation and Development (OECD), it seems that salaries alone cannot explain the quality of the teaching force or the achievement levels of students. On the other hand, Japanese teachers can move higher up the salary scale within a fifteen-year period, perhaps creating a stronger incentive for doing well, compared with teachers in Great Britain and North America, where salary structures are comparatively flat.

## School Effectiveness, Curricular Reform, and Classroom Practice

Governments around the world continue to debate the effectiveness of schooling in advancing equity and democratic participation and helping to pull peripheral or low-status groups into the mainstream. Early research conducted by the American sociologist James Coleman and others continues to prompt questions over the school institution's discrete effect in reducing economic and social inequalities—especially when governments fail to address structural barriers to jobs and social status. It remains unlikely that schools alone can enfranchise peripheral groups into civil society or integrate the poor into middle-class occupations. Research does show that schooling in low-income countries exerts a stronger effect on children's achievement, relative to family background, than it does on achievement or status attainment in wealthier nations.[10]

Comparative research prompts clearer thinking on how governments can best raise the effectiveness of local schools. Cross-nationally, for example, central or provincial governments differ in how they structure children's time in school, the nature of curricula, and the endorsement of pedagogical practices. These policies impart particular norms about what "official knowledge" is drilled into students, as well as the kinds of social participation expected and rewarded by institutions. Take the simple issue of instructional time. One 2002 study found that British students spend 940 hours per year in school, on average, compared with 875 in Japan and 980 in the United States.[11] But in Japan, fully 71 percent of all school-age children attend after-school tutoring programs (*juku*), compared with just 20 percent in the United Kingdom and 25 percent in the United States. Overall, exposure to formal schooling and instruction with private tutors varies markedly across nations.

The daily work of teachers cross-nationally, at least in the West, is remarkably similar in many ways. Most work in deeply entrenched learning organizations that exhibit a plethora of what the sociologist John W. Meyer terms "ritualized categories." This includes institutionalized contours such as age-graded classrooms, didactic delivery of the curriculum to largely passive students, and teacher reliance on textbooks and programmed curricular guides. One study of teaching in Germany, Japan, and the United States discovered that teachers structured their classrooms in similar ways, in terms of time spent in whole-class instruction, desk work, and explaining or discussing new material, at least when teaching mathematics.[12] But these researchers also found that teachers differ across nations in their beliefs about children's inborn intelligence versus the importance of effort, and what they do to remedy students' achievement difficulties. Other studies have found that Japanese teachers attempt fewer and more complex problems, prompting students to analyze questions from various perspectives, compared with more rote sequencing of material by teachers in U.S. classrooms.

Beyond the technology of teaching, other researchers have discovered that the locally situated meanings assigned to the same instructional materials can vary, across nations and regions. For example, Bruce Fuller and Prema Clarke report how textbooks are seen as essential tools for instruction in language arts by teachers in poor regions of southern Africa, whereas teachers in higher-quality schools rely on outside readers, such as novels, to encourage wider analysis by students. Even for young children attending preschools, studies in Japan reveal how children are socialized to abide by peer-enforced social norms that are at once participatory and intended to tacitly shape behavior, as opposed to the teacher being the constant didactic authority. And some nations or provinces, such as in northeast Brazil, explicitly encourage students to become engaged in the community or natural environment, following the educator Paulo Freire's call to teach literacy in ways that empower families to become critically engaged in civil society.[13]

## Crafting Citizens in Diverse Democracies

Contention involving our two core issues—how schools are governed and how pedagogy is organized—plays out globally in numerous ways. Political leaders and educators have debated whether centralized accountability and uniform curricula will raise children's achievement, or whether parental choice and decentralization of control works best. Similarly, witness the United States' so-called "culture wars" over phonics versus progressive approaches to language instruction, or the battle over how best to teach math and science. The root question is whether teachers are seen as all-knowing purveyors of facts or whether teacher-student relations are defined as more democratic, trusting and respectful of children's capacity to engage ideas and become participating citizens.

When Americans move outside their familiar context—into societies that exhibit different histories and tenets about education's role in the political economy—their tacit assumptions about the role and practices of schools within society are revealed. To illustrate this we next dig deeper into two cases, South Africa and Turkey, offering detailed evidence on how school governance and classroom social relations are constructed around the globe, with an eye on lessons for how democratizing elements of education might be better crafted in the United States.

Each country case is organized in three sections: (1) The changing nature of citizenship and schooling within civil society, (2) the reform of school governance, and (3) life inside schools and classrooms, and how it is situated within broader tensions, often linked to contention around political or cultural pluralism. We will see how democratic impulses—including new conceptions of the individual citizen—create fresh demands for the reform of school governance and social relations inside schools.

## South Africa: New Citizens, and the Search for Democratic Schooling

CITIZENS AND SCHOOLS WITHIN CIVIL SOCIETY. Questions involving individual rights and the inclusiveness of civil society lay at the heart of political struggles in South Africa. The Afrikaner-dominated National Party, after rising to power in 1948, created four separate school systems, one each for whites, blacks, coloreds (mixed race), and Asians (mostly from the Indian subcontinent). Each racial group had its own parliamentary body. But it was the assembly for whites that wielded political power under the segregationist regime. These separate education systems reinforced ethnic categories and stratified school resources. Bantu education, as it was called, prepared African children for their "proper destinations," menial jobs and general exclusion from civil society.

In 1991, three years before apartheid collapsed, the regime spent 4.6 times more per white pupil than for each black pupil. In the early 1990s, just under half of all adolescents living in the poorest one-fifth of the nation's households attended secondary school, compared with 83 percent of those in the richest one-fifth. Among the poorest 20 percent of families, one-half used wood as their main energy source. One-third of the children of these families showed signs of stunted growth due to chronic malnutrition. Two-thirds of all blacks, 21 million adults and children, lived beneath the poverty line. Schools effectively granted different degrees of citizenship and skills to particular groups: whites were full members of civil society, colored and Asian children became partial members, and all but a few blacks were denied the opportunity to become citizens.

South Africa's democratic movement, dating back to union organizing in the 1940s, sought full rights of citizenship for all adults, defined in classic liberal fashion, from the right to vote to protection against racial discrimination. The schooling regime became a prime target of attack as resistance intensified in the 1970s and 1980s, since it was such an egregious mechanism for reproducing racial inequalities in the labor force and civil society. "Liberation now, education later" became a rallying cry among adolescents and young militants, who repeatedly shut down government schools in the black townships. In 1993 the education ministry estimated that the number of days township schools had been closed equaled a full school term, or 6.6 million pupil days.

The People's Education Movement arose in the 1980s, powered by the African National Congress (ANC) and allied youth groups, sharply opposed to the authoritarian forms of schooling pressed by Bantu education policies. Outdated syllabi and textbooks were manifestations of the limited social and economic roles for blacks dictated by the Afrikaner regime. Pedagogy was didactic and controlling, situated in large classrooms with few materials. The curriculum continued to be regimented, pegged to matriculation exams. In contrast, the People's Education advocates pursued constructivist ideals, reminiscent of John Dewey, advancing active forms of pedagogy linked to children's everyday experience and position in the political economy. School-level organizing during the 1980s and early 1990s articulated how social relations of schooling, and its reform, should be a key part of the democratic movement. Nongovernment organizations grew dramatically during this period as Western aid agencies joined the resistance and began to prepare a new, multiracial generation of leaders.

But, following the first all-race elections in 1994, and the election of Nelson Mandela as president, the ANC government moved to the right politically in terms of macroeconomic policies. Some argue that neoliberal economists within the ANC necessarily aligned South Africa with the world economy, believing that the return of foreign investment and economic growth was a crucial precondition for political stability and redistributive policies. This bears on how South Africa's new leaders positioned the state and schools within a multicultural society. Mandela first appeared to side with old community-level activists in announcing a new "Reconstruction and Development Programme": "We have actively involved people and their organizations in their needs and aspirations. For those who have participated . . . it has been invigorating and reaffirmed the belief that the people of our country are indeed its greatest asset." Yet Mandela went on to emphasize the overarching importance of global economics: "Democracy will have little content, and indeed, will be short-lived if we cannot address our socio-economic problems within an expanding ... economy."[14]

SCHOOL GOVERNANCE AND REFORM. Post-apartheid policies initially emphasized racial integration and redistribution. The consolidation of the five separate education ministries (in addition to those for each of the ten black "homelands") represents a notable example, as does the effort to desegregate the old "Model C" schools that earlier served white children. South Africa's new constitution made nine years of basic education a right of all children. But government's incremental success in growing a more secure, racially diverse nonwhite middle class continues to complicate the integration process. Several economic and institutional forces constrain the school's effects in this long-term process of democratizing the new South Africa.

For example, a majority of independent (that is, private) school students are now nonwhite.[15] One increasing concern is that the rising black and colored middle classes will steadily leave government schools. These independent schools offer instruction in Afrikaans, Arabic, and regional African languages, countering the government's emphasis on English as the medium of instruction. Middle-class colored and Asian parents grew up learning that Afrikaans was the high-status language, allowing access to better jobs. Independent schools have opposed the introduction of "outcomes-based education," with learning objectives manifest in the central government's curriculum. Independent or private schools are named and protected in the new constitution and awarded public subventions. If an independent school charges more than 250 percent of the average tuition within a province, government provides no subsidy. The poorest schools, those charging the lowest tuition, receive from the provincial ministry an amount not to exceed 60 percent of per-pupil spending in government schools. The number of students attending independent schools has quadrupled since 1990, although this still represents just 2 percent of all students nationwide.

South Africa's new democratic constitution ensures that parents can apply to any school, a pro–school choice policy intended to hurry the pace of desegregation but one that by 2004 had yielded modest results at best. At the same time, parental choice also helps to ensure responsiveness to ethnic and language-based communities. Beyond a central curriculum and more equal allocation of teaching posts among the provinces, control has been largely decentralized to school governing councils. The cash-strapped government is eager to share the fiscal burden of education with provincial governments and local communities.

The ANC government has tried to decentralize authority to local school bodies, similar to the British model and experiments in the United States. South Africa's historical context, however, is quite different, stemming from the People's Education Movement and grassroots pressures for local control. But once government began crafting the new councils, the teachers' union initially opposed the idea of parents holding a majority of seats, then acquiesced when parents were no longer guaranteed a majority. The democratizing spirit faded a bit when government finally reached a compromise on decentralized school control, articulating expectations of local parents and teachers in a document titled "National Norms and Standards," a telling departure from the feisty days of People's Education when local schools were to devise a critical, liberationist form of curriculum and pedagogy. A national association of the nation's more than two thousand school councils has recently become a new lobbying group in Pretoria.

School finance reforms have aided poorer communities. For instance, a 1996 education act directed the provincial ministries to funnel 60 percent of their nonteaching resources to low-performing schools. To incrementally reduce disparities in class sizes and staffing levels, central government worked with the provinces to reallocate teaching posts, including severance packages for teachers in overstaffed, previously white schools. But countering this redistributive thrust, schools serving middle-class white, black, and colored families were given liberal freedom to raise their fees to finance quality enhancements or additional teaching posts. Some defined this policy move in the late 1990s as a way to stem further flight into the independent sector. If former white government schools were to be integrated, policymakers argued, better-off parents must be reassured that quality would not diminish.[16]

Student attendance patterns continued to reflect the ethnic stratification of South African housing and settlement patterns. In Western Cape province, which includes the cosmopolitan Cape Town region, in 2002, 99 percent of students in formerly African schools were black; 91 percent of children in formerly colored schools were colored. Formerly white schools had been integrated to some extent: 30 percent of students were colored and 5 percent were black. Formerly white primary schools charged annual fees of 2,077 rand in 2002, on average, compared with fees of 45 rand in previously African schools. This differential in revenue allowed formerly white schools to hire an additional four teachers on average, lowering class size, compared with black schools.

INSIDE SCHOOLS AND CLASSROOMS. Beneath these policy reforms—down at the school level—little is known empirically as to whether teachers and children are experiencing more democratic social relations and forms of participation. Government's new reform discourse has become quite technical, focusing on progressive school financing, specification of learning outcomes and student assessment, and bolstering the new school governing councils. In the early years of the twenty-first century only a few South African scholars were exploring whether social participation and engagement were any different inside classrooms a decade after the fall of apartheid.[17] Many political leaders have aimed to depoliticize the school setting for the sake of stability and to advance a "culture of learning." They also talk of a "culture of accountability," a "learner centered" set of policies that proscribe traditional forms of knowledge, aiming to advance children's basic skills largely through didactic instruction.

When Western aid agencies first arrived to advise ANC policymakers, prior to the fall of apartheid, constructivist pedagogies were quickly embraced, blending with the ideals of People's Education. Yet by the late 1990s, the new government was attempting to marry such Dewey-like strategies with more uniform learning outcomes, tighter alignment between curricular units and national exams, and concern with preparing children pragmatically for the labor market, captured under the government's Curriculum 2005 initiative. The original discourse concerning curricular change included talk of experiential and cooperative learning, aiming to "develop citizens who are imaginative and critical problem-solvers." Across traditional subject areas, which remain largely sacrosanct inside schools, teachers are to ensure that children learn effective communication skills, are able to identify and solve everyday problems, and can critically analyze new information. This, too, is reminiscent of late-twentieth-century curricular reforms in England. In both societies it remains unclear how national examinations assess and incentivize these virtuous learning aims, for teachers and students alike.

Despite all the policy talk it is unclear whether changes in democratic engagement or participatory forms of schooling are taking hold. Certainly the school governing councils, which involve community elections and local transparency, are nurturing grassroots participation. Yet research on the eve of free elections in 1994 revealed that many black principals in the townships had little understanding of what People's Education meant or the implications of these ideals for everyday life inside schools. Most black teachers grew up in schools characterized by control and routinized delivery of official knowledge, scripts that remain difficult to rewrite.[18] With resources scarce and strong demands on teachers to raise children's basic literacy, innovative programs and efforts to involve students in the community are difficult to enact. Government's post-apartheid press for outcomes-based education and accountability may further routinize classroom life and de-skill teachers, rather than advancing democratic social relations and civic engagement. As in the United States and Britain, the business of schooling, under centralized testing regimes, is to get the facts straight through efficient, habitually didactic teaching practices. Whether South Africa's millions of new citizens, given this dominant form of schooling, will become engaged in civil society, locally and nationally, remains a pressing question.

## Turkey: Multicultural Contention in State and School

Turkey is a society that remains at the edge of Western cultural and political traditions, bringing Westerners' assumptions about democracy and education into sharp relief. Despite growing Islamic influence and cultural pluralism more broadly, and recurring impulses toward distinctly nondemocratic politics, the Turkish state is pushing to democratize major institutions and elements of social life. The creation of individual citizens and their schooled membership in civil society are at times unfolding in rather non-Western ways across Turkey's diverse society.

CITIZENS AND SCHOOLS WITHIN CIVIL SOCIETY. Turkish society faces divisive challenges to the character of its modern state, how individual citizenship and civic membership are defined, and the role of secular and publicly funded Islamic schools. Since Kemal Ataturk presided over Turkish independence in 1923, military elites, with backing from the judiciary and business community, have dominated Turkey's strong, centralized state. Dissident Islamic parties, ascendant since the 1970s, envision a greater role for religion in public life, while at the same time Kurdish nationalists press for recognition and political autonomy. These pressures on a historically secular state directly shape education policy and the deeply cultural struggles over the character of schooling and civic participation.

In the 1920s Kemalists abandoned the Ottoman Islamic heritage of political, legal, and cultural institutions, developing a new order patterned after Western models of state and civil society. The schools served as a key site for this transformation. The 1924 Unification of Education Act abolished the parallel system of secular schools and traditional Islamic madrassa education for single-track public schools. The government conducted a literacy campaign to teach the Latin alphabet, replacing Arabic script and elevating Turkish above ethnic minority languages. Gradually the state raised support for Sunni Islamic institutions, originally to rein in the independence of Islamic actors, then to provide a counterweight to leftist political forces during the turbulent 1970s. This tandem strategy of containment and co-optation of Islamic symbols allowed the central state to broaden its legitimacy and soften Islamic opposition. The organized practice of religion in mosques and schools currently remains within the state's "public" jurisdiction.

Yet the rise of multiparty politics has spurred greater opposition to the military's rendition of a secular order. For example, the Islamist Welfare Party (WP) outpolled secular parties during the early 1990s in local and national elections, signaling a renewed popular commitment to religion and widening disaffection with the dominant regime. Then, in 1997, the military banned the WP and sought to diminish Islamic influence in civil society. Government bans on Islamic parties and individual leaders have not lessened the popularity of the movement, embodied most recently in the Justice and Development Party (AKP), which won many parliamentary seats in 2002. And while certain segments of civil society officially exclude Islamic symbols or citizens as such, public funds continue to support Islamic schools.

This contention plays out with education policy debates, as these diverse communities attempt to gain influence over how their children are raised and who gets to fully participate in civil society. The official aim of education in Turkey, as explained by the education ministry, is to forge a unified citizenry with a secular national identity, young graduates who "are conscious of their duties to the Turkish nation and who are embodied with a spirit true to Ataturk's nationalism." Turkey's schools are instrumental in advancing the state's secular ideals. To these ends, the national curriculum is far from hidden. Government requires that "Ataturk's reforms and principles are the basis for the curriculum level of the educational system."[19] A broader and more secular Turkish identity is to supercede religious or ethnic membership, a version of modern assimilation within this colorfully pluralistic society. Turkey offers an intriguing experiment in testing the compatibility of Islam and modern democracy, as a nation that for centuries has tried to bridge Europe and the Middle East, and a complicated publicly funded network of schools plays a central role

Turkey's commitment to widening children's basic access to school has yielded strong results. The education reform of 1997, for instance, lengthened compulsory schooling from five to eight years, and the net enrollment ratio for public schools rose from 76 percent in 1997 to 91 percent in 2000. Yet Turkey's child population has grown to one-third of the country's 71.3 million people, creating huge challenges for urban schools. Turkey's economic growth has been robust over the past generation, yet education spending has failed to keep up with enrollment gains. Since the mid-1990s government has reduced education spending as a proportion of GNP to 3.3 percent, the lowest of any OECD country. So macropolitical decisions have shaped the extent to which children can be incorporated into the secular ideals of this contested civil society.

SCHOOL GOVERNANCE AND REFORM. The Turkish education system has long been highly centralized, with strong bureaucratic controls. Central planning and authority offer little provincial or local autonomy. The most stable and powerful decision-making body, the National Education Council, includes military representation and meets every four years to make basic policy decisions. Western aid agencies, such as the World Bank, also play a role, actively inserting particular conceptions of education and democracy into Turkish policy circles.

International agencies have funded education projects in Turkey with mixed success, although Western ideologies and organizational forms flow steadily from these outside institutions. The World Bank now stresses that centralization, and attendant bureaucracy, undercut implementation of school reforms on the ground. The Bank has attempted to strengthen the central state's capacity to expand access and improve quality, while ducking issues concerning the content and social ideologies of the diversity of schools funded by government.

Private schools have grown rapidly, often providing higher-quality schooling, compared with government-funded institutions. The rise of neoliberal thinking in the education sector, and broadening of school choice, appear to most benefit afflu-ent families, those who can afford rising tuition fees while legitimating parents' choice of Islamic schools for their children. A new track of private tutoring gives the children of wealthy parents an advantage on national entrance exams. The private sector has experienced robust growth in higher education as well, with nineteen new private universities founded since 1986. While Turkey's fifty-eight public uni-versities retain the lion's share of students, they have lost faculty to the newer private institutions, which charge higher fees and offer professors more competitive salaries. The Islamic-oriented AKP, often siding with advocates for working-class families, is critical of the Western-style private universities, since they host secular, liberal ideals and customs. Thus the exclusion of poorer Islamic children from quality schools, constraining their long-term ability to become full citizens in civil society, may rein-force demand for Islamic schooling. The effect is that public and private schools alike reinforce class stratification, with students selecting into modern, largely secu-lar or Islamic tracks that often map families' social-class position.

Related conflicts arise with gains in primary school enrollments, financed by international agencies but weakening the parallel Islamic school system. Originally created as vocational schools designed to meet the need for preachers in mosques, the Islamic "imam-hatip" schools saw steady increases in enroll-ments between 1951 and 1997 with an enrollment of over five hundred thou-sand in junior high and high schools. The extension of compulsory primary education by three years to the eighth grade precipitated the closure of many religious junior high schools. Enrollment also dropped rapidly in imam-hatip high schools. Another factor leading to this decline was government's weighting practice, which puts religious school graduates at a disadvantage on national col-lege entrance exams, even though many civil servants have historically graduated from the Islamic school system.

Historically, girls have experienced more limited access to formal education of any kind. Just over three-fourths of all Turkish women report being literate, compared with 94 percent of men. As noted previously, secondary school enroll-ment rates for girls are much lower as compared with boys. In contrast, girls are represented equally in the imam-hatip schools, given that parents are more com-fortable with this form of schooling for their daughters. The secular state has had success in raising female enrollment rates, especially after the push to lengthen compulsory schooling to eight years.

The ability of girls to become full citizens in civil society is interwoven with religious commitments. For example, government has tried to ban girls from wearing the Muslim headscarf (*hijab*) at school. While this prohibition aims to signal secularization of government schools, it has had the unanticipated effect of discouraging school attendance by observant Muslim girls. This issue provided an election platform for the governing party and brought parents and women into activist roles. The fight for religious symbols is carried out vociferously at universities, from which some thirty thousand women were expelled in 1998. As Muslim women organized to protest the *hijab* ban, the character of political participation was reshaped—highlighting how competing social memberships arise in such culturally pluralistic societies.

The state's attempt to encourage ethnic and cultural integration has met with stiff opposition, especially from the nation's 12 million Kurdish families, which make up one-fifth of Turkey's population. They are concentrated in the economically isolated southeast and aspire to political self-determination. Schools in Kurdish areas display far lower quality levels. Under the Turkish constitution, the Kurdish language cannot be taught in schools. In response, Kurdish activists and professionals teach Kurdish in an informal, underground system. In public schools and universities a significant movement now presses for Kurdish language rights.

INSIDE SCHOOLS AND CLASSROOMS. Evidence remains scarce on the forms of participation and social relations found inside schools and classrooms. Studies confirm that Turkish pedagogy inside secular schools remains largely didactic and rote in character, although cultural differences persist with respect to the meaning of such pedagogy. As in other nations, the government approaches instruction simply through curriculum policy, notably introducing a required course on democracy and citizenship in the late 1990s. Another course focuses attention on human rights and the role of young citizens in the nation–state. These new curricula are tied to Western discourse around individual rights and responsibilities in a secular society. How local educators in government and Islamic school systems are interpreting and carrying out these innovations remains unknown empirically.

As discussed above, issues of achievement and school effectiveness are pivotal in determining which children become full members (citizens) of civil society. In Turkey, achievement levels remain unequal, stratified by class and ethnic background and gender. Comparisons across the secular and Islamic school systems are difficult, given that learning objectives and the social culture are different. And the growth of private schools and universities presents another challenge for scholars and policymakers who aim to learn what effects are yielded by schools of such uneven quality and character.

Finally, Turkey represents an intriguing force within the European community, prompting reflection on its core values and limits to cultural pluralism. The admittance of a Muslim-majority nation into the fold may intensify debate over what it means to be European. Extending democratic logic to the tolerance of Islamic groups and schools that at times oppose a secular state prompts deep questions for Western societies. How do schools prepare culturally diverse children to become "citizens" within contemporary civil society? And, does membership in civil society overlap with religious convictions, or is it segmented off under secular traditions?

## Lessons for the United States

In 1835 Alexis de Tocqueville, writing in *Democracy in America,* observed that "in democratic times . . . the tie of human affections is stretched and loosened. New families are constantly emerging from nowhere, other ones fall back into obscurity. You easily forget those who have preceded you, and you have no idea of those who will follow you. One takes an interest only in those who are closest to you."[20]

John Adams's optimistic claim, which was shared by early American democrats, was that the individual's rights and economic stake could be balanced by the mutual covenant with "the whole people" to advance the common good. Common schooling, of course, became pivotal in achieving this balance—to ensure that the individual child would gain skills leading to economic opportunity and acquire the collective responsibility of citizenship. Tocqueville, visiting America more than a half-century later, was not so hopeful. He feared that the democratic faith in individual opportunity and mobility, while seductive economically, was also eroding traditional forms of community, kinship, and spirit.

Many nations in the twenty-first century continue to struggle with this paradox, eagerly expanding schools and colleges to broaden the individual's economic fortunes while struggling to preserve universal cultural commitments and shared obligations to civil society. As the centrifugal forces linked to individualism gain strength—from rising consumption to the mass media's unrelenting images of self expression—the state's struggle to encourage obligations to the commonweal becomes ever more difficult.

The capacity of government to advance democracy locally—by employing and reforming the school institution—is constrained by long-running economic inequalities and more recent institutional shifts around the globe, as the case studies depicted here vividly illustrate. The core idea of common schooling for the masses, for example, stems from modern faith in a secular state that puts forward universal economic and moral goals for society. But this is weighed against the demands of layered labor markets and the interests of particular social classes that also use schooling to maintain or advance their class and cultural dominance. Efforts by various countries to enforce a common curriculum, then to hold schools accountable to deliver this "official knowledge," exemplify the state's universalist tenets. Yet the effectiveness of accountability reforms in closing achievement gaps and equalizing the odds of getting ahead remains unproven.

The modern state, habitually pressing for universal forms of citizenship, is plainly having difficulty convincing students—more and more self-consciously segmented by ethnic identity, social class, and religious conviction—that civic involvement is important in their lives. How we think about the quality of everyday life is becoming more distant from the ideals of community involvement and political action. The Western state's entrenched emphasis on individual rights, in the face of cultural pluralism, further contributes to the centrifugal forces that tear apart more public forms of community. It appears that individual consumption and self-expression, revolutionary tenets of the Enlightenment, are taking precedence over aging, modern conceptions of the commonweal.

In a sense, we have returned full circle to John Adams's idealized goal that schools would help each young citizen form a covenant "with the whole people ... for the common good." It is simply unclear whether older, modern institutional forms—including the bureaucratic state and school—will be able to accommodate the disparate forces of ethnic, religious, and class pluralism. The question, once so simple, is now perplexing: For which national or local communities should government schools socialize and educate children? Indeed, how we locate the head and heart of the state becomes a slippery question as societies become more diffuse, indeed more radically democratic, than Adams or Tocqueville could have ever imagined.

Part of the problem is that industrial forms of organization continue to dominate the modern state and its schools, constraining their ability to advance democracy within increasingly pluralistic and colorful societies. By the late nineteenth century mass schooling was infused with a tacit climate of "governmentality," in Michel Foucault's term, replete with formalized rules to pattern everyday behavior and beliefs in unobtrusive, highly legitimated ways. As John Dewey and progressives after him have long emphasized, the bureaucratized school continues to drift toward a utilitarian agenda, preparing children for capitalist expansion and didactically preaching the duties of mass citizenship, such as voting, paying taxes, and obeying traffic laws. What the Greeks defined as classical liberal training for broad civic engagement has been largely displaced by regimented instruction in many nations, simply to fit graduates into neoclassical tenets that advance markets and material consumption.

As the country cases given here detail, the central state attempts to regulate and hold schools accountable at the very same time that the identity and social authority of diverse groups is growing stronger, in part because of the earlier success of schooling and democratic tolerance. So the modern state is not trapped only by its philosophical foundations: the clumsy bureaucratic tools it habitually employs, via mechanical forms of schooling, also fail to motivate individuals or lend meaning to the daily lives of many social groups, teachers, and children. Then, as the bureaucratic state intensifies its attempts at control and homogenization of action, it grows more alien in the eyes of many local actors.[21] One need only visit a local high school in a working-class American community to sense youths' tenuous attachment to modern institutions.

So what lessons for American educators—concerned with the democratizing effects of education—can be discerned from this international tour of policy debates?

First, we must recognize that the classical foundations of civil society and how we socialize students to become efficacious citizens are weakening. These cracks, ironically, stem in part from the vibrant triumph of individual rights and democratic expression. Cultural groups and social classes—across the political and ideological spectrum—are seeking to advance their own rendition of schooling, advocating decentralized control and the shaping of their particular identities. The bureaucratic state, faced with this colorful panoply of local demands, attempts to regroup and engage in centralized reforms. Sometimes this advances the cause of more-egalitarian access to secondary schooling or higher education. At times, political leaders back the centralization of learning goals and national exams. But these mechanical responses often spur opposition from those who prefer the balkanized pursuit of individual and group interests. We see this tension in the push for charter schools in the United States, Britain's shift to a parental-choice system, South Africa's delegation of authority to school councils, and Turkey's delicate balancing act, funding secular and Islamic schools simultaneously. When states become fragile, faced with pluralistic pressures, they seem to convulse between centralized action and the decentering of certain "public" aims and forms of schooling.[22] We have much to learn internationally about whether these policy experiments are truly enhancing learning and nurturing youths' civic involvement.

Second, the intensifying challenges of cultural pluralism hold implications for education's unique role in advancing a more inclusive civil society. Many nations are struggling with where to find, indeed how to *define,* civil society as community action becomes more decentered, hosted by culturally diverse groups. As capitalist societies continue to be fractured along social-class lines, shared public space—indeed, government's overall interest in supporting public initiatives—comes into question. School vouchers, grant-maintained schools, and charter schools represent new institutional forms that allow the most affluent families to check out of public schooling—building what are essentially private schools with public dollars. Yet these mechanisms also serve the working classes as these families secede from what they have come to see as unresponsive, bureaucratic school systems. And as social enclaves become more isolated, the meaning of "citizenship" is restricted to membership in a particular social collective. The revival of ethnic or religious identity implies that pluralistic groups will demand social obligations of its members, further eclipsing youths' eventual engagement in a broader civic sphere. How will public schools respond to this dwindling degree of social integration, beyond trying to teach civics courses more effectively?

Third, the scarcity of empirical work on democratic social relations inside schools is distressing. Qualitative studies of teachers' work, classroom interaction, and curricular reform have been produced in the United States and Europe over the past decades. But very few scholars—or policymakers—have examined whether the distribution of social authority and engagement within schools reflects democratic ideals. The bureaucratic, at times paternal, mindset of many school administrators may well discourage democratic discourse inside schools, ensuring that the next generation will never have been asked to actively engage their immediate community. And when education reforms push to deskill the craft of teaching and standardize instruction, what are the odds that nurturing of more engaging and democratic social relations inside schools will flourish?

Finally, as Americans debate reforms that alter who controls schools and the social relations found inside, we should ask whether the reformation being advocated is being mindlessly imported from abroad or truly fits local conditions. Historically, the United States has borrowed and elaborated institutional tenets from European schools, while tailoring institutions in a more egalitarian fashion. Most recently, the press for national standards and even a national examination came from our European peers. Some contemporary reformers would implement both sides of the British design: centralizing curriculum and exams while radically decentralizing finance and control down to each school principal.[23] It remains unclear whether and how life inside schools, on either side of this policy formula, motivates greater innovation and pedagogical improvements. We must therefore think carefully and dig deeper empirically before simply acting on faith.

Reform inevitably evolves within a nation's own political culture and economy. The British push for school choice and cutting schools loose from their local education authority (LEA) was motivated by the neoliberal ideals of shrinking the welfare state and breaking monopolistic control of schools by unions and bureaucrats, freeing them to operate as agile market actors; whereas in South Africa a similar pro–school choice policy stemmed from quite different ideals, sprouting from the People's Education Movement and the old regime's decentralization of white schools during apartheid's dying days. Institutional diversity in Turkey provides a balance wheel for a secular government that must aid Islamic families and, for some, their sectarian schools. Cross-national lessons and school reform models are plentiful. Yet the problems of civil society, citizenship, and education will be cast and interpreted within particular national contexts.

Overall, the country cases given here illustrate how societies are becoming more colorful and politically pluralistic, while governments continue to rely on bureaucratic means and universal policy intentions. Achievement gaps persist—violating the ideals of egalitarian democracy—so governments centralize and simplify what children are to learn, often through routinized curricular packages that emphasize didactics and discourage social engagement by teachers and children. Similarly, the World Bank and fellow donors are spending hundreds of millions of dollars to test students more efficiently and reliably, ensuring that their allocation into stratified labor structures unfolds more smoothly.

Is this any way to prepare citizens for societies that are becoming more complex, in a sense more intensely democratic? Yes, if the state's pragmatic aim is to move graduates into entry-level jobs, or to limit the notion of citizenship to contributing to economic productivity. Certainly the modern state is responding to pluralistic pressures by narrowing its own role in society in several cases—portraying labor market needs and the nation's economic competitiveness as the remaining universal ideal to pursue from the political center. The modern state seems unable to articulate a theory of community and moral commonality, beyond preaching the utility of upward mobility through cultural assimilation. Indeed, the American Dream is one of a shrinking number of totems that signals a shared civic space in the United States.

The risk for policymakers and educators is that these centrifugal forces will subvert central political authority and the democratic forum that it attempts to uphold. It is unclear how the decentralization of school governance will close gaping inequalities in the structure of income and educational opportunity. The widening base of cultural pluralism, and its component constituencies, does prompt common cause in localism and particular, even private, forms of schooling. Many charter school parents in the United States, for instance, actively boycott government testing programs. It is doubtful that Anglican educators in England really believe in a centrally determined national curriculum. A variety of ethnically rooted schools in South Africa have expressed concern that Pretoria's outcomes-based education will push out the cultural and political particulars so necessary in preparing locally situated citizens.

The sticking point for policymakers—especially those trying to seriously reform schools around the globe—is that the modern state has historically pushed universal institutions and individual rights. The modern state often grasps in the dark when it tries to enrich civil society or recast social participation within increasingly pluralistic or class-stratified societies. The necessary tools are not available from its modern, individualist origins of three centuries ago. And the bureaucratic, regulatory habits of the state handicap its ability to get beyond a mechanical, culturally monochromatic conception of schooling. This is the frontier on which we must work, if government leaders and educators are to comprehend and speak back to the colorful, culturally democratic demands that are rising up in so many nations.

## Notes

1. National Center for Education Statistics, *The Condition of Education 2003,* sec. 3, "Student Effort and Educational Progress: Immediate Transition to College" (Washington, D.C., 2003), 42–43.

2. *World Education Encyclopedia: A Survey of Educational Systems Worldwide,* edited by Rebecca Marlow-Ferguson, 3 vols., 2nd ed. (Detroit: Gale, 2002).
3. Edward Fiske and Helen Ladd, "Balancing Public and Private Resources for Basic Education: School Fees in Post-Apartheid South Africa," in *Changing Class: Education and Social Change in Post-Apartheid South Africa,* edited by Linda Chisholm (Pretoria: Human Science Research Council, 2004), 57–88.
4. See Bruce Fuller et al., *Government Confronts Culture: The Struggle for Democracy in Southern Africa* (New York: Garland, 1999).
5. Quoted in Marie Parker-Jenkins, "Equal Access to State Funding: The Case of Muslim Schools in Britain," *Race, Ethnicity and Education* 5 (2002): 279.
6. See Alexander, *Culture and Pedagogy,* and Whitty, Power, and Halpin, *Devolution and Choice in Education.*
7. William G. Ouchi, with Lydia G. Segal, *Making Schools Work: A Revolutionary Plan to Get Your Children the Education They Need* (New York: Simon and Schuster, 2003).
8. Bruce Fuller, ed., *Inside Charter Schools: The Paradox of Radical Decentralization* (Cambridge, Mass.: Harvard University Press, 2000).
9. Organization for Economic Cooperation and Development, 2002.
10. David Baker and Gerald K. LeTendre, "Comparative Sociology of Classroom Processes, School Organization, and Achievement," in *Handbook of the Sociology of Education,* edited by Maureen T. Hallinan (New York: Kluwer, 2000).
11. Organization for Economic Cooperation and Development, *Education at a Glance* (Paris, 2002).
12. LeTendre et al., "Teachers' Work: Institutional Isomorphism and Cultural Variation in the United States, Germany and Japan," *Educational Researcher* 30, no. 6 (2001): 3–15.
13. Bruce Fuller and Prema Clarke, "Raising School Effects while Ignoring Culture? Local Conditions and the Influence of Classroom Tools, Rules, and Pedagogy," *Review of Educational Research* 64 (1994): 119–57; Susan P. Holloway, *Contested Childhood: Diversity and Change in Japanese Preschools* (New York: Routledge, 2000); Fuller et al., *Government Confronts Culture.*
14. Quoted in Motala and Pampallis, eds., *Education and Equity,* p. 58.
15. Hofmeyr and Lee, "The New Face of Private Schooling."
16. See Fiske and Ladd, "Balancing Public and Private Resources for Basic Education," for details.
17. These include Michael Cross, Ratshi C. Mungadi, and Sepi Rouhani, "From Policy to Practice: Curriculum Reform in South African Education," *Comparative Education* 38, no. 2 (2002): 171–87.
18. See Fuller et al., *Government Confronts Culture.*
19. Quoted in Ministry of National Education. *The Turkish Educational System.* General Directorate of Foreign Relations (Ankara, 1999), 1–2.
20. Alexis de Tocqueville, *Democracy in America* (New York: Knopf, 1986), 108.
21. See Fuller, *Growing Up Modern.*
22. Ibid.
23. For example, Ouchi, with Segal, *Making Schools Work.*

# Bibliography

Akarsu, Fusun. "Transition and Education: A Case Study of the Process of Change in Turkey." In *Education in a Global Society: A Comparative Perspective*, edited by Kas Mazurek, Margret A. Winzer, and Czeslaw Majorek. Boston: Allyn and Bacon, 2000.

Alexander, Robin. *Culture and Pedagogy: International Comparisons in Primary Education.* Malden, Mass.: Blackwell, 2001.

Carnoy, Martin. "Globalization and Educational Reform." In *Globalization and Education: Integration and Contestation across Cultures*, edited by Nelly P. Stromquist and Karen Monkman, pp. 43–62. Lanham, Md.: Rowman and Littlefield, 2000.

Dahl, Robert A. *On Democracy.* New Haven, Conn.: Yale University Press, 1998.

Education Policy Unit. *Democratic Governance of Public Schooling in South Africa: A Record of Research and Advocacy.* Durban: University of Natal, 1998.

Fiske, Edward, and Helen Ladd. "Balancing Public and Private Resources for Basic Education: School Fees in Post-Apartheid South Africa." In *Changing Class: Education and Social Change in Post-Apartheid South Africa,* edited by Linda Chisholm, pp. 57–88. London: Zed Books.

Fiske, Edward B., and Helen F. Ladd. *When Schools Compete: A Cautionary Tale.* Washington, D.C.: Brookings Institution Press, 2000.

Fretwell, David H., and Antony Wheeler. *Turkey: Secondary Education and Training.* Washington, D.C.: World Bank, 2001.

Fuller, Bruce. *Growing Up Modern.* New York: Routledge, 1992.

Fuller, Bruce. *Government Confronts Culture.* New York: Taylor and Francis, 1999.

Hofmeyr, Jane, and Simon Lee. "The New Face of Private Schooling." In *Changing Class: Education and Social Change in Post-Apartheid South Africa*, edited by Linda Chisholm, pp. 143–74. London: Zed Books.

Lemert, Charles. *Social Theory: Multicultural and Classic Readings.* Boulder, Colo.: Westview, 1999.

Lloyd, David, and Paul Thomas. *Culture and the State.* New York: Routledge, 1998.

Marty, Martin. *The One and the Many: America's Struggle for the Common Good.* Cambridge, Mass.: Harvard University Press, 1997.

Menand, Louis. *The Metaphysical Club: A Story of Ideas in America.* New York: Farrar, Straus and Giroux, 2001.

Migdal, Joel. *State in Society.* Cambridge, U.K.: Cambridge University Press, 2001.

Motala, Enver, and John Pampallis, eds. *Education and Equity: The Impact of State Policies on South African Education.* Johannesburg: Heinemann, 2001.

Parekh, Bhikhu. *Rethinking Multiculturalism: Cultural Diversity and Political Theory.* Cambridge, Mass.: Harvard University Press, 2000.

Seligman, Adam B. *The Idea of Civil Society.* New York: Free Press, 1992.

Smelser, Neil J., and Jeffrey C. Alexander, eds. *Diversity and Its Discontents: Cultural Conflict and Common Ground in Contemporary American Society.* Princeton, N.J.: Princeton University Press, 1999.

Steinmetz, George, ed. *State/Culture: State Formation after the Cultural Turn.* Ithaca, N.Y.: Cornell University Press, 1999.

Whitty, Geoff. *Making Sense of Educational Policy*. London: Paul Chapman, 2002.
Whitty, Geoff, Sally Power, and David Halpin. *Devolution and Choice in Education: The School, the State, and the Market*. Buckingham, U.K.: Open University Press, 1998.
Yildiran, Guzver, and John Durnin. *Recent Perspectives on Turkish Education: An Inside View*. Bloomington: Indiana University Turkish Studies Publication, 1997.

# TEACHING, LEARNING, AND WORKING

# 5

## CLASSROOM DELIBERATIONS

### *Katherine G. Simon*

MUCH OF THE INTEREST IN CIVICS EDUCATION IN the early years of the twenty-first century has been fueled by concerns about low voter-participation rates in the United States, particularly among young people; reportedly fewer than 20 percent of eighteen- to twenty-four-year-olds voted in 1998. Research on citizenship education suggests that these voting statistics reveal a much deeper problem. The American educational system is not producing enough young people who vote. Beyond that, however, it is not, by many measures, producing enough young people who have the potential of being *deeply informed* voters, voters who have the skills and inclination to participate actively and thoughtfully in democratic deliberation about a wide range of social issues.

This essay is based on the premise that if we want informed voters—and citizens who participate in civic life in other ways—schools must give students the opportunity to deliberate seriously about essential questions of governance. Most scholars who have analyzed this problem suggest that schools should provide students with much more practice in democratic deliberation, by making deliberation a key feature of classroom life, particularly in secondary social studies courses. Such scholars promote, among other things, the use of a host of what might be called "deliberative pedagogies" to help students gain the skills they need to address the complex problems facing society. Such pedagogies include, for example, discussions of controversial issues, simulations, debates, case studies, project-based investigations, and the like.[1]

While the view that democratic education requires deliberative pedagogies dominates the literature on democratic education, there is another school of thought. Emanating in large part from politically conservative think-tanks, this alternative stance argues that a key problem with U.S. social studies classes, in particular, is that they focus too much time on discussion, on consideration of diverse perspectives, and on exploring current social problems, and not enough on covering historical content in a coherent and sequential fashion.

Scholars from this school posit that the key to active American citizenship is gaining a thoroughgoing knowledge of the major documents on which the American system of governance is based and developing understanding of and pride in the contributions that American democracy has made to U.S. citizens and to the world. They contend that focusing on critical thinking skills or discussion of controversial issues distracts from these key aims and can dilute students' appreciation for the strengths and blessings of democracy. Opposition to deliberative pedagogies has also long come from members of the public, who have sought, for example, to ban a variety of books from schools, believing that it is the role of the public schools not to explore controversy, but to teach factual content.[2]

As in many ideological disputes, there are places in which the two schools of thought seem fundamentally irreconcilable, and places in which some common ground can be found. Certainly, both schools of thought seek to produce students who have the requisite knowledge and skills to participate in a democratic society. Those who promote deliberation as a core pedagogical strategy recognize the importance of grounding such deliberations in factual evidence and in democratic values. Those who emphasize the importance of the coverage of content, on the other hand, admit a role for deliberation—if only *after* the content is mastered.

Making deliberation subordinate to content, however, limits the possibilities of civic education. Joseph Kahne and his colleagues indicated this as they concluded their extensive study of school social studies classrooms:

> The findings are alarming. The 135 classrooms we examined provided very few high quality opportunities for students to develop the capacity to think clearly and deeply about complex matters, . . . to understand and respectfully consider diverse perspectives, or to examine and respond to social problems. If we are to attend to the rhetoric surrounding the democratic purposes of schooling, these opportunities and their impact must receive sustained and informed attention.[3]

Taking as a given Kahne's point that there are "few high quality opportunities for students to develop the capacity to think clearly and deeply about complex matters," this essay delves into the challenges inherent in bringing deliberative pedagogies to the classroom, through exploration of the following questions:

- What factors inhibit the practice of democratic deliberation in our classrooms, particularly on the secondary level? What factors promote it?
- What might be done to overcome the obstacles and to augment the factors that promote deliberation?
- What strategies are available to teachers committed to this work?

It is worth noting that what Kahne and his colleagues call the "complex matters" facing a democratic society are very often controversial. More narrowly, one might say that the particular matters that demand the skill of deliberation are those that provoke controversy. For where there is easy agreement in a society, there is little need for citizens to exercise their deliberative skills. This chapter, thus, explores pedagogical issues connected with deliberation not about safe or bland topics, but specifically about controversial social issues. It begins with a brief exploration of the skills traditionally promoted in American classrooms and contrasts those with the skills of democratic deliberation. We then turn to an exploration of the societal and pedagogical obstacles to an in-depth focus on democratic deliberation in public schools.

## Traditional Classroom Skills

Most of what passes for "discussion" in school classrooms follows this mode: the teacher asks a question to which he or she knows the answer, a student responds with a word or two, and the teacher confirms or corrects the response and moves on to another question. In *Classroom Discourse,* a landmark study published in 1988 that remains relevant to today's classrooms, Courtney Cazden reported that this three-part sequence, which Cazden calls IRE—teacher *initiation,* student *response,* teacher *evaluation*—is "the most common pattern of classroom discourse at all grade levels" (p. 29). With a brief example from a kindergarten classroom, Cazden illustrates the pattern and the degree to which it would seem bizarre in everyday life:

> *Teacher:* What time is it, Sarah?
> *Sarah:* Half past two.
> *Teacher:* Right. (p. 30)

In school, teachers typically raise questions in order to evaluate (and eventually to grade) what students know. Student talk, correspondingly, is supposed to display the students' knowledge. Student talk generally does not serve as an opportunity to think aloud, formulate ideas, or address authentic problems.

The IRE style of instruction continues to fit the content of much classroom work. For the most part, school demands that students assimilate discrete pieces of information—names, dates, terminology, and formulas. The focus on this kind of information dominates not only in elementary schools, where some might assume that students need to learn background material before getting to more complex questions, or in subjects like math, where one might assume that there are clear, unambiguous answers. (Both of these assumptions, however, deserve questioning.)[4]

High school social studies seems, on the face of it, to be a subject that would be given to inquiry and exploration—whether it be through discussion, case studies, debates, real-world projects, or simulations. Nevertheless, even in high school social studies classes, information-assimilation predominates. What John Goodlad reported in 1984 in *A Place Called School* remains true: the "preponderance of classroom activity" in high school social studies involves "listening, reading textbooks, completing workbooks and worksheets, and taking quizzes." Tests in social studies "rarely required other than the recall and feedback of memorized information—multiple choice, true or false, matching like things, and filling in the missing words or phrases" (pp. 212–13).[5]

The emphasis on "right answers" and the regular evaluation of those answers through tests and worksheets has a powerful effect on how students focus their energies at school. As Denise Pope describes in *"Doing School,"* the most successful and highly motivated students realize

> that they are caught in a system where achievement depends more on "doing"—going through the correct motions—than on learning and engaging with the curriculum. Instead of thinking deeply about the content of their courses ... the students focus on ... honing strategies that will help them to achieve high grades. They learn to raise their hands even when they don't know the answers to the teacher's questions in order to appear interested. They understand the importance of forming alliances and classroom treaties to win favors from teachers and administrators. Some feel compelled to cheat and to contest certain grades and decisions in order to get the score they believe they need for the future. (p. 4)

Pope then catalogs the overarching skills that "successful" students are practicing at school:

> figuring out what the teacher is going to ask on the test
> "cramming" into short-term memory the information predicted to be on
>    the tests
> arguing with the teacher about individual points on homework and tests
> "sicking out" of tests that one is unprepared for, and getting friends to share
>    the questions before retaking the test
> establishing "treaties" with adults that allow students to get by with doing
>    less (pp. 149–75)

It is hard to draw much of a connection between this list of skills, the ones our schools continue to promote, and the skills that are needed for democratic citizenship.

## Skills of Democratic Deliberation

Diana Hess defines "democratic deliberation" as follows:

> Democratic deliberation is a form of classroom discussion that focuses on important political issues in a manner that itself models and builds democracy. In such discussions, all students participate verbally as they

create, weigh and balance, and sift and winnow competing views on authentic political issues. The purpose of such discussions is to help young people build the knowledge, skills, and dispositions to make wise decisions and choices that are part and parcel of democracy. Such discussions do not propose to reinforce all prior beliefs, build students' self-esteem to the detriment of the critical challenge of ideas, or separate the classroom into polarized camps.[6]

While Hess focuses on a particular instructional strategy—the classroom discussion of controversial issues—there are numerous deliberative pedagogies that seek similar ends. Such complementary pedagogies, again, include the use of real-world projects, simulations, debates, and the like. Indeed, a wide range of written work, oral presentations, internships, and service learning, far beyond prototypical classroom discussions, can aptly fall into the category of deliberative pedagogies. The common thread among these pedagogies—or the criteria by which they could be considered "deliberative"—lies in the extent to which they succeed in supporting students to develop the following key capacities:

1. Understanding and engaging in the questions
   - grappling with issues that affect the common good
   - struggling to understand what is at stake in any given issue
   - reframing questions for clarification
2. Bringing alternate viewpoints, evidence, and history to bear
   - seeking and evaluating evidence garnered in a variety of ways and from a variety of sources, including primary sources
   - analyzing approaches to similar issues
   - demonstrating empathy for diverse perspectives
3. Developing an opinion and exploring solutions
   - valuating how various actions would meet the needs of various society members
   - seeking common ground
   - articulating ideas in ways that do not disparage others
   - digging deep for creative solutions that meet the needs of opposing sides
4. Reflecting on the process and moving forward
   - assessing one's own learning and growth throughout the process
   - establishing next steps for learning and action

One might tinker with the particular elements on this list, and again, there is a broad range of particular instructional strategies that teachers employ to serve these ends. One certainly might want to consider which sets of skills deserve most emphasis for students of different ages and instructional levels. But whatever specific sets of skills one seeks to promote, we face these broad questions of curriculum and instructional design: If we are aiming for high school graduates who possess these sets of skills, how shall we design our curriculum and instruction? What obstacles lie in the way of creating curricula and pedagogies of democratic deliberation?

## Challenges to Classroom Deliberation

Despite the strands of scholarly and public opposition to the idea of deliberation in classrooms, support in the educational community for discussing socially important issues in schools generally runs high—and there is widespread recognition that promoting deliberation about complex social issues does not imply ignoring important content. In 1996 the National Council for Social Studies published the *Handbook on Teaching Social Issues,* proclaiming in its foreword that issues-centered education is "the way all education should be approached to produce informed citizens who are involved in working out better solutions to our problems." The Carnegie Corporation and the Center for Information and Research on Civic Learning and Engagement (CIRCLE), to take another example, in 2003 published *The Civic Mission of Schools,* based on the work of a panel of fifty-six scholars and practitioners of civics education. Although the members of this panel represented "a diversity of political views, a variety of disciplines, and various approaches," they unanimously endorsed the following recommendation: Schools should "incorporate discussion of current local, national, and international issues and events into the classroom, particularly those that young people view as important to their lives" (p. 6).

Why, then, are classrooms so firmly stuck in the initiation-response-evaluation mode? Why is in-depth examination of complex issues so rare in schools? One of the answers comes easily: facilitating deliberation about complex and controversial social issues is challenging in any context—let alone in a room full of students. It is especially hard work, given that most teachers—like the rest of us—did not participate in this kind of deliberation as students. Few of us have much practice in it. If we were to take facilitating deliberation seriously as part of a teacher's role, we would have to incorporate facilitation skills in significant ways into teacher-education programs and ongoing professional-development efforts.

While the pedagogical challenges are real, they are the lesser challenges. Indeed, there are many teachers, even now, who have developed strategies for facilitating deliberations, and they have produced a wide variety of concepts and techniques that could be broadly put into practice. The more difficult challenges lie in society's conception of education and our choices about how to push teachers and students to achieve high standards.

## Social and Political Obstacles

CONCEPTION OF CURRICULUM. While the majority of educational theorists and policymakers would promote discussion as a valuable instructional strategy, many of them simultaneously hold a "knowledge mastery" view of the curriculum, a view which suggests that the central aim of the curriculum is to cover a wide range of relatively undisputed facts, typically arranged chronologically (or in the case of math and the sciences, arranged by perceived difficulty level or levels of abstraction).

There is, as noted above, a particularly snug fit between a knowledge-mastery view of the curriculum and the initiation-response-evaluation mode of discourse. The IRE mode can help meet the goals of a knowledge-mastery curriculum, by helping the teacher determine whether the students have gained the knowledge they are being asked to master. If students answer the teacher's questions correctly, it is time to move on to more-advanced material; if they answer incorrectly, the teacher knows that he or she must find another way to get students to understand the material or to memorize the information. Or perhaps more frequently, students who are unable to grasp the material simply receive low grades, and the teacher moves on.

The practice of classroom deliberation, on the other hand, can be at odds with some of the goals of a knowledge-mastery curriculum. Indeed, from the point of view of a knowledge-mastery approach, taking time to explore questions with no clear answers can be seen as a waste of time. As Linda Darling-Hammond reports, there are even teacher evaluation policies in several states that penalize teachers for asking questions that "call for a personal opinion or that are answered from personal experience."[7] Policies like these arise out of our deeply engrained societal conception of teaching and learning as the transfer and absorption of discrete units of knowledge.

There are, as we can see, widespread educational policies that reveal an understanding of the curriculum as a list of material to be mastered. There is widespread support, on the other hand, at least among leading social studies and civics educators, for the use of deliberative pedagogies. It is not surprising that we want both knowledge-mastery and deliberation. There is good evidence, in fact, to suggest that we can have both of these things in some measure: we can support students to gain impressive stores of factual knowledge while they simultaneously dig deeply into important social issues and learn the skills of deliberation. Indeed, the best deliberative approaches are extremely content-rich.[8]

But we must also face the fact that there is at least some level of mismatch between a curriculum that emphasizes the acquisition of uniform, specific, large sets of discrete units of information and instructional strategies that emphasize the skills of deliberation. It is not a question of either/or, but there is a significant question of emphasis, degree, and priority. Is the primary job of the teacher to deliver information, or to promote inquiry and foster deliberative dialogue? The answer to these questions results in very different actions at the classroom level.

To take an example: If a teacher is primarily in knowledge-mastery mode, she might ask a question like this: "Who wrote the Gettysburg Address, how does it begin, and what does it mean?" Neither the teacher nor the students are expecting to engage in deliberation, and what follows is the familiar routine of the teacher calling on one of the students, and then moving on to the next predetermined topic, let's say, Lincoln's appointment of Ulysses Grant as commander of the Union forces. If one were interested in deliberation, one would likely start with the same set of questions about the Gettysburg Address. But instead of moving on to the appointment of Grant, one would stay engaged in themes raised by Lincoln's speech, inviting a process of inquiry, and perhaps raising questions like these:

- What does it mean to try to construct a country that is dedicated to the proposition that "all men are created equal"?
- What do you understand "equal" to mean, given that there are obviously differences between people?
- What social issues in the news today hinge on people's varied understandings of the demands of equality?

In both cases, students would end up with some basic knowledge about the Gettysburg Address. But in the deliberation-based classroom, the conversation and projects (perhaps for the next several weeks) would then turn to an array of related and timely issues. There would be some topics that all students would be expected to know; but there would also be a considerable degree of individualization. As different students specialized in different issues and shared their findings, the whole class potentially would have the opportunity to deepen its understanding of the complexity of "equality." Some students might dig deeper into the evolution of understandings of equity over time, exploring, for example, how Lincoln's understanding of equality compared with that of the founders nearly a century before him and with civil rights leaders a century later. Other students might seek to understand how notions of equality influence current debates over affirmative action, tax policies, welfare policies, school vouchers, accessibility for the disabled, and others. To investigate these matters, students would need to engage in considerable research, including investigation of the Constitution, judicial decisions, public opinion, and more.

There would be quite a lot of "content" in this deliberation-based classroom. But even if the starting place were always the Gettysburg Address, the curriculum in the deliberation-based classroom would differ somewhat from year to year and would vary significantly over time. It would differ from one American history classroom to the American history classroom next door. The curriculum would be composed, with the teachers' guidance, of questions and topics that were most relevant to society's wider public debates and that most intrigued individuals and groups of students, keeping in mind that student interest can get piqued through learning about issues they originally find uninspiring.[9]

This is not a matter of process over content. Indeed, proponents of this approach argue that in the long run, students learn and retain more content knowledge through these kinds of explorations than they do through direct instruction. This is, however, a different vision of curriculum from that envisioned by some proponents of content-based approaches. Teachers who support inquiry are likely not to have time to "cover" all of the topics that appear on curriculum lists, so some systemic exposure to chronologically or topically arranged information can be lost. For those who are loath to let go of anything from the comprehensive curriculum lists, this presents a dilemma.

TESTING AND CONSTRAINTS ON INSTRUCTIONAL CHOICE. Another obstacle to enacting democratic deliberation is the deepening commitment in the United States to standardized tests. Many educators believe that it is possible to develop a testing system that could support high-level skills of democratic deliberation. Even if such a testing system is theoretically possible, however, current testing systems are inadequate to this task; they focus, rather, on evaluating whether students have absorbed discrete pieces of information from an assumed uniform curriculum.[10] Few of the habits and skills identified above as elements of democratic deliberation are measured well by standardized tests; neither can the more individualized and specialized content typical of deliberative classrooms be captured well by them.

The prevalence of tests that assume a standardized content heavy in chronologically arranged facts, the high-stakes nature of the tests with respect to promotion and graduation, and the public's satisfaction with tests as a means of raising standards have created an environment in which it is hard even for those educators drawn to democratic deliberation to enact their vision. Teachers who would like to teach the skills of democratic deliberation find themselves in a bind, whereby their concern for their students' success dictates that they provide testable answers. At a time when test scores hold so much sway, it is hard for teachers to spend time on skills the tests do not measure.

FEAR OF REPRIMAND. In addition to the pressure to cover material to prepare students for tests, teachers often report fearing that if they take class time to delve into controversial subjects, they will receive complaints or reprimands about their teaching. These fears have a basis in reality, as individual teachers around the country have faced disciplinary action for bringing up hot-button issues in the classroom, even if the teachers avoided stating their own views on the subject.[11] Indeed, if education is seen as the delivery of noncontroversial information, then teachers who introduce discussion of controversial issues may well be seen both as derelict in their duties and as provocateurs. Without public consensus that controversy belongs in the classroom, teachers who invite students to deliberate about controversial issues are at risk.

LACK OF MODELS. Another substantive obstacle to promoting democratic deliberation in schools is the lack of models of authentic democratic deliberation in society at large. While small-scale examples of democratic discourse occur around many family dinner tables and within numerous organizations and businesses, the more visible workings of the body politic often do not exemplify democratic deliberation. Watching the proceedings of a typical state legislature or even the U.S. Senate will not always provide a reliable portrait of rich democratic deliberation. Political opponents regularly attack one another's motives, values, and character, labeling those who disagree as ignorant, foolish, or malicious. Participants and hosts of talk shows on radio and television, the venues that perhaps have the most potential to serve as a modern town-square, too rarely demonstrate their skills at garnering evidence, listening with empathy, or seeking common ground.

Teachers who ask students to participate in democratic deliberation—in the name of learning to participate in society—are asking students to delve into something they might rarely have seen in action. This makes it more difficult both to teach the particular skills of democratic deliberation and to make a case that these skills are necessary for full participation in a democratic society.

## Classroom-Facilitation Obstacles

The challenges outlined above reside, or at least originate, outside the classroom. But as anyone who has tried to facilitate a discussion of a controversial issue will tell you, there are plenty of challenges inside the classroom itself.

DILEMMAS OF PARTICIPATION. Ask a classroom of students who are not practiced in democratic deliberation to address a controversial issue and you can bet on a situation involving at least some of the following behaviors: Some students will talk freely and vociferously; others will not speak at all. If a few students speak particularly strongly on one side of an issue, it will be even more difficult for those on the other side to speak up. In some cases, there will be strong advocates on each side, and a shouting match will ensue, during which no one is sufficiently heard, and nuances are lost, as class members take sides and present their ideas in extremes. Various speakers might recite misinformation, perhaps reinforcing misconceptions on the part of the rest of the class. As emotions run high, students might feel hurt or threatened, making it harder for the teacher to persuade class members to participate the next time around, or seriously damaging relationships. Or, in an alternate scenario, energy will be low, and there will be a sense of drifting chatter, the class talking the time away without saying anything important.

Perhaps the class will merely be silent. The teacher will ask what he or she thinks is a provocative question, and wait. And wait. The teacher will elaborate on the question, clarify it, and wait. No one speaks. The teacher feels confused and despairing. She asks a nice, safe, factual question. Someone answers. She says, "Good." She asks another. And everyone is back on the familiar terrain of initiation-response-evaluation.

As these scenarios suggest, one cannot count on an enthusiastic reception on the part of all students to a new form of pedagogy. This is ironic, because, of course, one of the key selling points for deliberation-based classrooms is that students will find deliberation engaging. In reality, while some students will immediately be thrilled at the invitation to inquiry, others will not be drawn to it, and may in fact gravitate to the more familiar filling-in-the-blanks. There are many factors at play here—including students' need for familiarity, their possible confusion about what the teacher wants, and their uncertainty about what would constitute "success" in this kind of work. In any case, change does not always come easily to students, even if the change is intended to meet their needs for involvement, contribution, and intellectual challenge.[12]

DILEMMAS OF GRADING. One of the reasons that students might resist jumping wholeheartedly into democratic deliberation involves their experience with grading systems. Students are used to teachers evaluating them on the basis of their right and wrong answers. When the teacher wants the students to participate in a dialogue where there are ostensibly no correct answers, students rightly wonder how they will be graded. Will they get more points for agreeing with the teacher? If they get points simply for talking, does that not unfairly reward the kids who dominate the conversation?

This swirl of issues can be as confusing for teachers as for students. Some teachers who seek to promote democratic deliberation refrain from grading students on their participation in classroom discussions, believing that such grades might inhibit students from speaking freely (or from remaining silent when that is warranted). Other teachers assign a relatively great number of points for participating in classroom discussions, hoping to emphasize the importance of these discussions and to motivate students to contribute.

However the teacher chooses to handle grading, it is hard to balance the competing roles of facilitator of democratic deliberation and teacher-as-evaluator. The dilemma faced by teachers when seeking to grade participation in democratic deliberation suggests the necessity for changes—beyond those already explored for curricula and assessments—in the role of the teacher. It suggests, in particular, a movement away from the current norm of teacher as constant evaluator and toward a view of teacher as "coach" or facilitator.[13] This, too, would require a shift in public will and perceptions of what it means to teach, and it would require the development of different sorts of accountability systems—ones based more on work produced by students and presented to groups of qualified adults than on the evaluations of individual tests or teachers.

CHOOSING APPROPRIATE TOPICS. Curriculum frameworks like those offered by E. D. Hirsch,[14] which value students becoming familiar with a list of topics, are easily criticized for being long, unwieldy, and random. Curricula that prize depth over coverage would seem to offer, at least, the advantage of being more streamlined and focused. One could, however, compose an almost limitless list of issues that merit democratic deliberation. How does one decide what topics to introduce to students? On what basis can one eliminate topics? An emphasis on democratic deliberation does not solve the curricular challenge of figuring out what topics really matter—and which ones to let go.

Deciding how to choose issues connects to the problem of how to frame issues. The way one frames a controversial issue—or whether an issue should be considered controversial—is often controversial in itself. Many people, for example, would see the following as a controversial issue: "Should two men be granted the right to marry one another?" People who land strongly on either side of this issue, however, might be hard-pressed to frame it as a controversy. For some people, the question is not controversial, any more than this one: "Should all human beings be granted basic human rights?" Those on the other side of the issue, alternately, might see the question as no more controversial than something like, "Should theft be legal?"[15] Even if we all agree that a given question is controversial, who gets to decide what constitutes a controversial issue worth investigating? And then, should teachers put aside their own strongly held convictions when framing questions for students? How could we possibly arrive at a curriculum of controversial issues that would not in itself evoke endless controversy? Developing a pedagogy of democratic deliberation will require some rationale or theory for choosing and framing topics of study.

TEACHERS' OPINIONS. Even if we had a rationale for choosing and framing topics of study, teachers would likely feel confused about how their own political or moral beliefs should inform their teaching. Certainly, parents may worry about teachers attempting to sway students to the teachers' particular belief systems. Recognizing this concern, some teachers stay away from controversial issues, wary that if they enter into these discussions, they might reveal their own opinions and thereby have undue influence on students' thinking. Others believe, on the other hand, that as part of their modeling of active participation in democratic life, they should let students know where they stand on important issues. This question deserves consideration. Is there a place for the teacher to share his or her convictions and commitments? Are there some topics about which teachers should express their opinions and others about which they should stay mum? How does one tell the difference? Teachers who seek to promote democratic deliberation need some guiding principles about how to incorporate—or omit—their own opinions.

## Deliberation and Democracy

There are many reasons a teacher might shy away from adopting the role of facilitator of democratic deliberation. "Sticking to the facts" keeps a teacher safe from the wrath of parents and administrators, and this stance also seems to address the demands of teaching in a climate of standardized tests. Teachers who avoid controversial issues do not have to decide how or how not to share with students their own passionately held commitments. If teachers avoid controversial issues, we all may feel more confident that they will not engage, wittingly or unwittingly, in indoctrinating students to their own beliefs. Additionally, avoiding democratic deliberation in the classroom relieves teachers of the myriad facilitation challenges inherent in this work. Why not, then, just stick to a "knowledge mastery" curriculum? What would motivate teachers—and whole schools and school systems—to place the skills of democratic deliberation at the core of their work?

Quite simply—and again, recognizing that there is another school of thought on this issue—a knowledge-mastery curriculum does not produce the kind of thinkers that a democracy needs. Several of the authors in this volume have investigated tensions between the individual and collective purposes of education. This essay argues that democracy rests on the notion that all citizens will have the skills and the predilection to participate actively in directing the course of society in a way that will promote the common good. We need, in the twenty-first century perhaps more than ever, a population that can think creatively, critically, and compassionately about the challenges that we face together as human beings. There is little documented connection between being able to memorize and recite facts and being able to bring knowledge to bear when it is needed—that is, to think.

If we want students to be able to think, we have to give them practice in bringing knowledge to bear on critical issues, which are by their nature both relevant and controversial. We have to give them practice in democratic deliberation. Few educational theorists in a democracy would dispute this—they simply argue that the facts need to come first and that students can study the controversies later. But if high schools, at least, are not focused on the skills of democratic deliberation, when and where do we imagine that our citizens will practice these skills? If these are skills that seem essential for our citizenry—for everybody—then school is the place.

## Addressing the Challenges to Classroom Deliberation

Given all of the political, social, and pedagogical challenges outlined here, what can be done to move us closer to a norm of democratic deliberation in our classrooms? The following are some promising directions both in the social and in the pedagogical spheres.

## Removing the Political and Social Barriers

REENVISIONING CURRICULUM AND ASSESSMENT. A pedagogy centered on democratic deliberation would require significant reconceptions of the nature of curriculum and of assessment. These alternative visions have been well articulated and even exist in practice in exceptional schools around the country. Enacting these changes more broadly in our public schools would enable a more central focus on democratic deliberation.

In *Curriculum as Conversation*, Arthur Applebee, for example, has argued for a reconceptualization of the curriculum that would make deliberation more central to pedagogy. Applebee contrasts the curriculum he believes is needed—a living exploration of open and exciting problems and questions—with the curriculum that currently predominates—a catalog of already-discovered facts or already-created solutions.

> Curricula can be thought about as culturally significant domains for conversations, and teaching and learning as the processes through which students become participants in those conversations. Such participation is a necessary step in transforming knowledge-out-of-context into knowledge-in-action. Through such conversations, students will learn not only the content that is important within each domain, but also the ways of thinking and doing that give content life and vitality. (pp. 126–27)

Nel Noddings, writing in a similar spirit in *The Challenge to Care in Schools*, has suggested a different framework for reconceptualizing the curriculum, based largely on student curiosity and passion:

> I . . . suggest that education might best be organized around centers of care: care for self, for intimate others, for associates and acquaintances, for distant others, for nonhuman animals, for plants and the physical environment, for the human-made world of objects and instruments, and for ideas. Within each of these centers, we will find many themes on which to build courses, topical seminars, projects, reading lists, and dialogue. (p. xiii)

Given pedagogies of deliberation, whether based upon Applebee's "culturally significant domains for conversations," Noddings's "centers of care" curriculum, or another conceptual framework, assessment systems would need to be redesigned to focus less on what facts students had mastered, and more on students' ability to grapple with authentic problems. One such approach to assessment, "the exhibition," was developed at length by Theodore Sizer in *Horace's*

*School* (1992). Building on Sizer's and others' work, Tina Blythe, in *The Teaching for Understanding Guide,* provides a brief outline of the characteristics of an assessment of this sort, which she terms a "performance of understanding":

> Performances of understanding are activities that require students show what they know in new ways or situations to build their understanding of unit topics. In performances of understanding students reshape, expand on, extrapolate from, and apply what they already know. Such performances challenge students' misconceptions, stereotypes, and tendencies toward rigid thinking.
>
> ... Although a "performance" might sound like a final event, performances of understanding are principally learning activities. They give both you [the teacher] and your students a chance to see their understanding develop in new and challenging situations over time. (pp. 62–63)

Performances of understanding require students to practice the same sets of skills that are crucial for democratic deliberation, including applying their knowledge to new situations and being able to explain cogently for others what they believe to be true. Like a deliberation-based curriculum, an assessment system of this sort gives practice in democratic citizenship, even when the *content* of the assessment is something other than a controversial social issue.

Many teachers and schools have worked to put these ideas into practice. A group of schools in New York founded the Performance Standards Consortium; it offers support to other schools and teachers seeking to develop performance-based assessment systems. Another organization, What Kids Can Do, seeks to "document the value of young people working with teachers and other adults on projects that combine powerful learning with public purpose." That organization's Web site highlights student work, underscoring the connections between academic achievement and the skills of democratic deliberation and action.[16]

EMBRACING CONTROVERSY AS CONTENT. In the public sphere, there is always controversy *about* schools: Should condoms be mentioned in sexual-education classes? Should students be asked to observe a moment of silence at the beginning of the day? Should students be given vouchers to pay for their education at whatever school they and their parents choose? Should *The Adventures of Huckleberry Finn* be included in the curriculum? Do standardized tests promote more academic rigor? Should students be required to wear uniforms? Currently, we fight hard to "solve" these issues outside of school. But a curriculum of democratic deliberation would invite pressing social issues such as these—the stuff of democratic deliberation—to become significant *content* for school inquiry.[17]

Schools that embrace controversy as curriculum may not meet the needs of parents who want to shelter their students from even knowing about such controversies or who want to ensure that students learn about the controversies from only one perspective. These parents may, indeed, decide that they want to opt out of the public system to avoid having their students exposed to certain issues. One can certainly argue, however, that it is within the purview of a democratic society to assert that all schools—even private schools—have a responsibility to provide students with the tools of democratic deliberation.[18]

REINVIGORATING DEMOCRATIC DELIBERATION OUTSIDE SCHOOL. Cynics might argue that schools do not need to teach the skills of democratic deliberation, because many adults in this culture neither need nor use these skills. Those who believe, however, that American democracy does need to be revitalized see a vicious cycle involving the lack of civic involvement in society and the lack of democratic education in the schools.

To break the cycle, it makes sense to address it both in school and in the wider social spheres. Schools' ability to teach the skills of democratic deliberation would be strengthened if democratic deliberation were a more visible part of the culture. It is intriguing to consider a few possibilities here: What if school boards, state legislatures, and popular talk shows made a serious attempt to practice deliberative democracy, where disputants did not attack one another and where people openly talked about having changed their minds based on an examination of the evidence? What if all of us, in each of our immediate neighborhoods, gathered together to deliberate on current election topics or to consider neighborhood needs, like building a playground or developing systems to share cars or childcare? What if the parent/teacher group at each school sponsored issuesforums to deliberate on matters of importance to the school and to the wider community? The more examples like these we can think of and collectively act upon, the more the notion of teaching deliberative democracy in schools will make sense to students as part of their initiation into the adult world.

## Engaging the Pedagogical Issues

The obstacles to facilitating the skills of democratic deliberation are largely systemic ones, involving such things as textbooks and tests, and even teacher accreditation and wider social mores. Traditional norms of pedagogy grew out of an interconnected system that mitigates against teachers being able to incorporate deliberation of substantive issues regularly into their classrooms.

To put it differently, democratic deliberation as suggested here is far-reaching. Individuals drawn to traditional ways of teaching are not necessarily people who have an interest in or propensity for facilitating classroom discussion. Even if they were, teacher-education programs do not typically support teachers in developing the skills they would need to do this work well. Even if teachers wanted to introduce deliberative strategies and were well prepared for their use, the demands of the curriculum, heavily constrained by mandated standardized tests, would inhibit their work. And even if it were not for the tests, one cannot rely on support from the public for schools to nurture in students the practices of democratic deliberation. On this level, the vision of education suggested here might seem unrealistic, as it would require a fundamental shift in society's vision of a valuable education.

And yet, even though promoting democratic deliberation on a broad scale would require systemic change, this vision is not unfeasible. Indeed, many individual teachers and communities of teachers are now placing primacy on helping their students develop the skills of democratic deliberation.

How do teachers address the predictable challenges involving participation, accuracy, nuance, and tradition, as outlined above? Several strategies are being used by teachers engaged in this work.

ENCOURAGING FULL PARTICIPATION. So often in classroom discussions, the students who find it easiest to speak are the ones who get practice expressing their opinions. Seeking to help less vocal students participate more fully, teachers design lessons that alternate between writing and speaking, individual thinking and reading time, and small-group and full-class discussion. Often, teachers find that students reluctant to speak in large groups do better if they have had a chance to write down their thinking first and perhaps to share it with a partner. Similarly, teachers find that eager talkers often deepen their thinking when they discuss in a small group or write before the whole group convenes.

AVOIDING POLARIZATION. Democratic deliberation seeks to help students to understand issues more deeply, bring new insights to bear, and develop creative solutions—not just to choose sides. While debate can be a useful classroom technique, it often serves to hone the skills of rhetorical one-upmanship more than those of listening and creative problem-solving. To help students develop these skills, teachers plan exercises that provide practice in uncovering gray areas, building consensus, and postponing drawing conclusions until considerable research and thinking have been done.

SUPPORTING INFORMED OPINIONS. So often, kids can get off the hook by saying, "This is what I think, and I have a right to my opinion." Everyone does have a right to an opinion. But the work of being a student—like the work of being an informed citizen—involves grounding one's opinions in a theoretical framework, empirical evidence, and persuasive interpretations of that evidence. Teachers work to help students see that theories, evidence, and interpretation—not just "the right to an opinion"—are the stuff of democracy.

ALLOWING FOR SHIFTS IN OPINIONS. Politicians regularly chastise one another for changing their opinions. And while it is true that politicians sometimes change their opinions for questionable reasons, the ability to change one's mind is a distinguishing feature of someone who is using his or her emotional and intellectual capacities. Teachers work to let students know that changing one's mind is not a weakness, and that through democratic deliberation, they will likely encounter exhilarating and humbling moments when they realize that they disagree with their former selves.

TEACHING DELIBERATION STRATEGIES ALONG WITH CONTENT. Teachers engaged in developing their students' capacity to deliberate teach discussion skills. One hears students in such classrooms use expressions like, "I would like to say back to you what I heard so that I can check if I understood you well" or, "I agree with Vanessa's first point, but I want to raise a question about her conclusion" or, "I want to build on what Brett said." They know how to elaborate on one another's ideas and they know how to disagree respectfully. They know that balanced airtime matters; they know that complex issues have important middle-grounds. Learning the characteristics of successful deliberation and analyzing how any discussion went—aside from its content—is part of the learning.

THINKING OF DELIBERATION AS A PRACTICE. As most teachers are used to focusing on content, we sometimes treat learning as if it has a beginning and an end—"Okay, we're done with photosynthesis, now we'll do genetics." Teaching the skills of democratic deliberation is more like teaching a performance art, a spiritual path, or a sport. It is a practice. Teachers engaged in this work find themselves developing basic skills and then spending years deepening the emotional and intellectual intensity of those skills and working on the fine points. They also support students to see that they are working on developing the *practice* of deliberation.

STEPPING OUT OF THE ROLE OF EVALUATOR. Most teachers have to give students grades at the end of each quarter or each semester. Teachers do not want students to be surprised by those grades, and they want to keep them posted about their progress, so they often give students points for almost every piece of writing, homework, or class activity. If we focus on the notion of democratic deliberation as a *practice,* we can see the downside of this kind of grading more clearly. What if every time a piano student sat down to practice, there was someone standing over his shoulder saying every few minutes, "That passage was an A. That one was a B-. That was a C." Or every time a young basketball player took to the courts, the coach rated every dribble and pass: "Ten points! Four points! Seven!" One thing is certain: it would be hard for the learner to concentrate on the music or the ball; it would be hard to get into any kind of flow; it would be hard to want to keep practicing. Teachers seeking to promote the skills of deliberation step as energetically as possible into the role of coach and away from the role of evaluator. To do this, many teachers strive to help students develop their own powers of self-assessment and enlist expert outsiders in the evaluation of final products.[19]

## *Classrooms and Controversy*

How do teachers put the principles of democratic deliberation into practice in the classroom? It is important to stress that there is no step-by-step formula or script for teaching about controversial issues. Facilitation of democratic deliberation demands, on the contrary, a huge pedagogical repertoire, a keen ear, and an appreciation for complexity and ambiguity. One cannot expect students to be able immediately to launch into unstructured whole-group discussions of complex issues that are productive and meaningful. Teachers engaged in promoting deliberation have developed teaching strategies that help them avoid the pitfalls described above and that can support students, over time, in building the skills of thoughtfulness that we strive for. Most of these strategies make use of the teacher's power to manipulate time and grouping structures to facilitate reflection, open communication, and evidence gathering.

As mentioned above, one question that inevitably arises when a teacher uses this power involves the teacher's own position on controversial issues. There is not a consensus among educational theorists or social science educators about whether or not a teacher should express his or her opinions about controversial matters. Nel Noddings, in *Educating for Intelligent Belief or Unbelief*, expresses a view in favor of a kind of "pedagogical neutrality": "Teachers have an obligation to present all significant sides of an issue in their full passion and their best reasoning. This is not to say that teachers should not disclose their own beliefs and commitments (although sometimes they should not), but that they should always help students to see why an issue *is* controversial" (p. 123).

In *Democratic Education*, Amy Gutmann argues that teachers in American society can be expected to uphold—and *not* to present as controversial—such shared values as religious toleration and mutual respect among races. Such standards would prevent, for example, a teacher from opening up as controversial a question about the superiority of one race over another.

There are, on the other hand, some issues that genuinely are controversial, however much one might wish that they were not. A teacher of any political stripe would have to agree that the question of whether two men should be allowed to marry by law is, from an empirical point of view, controversial in the United States in the early years of the twenty-first century. As we have seen, Nel Noddings would argue that it is incumbent upon the teacher to present all significant sides of the issue "in their full passion and their best reasoning." Others, of course, would argue that such a conversation has no place in the public schools. Indeed, in many school districts across the country, teachers would face sanctions for fostering any deliberation about this—or many other hot-button social issues—whatsoever. The question for all of us is whether we believe that schools are a fitting place for students to practice the skills that are essential to full civic participation.

125

## Conclusion

For teachers to take on the role of facilitator of deliberation about complex social issues will require not just adoption on their part of a set of teaching strategies, but a significant shift in the way society understands the role of education. American educational practice has traditionally been dominated by a conception of education that views students as recipients of packaged information, and teachers as regularly gauging how much students have received by asking short-answer questions in class and through administering multiple-choice tests. To foster the skills of deliberation, educators would need to give up seeking to cover all of the material that fills a textbook, and to focus more on the conversations that are alive in society, both among the public at large and among the active participants in specific fields of inquiry.

For schools and teachers that are ready to take this plunge, there would be much professional-development work to do. Such work would be aided, however, by a good number of existing frameworks and strategies designed to foster classroom exploration of controversial issues. While there is general agreement about the need to educate people for participation in a democracy, perhaps the greatest obstacle to meeting this need in the schools is uncertainty about the consequences. What would happen if all students—and eventually all citizens—thought deeply about the issues that face us? What changes would a population educated in democratic deliberation work for? It can be expected that such citizens would become actively engaged in critiquing social norms, exploring core questions of how the nation allocates resources, when it goes to war, how it cares for the sick, and the like. Citizens capable of such questioning would likely demand significant changes in the status quo. That might be unsettling for some. But if we believe in democracy, it makes sense to trust that students who learn to inquire, to sift through evidence, to think, and to consider the common good, will arrive at answers that contribute to the well-being of the world.

## Notes

1. Carnegie Corporation and the Center for Information and Research on Civic Learning and Engagement (CIRCLE), *The Civic Mission of Schools;* Evans and Saxe, eds., *Handbook on Teaching Social Issues.*
2. DelFattore, *What Johnny Shouldn't Read;* Thomas B. Fordham Foundation, *Back to Basics: Reclaiming Social Studies* (Washington, D.C., 2003).
3. Joseph Kahne et al., "Developing Citizens for Democracy? Assessing Opportunities to Learn in Chicago's Social Studies Classrooms," *Theory and Research in Social Education* 28, no. 3 (summer 2000): 333–34.
4. See, for example, Lampert, *Teaching Problems and the Problems of Teaching.*
5. For more recent observations of these same points across the curriculum and the grade levels, see Darling-Hammond, *The Right to Learn,* and Kohn, *The Schools Our Children Deserve.*

6. Diana Hess, "Developing Strong Voters through Democratic Deliberation," *Social Education* 64, no. 5 (September 2000): 294.

7. Linda Darling-Hammond, "Reframing the School Reform Agenda: Developing Capacity for School Transformation," *Phi Delta Kappan* 74, no. 10 (1993): 758.

8. See Meier, *The Power of Their Ideas,* and Sizer, *Horace's School.*

9. For more on this, see Diana Hess and Julie Posselt, "How Students Experience and Learn from the Discussion of Controversial Public Issues in Secondary Social Studies," *Journal of Curriculum and Supervision* 17, no. 4 (2002): 283–314; and Onosko and Swenson, "Designing Issue-based Unit Plans."

10. See Popham, *The Truth about Testing;* and Meier, *In Schools We Trust.*

11. Carnegie Corp. and CIRCLE, *The Civic Mission of Schools,* 15.

12. For more on this point, see Dewey, *Experience and Education,* and Wasley, Hampel, and Clark, *Kids and School Reform.*

13. See Sizer, *Horace's Compromise.*

14. E. D. Hirsch Jr., *Cultural Literacy: What Every American Needs to Know* (New York: Random House, 1988).

15. For more on this point see Hess and Posselt, "How Students Experience and Learn from the Discussion of Controversial Public Issues."

16. For more information on the New York Performance Standards Consortium, visit its Web site at www.performanceassessment.org. The What Kids Can Do Web site is located at www.whatkidscando.org.

17. For an elaboration of this view, see Nel Noddings, "Renewing Democracy in Schools," *Phi Delta Kappan* 80, no. 8 (April 1999): 579–87; and Gerald Graff, *Beyond the Culture Wars.*

18. For more on the issue of what democratic values private schools can be expected to promote, see Gutmann, *Democratic Education,* 115–21.

19. For more on these ideas, see Simon, *Moral Questions in the Classroom;* Meier, *The Power of Their Ideas;* Kohn, *The Schools Our Children Deserve;* Brookfield and Preskill, *Discussion as a Way of* Teaching; Hess, "Developing Strong Voters"; and Kessler, *The Soul of Education.*

## Bibliography

Applebee, Arthur N. *Curriculum as Conversation: Transforming Traditions of Teaching and Learning.* Chicago: University of Chicago Press, 1996.

Blythe, Tina, and the researchers and teachers of the Teaching for Understanding Project. *The Teaching for Understanding Guide.* San Francisco: Jossey-Bass, 1998.

Brookfield, Stephen D., and Stephen Preskill. *Discussion as a Way of Teaching: Tools and Techniques for Democratic Classrooms.* San Francisco: Jossey-Bass, 1999.

Carnegie Corporation and the Center for Information and Research on Civic Learning and Engagement (CIRCLE). *The Civic Mission of Schools.* New York: Carnegie Corp. of New York, 2003.

Cazden, Courtney B. *Classroom Discourse: The Language of Teaching and Learning.* Portsmouth, N.H.: Heinemann Educational Books, 1988.

Darling-Hammond, Linda. *The Right to Learn: A Blueprint for Creating Schools That Work.* San Francisco: Jossey-Bass, 1997.

DelFattore, Joan. *What Johnny Shouldn't Read: Textbook Censorship in America*. New Haven, Conn.: Yale University Press, 1992.

Dewey, John. *The Child and the Curriculum*. Chicago: University of Chicago Press, 1902.

Dewey, John. *Democracy and Education: An Introduction to the Philosophy of Education*. New York: Macmillan, 1916.

Dewey, John. *Experience and Education*. New York: Macmillan, 1938.

Evans, Ronald W., and David W. Saxe, eds. *Handbook on Teaching Social Issues*. Washington, D.C.: National Council for the Social Studies, 1996.

Glickman, Carl. *Revolutionizing America's Schools*. San Francisco: Jossey-Bass, 1997.

Goodlad, John. *A Place Called School: Prospects for the Future*. New York: McGraw Hill, 1984.

Graff, Gerald. *Beyond the Culture Wars: How Teaching the Conflicts Can Revitalize American Education*. New York: Norton, 1992.

Gutmann, Amy. *Democratic Education*. Rev. ed. Princeton, N.J.: Princeton University Press, 1999.

Hahn, Carol. "Research on Issues-Centered Social Studies." In *Handbook on Teaching Social Issues*, edited by Ronald W. Evans and David W. Saxe, pp. 25–41. Washington, D.C.: National Council for the Social Studies, 1996.

Hess, Diana, and J. Posselt. "How Students Experience and Learn from the Discussion of Controversial Public Issues in Secondary Social Studies." *Journal of Curriculum and Supervision* 17, no. 4 (2002): 283-314.

Hibbing, John R., and Elizabeth Theiss-Morse. *Stealth Democracy: Americans' Beliefs about How Government Should Work*. Cambridge, U.K., and New York: Cambridge University Press, 2002.

Kessler, Rachael. *The Soul of Education: Helping Students Find Connection, Compassion, and Character at School*. Alexandria, Va.: Association for Supervision and Curriculum Development, 2000.

Kohn, Alfie. *The Schools Our Children Deserve: Moving beyond Traditional Classrooms and "Tougher Standards."* Boston: Houghton Mifflin, 1999.

Lampert, Magdalene. *Teaching Problems and the Problems of Teaching*. New Haven, Conn.: Yale University Press, 2001.

Massialas, Brian. "Criteria for Issues-Centered Content Selection." In *Handbook on Teaching Social Issues*, edited by Ronald W. Evans and David W. Saxe. Washington, D.C.: National Council for the Social Studies, 1996.

Meier, Deborah. *The Power of Their Ideas: Lessons for America from a Small School in Harlem*. Boston: Beacon, 1995.

Meier, Deborah. *In Schools We Trust: Creating Communities of Learning in an Era of Testing and Standardization*. Boston: Beacon, 2002.

New York Performance Standards Consortium. A group of schools that has designed a rigorous assessment system. www.performanceassessment.org.

Noddings, Nel. *The Challenge to Care in Schools: An Alternative Approach to Education*. New York: Teachers College Press, 1992.

Noddings, Nel. *Educating for Intelligent Belief or Unbelief*. New York: Teachers College Press, 1993.

Onosko, Joseph, and Lee Swenson. "Designing Issue-Based Unit Plans." In *Handbook on*

*Teaching Social Issues*, edited by Ronald W. Evans and David W. Saxe, pp. 89–98. Washington, D.C.: National Council for the Social Studies, 1996.

Parker, Walter. *Teaching Democracy: Unity and Diversity in Public Life.* New York: Teachers College Press, 2003.

Passe, Jeff, and Ron Evans. "Discussion Methods in an Issues-Centered Curriculum." In *Handbook on Teaching Social Issues*, edited by Ronald W. Evans and David W. Saxe, pp. 81–88. Washington, D.C.: National Council for the Social Studies, 1996.

Pope, Denise Clark. *"Doing School": How We Are Creating a Generation of Stressed Out, Materialistic, and Miseducated Students.* New Haven, Conn.: Yale University Press, 2001.

Popham, W. James. *The Truth about Testing: An Educator's Call to Action.* Alexandria, Va.: Association for Supervision and Curriculum Development, 2001.

Rosenberg, Marshall B. *Life-Enriching Education: Nonviolent Communication Helps Schools Improve Performance, Reduce Conflict, and Enhance Relationships.* Encinitas, Calif.: PuddleDancer, 2003.

Schweber, Simone. *Making Sense of the Holocaust: Lessons from Classroom Practice.* New York: Teachers College Press, 2004.

Simon, Katherine G. *Moral Questions in the Classroom: How to Get Kids to Think Deeply about Real Life and Their Schoolwork.* New Haven, Conn.: Yale University Press, 2001.

Sizer, Theodore R. *Horace's Compromise: The Dilemma of the American High School.* Boston: Houghton Mifflin, 1984.

Sizer, Theodore R. *Horace's School: Redesigning the American High School.* Boston: Houghton Mifflin, 1992.

Wasley, Patricia A., Robert L. Hampel, and Richard W. Clark. *Kids and School Reform.* San Francisco: Jossey-Bass, 1997.

# 6

# THE STATE OF CIVIC EDUCATION: PREPARING CITIZENS IN AN ERA OF ACCOUNTABILITY

*Michael C. Johanek and John Puckett*

*Engaged citizens do not create themselves. We should no more expect spontaneous engagement than we do spontaneous combustion. The norms of the culture are against the former, just as the laws of physics are against the latter.*
The Civic and Political Health of the Nation (2002)

*The first and primary reason for civic education in a constitutional democracy is that the health of the body politic requires the widest possible civic participation of its citizens consistent with the public good and the protection of individual rights. The aim of civic education is therefore not just any kind of participation by any kind of citizen; it is the participation of informed and responsible citizens, skilled in the arts of deliberation and effective action.*
CIVITAS: A Framework for Civic Education (1991)

In an era of test scores and standards, how well do America's schools perform in preparing citizens? The answer depends on what is desired of citizens and what is expected from schools. This essay examines that relationship, mapping the range of expectations that Americans have with respect to citizenship and schools to conceptions of civic performance. It does so by looking at the current moment in civic education in historical context, in particular by examining a minor historical tradition in American education—that of the community-centered school. This tradition focuses intently upon citizen development as a commitment of public schooling, modeling institutionally for the community how to gain civic knowledge, how to be active civically, and how to demonstrate positive civic dispositions.

Our historical research highlights one such institution, Benjamin Franklin High School (BFHS) in East Harlem, New York City, during the 1930s and early 1940s. A "community-centered school" for boys, BFHS suggested what a multiethnic public school might look like if it modeled participatory and public work citizenship. For BFHS, public schooling served as the very foundation of a democratic republic. It would train youth to be local civic leaders through concrete community strategies, girding them with skills of social research, organizing, and political action, and in the process fostering locally based democracy and cultivating a richer citizen participation in resolving intercultural conflict.

Leonard Covello, the high school's indefatigable, visionary founding principal, and his professional allies in Italian Harlem (among them Vito Marcantonio, a powerful political leader, and New York's mayor, Fiorello La Guardia) built a community school that included community advisory committees; federally supported adult education and recreational services; street units for social clubs, community research bureaus and a community library; and a school-based community newspaper. Large-scale community organizing efforts such as housing and health campaigns, and partnerships with umbrella activist groups were undertaken to mobilize the community's educational resources in the service of the high school, to provide a training ground for active, engaged citizenship (for youth and adults alike), and to unify East Harlem's competing ethnic groups on the common ground of a shared democratic vision.

These community activities were linked to the high school curriculum through a multicultural education program, a community social research agenda, and various classroom projects. Every facet of BFHS's community program focused on civic education and reinforced the high school's instructional program and community work. Community advisory committees and social clubs, for instance, educated East Harlem parents about interethnic tolerance and cooperation at the same time that their sons were learning these lessons in the high school's intercultural education program. BFHS modeled the interconnectivity of the three domains of civic preparation and performance. Through its social research program, the high school was constantly improving its *knowledge*, which led it to adjust its *behaviors* to address its evolving role in engaging and reconciling civic and political issues. And through its behaviors—for example, the East Harlem housing campaign—it modeled the *dispositions* of engaged public work citizenship.

And yet community-centered schooling at BFHS could not be sustained beyond the 1940s. The withdrawal of federal funds at the end of the New Deal truncated the community program, postwar demographic shifts and ethnic tensions undermined community support, professionalization diminished the willingness of teachers to engage in community-centered work, and emerging educational policies targeted more individual and competitive ends. Both the promise and the demise of Benjamin Franklin High School reveal a great deal about current dilemmas of civic education.

Since the early 1990s there has been a growing revival of interest in civic education in the United States. Scholars in a variety of disciplines have contributed a raft of empirical research studies and theoretical essays. The Carnegie Corporation, the Pew Charitable Trusts, and the Kettering and Annenberg Foundations, among others, have sponsored research and curriculum development activities related to the teaching of democratic citizenship in the public schools. Their initiatives complement other innovative programs in this field, most notably a spate of widely used supplemental texts developed and distributed by the nonprofit Center for Civic Education, which receives most of its funding from the federal government.

What explains this increased attention to the school's role in civic education? The fall of the Berlin Wall in 1989, the collapse of the Soviet Union in 1991, and, with breathtaking speed, the rise of new democratic states in central and eastern Europe marked the starting point of increased attention. These developments spurred great optimism among American scholars and policymakers that democratic gains abroad would contribute to a renewal of democracy at home. Optimism soon turned to concern, however, as longitudinal studies, coupled with national report cards on the status of youth citizenship development in the United States, disclosed a continuous trend of decline in civic knowledge and political participation on the part of American youth during the second half of the twentieth century, a trend that appeared to be accelerating at the turn of the new millennium and significantly distancing contemporary youth and young adults from their counterparts in previous generations. Purported civic deficits have become a fire bell in the night for many of the actors and organizations involved in the multiple initiatives that seek to transform the field of civic education. More recent turns in foreign policy foregrounding a renewed proselytizing posture on behalf of democracy and the urgent need for civic reconstruction in troubled lands only complicate and highlight the challenge in preparing future citizens.

There are, of course, many factors that prepare citizens—home, community, media, peers, schools, and so on. Within this mix, how well do schools contribute to citizenship preparation? Unfortunately, even as we hold schools increasingly accountable for student achievement, we rarely seem to judge schools for their performance in citizenship preparation, an inauspicious "accountability gap" for a democracy. Contemporary school reform largely avoids citizenship education as a category of accountability.

Consistent with this observation, the sociologist David Labaree writes compellingly in *How to Succeed in School without Really Learning* (1997) that contemporary public education and reform are dominated by the goal of individual social mobility and status attainment, which justifies public schooling as a private good. Reflecting the primacy of this goal, the prevailing reform climate emphasizes students' scores on high-stakes standardized tests as near-exclusive indicators of school success. The emphasis on students' market viability contributes to reducing democracy to an economic concept—one that too often breeds selfishness, promotes a narrow conceptualization of the social responsibilities of citizenship, and undermines a vision of community. Inadequate attention is given to the public purposes that are necessary for schooling to be genuinely a public good—one that has far-ranging benefits that are more than simply an aggregation of private ends. While the inequities in academic opportunities mock any basic sense of fairness, and certainly impair societal development, it is also true that schools are not being held accountable for how well they prepare young people to be citizens. This is ironic, in that the primary justification for the school's existence as a publicly funded entity is citizenship training.[1]

To answer the question "How well do schools prepare citizens?" four key questions must be addressed:

1. *What is now happening in schools by way of civic education?* Here we focus on the *intentional* activities—curricular and extracurricular—that schools provide to prepare young people for citizenship.
2. *What is the "outcome" we desire for citizenship preparation?* To answer this we consider different meanings of citizenship and build on previous scholarship to designate a continuum of citizenship performance that ranges from "thin" to "strong" democracy.
3. *What do we know about citizen development outcomes for youth?* In particular, what do we know about three domains of citizenship performance: knowledge, behaviors, and dispositions?
4. *If we are not satisfied with these outcomes, what would be needed to advance a stronger concept of citizenship?* We conclude with a discussion of how to change significantly the outcomes of school-based civic education.

## Civic Education in the Schools

Schools train citizens most explicitly via three vehicles: *courses and standards,* whether actual civics/government courses or content within other social studies classes; *supplemental curricular programs,* such as debate forums on current issues; and *extracurricular activities,* such as student government. Social studies educator Carole Hahn aptly summarizes the status of formal civic education in the nation's public schools:

> The typical pattern is for primary grade children to learn several patriotic songs, to celebrate national holidays such as Presidents' Day and Thanksgiving with art projects and stories, and to say a daily salute to the flag. Primary grade children often study about "community

helpers," such as the police and firefighters, and about the need for rules and laws. In grades 4–6, children are usually introduced to United States history and the basic principles of the Bill of Rights and the United States Constitution. Most high school students take a year-long course in United States history and a semester-long course in government. Courses in state history, economics, law, and civics are also prevalent in many states and further contribute to the civic education of youth in the United States.[2]

## Courses and Standards

At least forty-two states (82 percent) require the study of civics or American government in some form in grades nine through twelve. As of the mid-1990s, 78 percent of graduating seniors had taken an American government class, and 95 percent had completed a U.S. history course, which likely included constitutional history. The central tendency, however, is a decline of formal civic education in the high school. According to *The Civic Mission of Schools* (2003), "Most formal civic education today comprises only a single semester course on government—compared to as many as three courses in democracy, civics, and government that were common until the 1960s" (p. 5). Civic education content is weighted heavily toward the structures and functions of U.S. government, primarily the Constitution, the three branches of government, and "how a bill becomes law."[3]

Primary responsibility for citizenship education in the nation's schools belongs to the social studies curriculum. Studies show that widely adopted social studies textbooks at different grade levels convey messages about citizenship that support mainstream values and acceptance of the status quo. More specifically, elementary social studies texts emphasize voting and obeying laws over other civic behaviors; middle school history and civics texts subordinate civic obligations and a conception of the public good to individual rights; and high school government texts encourage individual actions over communal participation. Teacher and student reports in surveys and national assessments suggest the dominance of textbooks and traditional didactic instruction in social studies classrooms.[4]

Standard-setting efforts in this field provide frameworks for textbooks and curricula. Enlisting the advice and contributions of more than three thousand teachers, scholars, national and international government officials, and other leaders, the Center for Civic Education, in conjunction with the Council for the Advancement of Citizenship, published the *National Standards for Civics and Government* (hereafter, National Civics Standards) in 1994, a set of voluntary content standards for grades K–12, divided into three grade groupings: K–4, 5–8, and 9–12. The precursor document to the national standards was the center's lengthy, elaborately detailed volume *CIVITAS: A Framework for Civic Education* (1991), which established a set of national goals for revitalizing K–12 public and private schools. More than 500 of the book's 665 pages deal with political knowledge—topics such as "the concept and purposes of law, types of legal systems, constitutional government, the Congress and the presidency, political parties, and the press;" to the limited extent that *CIVITAS* incorporated classical republican and communitarian perspectives, it stood as a departure from the minimalist conception of citizenship that imbued "mainstream civics" in the 1970s and 1980s.[5]

Enacted in 1994, the Clinton administration's Goals 2000: Educate America Act, which advocated rigorous state content standards and a corresponding alignment of curricula and assessments, provided a significant impetus to the promulgation of voluntary national civics standards. The National Civics Standards comprise roughly one hundred pages of behaviorally worded performance objectives, which focus on the principles, processes, and institutions of American government and politics, and are couched in such terms as "define," "describe," "explain," "identify," and "evaluate, take, and defend positions on" (the latter phrase appearing mostly in the grades-nine-through-twelve standards). The national standards are devoid of any language that would suggest agency in a political arena—a student's implied role is generally to be a spectator of government and politics.

In the mid-1990s, concomitant with the release of the National Civics Standards, a controversy raged over national history standards, casting in bold relief a long-standing, recurring issue that bears directly on the content of civics standards and curricula. As Gary Nash and his associates write in their recounting of the "history wars," *History on Trial* (1997), the issue is two competing visions of patriotism. On the one hand are those who argue that history studies should promote loyalty and pride in national achievements. They downplay the social injustices perpetrated in the country's history, which they view as short-lived aberrations in an otherwise consensual narrative of continuous progress and expanding freedom and opportunity. On the other hand are those who contend that history studies should expose students to the dark side of their history and the prominent role of conflict in building the nation. Proponents of this position, social historians for the most part, argue that the struggles of marginalized groups to overcome discrimination and exploitation should have parity with political, economic, and intellectual subjects in history textbooks.

The latter position was represented in the voluntary National History Standards produced in 1994 under the auspices of the nonprofit National Center for History in the Schools (NCHS) at the University of California at Los Angeles. The new history standards, which involved distinguished historians, veteran teachers, and hundreds of other stakeholders, were attacked by powerful conservatives who characterized them as "politically correct," "revisionist," and "postmodernist." Following a balanced review by the Council for Basic Education, a chastised NCHS published a thoughtfully revised version in 1996 which maintained the original document's social history perspective, yet eliminated contentious phrasing and controversial teaching examples. NCHS sent the revised standards to each of the nation's sixteen thousand school districts, and by the late 1990s at least twenty-eight states were using the standards.

When we turn to the states, we find in many cases that civics standards are conflated with social studies/history standards and are based on sources other than the National Civics Standards. As of the late 1990s only three states had separate civics standards. At least forty-one others included civics as an explicit section in their social studies standards or integrated civics in social studies or other standards; civics standards did not exist in any form in seven states, although five had plans under way to create them.[6]

The civics standards, themselves, are problematic. Most states overload their social studies standards (in some cases, they are merely wish lists), and many standards are exasperatingly vague; as, for example, this Illinois middle school standard: "Explain relationships among the American economy and slavery, immigration, industrialization, labor, and urbanization, 1700 to the present." The upshot, according to the historian Paul Gagnon, is that "most state standards for history/civics/social studies are not teachable." In addition, district-level analysis shows that most teachers are somewhat or completely unfamiliar with the civic content of state standards, and "even if teachers are familiar with the state standards, they still often pay little or no attention to them."[7]

## Supplemental Curricular Programs

A careful study of state policies and school district practices related to civic education in fourteen selected school districts in seven states (California, Florida, Indiana, Nebraska, New York, Ohio, and Texas) suggests that supplemental programs are becoming increasingly popular in school districts and classrooms. Regarding instructional materials, "a majority of responding teachers reported that textbooks influence their civics instruction at least somewhat, although the percentage of responding teachers reporting that textbooks have substantial influence is relatively small [16 percent]."[8] In this study many of the responding teachers reported using supplemental programs, notably the Center for Civic Education's civics materials.

Nonprofit organizations and foundations have taken the lead over commercial companies and forged ahead of the states in shaping the direction of civic education through their development or sponsorship of supplemental curriculum materials. The most influential of these organizations and the nonprofit with the longest history in this field is the Center for Civic Education, which was founded in California in 1965. Generously funded by the U.S. Department of Education, the center's publications, which focus primarily on political knowledge as the foundation of an informed and effective citizenry, hold the upper hand in what is now a crowded curriculum field vying for the attention of social studies teachers. Involving some 26 million students since its inception in 1987, the center's *We the People:The Citizen and the Constitution* program provides supplemental texts for elementary and secondary social studies classrooms. These materials are distributed through a network that includes 435 congressional district coordinators and 50 state coordinators, with distribution sites located also in the District of Columbia and U.S. territories.

The program's flagship series focuses on the history and principles of the Constitution and Bill of Rights and builds on the National Civics Standards.The high-school-level textbook is divided into six units and forty lessons.[9] The units include philosophical and historical foundations of the American political system; motives and actions of the framers and issues of the constitutional debates; organization of the new government, inclusion of the Bill of Rights, separation of powers and judicial review; development and expansion of the Bill of Rights, with particular attention given to Fourteenth Amendment protections and the civil rights movement; other protected freedoms and procedural due process; and roles and meanings of democratic citizenship. The culminating activity for the high school program is a simulated congressional hearing that involves groups of three to six students, each of which testifies on a unit in the textbook before a panel of community members who question the students on their political knowledge. High school teams have the option of participating in the We the People's national mock-hearing competition, which begins at the congressional-district level and leads to the national finals each spring in Washington, D.C.[10]

Supplemental programs sponsored by other foundations and nonprofits have different priorities. These programs are categorized below on the basis of the central activity they promote—deliberation, electoral participation, or citizen action. The following examples, briefly considered, illustrate the variety of approaches across and within these categories.[11]

DELIBERATION.  High school students participate in deliberative forums sponsored by the National Issues Forum (NIF) network in hundreds of communities nationwide. They deliberate with adults on complex public issues, like public education, racial and ethnic tensions, the Internet, and the national debt, consider the costs and consequences of alternative positions, and together reach "a reasoned, considered judgment about how to deal with an issue." Issues booklets prepared by the Public Agenda Foundation provide the grist for these deliberations, presenting three or four alternative positions on a complex issue, replete with pro and con arguments and supportive data.

Project 540 (the name denotes a 540-degree turn, or "a revolution and a half") encourages high school students to choose and construct their own issues for deliberation. Organized at more than 250 high schools, the project has purportedly involved over 140,000 students since 2002. A school leadership team, comprising ten to fifteen students, a lead teacher, and another adult, is designated at each high school to recruit and train the student facilitators who run the dialogue groups (ten students per group). The leadership team organizes the results of four dialogue sessions into a statement of key issues, a school map of civic resources, and a "civic action plan" for enhancing civic engagement in the school.

ELECTORAL PARTICIPATION.   Kids Voting USA, a national nonpartisan, nonprofit organization, was created in 1988 by civic-minded Arizona businessmen who wanted to bolster children's interest in the state electoral process and recognition of the importance of voting in a democratic society. The Kids Voting curriculum is introduced in a school eight weeks prior to a statewide election and engages children at different grade levels (K–12) in activities and special projects related to the electoral process and the history of voting, the candidates, and the issues. The project is designed to get the children talking with their parents about the campaign as a nudge for the parents to vote. On Election Day, students accompany their parents to the polls, where the students vote in a mock election, the results of which are reported in local newspapers.

CITIZEN ACTION.   Student Voices, a curriculum-based program of the Annenberg Public Policy Center at the University of Pennsylvania, focuses on the informed participation of high school youth in local government affairs. This program includes electoral participation in a broader context of citizen action. In 2003 approximately three hundred high schools in eleven large cities participated in Student Voices, with a statewide pilot project scheduled for Pennsylvania in 2004–2005. Under the program's auspices, students gather online information on local issues and electoral campaigns, exchange ideas with peers at other schools, and develop a Youth Issues Agenda. They discuss their ideas and opinions with candidates and local government officials during classroom visits and forums, and communicate their agenda to the general public through various media arrangements.

Public Achievement, a youth initiative (ages eight through eighteen) sponsored by the Center for Democracy and Citizenship at the University of Minnesota's Hubert H. Humphrey Institute of Public Affairs, provides guidelines for direct student action projects, either classroom-based or cocurricular, that are grounded in the theory of public work. Examples of children's public work include third and fourth graders organizing parents and neighborhood residents to march against violence, and fifth and sixth graders successfully campaigning to build a neighborhood park, raising $60,000 from public officials and businesses.

The Public Achievement guidebook, *Building Worlds, Transforming Lives, Making History*, is marketed as "a tool kit ... not a step-by-step recipe for public life" for use by both students and "coaches" (teachers or college student volunteers). The guidebook includes chapters on core concepts such as public work, politics, citizenship, democracy, power, responsibility/accountability, and public skills such as civic organizing, deliberating, and facilitating meetings.[12]

Active Citizenship Today (ACT), a supplemental curriculum published jointly by the Close Up Foundation and the Constitutional Rights Foundation, provides a more explicit framework for direct student action than Public Achievement and restricts its audience to high school and middle school students. The *Active Citizenship Today Field Guide*, the student text, is clearly written and attractively illustrated with cartoons, maps, and sidebar text. Students follow a step-by-step process that includes, in sequence, community mapping and local resource-charting; community surveying; deliberating to identify a problem area for class study and action; reviewing local public policies, actors, and interest groups that bear on the problem; through deliberation, identifying a specific problem; and designing a class project and a plan of action, including tasks, timeline, supporters, obstacles, evaluation plan, and budget. Examples include Jackson, Mississippi, high school students working with local community organizations to reduce the level of violence and crime in a ten-block area around the high school, and Omaha, Nebraska, middle school students organizing a book drive and donating more than one thousand books to a homeless shelter and the local literacy council.[13]

Any description of the varied landscape of formal civic education would be incomplete without discussion of service-learning. Service-learning is a particular form of community service that is explicitly linked to the school curriculum and (in theory, at least) is illuminated by information and concepts that students gain from their formal classroom studies. A scholarly consensus holds that bona fide service-learning involves systematic reflection on the community service experience in the form of class discussions, journals, and research papers and essays, through which a heightened awareness of social issues related to the service is achieved. Approximately one-third of the nation's public schools and one-half of public high schools offer service-learning opportunities involving a total of roughly 13 million students. Yet the implementation and quality of service-learning programs and classes, especially at the high school level, is highly variable, and in many cases service-learning programs fall far short of realizing the promise of community service as a medium for academic learning, critical thinking skills, and social insights.[14]

## Extracurricular Programs

Thus far, we have attended to civic education that takes place inside, or is linked directly to, the classroom. The school's extracurricular programs are often an intentional source of civic education. For example, most middle and high schools sponsor student councils and club activities that give youth opportunities to learn and practice leadership skills and the associational skills of self-governance. According to researchers at the Center for Information and Research on Civic Learning and Engagement (CIRCLE), two-thirds of students participate in at least one extracurricular activity, although only 12 percent are involved in student government and 9 percent in service clubs. Carole Hahn describes one California high school with a major student activities program:

> The [student body] officers meet in the mornings before school starts with a legislative council composed of students appointed from the freshman, sophomore, junior, and senior classes. The officers, council members, and representatives from various activities such as the school newspaper, yearbook, pep squad, band, and Reserve Officers' Training Corps (ROTC)—some eighty-five students in all—meet in a daily "leadership class." The leadership class organizes morning assemblies, lunch activities and after-school rallies. Its members also discuss proposed changes in school policy, such as one dealing with attendance. Also, they sponsor fund-raising activities to help finance homecoming, the prom, and teacher appreciation week. Interestingly, a goal of this extensive student activity program is to bring students together from diverse ethnic groups and to bridge their different interests.[15]

## Meanings of Citizenship

Given this profile of civic education efforts in the schools, their success or failure depends on our expectations for citizens. In brief, what is our target outcome for all these courses, supplemental curricular programs, and extracurricular activities? What do we want well-trained citizens to know and to be able to do?

These questions are not new; they have been the subject of debate for centuries. But beginning in the late twentieth century a number of American scholars, often with a critical bent, undertook anew the task of determining the nature of democratic citizenship—with major implications for civic education in the schools. The political theorist Michael Walzer writes that Western liberal democracies are legatees of two traditions that stand in uneasy tension with one another. A tradition of republicanism (a legacy of the ancient Greeks and Jacobin France) envisions citizenship as "an office, a responsibility, a burden proudly assumed," while liberalism (a legacy of imperial Rome and the Enlightenment) regards citizenship as "a status, an entitlement, a right or set of rights passively enjoyed." In theory, "the passive enjoyment of citizenship requires, at least intermittently, the activist politics of citizens"; in practice, however, "democratic citizenship in its contemporary form does not seem to encourage high levels of involvement or devotion."[16]

In a similar vein, Michael Sandel argues that liberalism is the dominant public philosophy of our era. Liberal political theory envisions a nation of individual citizens freely choosing their own ends and values within a framework of basic rights and liberties that are provided and protected by government. We are, in philosopher Sandel's apt phrase, a "procedural republic." This theory appeals to egalitarian liberals and libertarian liberals (conservatives, in contemporary political parlance) alike. The former argue that freedom to pursue one's own ends is contingent on the state's guarantee of "minimal prerequisites of a dignified life"; the latter defend the market economy and "a scheme of civil liberties combined with a strict regime of private property rights." On both views, liberal political theory has no vision of citizens deliberating about the common good or sharing in collective efforts to shape their political community. "The procedural republic cannot secure the liberty it promises," Sandel concludes, "because it cannot sustain the kind of political community and civic engagement that liberty requires."[17]

This critique is supported in Benjamin Barber's *Strong Democracy* (1984), in which the author makes an impassioned yet carefully reasoned plea for activist politics, taking direct aim at the passivity of contemporary democratic citizenship and sharply criticizing liberal democracy, which he derides as "thin," a "minimalist" conception that "is concerned more to promote individual liberty than to secure public justice, to advance interests rather than to discover goods, and to keep men safely apart rather than to bring them fruitfully together" (p. 4). Barber champions "strong" democracy, which he associates with communitarian politics. "In strong democracy," he writes, "politics is something done by, not to citizens. Activity is its chief virtue, and involvement, commitment, obligation and service—common deliberation, common decision, and common work—are its hallmarks" (p. 133).

The political theorist Amy Gutmann, in *Democratic Education* (1999), argues that a well-honed capacity and disposition for democratic deliberation are essential for effective political participation. According to Gutmann, the most critical factor in citizenship preparation is a school climate in which ample opportunities are provided for students to engage in collective deliberation and decision making. These participatory activities foster "the morality of association," whose hallmarks are the civic virtues of empathy, trust, benevolence, and fairness ("the cooperative moral sentiments"; p. 61). Through collective deliberation, children learn how to think critically about politics, to reconcile their political disagreements in mutually respectful ways, and to "live respectfully with those reasonable disagreements that remain unresolvable."[18] They are taught that collective decisions cannot be democratic if they involve discrimination or repression in any fashion. As guidelines for democratic deliberation, they are taught to honor the principles of proceduralism (regard for laws and rules of fair play) and constitutionalism (regard for the legitimacy of outcomes, the governing principle).

A coterie of American scholars have suggested ways of thinking about democratic citizenship and provided, usually implicitly, guidance on how expectations for citizenship might be translated into civic education in the schools. Others have been more explicit in extending their understanding of citizenship into the educational arena. A typology presented by the social studies educators Joel Westheimer and Joseph Kahne provides one such example, through their notion of the "personally responsible citizen" and the "participatory citizen." The personally responsible citizen, an individualistic conception, is described as the helping neighbor who picks up litter, donates blood, recycles, stays out of debt, obeys laws, and volunteers on an individual basis, perhaps at a soup kitchen or a senior center—salutary behaviors, yet insufficient to sustain an effective democratic society. By contrast, the participatory citizen has a collective orientation; according to Westheimer and Kahne, he or she is actively involved in community organizations and civic affairs, and helps organize such efforts as community economic-development initiatives and environmental cleanups.

Table 1, an adaptation of Westheimer and Kahne's novel schematic, shows the continuum of citizenship models on which the status and progress of citizenship preparation may be charted.[19]

TABLE 1
What Do We Mean by "Citizen"? A Continuum

| Personally Responsible Citizen | Participatory Citizen | Public Work Citizen |
| --- | --- | --- |
| *Helping citizen* obeys laws and performs individual acts that demonstrate social responsibility, kindness, and compassion. | *Corporate citizen* participates in collective action to address a need or alleviate a crisis—action that typically involves a self-selected "little public," i.e., one that is collectively not equivalent to the larger public in its range of interests and perspectives. | *Public-building citizen* engages with members of diverse groups constituting a non-self-selected "larger public" to address and resolve a problem by dealing with underlying causes—a resolution that requires the cooperation and resources of all groups with a compelling interest in the problem. |
| Volunteers in a homeless shelter. | Helps organize a clothing drive on behalf of the shelter. | Engages with members of diverse groups to address and resolve the problem of access to quality housing in a community. |

## Outcomes of Youth Citizenship Preparation:
### Knowledge, Behaviors, Dispositions

Given what schools do in civic education, and given the continuum of citizenship constructs as outlined in Table 1, what do we know about civic education outcomes? What do we know about youth civic development in terms of their knowledge, their behaviors, and their dispositions? The knowledge domain includes "political knowledge"; that is, knowledge of political structures and institutions, the law, political actors, and public policymaking; it also includes related analytic and participatory skills. Behaviors of interest range from voting to volunteer activity to public work. Dispositions include habits, attitudes, values, and motivations.[20]

Three questions guide our review of each domain. First, what is the status of youth vis-à-vis the domain; for example, what do we know about the political knowledge of youth? Second, what is the impact of civic education in the domain? Third, what role or importance does the domain have in relation to the other domains and wider citizenship preparation? We caution readers that keeping these domains analytically separate is difficult, and the distinctions occasionally blur in our analysis.

### Knowledge

What do we know about the status of contemporary youth's political knowledge and related skills? Indirect evidence provided by national surveys shows low levels of attentiveness to politics and public affairs among youth and young adults (for more details, see the discussion of "dispositions" below). Direct evidence reported by various authors discloses that "young people lack geography skills," "most students lack basic history knowledge," "the level of financial literacy has declined," and "civics eludes U.S. students." We concur with the political scientists Richard Niemi and Mitchell Sanders, though, that these studies have limitations.[21]

Perhaps the most controversial evidence derives from the oft-cited (and widely lamented) report of the 1998 National Assessment of Educational Progress (NAEP) decennial civics assessment, which reveals serious shortfalls in the political knowledge of young Americans. Roughly one-third of students in grades four, eight, and twelve performed below the basic level on the NAEP instrument, which measured political knowledge, intellectual and participatory skills, and civic dispositions. Thirty-five percent of twelfth graders scored below basic and only 26 percent scored at or above proficient. A brief example of a NAEP civics question may be illustrative of concerns. When asked to explain two ways that democratic society benefits from citizens actively participating in the political process, only 9 percent of twelfth graders answered completely and correctly; another 43 percent gained partial credit, and the balance was marked as either unacceptable, omitted, or off-task.

At all three grade levels, a majority of black and Hispanic students scored below basic (58 percent of black seniors, 56 percent of Hispanic seniors, for example), with whites outperforming both minority groups. Social class effects favoring students in higher income brackets may be cautiously inferred from this study. Racial and class disparities in civic achievement were evident in the 1999 Civic Education Study sponsored by the International Association for the Evaluation of Educational Achievement (IEA). By contrast, gender differences in both large-scale assessments were negligible.[22]

We the People supplemental programs appear to offer significant advantages to students in terms of knowledge outcomes on NAEP-like assessments. Reliable quasi-experimental studies consistently show that participants in *The Citizen and the Constitution* program significantly outperform comparison students on measures of political knowledge—and this was even the case when high school participants were compared with college students enrolled in political science courses at a major university. The political knowledge advantage holds for the high school participants whether the comparison group is another classroom or a national sample of high school students or adults. Generally positive results for We the People's Project Citizen are reported from a cross-national study of adolescent students in Indiana, Latvia, and Lithuania, which showed significant increases for the program students on measures of civic knowledge, sense of competence in civic skills, and propensity to participate in civic and political life. Notably, students who attempted to implement their action plans recorded the greatest gains in civic development.[23] (Supplemental programs that focus on deliberation, electoral participation, or citizen action have not been evaluated in terms of their political knowledge impacts. Similarly, the research literature is virtually silent on the relationship of service-learning to outcome variables in this domain.)

Why does civic knowledge matter? In their analysis of National Election Studies and other surveys of political knowledge and participation from World War II to the 1990s, political scientists Michael Delli Carpini and Scott Keeter, two of the leading theorists in this domain, meticulously document the strong linkage of political knowledge and citizenship. Specifically, their empirical analysis shows that "informed citizens are demonstrably better citizens. . . . They are more likely to participate in politics, more likely to have meaningful, stable attitudes on issues, better able to link their interests with their attitudes, more likely to choose candidates who are consistent with their own attitudes, and more likely to support democratic norms, such as extending basic civil liberties to members of unpopular groups. Differences between the best- and least-informed citizens on all of these dimensions are dramatic." These researchers assume links between civics education, political knowledge, and engaged citizenship, although beyond advocating a renewed emphasis on civics instruction in the elementary and secondary curriculum, they do not specify any particular content or pedagogy for strengthening these links.[24]

Delli Carpini and Keeter reflect a transformed climate of opinion in political science about civics coursework. As Niemi and Junn note in *Civic Education* (p. 62), a reigning assumption among political scientists, indeed the conventional wisdom, from the 1970s to the 1990s held that the high school civics curriculum was "largely redundant" with influences beyond the classroom and "therefore ineffectual" (never mind that political scientists had virtually nothing to say about the content of an effective program). Niemi and Junn, who analyzed the 1988 NAEP Civics Report Card, found that "students who have had no civics classes or who never studied the subject know less about all aspects of government; they are also less able to interpret written and graphic material about political matters" (p. 67). Put another way, in terms of civics knowledge, taking a civics course matters more than not taking one. That stated, Niemi and Junn imply that a great deal of improvement is still in order; they note that "too much civics teaching is still devoted to memorizing constitutional provisions and government-organization charts without comprehension of what these things mean" (p. 89). Their statistical analysis suggests that expanding the range of civics topics and including more classroom discussion of current events would bolster students' scores on NAEP-like assessments.[25]

Furthermore, from the perspective of cognitive-developmental theory, the heavy attention being paid the political knowledge of adolescents is rightly placed. Indeed this theory supports a heavy if not exclusive focus on civic education content in the upper secondary years, as opposed to childhood and preadolescence. Highly regarded studies demonstrate that during adolescence the individual acquires the cognitive frameworks (schemata) for hypothetical and deductive reasoning; as Joseph Adelson and Robert O'Neil noted in a seminal cross-age study in 1966, adolescents acquire "first, the capacity to reason consequently, to trace out the long-range implications of various courses of action; second, a readiness to deduce specific choices from general principles" (p. 302). Judith Gallatin, in *Democracy's Children* (1985), put it this way: "We believe that children enter their teens with only a rudimentary grasp of the relevant concepts. If you press them to define terms like 'government' or 'political party,' you are apt to find something close to a conceptual void. However, by the end of adolescence youngsters have managed to master the same principles that once seemed so foreign and obscure" (p. 2). Accordingly, political socialization theorists have shifted their field's earlier research focus from childhood, the period when loyalty and affective ties to the polity are established—in the 1950s and 1960s presumed to be the formative period for cognitive political development—to the years between ages fourteen and the mid-twenties, now regarded as "the period of maximal change."[26]

## Behaviors

Numerous surveys and research studies show that young Americans are disengaged from the political process. Voting trend analyses, for example, disclose a steady decline in young adult electoral participation since the 1970s. Between 1972, when eighteen-year-olds were first eligible to vote in a presidential election, and 2000, voter turnout among eighteen-to-twenty-four-year-old citizens declined between 13 and 15 percentage points, about one third, depending on the method of calculation. According to a 1999 report of the National Association of Secretaries of State (NASS), only about one-third of this age group voted in the 1996 election, and less than one-fifth voted in 1998. And as of 2002 only 60 percent of eligible DotNets, the generational cohort born after 1976, were even registered to vote. These young adults tend to avoid political activity of any kind, and they are highly unlikely to join any club or organization that has an explicit political agenda. DotNets are half as likely to contact public officials as boomers and their elders, and less than half as likely as GenXers, the generational cohort born between 1964 and 1976, to volunteer to address a social or political problem. "The evidence that young Americans are disconnected from public life seems endless," Delli Carpini observes.[27]

This withdrawal of young people from public affairs is properly viewed in the context of what political scientist Robert Putnam, in *Bowling Alone,* calls "a larger societal shift toward individual and material values and away from communal values"—a shift that Putnam attributes in no small way to an increasingly "habitual," even "mindless," reliance on electronic media, notably television (p. 272)—though such conditions are susceptible to change, as John Merrow suggests elsewhere in this volume. Even taking into account that young Americans might increase their levels of attentiveness and political participation (if not their identification with political parties and politicians) as they grow older, the fact remains that no previous youth cohort has lagged so far behind its counterparts in earlier generations as Generation Y and younger members of Generation X.

Paradoxically, at least at first blush, young people are volunteering in their local communities at an unprecedented rate compared to any previous generation. According to the results of a national survey conducted by CIRCLE in 2002, today's fifteen-to-twenty-five-year-olds, with 40 percent having served one group or another in the past year, have a significantly higher rate of volunteering than Generation Xers, baby boomers, or "matures." Young people are tutoring and working in homeless shelters, soup kitchens, and nursing homes; they are building houses for Habitat for Humanity and serving community groups in a myriad of other ways. Consistent with the findings of previous studies, most of their volunteer activity is self-consciously nonpolitical and is motivated by a desire to help others—though it is also episodic. Additionally, youth appear roughly as active in consumer activism as other age cohorts, behavior that warrants further exploration as a potent lens on evolving notions of civic involvement.[28]

The advantages of youth political activity and activism for producing participatory or activist adults are suggested by generational theorists whose studies demonstrate a strong link between the "in the trenches" social activism of young civil rights movement volunteers of the 1960s and their later adult civic/political engagement. These theorists argue that late adolescence/early adulthood is the pivotal age for the formation of a political ideology.[29]

The sociologist Doug McAdam compared former Freedom Summer student volunteers who had been in Mississippi in 1964 to Freedom Summer applicants who for various reasons had not participated in that formative experiment. McAdam found that the intensive Freedom Summer experience, in which students worked in sweltering, dangerous, stressful conditions to register African American voters and to organize Freedom Schools, radicalized these young people politically and spurred them to take prominent roles after that fateful summer in the free speech movement, the anti–Vietnam War movement, and (for the young women) women's liberation. More than twenty years later, most of the volunteers remained politically active, and their level of engagement was significantly higher than that of the Freedom Summer "no-shows."

The political scientist M. Kent Jennings writes, "If experiences during the formative years are to have long-term consequences, the protest era should serve as a textbook example." Using the construct of "generation units," Jennings tracks the political behavior of midlife adults who as high school seniors in the graduating class of 1965 had participated in the University of Michigan's national longitudinal study of political socialization, with resurvey points in 1973, 1982, and 1997. His sample of the class of 1965 for the thirty-year period includes 316 respondents, 94 (30 percent) of whom had been protesters in the movement era. Jennings highlights *inter*generational continuity in terms of political participation and issue positions for protesters and nonprotesters, comparing the protest generation (G2) to their parents (G1) and offspring (G3). He documents a continuing significant gap between protesters and nonprotesters—one that is moderately predicted by the parental generation and emergent in the offspring aged 15 and older—with the following stipulation: "Differential contact with a divisive political environment during their [G2s'] formative years served to perpetuate a sharp division in a fashion not applicable to either their parents or their children." This study has immediate relevancy for debates about volunteerism and service-learning; in his peroration, Jennings argues:

> Unless such activities include some form of group involvement or mobilization, it seems problematic that they could produce the kind of sustained high activity levels that stem from early, concrete involvement in the politics of mobilization and collective action, especially over emotionally charged issues. *Political* skills, experience, commitment, and networking are more likely to develop, flourish, and persist as a result of performance in manifestly political arenas.[30]

Lastly, some kinds of extracurricular activities appear to have salutary effects in terms of later political interest and engagement.[31] Participation in student government, an unsurprising source of civic development, is associated with increased reading of news sources on a weekly basis, greater understanding of politics, and increased tolerance of controversial books. Involvement in school clubs is associated with higher levels of post-high-school civic and political engagement. Some researchers reason that participatory experiences in clubs and other school organizations impart important communication and organizational skills that become critical resources for later political activity. Other researchers find that to be politically influential later, the participation has to have a political component; not just any school club will suffice.[32]

## Dispositions

Unsurprisingly, in light of their voting behavior and the apolitical orientation of their volunteerism, American youth report that they care little about politics. The *American College Freshman*, a highly regarded survey of the attitudes and behaviors of entering freshmen in the nation's colleges and universities, conducted annually since 1966 by the Higher Education Research Institute (HERI) at the University of California at Los Angeles, shows a clear trend of decline over a thirty-year period in habits and dispositions deemed essential for effective democratic participation. In fall 2000 only 28.1 percent of entering freshmen designated keeping up with politics as a "very important" or "essential" life goal—a record low, surpassing the previous year's all-time nadir of 28.6 percent—and only 16.4 percent reported discussing politics frequently; HERI researchers note a "persistent downward trend" in political interest. Cynicism toward politicians is part of this antipathy toward politics. According to the National Association of Secretaries of State, 64 percent of young people agree with the statement that "government is run by a few big interests looking out for themselves," and 58 percent say, "You can't trust politicians because most are dishonest."[33]

Some surveys and studies show that American young people hold a minimalist conception of citizenship, the defining traits of which they construe as being a "a good person," being a friend in need, voting, obeying the law, and acting patriotically; anything more is deemed to be uncommonly virtuous behavior or "above the line of duty."[34] Offering a concurring opinion based on interviews and hundreds of essays collected by the Stanford University Center on Adolescence, the psychologist William Damon avers that young people lack a strong "civil identity," which Damon describes as "allegiance to a systematic set of moral and political beliefs, a personal ideology of sorts, to which a young person forges a commitment. The emotional and moral concomitants to the beliefs are a devotion to one's community and a sense of responsibility to the society at large" (p. 127).

The potential of a well designed service-learning program to engender participatory or activist commitments integral to a strong civic identity is suggested in a number of studies. For example, in *Educating Citizens,* Anne Colby and coauthors argue that by deliberating to resolve conflicting moral issues encountered in their service-learning experiences, students advance their moral awareness and judgment. A study by the developmental psychologists James Youniss and Miranda Yates, detailed in *Community Service and Social Responsibility in Youth,* provides some empirical evidence of this. They studied a service-learning program at St. Francis, a predominantly African American parochial high school in Washington, D.C., in the mid-1990s. A total of 160 students, enrolled in five sections of a "social justice" class, provided direct service at a D.C. soup kitchen at least four times (quarterly, twenty hours in total) during the academic year. The soup kitchen sessions were followed by intense reflective discussions and essay writing on students' experiences. The service was also framed against the background of social issues that were studied in the social justice class and highlighted in exhibits and assembly programs throughout the high school—it had a political valence.

Youniss and Yates focused in particular on processes of cognitive moral development, an essential component of civic identity, observing that students' direct encounters with the "other" and small acts of kindness were precursors for taking a political perspective and searching for structural and root causes of the social problems that lead people to soup kitchens. As they note, "Service at the kitchen was no magic intervention that turned bored or cynical teenagers into instant activists. For some St. Frances students, however, service within the context of the social justice course triggered political awareness and steered the identity process in a useful direction toward political involvement" (p. 82). Questionnaire and interview data collected from 121 St. Francis alumni by Youniss and Yates show that the service-learning experience was formative for graduates, if not always in the direction the researchers might have predicted: "Even when alumni were not volunteering or disagreed with the ideology espoused in social justice, the message was recalled vividly either to pique their conscience or to serve as a point from which they have consciously departed" (p. 132).

What do we know about service-learning outcomes more broadly? Evaluation studies tell us something, but not a great deal. One problem is the great variability in implementation and quality of the programs that have been evaluated. Another problem is that only a small fraction of studies use control groups and even fewer look at long-term impacts; many rely on student self-reports and pre- and post-surveys of the service experience. Only a few involve a testable hypothesis or state the theoretical premises of the research. Nevertheless, some cautiously optimistic conclusions can be drawn from this literature: service learning appears to have positive developmental effects such as increased tolerance, self-esteem, and self-efficacy, and it seems to enhance students' sense of civic and social responsibility.[35] A national evaluation study of the Learn and Serve America program, which used control groups, suggests that a multiyear approach may be necessary to ensure the durability of these outcomes.[36]

In its present conception, service-learning as a mode of student citizen action is distinguishable from the approach of action-oriented programs such as Public Achievement and ACT by virtue of its emphasis on youth development as opposed to community development. In many cases purported service-learning activities do not require young people to think critically about their service or to consider the root causes of social problems, and they often reinforce a minimalist conception of citizenship by emphasizing personal responsibility and altruism as the purposes of youth community service.[37] That service-learning might include direct action by young people to *solve* community problems (moving a step further after identifying the causes and ramifications of problems) gets some heated attention in higher-education debates, but not in the world of precollegiate service-learning. In fact, the only hotly contested issue of any significance at this level is whether service-learning should be mandatory or voluntary.

In *An Aristocracy of Everyone*, Benjamin Barber argues passionately and persuasively that community service is simply too important for teaching democracy to make it an elective or extracurricular activity; in this particular case, he writes, coercion leads to liberation. Opponents of mandatory service-learning argue from legal theory that it is "involuntary servitude," hence banned by the Thirteenth Amendment; from democratic theory that it is oxymoronic to the democratic ideal; and from cognitive evaluation theory that it is externally motivated, hence unlikely to foster future volunteerism. A recent quasi-experimental (cross-cohort) study of participants in a required high school service program sheds empirical light on the last criticism. Here service-motivated students were not demotivated by the requirement, as evidenced by their high rates of continuing volunteerism after the course. Moreover, service-averse students who waited until their senior year to take the requirement reported that they planned to continue volunteering after graduation.[38]

## *Accounting for Civic Education*

Our review of civic education programs and activities supports Westheimer and Kahne's argument that schools are educating young people to be personally responsible citizens. In the lower grades they are taught, both formally and informally, that good citizenship means being patriotic, voting, helping others, obeying laws, and respecting individual liberties. At the high school level, the point of heaviest concentration, this version of citizenship is taught through a combination of a textbook-based civics or government curriculum, dominated by lecture and perhaps supplemented by a We the People program and/or some form of community service. In most cases, informed participation in conjoint civic or political activities is not emphasized as a hallmark of responsible citizenship. As we have seen, service-learning, an increasingly popular approach, usually takes the form of one-to-one volunteerism—it is less frequently participatory and rarely involves public work. Widely distributed supplemental programs such as We the People focus on political knowledge, a necessary but insufficient condition for the more advanced forms of citizenship. Innovative approaches that support participatory or public work citizenship operate in only a fraction of schools and even here an ambitious program such as Public Achievement is on the margins of the civics curriculum. In sum, civic education seems to be progressing out of its traditional *spectatorial* mode, largely by dint of service-learning and opportunities for volunteerism, but it is still a far cry from what might be called *change-agent* civics.

That the intentional activities of schools are oriented toward personally responsible citizenship does not necessarily mean that youth and young adults are positioning themselves at that point on the citizenship continuum outlined in Table 1. Most evidence suggests that young people have a limited understanding of the meaning of citizenship consistent with "thin" democracy. They view citizenship in terms of individual responsibilities and helping behaviors, and they do not consider collective civic participation or political engagement to be a citizen's responsibility. In fact, no generation since World War II has come of age so disconnected from the political process—a particularly worrisome gap as it obviates a vital mechanism for getting issues that are important to them into political arenas. Young people are volunteering in unprecedented numbers, but their volunteerism is largely individualistic and emphasizes altruism and charity. The increasing political interest of a growing minority of this generation manifested in surveys—especially connected to the September 11 tragedy and its aftermath—appears to be a response to events and social forces rather than the expression of a nurtured habit of mind and heart. A 2003 survey of college undergraduates reported by the Institute of Politics [at Harvard] suggests that a combination of September 11, the war in Iraq, and the sluggish economy may have jolted many DotNets to take a greater interest in politics. Whereas only 32 percent of eighteen-to-twenty-four-year-olds voted in the 2000 presidential election, 59 percent of college undergraduates (a cohort of roughly 9.5 million) stated that they would "definitely be voting" in 2004, with another 27 percent saying they "probably will vote." A large majority of them also said that they are keeping abreast of current events.[39]

We are inclined toward cautious optimism. Young people appear to be more tolerant and accepting of diversity than their counterparts in previous generations. *The Civic and Political Health of the Nation: A Generational Portrait*, a 2002 report by CIRCLE researchers led by Scott Keeter, finds that youth may be expressing both a generational political voice and a participatory orientation on a ground of their own choosing—consumer activism, "the unexplored path of civic engagement" (pp. 20–21). Alienated from conventional politics and disinclined even to vote, young people may be experimenting with a nonpublic political alternative for reconstructing civic participation—one that provides a creative outlet for their cynicism and certainly offers a social benefit. Consumer activism could be understood most generously as a deliberate route for civic influence in a market-dominant society where official political realms muster little respect and may appear closed to all but the financially well-heeled. In this sense, the market may be perceived as a reasonable if bounded route for collective civic influence, strangely consistent with the values of a society that uses the oxymoronic expression "private citizen" without so much as blinking. Consumer activism also appeals to those seeking international impact, as in sweatshop protests, expanding their civic influence beyond national political systems. Yet this behavior still orients them toward the "little publics" of issue-interested groups or groups sharing consumption patterns; it does not take sight of a larger public affected by a broad social issue, the realm of public work.

Accordingly, cautiously optimistic, we locate young people on the citizenship continuum shown in Table 1 between personally responsible and participatory citizenship, recognizing that they are groping toward new forms of civic and political participation, for which instructional support and new lines of research are demanded. Consumer activism is a case in point. Those who are comfortable with personally responsible citizenship are probably content with the current direction of civic education in the schools. Yet if citizenship means something that lies between participatory and public work, the evidence suggests the need for a significantly different approach than current activities. Certainly schools could do a great deal to promote movement along the continuum by adopting such participatory and social problem–focused service-learning programs as those illustrated in this essay. Some observers call for a comprehensive, or hybridized, model that combines some of the best examples of existing efforts.[40] Given the incremental impact individual components appear to cause, this would be a good start. Real movement toward public work citizenship, however, requires far more; namely, an *institutional commitment* and *institutional modeling of citizenship* are necessary, such as attempted, however imperfectly, by community-centered schools like Benjamin Franklin High School in the 1930s. While schools appear to have moved over the last few decades from traditional coursework to challenging supplemental components as the vehicles of civic education, the evidence suggests that schools would need to advance to the *institutional performance* of public work citizenship, if they are to move students beyond participatory citizenship closer to public work conceptions.

## Notes

1. See David Tyack, "Preserving the Republic by Educating Republicans." Some conservative critics question the appropriateness of school-based civic education, fearing either indoctrinating effects or the subordination of truth and academic achievement to "civic uplift"; see Chester E. Finn Jr., "Faculty Engineering," *Education Next: A Journal of Opinion and Research* 4, no. 2 (2004), http://www.educationnext.org/20042/16.html; and James B. Murphy, "Tug of War: The Left, the Right, and the Struggle over Civic Education," *Education Next: A Journal of Opinion and Research* 3, no. 4 (2003), http://www.educationnext.org/20042/10.html.
2. Hahn, *Becoming Political,* 17.
3. Statistics here are from Niemi and Junn, *Civic Education,* 63–64; and Richard G. Niemi and Julia Smith, "Enrollments in High School Government Classes: Are We Short-Changing Both Citizenship and Political Science Training?" *PS: Political Science and Politics* 34, no. 2 (2001), 281–287.

    Carnegie Corporation of New York and the Center for Information and Research on Civic Learning and Engagement (CIRCLE), *The Civic Mission of Schools* (New York: Carnegie, 2003).
4. Rahima C. Wade and Susan Everett, "Civic Participation in Third Grade Social Studies Textbooks," *Social Education* 58, no. 5 (1994), 308–311; Patricia G. Avery and Annette M. Simmons, "Civic Life as Conveyed in United States Civics and History Textbooks," *International Journal of Social Education* 15, no. 2 (2000/2001), 105–130; J. Cherie Strachan, Leah A. Murray, and Anne Hildreth, "In Search of Effective Civic Education Messages: A Content Analysis of High School Government Texts," paper presented at annual meeting of the American Political Science Association, Boston, August 2002.

    For the dominance of textbooks and didactic instruction, see Stephane Baldi et al., *What Democracy Means to Ninth-graders: U.S. Results for the International IEA Civic Education Study* (Washington, D.C.: National Center for Education Statistics, 2001, NCES 2001-096), 33, fig. 3.3; and Anthony D. Lutkus et al., *NAEP 1998 Civics Report Card for the Nation* (Washington, D.C.: National Center for Education Statistics, 1999, NCES 2000-457), 104.
5. See Policy Research Project on Civic Education Policies and Practices, *The Civic Education of American Youth: From State Policies to School District Practices,* project directed by Kenneth W. Tolo (Austin, Tex.: Lyndon B. Johnson School of Public Affairs, University of Texas, 1999, policy research report no. 133), 5; *CIVITAS: A Framework for Civic Education,* editorial director Charles N. Quigley, general editor Charles F. Bahmueller (Calabasas, Calif.: Center for Civic Education, 1991); and Harry C. Boyte, "Review of CIVITAS: A Framework for Civic Education," *Teachers College Record* 95, no. 3 (1994), 414–418.
6. Policy Research Project on Civic Education Policies and Practices, *The Civic Education of American Youth,* 24–25.
7. Paul Gagnon, *Educating Democracy,* 26–27, 30; Policy Research Project on Civic Education Policies and Practices, *The Civic Education of American Youth,* 91–92.

8. Policy Research Project on Civic Education Policies and Practices, *The Civic Education of American Youth,* 123.

9. *We the People: The Citizen and the Constitution,* general editor Duane E. Smith (Calabasas, Calif.: Center for Civic Education, 1995).

10. Another We the People supplemental curriculum, *Project Citizen,* introduces middle school students to public policy analysis and the collaborative development of a civic action plan for community improvement. A highly prescriptive handbook is used to complete a multistep process that includes identifying the problem and the level of government with purview, gathering and evaluating information, examining existing public policies, developing public policy, constructing an action plan, and reflecting on what was learned.

11. Here our use of the term "supplemental" includes programs that teachers may choose to use either in class or on a cocurricular (extraclass) basis. The National Issues Forum appears to be largely cocurricular though the network is presently marketing a curriculum kit, "The Campaign for the Classroom 2004." Similarly, Public Achievement has been largely cocurricular though the organization's goal is to embed the program in classrooms. Project 540 is used both inside and outside classrooms. Student Voices is designed expressly for classroom use, as is Active Citizenship Today.

12. Bridget Erlanson and Robert Hildreth, *Building Worlds, Transforming Lives, Making History: A Coach's Guide for Public Achievement,* 2nd ed. (Minneapolis: Center for Democracy and Citizenship, 1998).

13. *Active Citizenship Today Field Guide* (Los Angeles: Constitutional Rights Foundation; Alexandria, Va.: Close Up Foundation, 1994).

14. See Peter C. Scales et al., "The Effects of Service-Learning on Middle School Students' Social Responsibility and Academic Success," *Journal of Early Adolescence* 20, no. 3 (2000): 332–358.

   A peripheral trend in the 1980s, service-learning gained significant impetus and support from federal legislation in the 1990s, the capstone of which was the bipartisan National and Community Service Trust Act of 1993. This law created the Corporation for National Service and the Learn and Serve America program, through which the corporation awards service-learning grants to states and national organizations for selective distribution among school districts and community organizations. About half the states either honor community service or service-learning credits toward graduation or provide appropriations to support such activities. See Katy Anthes, *Institutionalized Service-Learning in the 50 States* (Denver, Colo.: Education Commission of the States, 2001).

15. Hahn, *Becoming Political,* 99.

16. Michael Walzer, "Citizenship," 217, 218.

17. Michael Sandel, *Democracy's Discontent* , 11, 24.

18. Amy Gutmann, "Why Should Schools Care about Civic Education?" 75.

19. Joel Westheimer and Joseph Kahne, "What Kind of Citizen? The Politics of Educating for Democracy," *American Educational Research Journal* 41, no. 2 (2004), 237–269; Table 1, 240. The critical factor that distinguishes education for participatory citizenship from a more politicized, social change conception is the latter's

depth of critical attention to the structural causes of social problems. Westheimer and Kahne call it the "justice-oriented citizen," the third and most advanced category of their typology. We believe, however, that public work citizenship is a more powerful conception, as it embraces the goal of "larger public" building and suggests a set of operational criteria for the justice-oriented conception. For more on public work, see Boyte and Kari, *Building America*; for the "larger public" and the problem of "little publics," see Walter C. Parker, "'Advanced' Ideas about Democracy: Toward a Pluralist Conception of Citizen Education," *Teachers College Record* 98, no. 1 (1996), 104–125.

20. The analysis here focuses on the present generation of youth and young adults, so-called DotNets (alternately dubbed Millennials, Generation Y, Generation NeXt, and Generation Dot.com). Born after 1976, at ages fifteen through twenty-five as of 2002, this cohort numbers about 40 million, according to Scott Keeter et al., *The Civic and Political Health of the Nation,* 6. Some studies conflate Generation Y and younger members of Generation X, the youth cohort born between 1964 and 1976; some eschew these labels, referring simply to "eighteen-to-twenty-four-year-olds" as the category of analysis.

21. Richard G. Niemi and Mitchell S. Sanders, "Assessing Student Performance in Civics: The NAEP 1998 Civics Assessment," *Theory and Research in Social Education* 32, no. 3 (2004), 326-348. As their major focus, Niemi and Sanders put a cautionary flag on the 1998 national civics assessment (NAEP Civics), arguing that "there are major limitations on the insights it can provide about the quality of civic education and the resulting knowledge levels of today's students. How much students are learning, what they are learning, and whether they are learning enough, are not at all clear." One design flaw, for example, is the failure of the test to distinguish between relative areas of strengths and weaknesses in the civic knowledge and skills of students. This analysis also highlights a concern about the meaningfulness of questions students are asked. Elsewhere, comparing NAEP results on student knowledge of civics and government over time, Niemi and his coauthors report "some decline in civic knowledge in the past quarter century" in grades eight and twelve, though they argue that the decline is not catastrophic. Their comparison of the test performance of recent twelfth graders to students in the 1930s through the 1960s shows, though somewhat ambiguously, that contemporary students are stronger on certain civics skills than the earlier students. See Richard G. Niemi, Mitchell S. Sanders, and Dale Whittington, "Civic Knowledge of Elementary and Secondary School Students, 1933-1998," working paper provided by first author, August 2004.

22. See Lutkus et al., *NAEP 1998 Civics Report Card for the Nation,* Table 3.2, 51, and Baldi et al., *What Democracy Means to Ninth-Graders,* 29–30, 40–43. IEA CivEd is an eight-year study of the civic education of adolescents in twenty-eight countries. Comparative data are reported for U.S. ninth graders (fourteen-year-olds) on separate measures of political knowledge and political interpretive skills, and a composite measure of civic competence. It is worth noting, though difficult to interpret, the CivEd finding that U.S. fourteen-year-olds outrank the other nations in interpreting simple messages in political leaflets and cartoons.

23. Suzanne Soule, *We the People . . . The Citizen and the Constitution: Knowledge and Support for Democratic Institutions and Processes by Participating Students: National Finals 2001* (Calabasas, Calif.: Center for Civic Education, 2001).Thomas S.Vontz, Kim K. Metcalf, and John J. Patrick, *Project Citizen and the Civic Development of Adolescent Students in Indiana, Latvia, and Lithuania* (Bloomington, Ind.: ERIC Clearinghouse for Social Studies/Social Science Education, 2000).

24. Delli Carpini and Keeter, *What Americans Know about Politics and Why It Matters,* 272. Delli Carpini and Keeter's over-time trend data reveal persistent knowledge gaps along gender, racial, class, and generational lines; the least-informed citizens "are most likely to be found among . . . women, blacks, the poor and the young" (177); Judith Torney-Purta, "Links and Missing Links between Education, Political Knowledge, and Citizenship," *American Journal of Education* 105 (1997), 446–457.

25. Classroom discussion was a predictor of civic knowledge in the IEA civics education study; see Judith Torney-Purta, "The School's Role in Developing Civic Engagement: A Study of Adolescents in Twenty-eight Countries," *Applied Developmental Science* 6, no. 4 (2002), 203–212.

26. Joseph Adelson and Robert O'Neil, "Growth of Political Ideas in Adolescence: The Sense of Community," *Journal of Personality and Social Psychology* 4, no. 3 (1966), 295–306; Richard Niemi and Mary Hepburn, "The Rebirth of Political Socialization," *Perspectives on Political Science* 24 (winter 1995), 8–16; Constance A. Flanagan, "Volunteerism, Leadership, Political Socialization, and Civic Engagement."

27. Statistics here are from Peter Levine and M. Lopez, *Youth Voter Turnout Has Declined by Any Measure* (College Park, Md.: Center for Information and Research on Civic Learning and Engagement [CIRCLE], University of Maryland School of Public Affairs, 2002); National Association of Secretaries of State, *New Millennium Survey: American Youth Attitudes on Politics, Citizenship, Government and Voting* (Washington, D.C.: NAAS, 1999); and Keeter et al., *The Civic and Political Health of the Nation,* 10, 14, 20.

    Michael X. Delli Carpini, "Gen.Com: Youth, Civic Engagement, and the New Information Environment," working paper, n.d., http://depts.washington.edu/cce/events/carpini.htm.

28. Keeter et al., *The Civic and Political Health of the Nation,* 19–22.

29. See Flanagan, "Volunteerism, Leadership, Political Socialization, and Civil Engagement."

30. Doug McAdam, *Freedom Summer;* M. Kent Jennings, "Generation Units and the Student Protest Movement in the United States: An Intra- and Intergenerational Analysis," *Political Psychology* 23, no. 2 (2002), 303–324.

31. For a pioneering study on extracurricular activities and political involvement, see Paul A. Beck and M. Kent Jennings, "Pathways to Participation," *American Political Science Review* 76, no. 1 (1982), 94–108.

32. See Richard G. Niemi and Chris Chapman, *The Civic Development of 9th- through 12th-grade Students in the United States: 1996* (Washington, D.C.: National Center for Education Statistics, 1999, NCES 1999, 131). Verba, Schlozman, and Brady, *Voice and Equality;* Mary Kirlin, "Civic Skill Building: The Missing Component in Service

Programs?" *PS: Political Science and Politics* 35 (2002), 571–575; and Keeter et al., *The Civic and Political Health of the Nation*, 34.

33. Linda J. Sax et al., *The American College Freshman: National Norms for Fall 2000* (Los Angeles: University of California Higher Education Research Institute, 2000); Higher Education Research Institute, "College Freshmen More Politically Liberal Than in the Past, UCLA Study Reveals," University of California at Los Angeles, press release for *The American Freshman: National Norms for Fall 2001,* January 28, 2002, http://www.eurekalert.org/pub_releases/2002-01/uoc—cfm012802.php.

    National Association of Secretaries of State, *New Millennium Survey*; for a later study showing a similar pattern of low levels of political knowledge and engagement, see North Carolina Civic Education Consortium, Measures of Citizenship: The North Carolina Index (2003), http://ncinfo.iog.unc.edu/programs/civiced/media/finalreportci.htm.

34. See especially Pamela J. Conover and Donald D. Searing, "A Political Socialization Perspective."

35. Shelley H. Billing, "Research on K–12 School-based Service-learning: The Evidence Builds," *Phi Delta Kappan* 81, no. 9 (May 2000), 658–664. See also Flanagan, "Volunteerism, Leadership, Political Socialization, and Civic Engagement"; James L. Perry and Michael C. Katula, "Does Service Affect Citizenship?" *Administration and Society* 33, no. 3 (2001), 330–365; and Mary A. Hepburn, "Service Learning and Civic Education in the Schools."

36. Alan Melchior, *Summary Report: National Evaluation of Learn and Serve America* (Waltham, Mass.: Brandeis University Center for Human Resources, 1999).

37. Tobi Walker, "Service as a Pathway to Political Participation: What Research Tells Us," *Applied Developmental Science* 6, no. 4 (2002), 183–188; Westheimer and Kahne, "What Kind of Citizen?"; Sally Raskoff and Richard A. Sundeen, "Youth Socialization and Civic Participation: The Role of Secondary Schools in Promoting Community Service in Southern California," *Nonprofit and Voluntary Sector Quarterly* 27, no. 1 (1998), 66-87; Harry C. Boyte, "Community Service and Civic Education," *Phi Delta Kappan* 72 (1991), 765-767.

38. Beth A. Covitt, *Middle School Students' Attitudes toward Required Chesapeake Bay Service-Learning* (Washington, D.C.: Corporation for National and Community Service, 2002); Edward Metz and James Youniss, "A Demonstration That School-based Required Service Does Not Deter—But Heightens—Volunteerism," *P.S.: Political Science and Politics* 36, no. 2 (2003), 281-285.

39. Megan Rooney, "Freshmen Show Rising Political Awareness and Changing Social Views," *Chronicle of Higher Education,* January 31, 2003; J. Della Volpe, "Campus Kids: The New Swing Voter," Memorandum, May 21, 2003, Harvard University Institute of Politics, http://www.iop.harvard.edu/iopstudents/survey/spring_2003.pdf. For voting as a means to advance DotNet generational issues, see Alison Bryne Fields, *The Youth Challenge: Participating in Democracy* (New York: Carnegie Corporation of New York, 2003), 3-5.

40. See Cynthia Gibson, *From Inspiration to Participation: A Review of Perspectives on Youth Civic Engagement* (Berkeley, Calif.: Grantmaker Forum on Community and National Service, 2001).

# Bibliography

Barber, Benjamin R. *Strong Democracy: Participatory Politics for a New Age.* Berkeley: University of California Press, 1984.

Barber, Benjamin R. *An Aristocracy of Everyone: The Politics of Education and the Future of America.* New York: Ballantine, 1992.

Barber, Benjamin R. *A Place for Us: How to Make Society Civil and Democracy Strong.* New York: Hill and Wang, 1998.

Boyte, Harry C., and Nancy N. Kari. *Building America: The Democratic Promise of Public Work.* Philadelphia: Temple University Press, 1996.

Colby, Anne, et al. *Educating Citizens: Preparing America's Undergraduates for Lives of Moral and Civic Responsibility.* San Francisco: Wiley, 2003.

Conover, Pamela J., and Donald D. Searing, "A Political Socialization Perspective." In *Rediscovering the Democratic Purposes of Education,* edited by Lorraine M. McDonnell, P. Michael Timpane, and Roger Benjamin, pp. 91–124. Lawrence: University Press of Kansas, 2000.

Damon, William. "To Fade Away: Restoring Civil Identity among the Young." In *Making Good Citizens: Education and Civil Society,* edited by Diane Ravitch and Joseph P. Viteritti, pp. 122–141. New Haven, Conn.: Yale University Press, 2001.

Delli Carpini, Michael X., and Scott Keeter. *What Americans Know About Politics and Why It Matters.* New Haven, Conn.: Yale University Press, 1996.

Gagnon, Paul. *Educating Democracy: State Standards to Ensure a Civic Core.* Washington, D.C.: Albert Shanker Institute, 2003.

Gallatin, Judith. *Democracy's Children: The Development of Political Thinking in Adolescents.* Ann Arbor, Mich.: Quod, 1985.

Gutmann, Amy. *Democratic Education.* Rev. ed. Princeton, N.J.: Princeton University Press, 1999.

Gutmann, Amy. "Why Should Schools Care about Civic Education?" In *Rediscovering the Democratic Purposes of Education,* edited by Lorraine M. McDonnell, P. Michael Timpane, and Roger Benjamin, pp. 73–90. Lawrence: University Press of Kansas, 2000.

Hahn, Carole L. *Becoming Political: Comparative Perspectives on Citizenship Education.* Albany: State University of New York Press, 1998.

Hepburn, Mary A. "Service Learning and Civic Education in the Schools: What Does Recent Research Tell Us?" In *Education for Civic Engagement in Democracy: Service Learning and Other Promising Practices,* edited by Sheila Mann and John J. Patrick, pp. 45–59. Bloomington, Ind.: ERIC Clearinghouse for Social Studies/Social Science Education, 2000.

Keeter, Scott, et al. *The Civic and Political Health of the Nation: A Generational Portrait.* College Park, Md.: Center for Information and Research on Civic Learning and Engagement (CIRCLE), University of Maryland School of Public Affairs, 2002.

Labaree, David F. *How to Succeed in School without Really Learning: The Credentials Race in American Education.* New Haven, Conn.: Yale University Press, 1997.

Macedo, Stephen. *Diversity and Distrust: Civic Education in a Multicultural Democracy.* Cambridge, Mass.: Harvard University Press, 2000.

Mann, Sheila, and John J. Patrick, eds. *Education for Civic Engagement in Democracy: Service Learning and Other Promising Practices.* Bloomington, Ind.: ERIC Clearinghouse for Social Studies/Social Science Education, 2000.

McAdam, Doug. *Freedom Summer.* New York: Oxford University Press, 1988.

McDonnell, Lorraine M., P. Michael Timpane, and Roger Benjamin, eds. *Rediscovering the Democratic Purposes of Education.* Lawrence: University Press of Kansas, 2000.

Nash, Gary B., Charlotte Crabtree, and Ross E. Dunn. *History on Trial: Culture Wars and the Teaching of the Past.* New York: Knopf, 1997.

Nie, Norman H., Jane Junn, and Kenneth Stehlik-Barry. *Education and Democratic Citizenship in America.* Chicago: University of Chicago Press, 1996.

Niemi, Richard G., and Jane Junn. *Civic Education: What Makes Students Learn.* New Haven, Conn.: Yale University Press, 1998.

Putnam, Robert D. *Bowling Alone: The Collapse and Revival of American Community.* New York: Simon and Schuster, 2000.

Ravitch, Diane, and Joseph P. Viteritti, eds. *Making Good Citizens: Education and Civil Society.* New Haven, Conn.: Yale University Press, 2001.

Sandel, Michael J. *Democracy's Discontent: America in Search of a Public Philosophy.* Cambridge, Mass.: Harvard University Press, 1996.

Schudson, Michael. *The Good Citizen: A History of American Civic Life.* New York: M. Kessler, 1998.

Tyack, David, "Preserving the Republic by Educating Republicans." In *Diversity and Its Discontents: Cultural Conflict and Common Ground in Contemporary American Society,* edited by Neil J. Smelser and Jeffrey C. Alexander, pp. 63-83. Princeton, N.J.: Princeton University Press, 1999.

Verba, Sidney, Kay Lehman Schlozman, and Henry E. Brady. *Voice and Equality: Civic Voluntarism in American Politics.* Cambridge, Mass.: Harvard University Press, 1995.

Vinovskis, Maris A. "Missed Opportunities: Why the Federal Response to *A Nation at Risk* Was Inadequate." In *A Nation Reformed?: American Education 20 Years after A Nation at Risk,* edited by David T. Gordon. Cambridge, Mass.: Harvard Education Press, 2003.

Walzer, Michael. "Citizenship." In *Political Innovation and Conceptual Change,* edited by Terence Ball, James Farr, and Russell L. Hanson (Cambridge: Cambridge University Press, 1989), 211-219.

Youniss, James, and Miranda Yates. *Community Service and Social Responsibility in Youth.* Chicago: University of Chicago Press, 1997.

# 7

## WORKING IN SCHOOLS

*Susan Moore Johnson*

" "THE CENTRAL QUESTION POSED BY DEMOCRATIC education," Amy Gutmann contended in 1987, is "Who should have authority to shape the education of future citizens?" (p. 16). While federal, state, and local officials all play their part in determining what schools should teach, it is teachers who have the greatest potential influence on what and how those "future citizens" think. Thus, it is not surprising that questions about the legitimate role of teachers in shaping students' education evoke contentious debate. In *Democratic Education,* Gutmann frames the issue simply: "Do teachers determine what should be taught, or does the public determine what should be taught and hire teachers to do their bidding?" (p. 71).

Students learn about democracy both directly, through the content of their lessons, and indirectly, through the conduct of their classes and school. They learn explicitly about democratic education by studying topics such as First Amendment rights and the electoral process. Deeper lessons about democratic institutions are conveyed implicitly, through what is sometimes called "the hidden curriculum." In their interactions with teachers and their observations about whether their schools encourage faculty and students to exercise voice and influence, these future citizens learn lessons that can last a lifetime.

One can reasonably argue that teachers who have little or no say in determining the policies and practices of their schools cannot effectively educate students to live in a democratic society. For when there are excessive constraints on teachers' authority within the school, students may dismiss lessons about access and equity that are taught in the formal curriculum, absorbing instead lessons about compliance, deference, and impotence that are conveyed by the hidden curriculum.

Terry Moe takes the opposing view, arguing that it is the public's right, not the teachers', to exercise control over its schools: "The public schools are agencies of democratic government, created and controlled by democratic authorities. They are not free to do what they want. Everything about them, from goals to structure to operations, is a legitimate matter for decision by their democratic superiors and subject to influence by the political processes that determine who those superiors are and how they exercise their public authority."[1] From this perspective, schools and their staff are beholden to the government, and thus teachers have no right to make independent decisions. Lorraine McDonnell explains that there has been an "uneasy truce" since the Progressive era between these competing forces of democratic control and professionalism. She elaborates: "Democratic control assumes that as a governmental institution, schools derive their legitimacy from the consent of the electorate," and thus "should be held publicly accountable." It further assumes, she explains, that there should be "externally imposed" constraints on teachers, because they are public employees. However, "professionalism assumes that educators possess a specialized body of knowledge and that, because their work poses complex and nonroutine problems," they should be "guided by a code of ethics internal to their profession."[2]

McDonnell's analysis suggests that there is merit in both Gutmann's and Moe's positions, but in the extreme, each is problematic. If a school is guided solely by teachers' views and operates with cavalier disregard for the priorities of parents and the public, students learn negative lessons about what prospects public life provides for active and effective engagement in their schools. However, if a school discounts teachers and their acquired knowledge about instruction, students learn a different set of lessons—that their teachers act without freedom, judgment, and conviction. Moreover, public education fails to be enriched by teachers' expertise.

The potential impact that either stance might have on curriculum is great as well, for a school that is entirely subject to local, public control, as Moe proposes, may teach unfounded truths such as those of creationism, or it may rely excessively on inadequate modes of teaching, such as rote learning. On the other hand, a curriculum controlled exclusively by teachers, as Gutmann proposes, may disenfranchise a public preferring that lessons be grounded in patriotic rather than global values or that students learn through lectures rather than student discussions or projects. Complete control by either the teacher or the public is arguably unwise, but debate persists about where the balance between the two should be.

Analysts will continue to argue about how best to resolve this issue. The answer to Gutmann's question has no simple answer. However, it is crucial that teachers play a central role in addressing it. For if teachers are ignored or undervalued, if they function only as employees who do the public's bidding, they cannot be good models for their students and teach in ways that encourage independent thought and action. The resolution of this issue will depend greatly on the role, standing, and influence that teachers hold in public education. To the extent that teachers, as a group, are highly regarded, well compensated, and positioned to exercise influence in policy and practice, the balance is likely to shift in their favor. To the extent that teachers are dealt with as inferior workers who are poorly paid and excluded from important decisions in public education, there is likely to be more public control of instructional practice.

The following discussion examines the constellation of factors that, over time, have contributed to the positions and careers that teachers hold. It moves on to review efforts by teachers' unions to improve teachers' pay, working conditions, influence in educational policy and practice, and status in the society. Finally, it examines the characteristics of today's new teachers and the environment they enter. The essay concludes with an analysis of whether, going forward, public education is likely to be controlled by the public or the teachers, and what this might imply for the future of democratic education.

## Subordinate Status of Teachers: Contributing Factors

A variety of factors have interacted over time to establish the role and standing of teachers in U.S. public schools. Some result from features of the job market. Others grow out of the organizational practices and norms of schools. Yet others are a consequence of public policy.

### Teaching as Itinerant, Women's Work

From the early days of the American republic, teaching was short-term, itinerant work, a fact that has long made it hard for teachers to command high pay and respect. In *Schoolteacher: A Sociological Study,* Dan Lortie observed that during the colonial period, "those who taught did so for limited periods of time, for most of them were on the way to something else—ministerial students preparing for a pulpit, indentured servants accumulating the price of their bond. Incomes and prestige were low" (p. 17). With the expansion of urban schooling during the late nineteenth century, teaching gradually became the work of young women. However, like the men who preceded them, these women never committed to teaching as a long-term career, for school districts routinely prohibited women teachers from remaining in the classroom once they were married or became pregnant. It was not until a teacher shortage developed during the 1950s that school districts lifted such restrictions, opening the way for teaching to become a long-term career.[3]

In 1870 two-thirds of all teachers were women; by 1900 women teachers comprised three-fourths of the teaching force.[4] The common assumption was that women were more suitable for teaching and could be paid less. Given women's history of second-class citizenship, it is no surprise that U.S. teachers, 80 percent of whom, in 2004, were women, continued to have second-rate standing. Gary Sykes observed in 1983 that, although teaching "has enjoyed a measure of public esteem and gratitude through the years, . . . there is a long-standing taint associated with teaching and corresponding doubts about those who chose this occupation."[5] That negative view of teaching has, if anything, intensified in the years since Sykes made this comment.

## A Profession Dominated by Administrators

Throughout the history of public schooling in the United States, teachers have held explicitly subordinate positions in a school hierarchy headed by administrators, most of whom have been men.[6] Control of curriculum and school policies remained not in the hands of teachers who carried out the core work of the enterprise, but in the hands of male administrators who managed it. Teachers' subordinate position became especially apparent between 1905 and 1930 when administrators, drawing upon popular practices in business, claimed expertise in "scientific management." Educational "efficiency experts" across the nation, led by influential university faculty such as Ellwood P. Cubberley, dean of the School of Education at Stanford University, assessed schools and the performance of teachers in large school districts. They recommended schemes for rating and paying teachers, based on scales that assessed teachers' appearance, preparation, demeanor, cooperation, and instructional skills. Teachers resented these early approaches to merit pay, but are reported to have tolerated them "meekly."[7] During this period when business practices were in vogue, teachers functioned explicitly as subordinate workers whose job performance was closely monitored and whose independence in doing their work was tightly circumscribed. This hierarchical relationship has largely continued to the present.

## Low Pay

Teachers' low status also has long been reflected in their pay and working conditions, which continue to compare poorly with those of other fields that require comparable training. Research has repeatedly documented that teachers choose teaching for its intrinsic rewards—meaningful work that offers personal satisfaction. Portrayals by the media of good teachers as selfless workers further reinforce the public perception that pay and working conditions matter little to the best of teachers. According to Gerald Grant and Christine Murray, the public expects a "true teacher" to exhibit "professional altruism," which is often taken to mean being satisfied with a salary that is considerably lower than that earned by individuals with comparable education. A 2000 report by Public Agenda expressed a similar sentiment when reporting on survey responses by teachers.[8]

Although many teachers express the belief that teaching is a calling, rather than simply a job, pay and respect also matter. They rarely report that they have entered teaching for the pay and certainly do not expect to get rich on a teacher's salary. However, they do anticipate having a secure job and living a middle-class life. Low pay surely dissuades many prospective teachers from considering a career in teaching and drives out novice teachers when they discover that they cannot buy a home or educate children on a teacher's salary.[9]

Until the mid-1900s, elementary teachers, who were virtually all women, earned less than secondary teachers, the majority of whom were men. Administrators, almost all male, also earned more than teachers. Today, salary discrepancies no longer exist between elementary and secondary teachers within a district, and in some school districts, principals earn little more than the teachers at the top of the salary scale. Based on salary comparisons with teachers in other countries, researchers in 1999 concluded that "American teachers are well paid."[10] However, U.S. teachers still find that their pay compares poorly with that of peers who have attained a bachelor's degree and are employed in other lines of work. An analysis conducted by *Education Week* in 2000 shows that the 1994 salary gap between teachers with bachelor's degrees and nonteachers with bachelor's degrees was $11,035. Just four years later, in 1998, this gap was $18,006. For master's degree recipients, the analogous salary gap between teachers and nonteachers was $12,918 in 1994 and $24,648 in 1998. Further, in 1998 young teachers (ages twenty-two to twenty-eight) with only a bachelor's degree earned an average of $21,792, which was $8,192 less than their nonteaching peers.[11]

A report from the National Center for Education Statistics also provides evidence that teachers have lost ground to their nonteaching peers in the area of salary. Among bachelor's degree recipients who graduated in 1992–1993 and were working full time five years later, teachers had the lowest annual salaries of their college cohort. Many teachers today find that they cannot afford to teach on the wages they earn, unless they are subsidized by a partner's income.[12]

## Public Funding and Public Accountability

Low pay and its corollary, low status, indirectly limit teachers' role in determining how schools educate students. Because teachers' salaries are publicly funded, there are inevitable limits on what they can be paid, a fact that has implications for the autonomy they are afforded in their work. Although the process of collective bargaining has standardized pay for teachers,[13] local budgets restrict negotiated salary settlements. Cities and towns often require that officials establish equity with other groups of public service employees, such as firefighters and police, making it virtually impossible for teachers to achieve financial standing and status comparable to that held by professionals in other fields, such as engineering, finance, medicine, or law.

Since teachers' salaries are funded with tax dollars, citizens at both the local and state levels claim the right to hold teachers accountable for their work. Formally, this responsibility is exercised by central office administrators, appointed by publicly elected school boards. Although many who analyze teachers' work note that they can teach however they choose once their classroom door is closed, the autonomy they exercise within those walls is unintentionally, not deliberately, granted by administrators. Also, this autonomy is somewhat illusory in that the scope of teachers' independence is limited; often teachers are not permitted to choose their own textbooks or select instructional equipment and supplies.

In the mid-1980s, teachers started to challenge their subordinate status through their unions. Ironically, though, relying on collective bargaining—a formally structured, legally sanctioned process—to achieve higher standing calls attention to the fact that teaches are public employees who are publicly paid and publicly accountable for their work.

## Working Conditions

Although teachers are often criticized for their short workdays and long summer vacations, their assignments and schedules are in fact intense and demanding. At the elementary level, teachers spend six or seven hours each day instructing classes of 20 to 35 students. Secondary school teachers often teach five classes of 20 to 30 students each day, for a total student load of 100 to 150 students. Elementary school teachers typically are responsible for preparing lessons in all major subjects, and secondary school teachers typically must prepare for two or three different courses with several sections each. There are few breaks in a teacher's day and lunch is often no more than twenty to thirty minutes. Teachers cannot do a good job in the classroom without committing more time after official school hours planning for the next day's classes, gathering materials, and grading students' work, time that must come from evenings and weekends. The relentless schedule and intense demands of working with so many students in an institutional setting make teaching exhausting work, no matter how exhilarating or rewarding it might be.

Teachers work in settings that are arguably substandard, particularly when compared with those in many other lines of work. Colonial-era teachers were responsible for heating their classrooms and had to make do with primitive supplies. Although most teachers today are not expected to carry out basic custodial services, schools often fail to provide a setting for teaching that is well maintained and adequately supplied. Many teachers lack basic instructional supplies and equipment, such as chemicals for experiments or specimens for dissection in science; up-to-date texts in history; current maps in geography; graphing calculators in mathematics. Classrooms commonly lack phones, computers that are wired to the Internet, and clocks that work. Schools often have but one photocopy machine, which routinely is in disrepair, even though teachers who lack curriculum materials must rely on it for teaching day to day. Despite their relatively low pay, teachers routinely spend their own money to meet basic classroom needs—food to feed the class gerbils, paperback books to stock the in-class library, shiny stickers to reward students for good work, crayons, paints, and even lined paper for student work. A 2002 survey revealed that, on average, a first-year elementary school teacher spends $701 of her own money on classroom materials.[14] This figure probably underestimates what teachers who work in severely underfunded schools spend. Such deficiencies signal the public's lack of support for schooling and a prevailing disrespect for teachers' work. Students who observe these attitudes might well question whether the work that their teachers do is important.

## Organization of Schools

The organizational structure of schools, which is flat and undifferentiated, also contributes indirectly to teachers' lack of standing and influence in public education. Schools today have their origins in the one-room schoolhouse of colonial America, when each school was a single classroom, and each classroom housed one teacher and a multi-aged group of students. When the cities began to grow and student enrollments expand in the mid-1800s, public support grew for grouping students by age, and communities created what has come to be called the "egg-crate school," where classrooms were assembled in rows, sometimes stacked several floors high. The organizing principle of one teacher, one classroom, persists, and teachers continue to work in isolation. Dan Lortie observed in 1969 that "throughout the long formative decades of the modern school system," in which the "multiple-unit school" developed, "schools were organized around teacher separation rather than teacher interdependence." Lortie likened this expansion to the undifferentiated cellular growth of an organism and observed that school administrators dealt with schools as "aggregates of classroom units, as collections of independent cells," rather than as "tightly integrated organisms."[15]

This egg-crate approach to organizing teachers and schools has had far-reaching implications for management, teaching, and learning. Having a collection of independent classroom units made it easier for school boards and administrators to manage the growth and decline of student populations, because they could either add or close a classroom, one unit at a time. However, the administrative convenience that this organizational structure provided came at a price, since it required that teachers be trained and dealt with as interchangeable workers, who could be called upon to do the same task (adjusting for age or subject specialty) wherever they were assigned. Teachers were not expected to distinguish themselves as individuals equipped with specialized skills for particular schools, but rather to quickly adapt to generic assignments. Since it first emerged, this rather primitive organizational structure has been incredibly hardy; most schools today continue to function according to its principles. As a result, teachers' work is far more often independent than interdependent, and schools are much less coherent and effective organizations than they might be.

One consequence of this organizational structure for teachers has been that the principal, rather than the teachers, retains control over policy and practice. Teachers are expected to focus on their classroom rather than the whole school, and their formal influence seldom extends beyond that domain. Students rarely see their teachers enacting the kind of participation in the larger school setting that those same teachers may espouse in their classes.

Thus, the traditional egg-crate school prolongs teachers' isolation and subordinate standing in public education. Despite their advanced training, teachers continue to function as employees who have little say in how their schools will work. Most schools treat teachers as replaceable workers with minimal, generic skills, rather than as specialists with advanced training who could assume expert roles in school reform. It is important to note that most teachers, themselves, have long stressed their responsibilities as classroom teachers rather than as agents of school improvement and, thus, have perpetuated this arrangement.

## An Undifferentiated Career

One of the most striking features about the career of teaching is that it is so uniform. It is often said that teachers have the same assignment—classroom teaching—on the first and last days of their career. When teaching was short-term, itinerant work, this was understandable, since individuals could move in and out of teaching positions with little special preparation. However, between 1960 and 2000, teaching became a lifelong career for a large cohort of teachers, leading some to question the wisdom of maintaining an undifferentiated career.

A career ladder or a set of differentiated roles might sustain teachers over time. More important, identifying and compensating experienced, expert teachers who are prepared and authorized to play a greater role in decision making might greatly enhance teachers' influence in school governance and elevate them as models for their students. Although a case can be made that administrators have withheld opportunities for teachers to decide important matters of school policy and practice—for example, by limiting a school-site council's scope of authority—it is also clear that teachers' undifferentiated career is, in part, self-imposed. Wary of patronage and administrative favoritism that thrived in the early decades of public education, teachers as a group have long supported rules designed to ensure that they will be treated uniformly.[16] Thus, teaching assignments and pay have been regulated by standardized rules and seniority-based criteria, and in the name of equity, teachers have denied themselves opportunities for advancement and expanded influence.

Researchers who studied teachers' views of their careers in the 1970s and 1980s confirmed that teachers expressed more interest in developing instructional competence within their classrooms than advancing professionally in a broader arena. In response to school reformers' proposals for career ladders in the mid-1980s, Milbrey McLaughlin and Sylvia Yee explored teachers' conceptions of a teaching career. They wondered whether the "vertical" careers and differentiated roles proposed by reformers would interest teachers. They distinguished between two conceptions of career, one defined by the institution and another by the individual. The first, they explained, is "conceived in largely external terms of vertical mobility," while the second is more subjective and takes "meaning from personal motivations and goals." McLaughlin and Yee concluded that the eighty-five teachers they interviewed did not aspire to greater levels of responsibility, influence, and compensation, but rather found satisfaction in, and built their careers within, the classroom, seeking to achieve depth rather than breadth of influence.[17] Administrators and school officials who view teachers as employees obliged to comply with public orders rather than free to expand their influence as educators can find support in teachers' own reluctance to extend their authority.

## A Limited and Contested Knowledge Base

If teaching was fully grounded in a widely respected knowledge base and teachers were known to have specialized expertise, they might be accorded more status and granted a greater say in decisions about curriculum and pedagogy. In turn, they might be more likely to teach in ways that encourage students to think for themselves and confidently address society's problems. However, compared with a field such as medicine, the knowledge base of education is underdeveloped and contested. Based on what Linda Darling-Hammond calls the "apprenticeship of experience," many adults believe that they know how to teach simply because they once attended school.[18]

Lortie observed that teachers' special expertise rests in knowing effective pedagogy, rather than knowing the content of the subjects they teach. It is historians, not high school history teachers, who are seen as experts in the discipline. Meanwhile, publicly elected education officials debate whether history should be taught as a compendium of facts (dates of wars or names of explorers) or as a sequence of complex social movements, and although teachers may present informed views about this, their answers are not grounded in solid research findings. Before 1980, there was little systematic study of how best to teach and, although steady progress has been made in some subject areas since then, the knowledge base of teaching remains scant and, thus, teachers' views about what and how they teach are readily contested.

Moreover, even when good evidence exists about effective teaching practice, for example, in the field of bilingual education or literacy, that evidence is frequently rejected or ignored if it does not conform to public priorities and predispositions. In this regard, U.S. teachers are at a special disadvantage, for they must contend with or adjust to the inclinations and interests of nearly fifteen thousand local school boards and their appointed administrators. In other countries, such as Japan or France, where education is far more centralized and policies are set by nationally appointed experts, instructional strategies are more widely endorsed and teachers are thus regarded as having the knowledge and authority they need to do their work without the daily oversight of local public agencies and citizens.[19]

## Teachers' Unions and Teachers' Work

The constellation of factors described above reinforces the image of teachers as deferential, compliant employees rather than as confident, outspoken advocates of instructional excellence. In such circumstances, the lesson that the hidden curriculum teaches students is clear: doing well in school requires submission and conformity. These factors are also somewhat self-fulfilling in that teaching, on the whole, does not attract and retain individuals who hold independent views or are inclined to challenge the authority of the state or school officials to specify what and how they should teach.

Despite this conservative force within their ranks, some teachers have sought to advance their standing and expand their influence through their unions. These organizations and their leaders have, in some cases, sought to protect teachers by limiting the scope of their responsibilities and ensuring uniform treatment, while in other cases, they have tried to expand teachers' domain of influence, develop differentiated roles, and promote greater control of public education by educators.

Teacher unions and their role in public education have been severely criticized by those who would deny teachers greater influence and control in public education. Calling unions the "'500 pound gorillas' in the educational arena," Terry Moe contends that they are self-interested organizations that concern themselves excessively with "job security, working conditions, and collective bargaining rights." Moe argues that such priorities are wrongheaded: "What is good for unions is not necessarily what is good for children or for education." Gutmann, however, argues that through their unions, teachers can "cultivat[e] the capacity for democratic deliberation" and resist the oppression of those who require schools to "perpetuate the beliefs held by dominant majorities."[20]

### The Growth of Unions

Since the late nineteenth century, union organizers have drawn attention to teachers' low pay, inadequate working conditions, and inability to control their work. Early reformers were at once classroom teachers and feminists, and their labor movement was concurrent with the campaign for woman suffrage. Unquestionably, the most influential of all early union organizers was Maggie Haley, a Chicago teacher of twenty years' experience who organized the Chicago Federation of Teachers (CFT) in 1889. In making the case for teacher unions, Haley made no distinction between efforts to improve the lot of teachers and efforts to improve schools for children. What benefited one, she argued, would benefit the other; if teaching did not satisfy teachers' basic personal needs, they would discontinue their work with children. While they were striving to improve their salaries and working conditions, Haley urged her fellow teachers to "take up the knapsack of service," by supporting social causes that would improve the lot of children and their families.

Organizing teachers proved to be challenging work for early union leaders. In 1916 the Chicago Board of Education denied Haley's CFT the right to affiliate with a trade union and fired sixty-eight teachers, including all the CFT officers. The board publicly branded Haley and her associates as "lady labor sluggers," and thus "conveyed the image that these foes of entrenched privilege themselves served a 'special interest' detrimental to the public good."[21] Moreover, some organizations that appeared to represent teachers' interests did not. Between 1857, when the precursor of the National Education Association, now the largest national teachers' union, was formed, and the mid-twentieth century, the NEA was deliberately maintained as a professional association, including both administrators and teachers as members. Although the NEA language implied that teachers had elevated professional standing, that was not so. Teachers did not run this professional association, and control remained in the hands of male administrators and college professors through the 1950s.

By the mid-1960s, however, the NEA was competing vigorously for new members with the American Federation of Teachers (AFT), avowedly a union. The NEA shifted its focus from administrative matters to the concerns of classroom teachers, and began to behave more like a traditional union. At the same time, teachers in a number of states won the right to bargain collectively, and they negotiated early contracts specifying teachers' hours, work responsibilities, and pay. Gradually, collective bargaining gained acceptance among teachers as a means to control at least the basic elements of their work.

The model for collective-bargaining statutes was the 1935 National Labor Relations Act, which regulates private-sector labor practices. The adversarial relations between teachers and administrators that were established by statute further institutionalized a management-controlled hierarchy in public education in which teachers were subordinates. The template for the process that regulated the creation of teacher unions and the process of collective bargaining was crafted with the needs of industry, not schools, in mind. Like the factory, schools have supervisors and subordinate workers, bound in a formal, hierarchical work relationship. However, unlike workers on the assembly line, teachers necessarily must exercise discretion in their work if they are to do their job well. This is largely because the "raw materials" of schooling—students—are varied and unpredictable, while the process of pedagogy is far more difficult to specify than are the tasks of skilled workers on an assembly line.

Despite the professional aspirations of teachers and the unique nature of their work, union leaders in the 1960s and 1970s modeled their approaches to collective bargaining on the confrontational practices that worked for industrial labor leaders. Meanwhile, school managers, charged with representing the public in negotiations, were far less prepared for the process of collective bargaining than their union counterparts. As a result, school boards and administrators all too often relinquished important management prerogatives and acquiesced to the use of conventional labor decision rules in education, most notably the use of seniority in determining teachers' assignments.

As states passed labor statutes mandating collective bargaining with teachers, they designated the range of topics that management could be required to negotiate, typically, wages, hours, and working conditions. Certain topics, such as layoff procedures, were widely interpreted to be within the legal scope of bargaining. Others, such as class size limits or the school calendar, often were disputed. However, throughout the first three decades of collective bargaining, broader educational concerns about issues such as curriculum, school governance procedures, and the budget were widely agreed to be the province of management and, thus, to be beyond the legal limits of collective bargaining.

Therefore, while successful union organizing won for teachers the right to bargain about the conditions of their work, it also explicitly denied them the right to control—and sometimes even to participate in—decisions about curriculum, instruction, and the use of educational funds. Charles Kerchner and Douglas Mitchell noted in 1988 that the formally defined scope of bargaining was very important symbolically. It "became the substitute for the doctrine of sovereignty, a way of asserting that collective bargaining had not contaminated the policymaking process. A legal line is drawn between contract and policy."[22] Thus, a tightly defined scope of bargaining reinforces the rights of management, ensuring that the public, not teachers, control educational policy.

It is important to note, however, that at the local level, where teachers' contracts are negotiated, labor and management did not always abide by the state's defined scope of bargaining, and contracts often dealt with issues that were technically off limits, such as teachers' right to participate in textbook selection. In a 1979 study titled *Organized Teachers in American Schools,* Lorraine McDonnell and Anthony Pascal found that those who negotiated contracts often were not aware of the legal scope of bargaining in the prevailing statute, and they bargained about whatever they chose to. As a result, the actual scope of bargaining expanded over time, primarily as a consequence of local practice, not legislation.

There is no doubt that collective bargaining has increased the leverage that teachers and their unions have on school officials' decisions. Once a contract is signed and ratified, it places demands for compliance on both district administrators and school site principals. Because a contract applies to all teachers within the bargaining unit (which coincides with the school district), that contract specifies practices for an entire school district. Consequently, individual schools are discouraged or prohibited from devising their own ways of operating. Researchers studying the impact of teacher contracts on the schools have found that these formal agreements tend to standardize practice across schools, centralize administration of the district, and promote conformity among both teachers and administrators.[23]

Individual schools that set out to create their own workplace rules may find this problematic in a unionized district, although not impossible. For there is also considerable evidence that exactly the same contract language can be interpreted differently by different districts. Moreover, within the same district, schools can vary substantially in how they implement particular provisions.[24] For example, a district's contract may call for establishing a school-based faculty senate at each school, yet one school within the district may have an active and influential senate, another may have a senate that barely functions, and a third may have no faculty senate at all.

Repeatedly, the school principal has been shown to be the key agent in determining what effect a teachers' contract will have at a particular school. In 1979, McDonnell and Pascal concluded: "Truly effective principals usually accept collective bargaining and use the contract both to manage their building more systematically and to increase teacher participation in school decision making. Less effective principals may view the contract as an obstacle to a well-run school and then use it as an excuse for poor management" (p. 81). In her 1984 text *Teacher Unions in Schools,* Susan Moore Johnson studied six school districts and found that few contract provisions were fully implemented throughout the schools of any district, "most being subject to interpretation, amendment, or informal renegotiation at the school site" (p. 165). Therefore, a principal with a collaborative bent might engage teachers in adapting the contract provisions to meet their school's and students' needs.

It is the grievance procedures of a contract—often called the "heart of the contract" by union leaders—that give teachers the power to enforce its terms. There is considerable evidence that teachers try to avoid adversarial interactions with administrators and, thus, most are reluctant to file grievances, even in the face of obvious contract violations. Except in unusually hostile circumstances, the number of grievances actually filed is very small. However, the threat of a grievance can, in itself, provoke compliance by a principal wanting to avoid conflict. In 1984 Douglas Mitchell dubbed grievances "communication mechanisms," and explained that they force management to pay attention to issues that they might rather ignore.

It is difficult to know, on the basis of formal challenges, to what extent collective bargaining has compromised management's authority and, thus by extension, the public's interest. Some critics, such as Myron Lieberman and Terry Moe, argue that the effect has been far-reaching and negative. Kerchner and Mitchell, however, contend that in some cases collective bargaining actually has heightened the profile and influence of management in public education: "Managers often find that the new rules work in their favor and proceed to use them aggressively. In some respects, management authority increases. At least the attention given to explicitly managing schools increases, as does the recognition of school administrators as 'managerial.'"[25]

Before the mid-1980s, some principals chose to engage teachers in decisions about matters such as student assignments, professional development, and curriculum, but they were not obliged to do so. Teachers were only entitled to file grievances about an alleged violation of some specific provision in their contract, for example, a procedural error in how their principal conducted an evaluation. Because most contracts did not address matters of instruction or school governance, teachers had no formal grounds to protest actions taken about such matters, for example, banning a text or hiring an unqualified teacher. However, things began to change in the mid-1980s.

## Efforts to Professionalize Teaching, 1985–2000

When the federal government issued *A Nation at Risk: The Imperative for Educational Reform* in 1983, the work and career of teaching had changed little since the mid-1950s. Teachers continued to work alone, seemingly independently, in their classrooms, yet they had little authority to control the basic aspects of their work or to improve their workplace. Responding to the report's warnings about "a rising tide of mediocrity" in public education, states and local districts widely adopted policies designed to regulate teaching. However, not only were efforts to compel teachers to follow prescribed curricula incomplete and largely ineffectual, students' performance improved little, if at all. In response, some reformers turned to teachers as the agents, rather than the objects, of reform.

Initiatives to increase teachers' influence in the mid-1980s were grounded in assumptions about the teacher's legitimate role in directing reform in public education, and were fueled by the conviction that schools would not improve until teachers had a greater say in what changes were warranted. Thus reformers devised a strategy whereby teachers would gain autonomy and control of instructional practice in exchange for adhering to standards of instructional practice. At the time, Gary Sykes explained: "A profession agrees to develop and enforce standards of good practice in exchange for the right to practice free of bureaucratic supervision and external regulation. At the policy level, this contract applies to standards for licensure, certification, and program accreditation. . . . At the practice level, this contract applies to the organization and management of work. Collegial norms and peer evaluation direct work that is amenable neither to administrative oversight nor to routinization."[26] Sykes proposed that teachers' work should be organized to encourage greater collegiality, more reliance on shared norms, and increased attention to the specialized knowledge and skills of teachers. Given the history of teaching as subordinated, regulated work, this proposed trade of autonomy for adherence to professional standards was unprecedented. If fully implemented, it would fundamentally change the teacher's role and the conduct of schooling, with students and the public as the ultimate beneficiaries.

Broad coalitions of teacher union leaders, teacher educators, education scholars, politicians, and prominent businesspeople formed several key alliances to advance the standing and influence of teachers. The most noteworthy of these was the Task Force on Teaching as a Profession, sponsored in 1985 by the Carnegie Forum on Education and the Economy and composed of leaders from business, government, and teacher unions. This group's report, *A Nation Prepared: Teachers for the 21ˢᵗ Century,* emphasized the importance of autonomy for teachers, noting that "if the schools are to compete successfully with medicine, architecture, and accounting for staff, then teachers will have to have comparable authority in making the key decisions about the services they render" (p. 58). Calling for teachers to assume greater leadership in their schools, the report likened teaching to a profession and noted that "in most professional organizations those who are most experienced and highly skilled play the lead role in guiding the activity of others" (p. 58). Thus, between 1985 and 2000, coalitions of reformers joined to advance a far-reaching agenda—creating an advanced level of teacher certification; introducing local peer review and career ladders for teachers; and decentralizing school governance and granting teachers greater influence in matters of school policy and practice. Notably, often these were developed and adopted within the context of collective bargaining.

### Creating a System of Advanced Certification

*A Nation Prepared* called for creating a National Board for Professional Teaching Standards (NBPTS), which would "establish high standards for what teachers need to know and be able to do, and ... certify teachers who meet that standard." Teachers who achieved this advanced level of certification could subsequently serve as lead teachers in their schools, "guid[ing] and influence[ing] the activity of others, ensuring that the skill and energy of their colleagues [would be] drawn on as the organization improve[d] its performance" (p. 56).

Over the next decade, this idea became a reality. By 2004 the NBPTS had developed performance-based assessments of teachers' work in twenty-seven instructional fields. A majority of the board's members were classroom teachers, in keeping with plans to create a self-regulated occupation. By 2004 the national board had certified thirty-two thousand "accomplished" teachers.[27] The board has received many accolades for its accomplishments, but opponents criticize both the assessment process, which they contend favors a constructivist, student-centered approach to instruction, and the large sums of federal money that have funded the initiative.[28] Many states and local districts offer substantial financial incentives and recognition for board-certified teachers. Among the most generous are those granted by North Carolina, which increases by 12 percent the portion of board-certified teachers' salaries paid by the state, and Mississippi, which pays teachers who achieved advanced certification an additional $6,000 per year for the ten-year life of the certificate. The vision of a teaching career advanced by *A Nation Prepared* would have board-certified teachers assuming leadership roles and transforming their schools into learning organizations. However, the number of certified teachers remains relatively small. Even if the board were to achieve its 2000 goal of certifying one hundred thousand teachers by 2006, that would still be considerably less than 5 percent of the teaching ranks. Also, teachers who have achieved advanced certification tend to be clustered in suburban rather than urban districts, thus potentially increasing the gap in teacher quality between wealthy and low-income communities. As yet, few local districts have developed roles for board-certified teachers, a practice that might do a great deal to advance and institutionalize collegial control of teaching. Lacking such roles, most board-certified teachers simply return to their classrooms, accepting the limited influence that schools traditionally grant classroom teachers. Even though the NBPTS developed the means to certify large numbers of accomplished teachers, the task force's vision for teacher leadership has not been fully realized.

## Introducing Peer Review and Career Ladders

While the NBPTS was developing its assessments, local union leaders and school administrators in some districts experimented with ways for teachers to exert greater control over entry into teaching. Starting in 1983, a small number of unionized districts began to experiment with new approaches to collective bargaining that encouraged labor-management collaboration. The resulting policies and programs expanded teachers' roles in the induction and assessment of their peers.[29]

Toledo, Ohio, is the site of the first and longest-running peer-review plan in the United States, created jointly by labor and management in 1981.[30] A committee of teachers and administrators oversees the program, selecting and training a group of experienced teachers who serve full-time for two years as mentors and evaluators of novice teachers. These peer reviewers, who spend months closely supervising new teachers' work and modeling expert practice, eventually recommend whether the novices should be re-employed or terminated. With few exceptions, their recommendations hold. After several years, peer reviewers also began to assist and assess experienced teachers who had been judged by peers or administrators to be in need of assistance.

Peer assistance and review in Toledo gained respect and recognition for two reasons. In a cost-effective manner, it provided the support that new teachers needed in order to succeed in the classroom and it enabled the district to dismiss ineffective teachers. As a result, Toledo's plan served as the model for comparable programs in Cincinnati, Rochester, Columbus, and other districts.

Notably, this was the first time that classroom teachers, led by their unions, had assessed their peers and recommended re-employment or termination. For those who opposed unions and the move toward increasing teachers' control of schooling, these programs breached the boundary dividing the responsibilities of school officials from those of teachers and their union. There was also opposition from many union leaders, who objected because peer assistance and review plans seemed to violate deeply held beliefs about equity among teachers, which would preclude teachers from assessing one another.

In Rochester, New York, union president Adam Urbanski and superintendent Peter McWalters not only created a peer-review plan modeled on the Toledo plan, but also established a career ladder, which had several steps for teachers with increasing levels of experience and expertise. They introduced the position of lead teacher—first proposed by the Task Force on Teaching as a Profession—for those who would be peer reviewers in Rochester's Peer Assistance and Review Program. When their 1987 contract was approved, teachers' salaries had increased by 40 percent, and lead teachers could make as much as $70,000 a year, an unprecedented wage at the time. [31]

Although a very small number of districts were adopting collaborative approaches to collective bargaining and creating reforms meant to elevate the standing and influence of teachers, the rest were settling their contract disputes with conventional, confrontational approaches drawn from industry. Rather than redefining roles and creating new programs, they were splitting the difference between extreme positions laid down by each side. Instead of collaborating candidly to solve educational problems shared by all, they concealed their interests, dissembled about their intentions, and held out to wrest greater concessions from the other side. As a result, contracts that spell out the details of management rights and narrowly define teachers' responsibilities perpetuate the image of teachers as public employees and laborers. [32]

## Decentralizing School Governance

While union reformers in Rochester, Toledo, and Cincinnati were developing peer assistance and review programs and career ladders, their counterparts in Miami-Dade, Florida, were introducing shared decision-making councils in their schools, which included teachers, administrators, and parents. [33] Also called school-based management committees or school-site councils in other districts, they were introduced as a mechanism for moving more decisions about policy and practice from the district office to the schools. In a small number of districts, school-site councils gained substantial authority for hiring staff and for allocating the nonpersonnel part of the budget. When school-site management was approved through collective bargaining, teachers typically claimed the majority of seats on such councils. However, in some districts, such as Boston, principals held veto power, even though teachers had the majority of votes.

School-based management proved to be a much more popular reform than peer assistance and review or career ladders, both because it was easier to initiate and because it did not challenge any traditional union values. Thus, by the early 1990s many districts had formally devolved more decision-making authority to the schools, although in practice, district offices often withheld the budgetary control that had been promised. In most districts, school-site council members were unprepared and sometimes unwilling to make decisions. Frequently, they became enmeshed in the details of administration and school maintenance and seldom addressed more central concerns of instructional policy and practice. In 1994 Rodney Ogawa and Paula White concluded that there was "little evidence that [school-based management] has significantly enhanced conditions in schools and districts or improved students' academic performance."[34]

One rationale for school-based management was that teachers would be far more likely to embrace reforms that they had participated in fashioning. However, there is not much evidence that teachers managed to achieve greater control of their schools as a result of this reform. Analyzing principals' responses to a question on the 1990–1991 Schools and Staffing Survey about the extent of teachers' authority in "decisions concerning curriculum, discipline, and hiring in schools," Richard Ingersoll found that "in comparison to principals, teachers appear to have had limited professional authority over these school educational decisions."[35]

Charter schools, a subsequent reform that embodied the principles of school-site management, also had the promise of giving teachers greater influence in their school. A small number of charter schools are teacher-run and some do grant teachers considerable say in policy and practice. However, many are tightly controlled by administrators—some being managed externally by for-profit corporations—and they afford teachers even less influence and assurance of fair treatment than most conventional schools.[36]

### The Current State of Union Reform

It is difficult to sum up the overall impact of fifteen years of negotiated reforms, largely because it is so uneven. Some local districts have introduced a range of progressive changes augmenting the teacher's role in decision-making, both in the schools and at the district level. They have acknowledged the shared interests of teachers and administrators, by establishing joint labor-management committees to solve problems and oversee programs. They have affirmed the importance of nonstandardized, flexible practices by granting school sites greater autonomy and reducing the role of seniority in staffing decisions. They have created differentiated roles for expert teachers as peer reviewers, lead teachers, mentors, and coaches.

However, many other districts have advanced little beyond the industrial practices and adversarial relations typical of educational collective bargaining from the start. These districts continue to draw firm lines between the rights and interests of teachers and management. They promote standardized practices for all schools and individuals. They treat teachers as an undifferentiated group of similarly skilled workers, no matter what their training, experience, or expertise.[37] They reinforce the culture of schools as industrial rather than democratic workplaces.

Management has promoted a far more collaborative relationship with teachers in some districts than in others. However, many local teacher unions also have done their part to resist labor-management collaboration, preferring instead to maintain traditional, confrontational relationships. Experienced teachers, too, have proven less willing than reformers initially expected they would be to actively engage in reforms and to assume increased responsibility for their schools.[38] Notably, however, as the cohort of teachers who have encountered and often resisted reform since 1985 approach retirement, it is important to ask whether tomorrow's teachers will be more inclined to exercise leadership in their schools than their predecessors were. To answer that, we must know who those new teachers will be and what they are likely to value and do.

## The Next Generation

The cohort of teachers who now approach retirement were hired between the mid-1960s and mid-1970s, a time when many professions were not open or welcoming to women and people of color. As a result, public education attracted many well-educated individuals at relatively low wages, a phenomenon that has been called the "hidden subsidy" of education. Unlike their predecessors, women who entered teaching at this time were permitted to continue working after marriage and childbearing and, as a result, this cohort of teachers became the first in U.S. history to make teaching a lifelong career.[39]

Prospective teachers today have many more career choices than the retiring generation of teachers had when they were hired. Like their counterparts in other fields, new teachers today are far less likely than they would have been in the 1960s or 1970s to make a lifetime commitment to any career. In fact, serial careers have become the norm rather than the exception in American society, and there is increasing evidence that teaching during the early decades of the twenty-first century will reflect that trend. In fact, attrition rates among new teachers, largely driven by low pay and poor working conditions, are extremely high and seem to be accelerating. In 2003 researchers found that, nationally, approximately one-third of new teachers leave within three years of entry, one-half within five years.

A four-year study of fifty new teachers reveals that remarkably few expected to make a long-term commitment to classroom teaching. Only three of the respondents in this study had entered teaching as a first career and planned to be teachers until they retired. Those who had entered teaching tentatively intended to explore the possibility of staying longer. If they found teaching rewarding they would stay, but if not, they would move on to another field. Other new teachers entered the classroom planning to contribute to public education for a few years before moving on to other work. Many participants intended to remain in education—but not the classroom—for the rest of their careers. They hoped that, after teaching for several years, they might become administrators or take on hybrid roles that would allow them to teach part-time while also serving as curriculum writers, mentors, or professional developers, roles that districts have only begun to establish and refine. After four years, seventeen of these fifty respondents had left their jobs as public school teachers, and many others expressed doubts that they would stay. In their tentative commitment to classroom teaching, this new cohort differs significantly from that of their retiring colleagues, who entered teaching as a first career and remained full-time classroom teachers over time.[40]

There is considerable evidence in this study and others that teachers leave the classroom because of poor working conditions—inappropriate or excessively difficult teaching assignments; insufficient curriculum, supplies, and equipment; student disorder and ineffective discipline policies; isolation from colleagues; and lack of influence in school governance. Many entrants to teaching today are accustomed to working in teams and they express dismay at the extent of isolation they encounter in their schools, which continue to have an egg-crate organizational structure. Teachers who are dissatisfied with their schools often blame administrators for neglecting their responsibilities, being authoritarian, or playing favorites, while those who are satisfied often attribute their school's effectiveness to a collaborative, well-organized principal who understands good teaching.

An increasing proportion of new teachers today enter the classroom through alternative routes, which offer substantially abbreviated pre-service training. Often such fast-track programs provide five to seven weeks of summer coursework and student teaching, much less than the academic year typically required by university-based programs. These programs are attractive, particularly for mid-career entrants, because they are inexpensive and reduce the time it takes to move into a paid teaching position. They are designed to encourage job-embedded learning, by moving much of the training and support for new teachers into the schools. Often, however, that on-the-job training and support fail to materialize. Given the brief coursework and uneven induction practices, participants in alternative certification programs are less likely than traditionally trained teachers to become informed about the knowledge base in education. And the proliferation of fast-track programs may further diminish rather than enhance the public's regard for the specialized expertise of teaching.

In the coming years, much more evidence will emerge about the character of the next generation of teachers. Initial research suggests, however, that they come to teaching expecting to have opportunities for growth and career development, to exercise influence beyond their classrooms, and to have their pay reflect, in some way, their skills and accomplishments. If schools are organized to promote interdependence rather than isolation among colleagues, to grant teachers a meaningful role in governance, and to offer differentiated roles that enable teachers to build careers that reach beyond the classroom, a large proportion of this cohort may well remain in education and elevate the standing and influence of teachers within their schools and in their communities. We might reasonably expect that by their example and pedagogic approaches, these teachers will influence students to become well-informed and to think and act for themselves.

However, if traditional school structures persist and teachers continue to be treated as subordinates, it seems likely that those teachers who have alternative career options will leave, and schools will be staffed with their peers who had nowhere better to go. Overall, the teaching of those who stay behind is likely to be less informed and less creative than it was among those who left, leaving classroom settings focused even more on eliciting compliance rather than encouraging agency among students.

## The Standards and Accountability Movement

One of the most important changes in the context of new teachers' experience is the emergence of the standards and accountability movement, first introduced by states and subsequently embodied in federal legislation, the No Child Left Behind Act of 2001. This large-scale reform, designed to improve student learning especially in low-performing, urban and rural schools, is arguably the most far-reaching education policy initiative since 1985. This policy introduces sanctions for schools that fail to reach acceptable levels of performance, as measured by standardized tests. In part, it is a response to the slow pace and inadequate gains in students' performance as a result of the reforms of 1985–2000 discussed above, which were designed to increase teachers' standing and influence. There is great variety in how the states conceive of standards and what the prospect of annual testing means for teachers' work, classroom instruction, and student learning. In some cases, these reforms have led districts to impose rigidly scripted curricula and to require teachers to conduct repeated sessions of test preparation. In other cases, they have led to greater curricular coherence and more focused, challenging instruction.

Initially, the standards and accountability movement seemed to be entirely compatible with building a well-informed, skilled, and influential teaching force. Because early reformers envisioned a challenging curriculum that would require extensive professional development, it seemed likely that there would emerge new roles for expert teachers to provide professional development for less experienced peers. Widely publicized experiences in District 2 in New York City provided an encouraging model. However, some states have adopted standardized tests that require mastery of rudimentary rather than advanced skills and emphasize the recall of facts rather than expression of original thought. Many districts have responded by issuing top-town directives calling for uniform instructional practice, reducing the scope and depth of the curriculum, and specifying what teachers must do day to day in their classrooms. Teachers frequently report that their lesson plans are regularly checked and that they have far less freedom than they once did to devise curriculum, choose texts, and create interdisciplinary projects. It is important to note that teachers differ among themselves about the value and impact of these changes. Some judge the reforms favorably and welcome the deliberate order and increased resources that have accompanied them. Others, however, find the demands oppressive and resent what they see to be administrative intrusion into the classroom. Initial research suggests that new teachers tend to support initiatives that lead to increased student learning, but reject those that focus excessively on rote skills, severely reduce their instructional options, or diminish their standing as teachers.

Schools might become more purposeful, interdependent, and differentiated organizations in response to a set of challenging, fair, and aligned standards, curriculums, and assessments. If the principal and teachers in a school join together to ensure that all students succeed, expert teachers could play an expanded role in defining the school's policies and practices. Alternatively, increased pressures to deliver higher test scores at nearly any cost and to hold individual teachers narrowly accountable for the results may further isolate and divide teachers, discouraging contributions that the best among them have to offer, and diminishing the quality of the instructional program that the school provides.

## *Taking Stock and Moving Ahead*

To what extent, if any, have teacher unions and collective bargaining, post–1985 professional reforms, and the standards and accountability movement changed the standing, role, and career of teachers? The effects are varied and highly dependent on local and state context. Overall, there is greater potential today than there was in the 1970s and 1980s for teachers to achieve higher status, to earn more pay, and to exercise greater influence in public education. There are union leaders and school administrators who collaborate regularly and adopt progressive policies. There now are collective-bargaining agreements that have established peer assistance and review plans, the basic elements of a career ladder, and school-site councils with the authority to hire teachers and allocate funds. The NBPTS has a well-established assessment system that can be used to identify expert teachers who then can serve as teacher leaders. There are experiments with career ladders that offer differentiated roles and performance-based pay for teachers. Each of these has promise for enhancing the standing and influence of teachers. Combined, they might substantially transform the career of teaching

and the character of schools. Such a scenario would substantially augment teachers' formal and informal authority in public education. With their increased
responsibility and status, teachers could take a greater role in defining how
schools work and what is taught. They could oversee a program in which students are educated to think critically and to value and defend democratic principles, not only in school, but beyond.

However, that potential has yet to be realized, and there are substantial countervailing forces—authoritarian administrators who seek to keep teachers in
their place, unyielding union leaders who refuse to compromise hard-won
industrial protections, budget shortfalls that suddenly halt the implementation of
progressive reforms, and teachers who resist the responsibility and are apprehen-
sive about the recognition that accompany new roles. Such conditions will not
attract and sustain teachers who question authority or impress upon students the
importance of taking responsibility for their own learning.

The prospects for greater influence by teachers are further complicated by a
new generation of teachers entering schools within the context of the standards
and accountability movement. These recruits to teaching, many of whom are
starting to teach with less formal preparation than their predecessors, expect
more of a teaching career than it can currently deliver. They look forward to
working collaboratively, rather than in isolation, and to being paid and recognized in keeping with their accomplishments. They do not expect to be full-time
classroom teachers long-term, but rather seek opportunities to acquire new
skills, have varied responsibilities, and develop in their careers as teachers.
Because they have many other employment options and live at a time when
serial careers are common, these novices will not patiently wait for schools to
adopt the reforms that matter to them. If they are dissatisfied with teaching—and
current attrition figures suggest that they are—they may leave after a short time,
making teaching once again itinerant work, with all the diminished influence
that would bring.

Notably, however, new teachers, as a group, appear to support the standards
and accountability movement. If they have curricula and instructional supplies
that are well aligned with state frameworks and assessments, and if they receive
the support of first-rate professional development, they may succeed in preparing students in accord with the public's expectations for their schools. For
once, teachers' judgment would be well aligned with public preferences.
However, given the tremendous variation that exists across schools and districts, it seems virtually certain that in most settings the tension between teachers and the public about who should determine what and how students learn
will persist.

It is worth considering whether that tension is inevitably unproductive or
could have promise for democratic education. This discussion opened with
Amy Gutmann's simple but challenging question: "Who should have the

authority to shape the education of future citizens?" Given unresolved debates about the goals of schooling and persistent uncertainty about how best to teach the full range of students, neither the public nor teachers should or even could have exclusive authority to decide the shape of education. In some settings, there will be an ongoing, adversarial struggle for control, as school boards and unions reach impasse in negotiations, teachers resist the directives of principals, and parents threaten legal action on behalf of their children. But in more productive settings, participants—whether they be teachers or parents, school administrators or union leaders, legislators or the heads of state professional associations—will collaborate to establish policies and practices that are consistent with best practices in teaching and learning, while also meeting citizens' priorities for their schools. In such situations, the public will not stubbornly impose an unwise educational plan; nor will it be cowed to accept unjustified practices. Teachers will not brandish their professional expertise; nor will they routinely comply with dictates that violate informed judgments about best practices. There will be give and take, an exchange of views and information, gradual compromise and agreement.

The question of who should control education probably will never be settled fully in favor of either teachers or the public because so many factors combine to influence the outcome—the history and status of teaching, the composition of the teaching ranks, the dynamic character of local control, the limited knowledge base in education, and the shifting priorities and practices of teachers' unions. But this is not a bad state of affairs. Assuming that a reasonable balance of influence and control can be achieved, both the schools and the students they serve stand to benefit. Open discussion and informed debate about what and how to teach might occur in many settings—during a parent conference, a school board meeting, a class discussion, or a legislative hearing. Such exchange offers the best opportunity to identify and adopt sound and appropriate instructional practices. And as it occurs, students can witness the day-to-day process of democratic participation in schooling, observe their teachers as agents of change, and anticipate their future roles as active, influential citizens.

## Notes

1. Moe, "The Two Democratic Purposes of Public Education," 127.
2. McDonnell, "Defining Democratic Purposes," 8.
3. See John L. Rury, "Who Became Teachers?" and D. A. Spencer, "Teacher's Work in Historical and Social Context."
4. Grant and Murray, *Teaching in America.*
5. Sykes, "Public Policy and the Problem of Teacher Quality," 98.
6. See Tyack and Hansot, *Managers of Virtue;* and Rury, "Who Became Teachers?"
7. See Callahan, *Education and the Cult of Efficiency,* 104–11.

8. Grant and Murray, *Teaching in America,* 92; Steve Farkas, Jean Johnson, and Tony Folema, *A Sense of Calling: Who Teaches and Why* (New York: Public Agenda, 2000).

9. Johnson, *Teachers at Work;* Johnson and the Project on the Next Generation of Teachers, *Finders and Keepers.*

10. Grant and Murray, *Teaching in America,* 21.

11. Lynn Olson, "Sweetening the Pot," *Education Week* 19, no. 18 (special report, *Quality Counts 2000*): 28–34.

12. Robin R. Henke, Xianglei Chen, and Sonya Geis, *Progress through the Teacher Pipeline: 1992–93 College Graduates and Elementary/Secondary School Teaching as of 1997* (Washington, D.C.: National Center for Educational Statistics, 2000); Johnson and the Project on the Next Generation of Teachers, *Finders and Keepers.*

13. Odden and Kelley, *Paying Teachers for What They Know and Do.*

14. Quality Education Data, *QED's School Market Trends: Teacher Buying Behavior and Attitudes 2001–2002* (Denver, Colo.: QED, 2002).

15. Lortie, "The Balance of Control and Autonomy in Elementary School Teaching," 15–16.

16. See Johnson, *Teachers at Work.*

17. McLaughlin and Yee, "School as a Place to Have a Career," quotes at 23–24.

18. Darling-Hammond, "Standard Setting in Teaching," 761.

19. See Stigler and Hiebert, *The Teaching Gap.*

20. Terry M. Moe, "Education Taking on the Unions," *Hoover Digest* 1 (2001): 133–34, article available at http://www-hoover.stanford.edu/publications/digest/011/toc011.html; Gutmann, *Democratic Education,* 76.

21. Information on Haley is in Robert L. Reid, ed. *Battleground: The Autobiography of Margaret A. Haley* (Urbana: University of Illinois Press, 1982); quotes are at x, xvii.

22. Kerchner and Mitchell, *The Changing Idea of a Teachers' Union,* 139.

23. See Johnson, *Teacher Unions in Schools,* and Kerchner and Mitchell, *The Changing Idea of a Teachers' Union.*

24. Johnson, *Teacher Unions in Schools.*

25. Kerchner and Mitchell, *The Changing Idea of a Teachers' Union,* 190.

26. Sykes, "Reckoning with the Spectre," p. 19.

27. Information on the National Board for Professional Teaching Standards was obtained from the board's Web site at www.nbpts.org.

28. See Wilcox, "The National Board for Professional Teaching Standards."

29. See Kerchner and Caufman, "Building the Airplane while It's Rolling Down the Runway."

30. Gallagher, Lanier, and Kerchner, "Toledo and Poway."

31. See Grant and Murray, *Teaching in America,* and Koppich, "Rochester: The Rocky Road to Reform."

32. Johnson and Kardos, "Reform Bargaining and Its Promise for School Improvement."

33. Phillips, "Miami: After the Hype."

34. Ogawa and White, "School-based Management," 54.

35. Richard M. Ingersoll, *An Agenda for Research on Teachers and Schools: Revisiting NCES's Schools and Staffing Survey* (Washington, D.C.: National Center for Education Statistics, 1995).

36. See Susan M. Johnson and Jonathan Landman, "'Sometimes Bureaucracy Has Its Charms': The Working Conditions of Teachers in Deregulated Schools," *Teachers College Record* 102, no. 1 (2000): 85–124.
37. See Johnson and Kardos, "Reform Bargaining and Its Promise for School Improvement."
38. See Evans, *The Human Side of School Change.*
39. Thomas Smith and Richard M. Ingersoll, "Reducing Teacher Turnover: What Are the Components of Effective Induction?" Paper presented at the American Educational Research Association, Chicago, April 2003.
40. Johnson and the Project on the Next Generation of Teachers, *Finders and Keepers.*

## Bibliography

Callahan, Raymond E. *Education and the Cult of Efficiency: A Study of Social Forces That Have Shaped the Administration of the Public Schools.* Chicago: University of Chicago Press, 1962.

Carnegie Forum on Education and the Economy. *A Nation Prepared: Teachers for the 21st Century: The Report of the Task Force on Teaching as a Profession.* Washington, D.C.: Forum, 1986.

Darling-Hammond, Linda. "Standard Setting in Teaching: Changes in Licensing, Certification, and Assessment." In *Handbook of Research on Teaching*, edited by Virginia Richardson, 751–76. 4th ed. Washington, D.C.: American Educational Research Association, 2001.

Evans, Robert. *The Human Side of School Change: Reform, Resistance, and the Real-life Problems of Innovation.* San Francisco: Jossey-Bass, 1996.

Gallagher, James J., Perry Lanier, and Charles Kerchner. "Toledo and Poway: Practicing Peer Review." In *A Union of Professionals: Labor Relations and Educational Reform*, edited by Charles T. Kerchner and Julia E. Koppich, with William Ayers et al., 158–76. New York: Teachers College Press, 1993.

Grant, Gerald, and Christine E. Murray. *Teaching in America: The Slow Revolution.* Cambridge, Mass.: Harvard University Press, 1999.

Gutmann, Amy. *Democratic Education.* Princeton, N.J.: Princeton University Press, 1987.

Ingersoll, Richard. *The Status of Teaching as a Profession: 1990-91*, 97–104. Washington, D.C.: National Center for Education Statistics, January 1997.

Johnson, Susan M. *Teacher Unions in Schools.* Philadelphia: Temple University Press, 1984.

Johnson, Susan M. *Teachers at Work: Achieving Success in Our Schools.* New York: Basic, 1990.

Johnson, Susan M., and Susan M. Kardos. "Reform Bargaining and Its Promise for School Improvement." In *Conflicting Missions? Teachers Unions and Educational Reform*, edited by Tom Loveless. Washington, D.C.: Brookings Institution, 2000.

Johnson, Susan M., and the Project on the Next Generation of Teachers. *Finders and Keepers: Helping New Teachers Survive and Thrive in Our Schools.* San Francisco: Jossey-Bass, 2004.

Kerchner, Charles T., and Krista D. Caufman. "Building the Airplane While It's Rolling Down the Runway." In *A Union of Professionals: Labor Relations and Educational Reform*, edited by Charles T. Kerchner and Julia E. Koppich, with William Ayers et al., 1–24. New York: Teachers College Press, 1993.

Kerchner, Charles T., and Douglas E. Mitchell. *The Changing Idea of a Teachers' Union.* New York: Falmer, 1988.

Koppich, Julia E. "Rochester: The Rocky Road to Reform." In *A Union of Professionals: Labor Relations and Educational Reform,* edited by Charles T. Kerchner and Julia E. Koppich, with William Ayers et al. New York: Teachers College Press, 1993.

Lieberman, Myron. *Public Education: An Autopsy.* Cambridge, Mass.: Harvard University Press, 1993.

Lortie, Dan C. "The Balance of Control and Autonomy in Elementary School Teaching." In *The Semi-professions and Their Organization: Teachers, Nurses, Social Workers,* edited by Amitai Etzioni, 1–53. New York: Free Press, 1969.

Lortie, Dan C. *Schoolteacher: A Sociological Study.* Chicago: University of Chicago Press, 1975.

McDonnell, Lorraine. "Defining Democratic Purposes." In *Rediscovering the Democratic Purposes of Education,* edited by Lorraine McDonnell, P. Michael Timpane, and Roger Benjamin. Lawrence: University Press of Kansas, 2000.

McDonnell, Lorraine, and Anthony Pascal. *Organized Teachers in American Schools.* Santa Monica, Calif.: RAND, 1979.

McLaughlin, Milbrey W., and Sylvia M.-L. Yee. "School as a Place to Have a Career." In *Building a Professional Culture in Schools,* edited by Ann Lieberman, 23–44. New York: Teachers College Press, 1988.

Mitchell, Douglas E. "The Impact of Collective Bargaining on School Governance and Politics." In *Collective Bargaining in Education,* edited by Anthony Cresswell and Michael Murphy, with Charles Kerchner. San Francisco: McCutchan, 1984.

Moe, Terry M. "The Two Democratic Purposes of Public Education." In *Rediscovering the Democratic Purposes of Education,* edited by Lorraine McDonnell, P. Michael Timpane, and Roger Benjamin. Lawrence: University Press of Kansas, 2000.

Moe, Terry M. "Education Taking on the Unions." *Hoover Digest* 1, 24–26, 2001, available at http://www-hoover.stanford.edu/publications/digest/011/toc011.html.

Odden, Allan, and Carolyn Kelley. *Paying Teachers for What They Know and Do: New and Smarter Compensation Strategies.* Thousand Oaks, Calif.: Corwin, 1997.

Ogawa, Rodney T., and Paula A. White. "School-based Management: An Overview." In *School-based Management: Organizing for High Performance,* edited by Susan A. Mohrman and Priscilla Wohlstetter. San Francisco: Jossey-Bass, 1994.

Phillips, LeRae. "Miami: After the Hype." In *A Union of Professionals: Labor Relations and Educational Reform,* edited by Charles T. Kerchner and Julia E. Koppich, with William Ayers, 116–35. New York: Teachers College Press, 1993.

Rury, John L. "Who Became Teachers?: The Social Characteristics of Teachers in American History." In *American Teachers: Histories of a Profession at Work,* edited by Donald Warren, 7–48. New York: Macmillan, 1989.

Spencer, Dee. A. "Teachers' Work in Historical and Social Context." In *Handbook of Research on Teaching,* edited by Virginia Richardson, pp. 83–85. Washington, D.C.: American Educational Research Association, 2001.

Stigler, James W., and James Hiebert. *The Teaching Gap: Best Ideas from the World's Teachers for Improving Education in the Classroom.* New York: Free Press, 1999.

Sykes, Gary. "Reckoning with the Spectre," *Educational Researcher 16,* no. 6 (August–September 1987): 19–23.

Tyack, David B. *The One Best System: A History of American Urban Education.* Cambridge, Mass.: Harvard University Press, 1974.

Tyack, David B., and Elisabeth Hansot. *Managers of Virtue: Public School Leadership in America, 1820–1980.* New York: Basic, 1982.

Wilcox, Danielle D. "The National Board for Professional Teaching Standards: Can It Live Up to Its Promise?" In *Better Teachers, Better Schools*, edited by Marci Kanstoroom and Chester E. Finn Jr., 163–97. Washington, D.C.: Thomas B. Fordham Foundation, 1999.

# 8

# YOUTH, MEDIA, AND CITIZENSHIP

## *John Merrow*

C HILDREN AND YOUTH IN THE TWENTY-FIRST CENTURY swim in a sea of media. They learn lessons about citizenship and their role in society from such sources as television, computers, magazines, and talk radio. Given that media portrayals of children are often negative, however, one has to wonder how youth development is affected by their constant exposure to these forms of mass communication.

Computers and television have the potential to transform education, but the basic structure and purpose of school, as well as teacher training, may be obstacles to the optimum use of these technologies as tools to develop habits of citizenship and promote active participation in a democratic society.

### *Media and the Stereotyping of Youth*

In the fall of 2002 the Josephson Institute of Ethics released a survey documenting what it called "a decade of moral deterioration." Kids are more likely to cheat, steal, and lie than kids ten years ago, it headlined. Girls cheat and lie just as much as boys but are less likely to steal. And apparently athletics does not build character, because varsity athletes were more likely to cheat on exams. Those who said their religion was essential to them were just as likely to cheat and lie as others, although they didn't shoplift as much.

If you believe these results, you probably also have to conclude that the sky is falling. On the Josephson Institute's Web page are found opportunities to improve the character of American youth: curriculum guides, posters, bumper stickers, neckties, and other items for sale. This is not to pick on the institute, because literally thousands of organizations draw attention to themselves with dire warnings about the decaying fiber of youth—a view that has existed in America since the Puritans established schools to ward off the influence of Satan.[1]

The media's frequent portrayal of "youth gone bad" is clearly overdrawn. "God don't make no junk," blues singer Ethel Waters once said, explaining why she mattered. All of our children matter, and all deserve opportunities to achieve and grow. Unfortunately, there is what might be called an "anti-youth virus" in the United States, fed by warnings of youth's increasing decadence, as evidenced by isolated incidents of criminal behavior, and by media stereotyping of youth.

Adult perceptions of kids are strikingly negative. An astonishing 74 percent of parents say that teenagers are "rude, irresponsible and wild," and 58 percent describe children as "lazy and spoiled." As to the future, 57 percent of parents say that today's teenagers will make little difference in the nation's progress—and might even prove to be detrimental. That 1997 Public Agenda survey of adult attitudes also reported, "Most Americans look at today's teenagers with misgivings and trepidation, viewing them as undisciplined, disrespectful, and unfriendly." The report indicated that adults feel this way about teens regardless of race, gender, and economic status. Such sentiments reflect a traditional generation gap that is widened by media stereotypes and sensational news coverage.[2]

In *Ordinary Resurrections*, a sensitive portrayal of young kids in the South Bronx, Jonathan Kozol writes, "The emphasis on 'differentness' in inner city kids has been a part of sociology as long as inner cities have existed, I suppose. When I was a young teacher, 'the culture of poverty' was an accepted phrase. Similar phrases have been canonized in decades since." Kozol goes on to condemn the "wholesale labeling of inner city children," particularly by those who suggest in their writings that children in the inner city are not really children but "'premature adults,' perhaps precocious criminals, 'predators'" (p.116).[3]

The anti-youth virus is widespread. A story in *U.S. News & World Report* in 2000 reported that only 15 percent of American adults believe that young people had a strong sense of right and wrong, a sharp contrast to the 52 percent of adults who felt that way about kids in 1952.[4] Consider the media—particularly television, magazines, and talk radio. The years since 1990 have seen a spate of sensational coverage of youth crime, coverage that suggests that the nation is in the grip of a teenage crime wave of unprecedented proportions, even though the opposite is true.

A "child free" movement is growing in the United States, encouraged by books like Elinor Burkett's *Baby Boon: How Family-Friendly America Cheats the Childless.*

Some gated communities ban children, some "planned communities" consist of homes with a maximum of two bedrooms, to discourage families, and some hotels warn patrons that children under eighteen are not allowed on the premises even as paying guests. In 2004 the organization No Kidding, which celebrates a 'life style' that purposely does not include children, had forty-seven chapters, up from two chapters in 1997. Child-free Web sites are sprouting, visited by childless baby boomers, who now number 13 million, as Lisa Belkin reported in the *New York Times Magazine.*[5]

In the three-year period from 1997 to 1999, virtually every publication in the magazine food chain put adolescents on its cover: *Time, Newsweek, U.S. News & World Report, People,* the *National Enquirer,* and on down the ladder. While isolated crimes like the 1999 murders at Columbine High School in Colorado are indeed horrifying, the overall effect of prolonged coverage of such events has been to suggest that young people in America as a group are antisocial, depraved, and dangerous. As Karen Hein, former president of the William T. Grant Foundation, commented, "Adult attitudes can be toxic for teens."[6]

What adult attitudes? One young high school student in Alaska shocked an audience of state superintendents of education with her blunt analysis. "Adults don't respect teenagers or youth," she said. "Students are not seen as people. They're babysitting charges. You don't get respected. You don't get looked at, just glared at.... It's terrible the way they pounce on you."

Just as harmful may be the attitudes of policymakers who view youth not as a public good but as a social investment that must be "cost effective." Kozol writes of adults whose policy discussions "seem to view [children] less as [individuals] who have fingers, elbows, stomachaches, emotions, than as 'economic units'—pint-sized deficits or assets in blue jeans and jerseys, some of whom may prove to be a burden to society, others of whom may have some limited utility" (p. 137).

Can adults who speak of children and adolescents in these terms, and see them through an economic lens, connect with them on a human level?

Even adults who care about young people may add to the problem when they emphasize the uniqueness of adolescence. When they do that, those sympathetic observers inadvertently contribute to the view that young people are themselves the *cause* of their problems. Once you believe that adolescent problems are the adolescents' fault, the range of possible solutions is limited to finding ways to either change the kids or isolate them from the rest of society.

An even greater danger is the search for a mythical "silver bullet" that will make all problems disappear. So we find state legislatures debating the death penalty for children, for example, as if that would solve complex social problems, and initiatives for "getting tough on" juvenile crime. Massachusetts law allows fourteen-year-olds to be sent to adult prisons. In Oregon, the age is twelve; Wisconsin, ten. Between 1985 and 1997 the number of young people under eighteen incarcerated in adult prisons more than doubled, from thirty-four hundred to seventy-four hundred. One in ten juveniles being held is locked up in adult jails or prisons. In 1994, according to the American Civil Liberties Union, forty-five children met their deaths in adult prisons. All of this is happening even though juvenile crime has been *decreasing* for a decade.[7]

Just as it is illogical and wrong to assume that adolescents are the problem, so too is it wrongheaded to think that the solution is to punish, restrict, curtail, or refuse to support them.

## *The Kids* Are OK

*The Merrow Report,* a series of programs on education for the Public Broadcasting System (PBS) and National Public Radio (NPR), goes right to the source. "It's not racism. They just don't like kids," said thirteen-year-old Paul, a streetwise Latino boy from Manhattan, and the insight was echoed by other young adolescents, black, white, and Latino. "Sometimes grown-ups will cross the street when they see us coming," another young adolescent in the "Growing Up in the City" segment, broadcast on PBS in 1999, observed.[8]

Teacher Alec Mahre supported the observation. "I've heard policemen refer to the kids as 'animals' just because they were laughing and talking loudly on the street," noted Mahre, a science teacher at a Manhattan middle school. Mahre understands what kids are really like. "They want to be grown up, and they think they're grown up, but they're still at an age where they need others to solve their problems or they need attention about something."

Adults may admit to crossing the street if they see a group of urban teenagers coming their way. "I know I shouldn't react that way because they're just kids," goes a common complaint, "but I can't help being scared."

Actually, the young kids have fears of their own, and what they are afraid of can be surprising. "I'm afraid of the world coming to the end," Miguel Molina admitted on "Growing Up in the City." Renata Mills said she's afraid of aliens, while Stephanie Dowie shared the following: "I sometimes worry about waking up in the morning, and my mom won't be there." Davon Carter, a twelve-year-old boy who watches a lot of TV, said he worries about "kidnappers and rapists. Sometimes that kind of scares me."

"Growing Up in the City" followed fourteen young adolescents, ages eleven to fourteen, as they made their way around New York City. These were typical kids, grappling with issues of identity, belonging, freedom, and control, just as adolescents always have. They may be defiant, and they may look and sound older, but they are still in need of adult guidance.

What has changed for adolescents today? For one thing, fewer supports and services are available. Most young adolescents are left on their own every day after school until a parent or guardian gets home from work. Few supervised activities are available for these kids, and much of what is available costs money, putting such care out of reach of many working families.

Many of the messages that kids are bombarded with on a daily basis urge them to act older, be sexy . . . and buy, buy, buy! Sexual messages dominate the media, and several young girls, ages twelve to fourteen, told stories about predator males, usually nineteen to twenty-five, who tried to entice them into sexual relationships. "When one of them asks me for my phone number," one thirteen-year-old girl said, "I smile and ask him for his number and tell him that I will call him. Later on I just throw the paper away."

Their teacher, Theresa Jinks, was appalled by this predatory behavior. "We need to watch out on the street for people who don't seem to care about their growth. We need to let these children take their time to grow because they need to catch up emotionally and socially with their bodies. If we, as adults, are infringing on that time by making passes at them because their bodies look appealing, then we have, as a society, lost our way."

Data about American youth contradict myths and stereotypes. Declines in youth crime, teen pregnancy, and high school dropouts have been accompanied by increases in educational accomplishments. SAT and ACT scores are up, as is enrollment in Advanced Placement courses. Between 1984 and 1999, the number of AP exams taken by high school students tripled. Minority students make up 30 percent of test takers, up from 22 percent a decade ago.

More girls are taking higher-level math and science courses including Chemistry and Physics, and enrollment in Algebra II and Trigonometry increased by more than 50 percent between 1982 and 1994. According to the National Assessment of Educational Progress (NAEP), science achievement is improving, with black and Hispanic students making the largest gains. Reading scores have not improved very much, and math scores are mixed, with kids doing well on more complex mathematical thinking, less well on basic skills. And the United States still ranks below most industrialized nations, in case anyone thinks that the reforms of the last decades have succeeded.[9]

But what about that Josephson Institute poll? Are young people today less moral than their parents? Certainly they have been stealing music, using Napster and its successors, including KaZaA. Before free downloading, the best-selling albums sold 60 million copies in 2000. That dropped to 33 million units in 2002, a decline the industry blames on youth theft. Frank Rich notes that the spread of piracy coincided with dramatic increases in the price of a CD (ten tracks for $30), and he predicts that theft will decline now that Apple and others are making songs available for less than a dollar. "Far from being a particularly unethical generation, [they] may be no more or less moral than those that came before."[10]

Or consider how much is accomplished by the fifty thousand young workers in AmeriCorps, the national network of 2,100 service programs that touches the lives of two million Americans every year—eleven thousand homes built; 650,000 senior citizens assisted; 4.4 million children tutored; 1 million at-risk children enrolled in after-school programs; and, along the way, 2.5 million part-time volunteer workers recruited to help them: not bad for a generation whose morals are deteriorating.[11] Karen Pittman has observed that until recently the one certainty for American youth was schooling—the right to an adequate education. "But increasingly the rights of individual young people are being cut off," Pittman wrote in *Youth Today*, the monthly paper published by the American Youth Work Center. "Education is headed down the slippery slope toward becoming not a right but a privilege. This willingness to suspend individual educational rights . . . reflects the development of a new certainty for U.S. youth: jail."[12]

Is Pittman's pessimism warranted? Can schools serve as a counterweight to the social messages and embrace technology's potential to develop habits of inquiry and citizenship?

## Television in School

"You can't just use traditional media like TV these days," Tina Wells, the twenty-three-year-old CEO of Buzz Marketing, told the Associated Press. She recommends contests on Web sites and text messaging on cell phones.

That view may represent the newest thinking in how to reach—and sell to—youth. However, in most schools, a TV set, not a cell phone or Web site, is the marketing device of choice. It is unfortunately true that most schools have not figured out how to harness the power of television to the creative energies of students. If they did, they would help create an informed citizenry, capable of resisting the hard and soft sell of adults trying to separate them from the billions of dollars they collectively have to spend.

Television is a fact of young children's lives. Young people between the ages of six and eleven watch, on the average, between twenty-one and twenty-eight hours of television a week. Put another way, children are spending the equivalent of two months of the year watching television. The average family with children between the ages of two and seventeen has three television sets, 97 percent have VCRs or DVD players, and 78 percent have cable or satellite.[13]

Television is also a fact of life in many school homerooms, thanks to Channel One, the twelve-minute news program—with two minutes of commercials—that is required viewing in many schools (except California and New York, which ban it). Chris Whittle, the entrepreneur who dreamed up Channel One, sold educators on the concept by offering free video equipment to schools in return for the opportunity to sell products to students. His sales pitch was: "We want our children to know, for example, where Beijing is. Suppose the price of their learning that is two minutes of commercials? Do we still want them to know where Beijing is?" And most school districts, pressed for financial resources, said yes.

Television is used to make young children aware of social values and civic responsibilities, and to teach basic skills. *Sesame Street, Mister Rogers' Neighborhood, Barney & Friends, The Electric Company,* and many other programs for children have long been the staple of public television. Earlier children's programs like *Captain Kangaroo* and *Howdy Doody* also tried to teach young viewers the importance of cooperation, determination, tolerance, and other generally accepted values.

Many more children today are watching what I would call "semi-adult" and often cynically hip programs like *Rugrats, Hey Arnold!,* and *SpongeBob*

*SquarePants,* however, or perhaps nakedly commercial series designed around products like My Little Pony. Other children are watching adult fare, with or without adults around.

Watching TV is not particularly good for children because the content of shows is so often violent. "Children who watch the violent shows, even 'just funny' cartoons, were more likely to hit out at their playmates, argue, disobey class rules, leave tasks unfinished, and were less willing to wait for things than those who watched the nonviolent programs," says Aletha Huston, coauthor of *Big World, Small Screen: The Role of Television in American Society.*

Dry statistics about TV's ubiquity come to life in conversations with young people everywhere. In a sophomore English class visited by *The Merrow Report,* most of the students said that TV was "boring and repetitive," but what is perhaps most significant about their revelations is not the shows they said they watched or the number of hours they admitted to viewing; it was the number of TV sets in their home. Three-quarters of these young people had their own TV sets; every household had at least two, and a few had as many as five. The youngsters reported that at least one set was on "all the time."

Who picked the programs? One young girl's answer: "Nobody really chooses. We just watch whatever's on. Mom or Dad may be in the same room with us, watching the same shows, but they're not really with us, if you know what I mean."[14] That conjures up images of television as a soporific, enervating experience that leaves viewers tired, frustrated, and angry—without knowing why.

## Television and Citizenship Education

Not everyone is anti-television, however. Since the 1960s researchers have produced more than thirty-five hundred reports and commentaries about television and children, often calling for more children's programming, for more public-access channels, and for "media literacy" training in schools.

In the early 1980s, the Markle Foundation recommended the following five objectives for realizing the educational potential of television.[15]

1. Availability. Programs directed at children should be aired at the hours when children watch television.
2. Diversity. The range of content, style, and subject matter should be as broad as a child's curiosity and needs.
3. Selectivity. Programs should use television for purposes it meets better or more efficiently than other forces influencing children.
4. Focus. Different programs should be made for children of different ages.
5. Innovation. Programs should try concepts and tasks not yet extensively explored.

More recently, others have suggested a sixth objective: *access*. Give children access to information about how television is made and to the TV-making equipment itself. Access invites inquiry and encourages curiosity and creativity. And with access, young people are given more control over their own learning. Let children be *around, in, and on* television. Children want desperately to "be on TV," as any reporter who has taken a camera crew into a school can attest. Children flock around TV reporters, clamoring for attention and demanding to know what channel they will be on.

Making young people part of the production process itself, sitting down with them and explaining everything and answering every question, gives them power and a stake in the outcome. Understanding how television is made—actually helping to make it—provides young people with an even greater sense of self.

Because children learn quickly what they want to understand, only rarely does something have to be explained more than once when the subject intrigues them. Television is a part of their lives, their "friend and neighbor." But it is more than that: television is their common language and the collector of their experiences.

More proof of TV's power with children can be gained by watching them watch the tube. Children often like commercials best of all because the razzle-dazzle (what we call "production values") draws them in. Once students understand television, the seductive power of television advertising does battle with their desire to understand the how and why of message construction. They learn that ads can tell them about more than the attractions of such-and-such a product; ads can tell them about the marketer's target audience and the techniques used to sell the product.

Some may not want children to understand television's power to sell. After all, businesses market to teens and younger children because they have money to spend, an estimated $170 billion in 2003, up from about $155 billion in 2000, according to Teenage Research Unlimited, a Chicago firm. Just as young people who learn to make their own television programs become more discerning in their viewing, so are youth who study marketing—by making their own ads—less likely to "have to have" whatever the latest new thing is.

Unfortunately, schools often join with businesses to advertise to children, another dubious lesson in citizenship. Some schools contract with McDonald's and other fast-food chains, so much so that the CDC has estimated that 20 percent of schools offer brand-name fast food in their cafeterias. Fast-food businesses spent an estimated $15 billion in 2003 to reach the youth market, according to research done at Texas A&M and reported in the *New York Times.*[16] James McNeal, a professor of marketing at Texas A&M, says that kids ages four through twelve spend about $30 billion on their own but, more importantly, "Their influence on what their parents spend is $600 billion. That's blue sky."

Schools make what some call a bargain with the devil because they are strapped for money, which is a classic example of a short-term gain that does not come close to offsetting the long-term losses. Schools are missing "teachable moments" at an alarming rate when they become complicit in creating consumers.

There is a message for the schools in all of this, a message that excellent schools already understand. Most schools generally use television as a medium of instruction. Draw the shades, dim the lights, and watch videotapes in science or social studies class. Teachers attuned to the importance of media literacy often acquire scripts of network series and build lessons around them, as a way of teaching writing and other skills.

High schools and a few middle schools in prosperous districts have their own production facilities, perhaps even closed-circuit channels; a few cable systems broadcast programs produced entirely by children, for children. The advent of low-cost digital cameras and computer-based editing systems means that most schools can afford one or more complete systems.

Excellent schools have this equipment *and* use it creatively. Some schools produce news programs, complete with pseudo-commercials, to be shown on closed circuit throughout the school. Today, however, the gates are down, and school productions do not have to rely on traditional broadcasting. Student programs can be streamed on the Internet to audiences everywhere in the world.

The possibilities for using TV positively, productively, and democratically in schools seem endless. For example, every junior high school social studies class could make a news program about a particular historical period, and a panel of judges could choose the best one. Or a chemistry experiment could be videotaped and tightly edited to teach both specific content and lab techniques. Any innovative music, art, physical education, or dramatic arts teacher could think of dozens of creative ways to have students use the equipment. Such projects might also become lessons in cooperation, decision making, information gathering, and current events.

It is time to recognize that television, the most powerful medium of mass communication ever invented, is also a wonderfully effective way to acknowledge individuality, and a powerful educational tool in the fostering of citizenship.

Hands-on involvement with television makes schools places that young people want to attend, and interested students make school a more satisfying place for everyone else. Hands-on experience with television makes children better educated, better informed consumers of television, which will lead them to demand better television—and to avoid inferior programming. It fosters in children media literacy, a level of understanding that is essential in the information age.

To those who worry that TV and other media will replace the textbook, there is a real possibility that the text*book* may go out of fashion, but *text* itself will not disappear. Words will always matter. Students who become avidly media literate remain curious about the world around them. They read to learn. The founder of Syms, a discount clothing retailer, is credited with the slogan "An educated consumer is our best customer." This catchphrase would well be adapted to education: "An educated citizen is democracy's best hope."

## Computers in School

A teacher in Detroit wanted to join the national Listen Up! youth media network, which trains disadvantaged youth to be media producers and reduces the probability of students' dropping out of school. Detroit's leaders, from the mayor on down, had made it clear, however, that any proposed new activity that was not directly related to test score improvement would not be approved. The school administrators were "walking on pins and needles," in the words of the teacher, and the tension prevented the project from ever getting under way.

Technology teaches. It is not just an instrument for school use but an indicator of educational values. How schools adapt to technology, and how youth are encouraged to use technology, reveal a great deal about values. It is not too much of a stretch to say that *how* technology is employed provides an object lesson in citizenship education.

And when those adult leaders in Detroit denied youth opportunities for immersion in technology on the grounds that it would cut into test preparation and other study, those adults revealed a profound misunderstanding of genuine education.

Contemporary society uses the computer as its central tool for communicating and creating knowledge, but many public schools misuse computers, and some cannot use them at all. Three significant obstacles stand in the way of the technological revolution schools desperately need: (1) inappropriate teaching methods; (2) stereotyping of students; and (3) obsolete facilities.

Technology is a profound threat to organized education. Simply put, if schools remain the technological equivalent of a desert while kids are growing up swimming in a sea of technology, kids will simply turn their backs on schools and classes that reject technology. One middle school student compared two of his classes: "It's sort of like going from the future to the Stone Age. We have all these computers in this class, and it's really fun, because you get to explore on the computers and you know what you're doing half the time, the other half you're just exploring. But when the bell rings, we're back in the Stone Age. You just sit there and work in the book for thirty or forty minutes, and you're just so bored of it that you want to scream and leave." At the same time, technology offers remarkable potential for learning. As Luyen Chou, a New York educator and developer of interactive technologies, commented, "This change is just as dramatic as the invention of the printing press, and maybe as important as the invention of written language back in the fifth century B.C. in Greece."[17]

Technology is a threat because it creates an unparalleled opportunity for cheating, for widespread dishonesty. Most people know how easy it is now for a student to download something from somewhere else and say: "This is my work." In fact, 77 percent of high school students say they use the Internet to do research for school assignments, according to *Who's Who Among American High School Students* (1999). How is a teacher to recognize an individual's work under current conditions: too many students, a broad curriculum that must be raced through, and, most likely, standardized, multiple-choice tests at course conclusion?[18]

Teachers who attempt to control the uses of technology the way they have traditionally controlled classrooms will not succeed. For example, the teacher who is accustomed to prescribing to the last detail exactly how a research paper must be done will be frustrated if she insists that students use the Internet and other resources precisely according to her plan. In the end, students will ignore her, or cheat, or become disillusioned and do poorly in the class. Technology rewards flexibility and innovation, and is resistant to efforts to restrict use.

Technology may be value-free, but those who control it are not. If technology is used to make schooling more efficient and cheaper, it may drive people away from learning. For example, if technology is harnessed to produce a single measure of learning, schools will end up with even more machine-scored, multiple-choice exams, which inevitably will narrow the curriculum to knowledge that can easily be tested.

Here is one example of the potential of technology: A history teacher and class are studying the Civil War. The teacher says to the twenty students: OK, each one of you is responsible for the life of a single soldier in the Civil War. As a student, you would pick—let's just make up a name—Jonathan Logan from the Hartford 108th regiment. Your job would be to become, in effect, the world's foremost expert on the life and experiences of Jonathan Logan and the 108th in Hartford. The teacher's job is to keep track of you, to orchestrate the tapestry, to make sure you and every other student in the class see the whole Civil War. As students dig up information on the Web, it is difficult to cheat because no one has ever done a life history of someone like Jonathan Logan before—information cannot be copied; original work must be done. Students are encouraged to create knowledge, and they may discover what others do not know.

Professor Edward L. Ayers and his colleagues at the University of Virginia are enabling technology to be used in just this way. Their "Valley of the Shadow" project is an online digital archive that allows anyone with an Internet connection to explore the intimate details of Augusta County, Virginia, and Franklin County, Pennsylvania, before, during, and after the Civil War. The archive contains original letters and diaries, newspapers and speeches, census and church records left by hundreds of men and women of the time. It is a treasure trove for students. As Professor Ayers observed in his essay "History in Hypertext,"

> The computer provides a powerful environment for thinking more rigorously, revealing patterns we simply could not see before. The machine is equally felicitous with numbers and words and images, across time or space, in political, cultural, or social history. Students working with large but finite bodies of evidence experiment with various perspectives and questions. The computer amplifies students' critical abilities, allowing them to refine their questions and quickly follow up with new ones. It permits them to build archives and interpretations of their own and share them with others far beyond their own classroom."[19]

In order for technology to reach its potential as an educational tool, the paradigm of schools and their accepted practices must adapt and change. As powerful as technology can be, under current conditions in many schools—with teachers responsible for 120 to 150 students per day—technology will have only a marginal impact on teaching and learning. Under these circumstances, teachers can only use computers to do such activities as programmed drill exercises.

The persistent stereotyping of children has further complicated the effective use of technology in learning. Basically, schools with large numbers of poor children are likely to use technology to control students. "Qualifies for free or reduced-price lunch" is a common proxy for "poor," and in schools with 71 percent or more students qualifying for this government program, drill is the favored application (35 percent). However, in schools with less than 11 percent on free or reduced-price lunch, "research using the Internet" is the most common use of computers (39 percent), according to the National Center for Education Statistics.[20]

Many schools in poor neighborhoods have computer laboratories equipped with drill-and-practice tutorial programs called integrated-learning systems, where students sit in front of computers and follow a programmed routine, typing in answers to problems like "12 + 4 − 2 = ?" Critics call this the "drill and kill" approach, and it would be hard to find a student who would disagree with this designation. But in many suburban schools, students control the technology. They are doing research on the Internet, or they are creating databases and manipulating spreadsheets and using computer-aided design (CAD) programs—all of which allow them to create. They are able to express themselves and their thoughts and share that information with one another.

The balance sheet might show per-pupil spending for technology among schools as equitable when the programs and their impact on students could not be more different. In other words, middle-class students, who probably have access to technology at home, are given the opportunity to use technology in ways that will make them controllers of their lives. Poor children, probably without computers at home, are being denied that power in the one place that could provide it, school. Practices like these serve to divide our society. They also contradict the American myth of public education as the great equalizer, the road to advancement.

As Larry Cuban notes in *Oversold and Underused,* schools have bought more than their share of technology. In 1983–1984, there was one computer for every ninety-two students, a ratio that improved to 1:6 by 1999. Cuban notes that, while only 3 percent of classrooms were connected to the Internet in 1994, by 1997, 27 percent were wired.[21] No doubt these conditions have continued to improve.

The use of technology in optimum ways is further hindered by requirements to teach a curriculum that is a mile wide and a foot deep. Teachers are required to teach what are essentially surveys—cover so many years, so many battles, or so many literary genres. This is the case when, at least for older students, less is more, and mastery of one area kindles the desire to know more. On the other hand, racing through history or literature (or almost any subject) at a breakneck pace leaves no time for questions and smothers curiosity, thereby undermining the very strengths technology brings to the classroom.

In the past, schools have resisted technology successfully, but that is no longer possible because most children live in the world of technology that exists outside of school. When schools resist technology or refuse to take advantage of its capacities, young people are likely to turn off. That means more discipline problems, a higher dropout rate, and greater waste of human potential. When educators use technology to standardize schooling, they treat students as objects to be manipulated. A desperate search for higher test scores puts short-term gains ahead of the more complex and important task of developing citizens. We may get the higher scores, but at what cost? What lessons have our young people learned? Schools that resist technology or deny its promise run the risk of seeing young people merely as objects to be controlled, rather than as the next generation, as, quite literally, our future. How likely are today's youth, when they become parents, to support a public education system that they see as having manipulated them?

## *"Do As I Say" Citizenship*

When ninth graders in upscale Hanover High School in New Hampshire wanted to start a debate team, no teachers were willing to serve as faculty adviser. When one teacher was finally persuaded to serve and debates began, the kids and the teacher found themselves in trouble, because the students were debating abortion rights, drug abuse, and other controversial issues.

The most common assumption about citizenship education in schools is that it should avoid serious controversy. Even when teachers agree that preparing for democratic citizenship requires learning about, debating, and making decisions about controversial issues, they often find themselves unable to implement their values because controversy and schooling are supposed to be kept separate. Such views fly in the face of the technological reality that surrounds schools: young people everywhere can connect to controversial topics within a matter of seconds and the material they discover is often presented attractively and authoritatively.

For a host of reasons, schools and teachers have not made the connections between teaching democratic citizenship and the new technological universe, tending instead to be reactive, preferring to avoid controversy and possible litigation. Where the "safe road" eventually leads ought to be of concern to everyone.

It is often said that teachers teach the way they were taught, not the way they were told to teach. What if young people grow up to practice citizenship the way they are treated in schools? Schools and the adults in them cannot help but teach lessons in citizenship, but because schools are—by definition—both hierarchical and authoritarian, the lessons they teach are not obvious preparation for effective citizenship. Schools deliver an overt curriculum that is knowledge based, but the institution's "hidden curriculum" values control and order over inquiry and learning. Stated simply, schools and teachers do not like to pose questions that they do not already know the answers to.

The new technologies do not guarantee that notions of citizenship based on inquiry and active learning will take root. But the new technologies, much more readily than the current organization of schools, do lend themselves to inquiry, in large part because almost any question that is posed can be answered—or at least explored in depth—through technological inquiry.

It is clear that schools are making efforts to bring civic values, teaching, and technology together, by harnessing technology to extend classroom lessons. The schools in Stafford County, Virginia, for example, proudly "recognize the importance of teaching children appropriate ways in which to work with others in classrooms, workplace, and community." Stafford schools have a citizenship-building "Word of the Month," which is posted on the District's Web site. This is Stafford's message about "patience":

> At home, as well as at school, exercising patience is a good way to avoid conflicts with brothers, sisters, and classmates. Sometimes self-control is a key ingredient of patience, for example, "holding your tongue" when someone says something you think is "dumb." Waiting your turn is another way of showing patience, whether you are standing in line at the water fountain, raising your hand to speak in class, or waiting your turn to receive dessert at the dinner table at home.[22]

There is, however, no recognition of the value and importance of occasionally being *impatient*—with sloppy thinking, blatant appeals to authority, or irrationality, for example.

The power and ubiquity of technology are in direct conflict with the *structure* of schools and the *training* of teachers. In most schools students are rarely encouraged to explore controversy or to question conventional wisdom. Take that ninth-grade debate team in Hanover, the small town that is home to Dartmouth College. The idea of students openly discussing drug use or abortion or similar complex concepts apparently frightened the adults in charge. Their response was to shut down the organized discussion, perhaps in the hope that, if ignored, complexity would go away.

I asked a veteran high school teacher with tenure what he does when a student wants to talk to him about disagreements that the student has with his or her parents on complex social issues or values. The teacher didn't hesitate. "My only reaction is, 'You're living in your parents' house, so act accordingly.'"

I pushed. "What if the student holds a value that you personally admire— tolerance for people of another religion—and a student comes to you and says, 'Sir, my parents are really anti-Semitic, or anti-Amish. I don't think that's right but I don't know what to do.'"

Again the teacher did not hesitate to support the parents, so I kept on pushing. "Suppose the kid is in tears and asks you directly, 'How can I love my mother and my father when they have so much hate for the Amish or the Jews?' What would you say?"

The teacher squirmed. "I can't comment; I don't know." After a minute he said, "I'd say, 'They are your parents. When you're with your parents, you better do as your parents say. When you leave home, then you make your own decisions.'"

Did he always try to avoid tough issues, I asked. He laughed nervously, "I won't say I always succeed, but I try to."

He agreed that he was teaching a value lesson right there but defended his position. "I have to be very, very careful, because I could be sued. A parent could take me to task on this. I try not to interfere with what the parent is trying to pass on to their children, and I don't find that cowardly at all." Fear of ideas, fear of conflict, and blind obedience—that is one heck of a lesson to teach students. But don't be too quick to blame the teacher, who is behaving sensibly, given a climate of inflamed passions. Unfortunately, however, children who are taught to be afraid of ideas have a good chance of growing up to be ignorant, easily led adults. What's more, older students recognize the "retreat from controversy" approach to education for what it is, and hold it in contempt.

Teacher training may be at fault as well. In a thoughtful 1999 essay, Charles Glenn placed the blame for widespread confusion among teachers over values squarely upon those who trained them, the teacher educators. The professors taught neophyte teachers to be "even-handed" and "value free." Above all, they were told, do not "impose your values" on your students. "But good teaching," Glenn wrote, "is all about urging those we teach to accept what we believe to be true and worthy of their acceptance. Bad teaching imposes values, too, and schools that are incoherent are not neutral or 'value free.' Cynicism, indifference to truth, disinclination to carry out tasks thoroughly, and disrespect for others—all of these can be learned in school." If those are the lessons learned, then democracy in America will not survive. As Paul Gagnon wrote in "Educating Democracy: State Standards to Ensure a Civic Core," "A democracy has a right to ask every student to master a civic core, and students have the right as citizens *not* to be allowed to avoid it."[23]

Given that so many schools shrink from controversial ideas, it is not surprising that young people do not seem to grasp fundamentals of American democracy. The 2001 National Assessment of Educational Progress (NAEP) found that only 17 percent of eighth graders, and just 11 percent of twelfth graders, scored at "advanced" or "proficient" levels in U.S. history.[24]

In "Educating Democracy," Gagnon reported that only one-third of seniors knew what the Progressive Era was, and many were unsure whom the United States fought in World War II.

However, idealism, which may be youth's natural state, is hard to extinguish. Exhibit one is the fact that 69 percent of college students do volunteer community service, according to Harvard's Institute of Politics. But only 27 percent are involved in political or governmental organizations, evidence of the school system's failure to model and teach citizenship. And more than half of fifteen-to-twenty-five-year-olds say they are "completely disengaged from civic life," according to a study done by researchers at Rutgers, DePaul, and George Mason Universities.[25]

## Conclusion

Deep democratic principles, particularly the belief that individuals, given the proper tools, will take on the responsibility of democratic citizenship, have been the bedrock of American education for over two centuries. But our understanding of citizenship changes, and the intricate relationship between public education and democratic citizenship is not guaranteed. Today, public education is clearly in transition. Education seems to be less a social investment and public good, more a commodity that benefits the individual. Evidence of this trend abounds, whether it is the privatizing of entire schools, the rise of charter schools, a federal law allowing public funds to be spent on private tutoring, or the approval of voucher systems in Cleveland, Milwaukee, the District of Columbia, and other places. Critics on the Right routinely refer to public schools by the pejorative "government schools."

Ironically, this growing mistrust of government institutions has been accompanied by increasing central control of education. Schooling's focus has narrowed to emphasize skills that can be measured by machine-scored, multiple-choice tests.

Throughout most of the twentieth century public schools were accepted as the main road to achieving the American dream. While the American dream is private in nature—individuals using education to achieve personal goals—the public institution of school has always played a prominent part. In effect, families entered into a bargain with educators: "We'll send you our children, and you make sure they learn what they need to know to be successful." There is, however, an increasing mistrust of the road that schools provide; it is seen as bumpy, unlit, and full of potholes—a road to nowhere.

Media continues to be part of public education's problems, by contributing to the continuing deterioration in public discourse. Talk radio, where rumor and titillation rule, and sensationalized coverage on television do substantial harm to the public image of schooling, and thus to public support for the institution.

Media must be part of a solution, however. In its many forms, it can be an alternate source of democracy and a democratizing influence. If embraced by proactive public educators, media (particularly the Internet) can be a "walled garden" allowing students to embark on educational journeys that could not even have been imagined in 1985, even as responsible adults are protecting the young from the very real dangers of unlimited access. Many homeschooling parents know this and take full advantage of the Internet.

If schools and the adults in them are to benefit from the opportunities that media and technology provide, significant changes must occur. Schools, and the adults in them, must become less reactive and controlling and more open to learning and changing. They must embrace media and its many forms. That is, to advance student learning and the democratic habits of thoughtfulness and reflection, they must first become learners.

Whether public schools, long accustomed to a largely custodial role and in the early twenty-first century under harsh attack, can make these changes is questionable. The United States' future as a healthy democracy may hang in the balance.

However, there is ample reason to applaud American youth, giving them at least two cheers—and probably three—considering that media stereotyping and unimaginative or wrongheaded use of technology in schools put many hurdles in their path to becoming successful, productive citizens in a stronger democracy.

Children and adolescents need and want adult guidance, support, and companionship. As the number of children increases from 61 million in 2000 to nearly 71 million (projected) in 2030, we cannot disinvest in young people, turn our backs on them, use technology to manipulate them, and then dismiss them as "dangerous" or worse.[26] In doing so, more than voicing a self-fulfilling prophecy, we become complicit in democratic failure.

## Notes

1. Josephson Institute, "Report Card on the Ethics of American Youth," 2002. For the full survey, see www.josephsoninstitute.org.

   An earlier survey for *Who's Who among American High School Students* (2000) produced similar findings: "While 44 percent of top-achieving teens cite 'moral and social breakdown' as the biggest problem facing their generation, an alarming number—78%—admit to cheating. Degrees of dishonesty vary, with 39% admitting they've cheated on a test and 65% saying they've copied someone else's homework. And consequences are virtually nonexistent; over nine out of ten (95%) of students who cheated say they weren't caught." *Who's Who Among American High School Students* is published by Educational Communication, and is one of many incarnations of *Who's Who* publications. ECI notes that it is not part of Marquis, the original publisher of *Who's Who*. The reader is advised to be skeptical of these publications, because self-nomination seems to be the means of gaining recognition. Survey findings cited here might best be taken with a grain of salt.

2. Steve Farkas, with Jean Johnson, "Kids These Days: What Americans Really Think about the Next Generation" (Washington, D.C.: Public Agenda, 1997). Public Agenda, which was founded in 1975, may be the single best source of reliable information about public attitudes toward complex issues. For more information, see www.publicagenda.org.

3. Jonathan Kozol, *Ordinary Resurrections: Children in the Years of Hope* (New York: Crown Books, 2000). In this book, the author of *Death at an Early Age* discusses children who survive despite the injustices and indignities of their world.

4. Angie Cannon and Carolyn Kleiner, "Teens Get Real," *U.S. News & World Report,* April 17, 2000.

5. Elinor Burkett, *Baby Boon: How Family-Friendly America Cheats the Childless* (New York: Free Press, 2000); Lisa Belkin, "Your Kids Are Their Problem," *New York Times Magazine,* July 23, 2000.

6. Personal communication with author.

7. Karen Pittman, "The Cost of Being Certain," in *Youth Today* 7, no. 5 (September 1998). More recent data provide a picture that is at least as grim. According to a 2003 report by the Sentencing Project (a non-profit organization and a grantee of the Open Society Institute), two hundred thousand juveniles are prosecuted each year as adults in criminal court. According to "Kids, Crime, and Punishment," in the spring 2003 issue of *AdvoCasey,* the report of the Annie E. Casey Foundation, the number of juvenile offenders confined in residential corrections institutions from 1993 to 1999 increased 48 percent, although the juvenile arrest rate for violent index offenses from 1993 to 1999 declined 33 percent. Forty-nine states and the District of Columbia have made it easier to try juveniles as adults. The percentage change of spending per resident from all states' general tax revenues from 1980 to 2000 is up 189 percent for prisons and 32 percent for higher education. According to the Office of Juvenile Justice, arrests of people age eighteen and under dropped 15 percent from 1996 to 2000, but juvenile facilities report more delinquents in residential placement in1999 than ever before. See also Amnesty International, "Betraying the

Young: Human Rights Violations against Children in the U.S. Justice System," Amnesty International USA, 1998. *The American Civil Liberties Union regularly presents its data in full-page advertisements in newspapers and magazines.*

8. The Merrow Report, anchored by the author, is produced by Learning Matters Inc. "Growing Up in the City" was broadcast on PBS. Complete archives are at www.pbs.org/merrow.

9. Nancy Kober and Diane Stark Rentner, "Do You Know the Good News about American Education?" (Washington, D.C.: Center on Education Policy, January 2000). AP exams are annual tests offered in many different subject areas that give students an opportunity to demonstrate college-level achievement. Many colleges and universities offer college credits to those scoring at least a 3 on a 0–5 scale. In a more recent report (August 2003), however, CEP notes that states are pressing ahead with so-called "exit exams" even though gaps in pass rates for poor, minority, and disabled students are increasing, diplomas are being withheld in surprising numbers, and dropouts and "pushouts" are increasing. See also "From the Capital to the Classroom," published by CEP in January 2003.

10. Frank Rich, "Harry Crushes the Hulk," *New York Times,* June 29, 2003, Arts and Leisure sec., 1.

11. http://www.americorps.org.

12. Karen Pittman, "Just Let Them Do It!" *Youth Today* 5, no. 5 (September–October 1996). Information about Pittman's organization, the International Youth Foundation, can be found online at www.iyfnet.org.

13. Emory H. Woodward, with Natalia Gridina, "Media in the Home 2000," a report by the Annenberg Public Policy Center of the University of Pennsylvania. The research was directed by Kathleen Hall Jamieson, the dean of the Annenberg School for Communication. Among the findings: 57 percent of the children (ages eight to sixteen) surveyed have a TV set in their bedroom; children from low-income families were more likely to have TV in the bedroom. The center produces dozens of valuable reports about media, many dealing with children's issues. More information can be found at www.appcpenn.org/reports.

14. *The Merrow Report,* "Your Children, Our Children," PBS, 1985.

15. Markle Foundation/Boys Town Conference, *The Future of Children's Television: Results of the Markle Foundation/Boys Town Conference,* edited by John P. Murray and Gavriel Salomon (Boys Town, Neb.: Boys Town, 1984).

16. David Barboza, "If You Pitch It, They Will Eat," *New York Times,* August 3, 2003. section 3, p. 1.

17. Quotes in this paragraph from *The Merrow Series,* "Promises, Promises," PBS, 1999.

18. For student misuse of the Internet, see Kelly Heyboer, "Cut-and-Paste, Turn It In— You Call That Cheating?" Newark (N.J.) *Star-Ledger,* August 28, 2003. This report, based on interviews with eighteen thousand students, was conducted by the Center for Academic Integrity at Duke and headed by Don McCabe of Rutgers. The survey found that nearly 40 percent of college students have plagiarized material from the Internet by simply using the cut-and-paste function on their computers. That is an increase of 10 percent in two years.

Among the other findings, wrote Heyboer: "Old-fashioned cheating is just as popular. Forty percent of undergraduates admitted to lifting parts of books and other written sources for their papers. But less than 5 percent of students said they turned in assignments entirely downloaded from a Web site or purchased from a term-paper mill.

"Twenty-two percent of undergraduates admitted to at least one instance of serious test cheating in the last year, including using crib notes, copying from another student or sharing answers.

"Business majors admitted to the most cheating, with 63 percent saying they cheated at least once in the last year. They were followed by education majors (60 percent) and journalism and communication majors (59 percent). Science majors reported the least cheating, with about half admitting to some academic dishonesty."

19. Edward L. Ayers, "History in Hypertext," 1999, available at http://www.vcdh.virginia.edu/Ayers.OAH.html. The Valley of the Shadow digital archives is at http://valley.vcdh.virginia.edu.

20. "Teacher Use of Computers and the Internet in Public Schools" (Washington, D.C.: National Center for Education Statistics, 2000). Full report available at http://nces.ed.gov/pubsearch/pubsinfo.asp?pubid=2000090.

21. Cuban, *Oversold and Underused*, p. 82.

22. Stafford County, Virginia, school district Web site is at www.pen.k12.va.us/Div/Stafford; however, postings change regularly.

23. Charles Glenn, "The Teachers' Muddle," *Wilson Quarterly* 23 (autumn 1999); Paul Gagnon, "Educating Democracy: State Standards to Ensure a Civic Core" (Washington, D.C.: Albert Shanker Institute, 2003).

24. National Assessment of Educational Progress, available at http://nces.ed.gov/nationsreportcard.

25. "The Campus Attitudes Towards Politics and Public Service" annual survey, Harvard University Institute of Politics, 2002; "The Civic and Political Health of the Nation: A Generational Portrait" (College Park, Md.: Center for Information and Research on Civic Learning and Engagement, 2002).

26. http://www.census.gov/ipc/www/usinterimproj.

## Bibliography

Colby, Anne, et al. *Educating Citizens: Preparing America's Undergraduates for Lives of Moral and Civic Responsibility.* San Francisco: Jossey-Bass, 2003.

Cuban, Larry. *Oversold and Underused: Computers in the Classroom.* Cambridge, Mass.: Harvard University Press, 2001.

Federal Trade Commission "Marketing Violent Entertainment to Children: A Review of Self-Regulation and Industry Practices in the Motion Picture, Music Recording and Electronic Game Industries," Washington, D.C., September 2000. The report revealed how major media companies deliberately target their advertising for R-rated movies to young children. An FCC review of the report in June 2002 found that the motion picture industry had cut back advertising R-rated movies in some venues, but continued to advertise "R-rated films on television shows that are very popular with teens." And there were "Still many advertisements with ratings that were difficult to read." "Virtually no change in industry practices since the September 2000 report" was shown with respect to explicit-content music ad placements.

Fink, Kristin, and Linda McKay. "Making Character Education a Standard Part of Education." Washington, D.C.: Character Education Partnership, 2000. CEP has developed eleven principles of effective character education but does not endorse separate classes in the subject. Its Web site is at www.character.org.

Gordon, David. "Myths and Realities about Technology in K–12 Schools." In *The Digital Classroom: How Technology Is Changing the Way We Teach and Learn*, edited by David T. Gordon. Cambridge, Mass.: Harvard Education Letter, 2000.

Huston, Aletha C., et al. *Big World, Small Screen: The Role of Television in American Society*. Lincoln: University of Nebraska Press, 1992.

James, Donna Walker, and Glenda Partee. "No More Islands: Family Involvement in 27 School and Youth Programs." Washington, D.C.: American Youth Policy Forum, 2003.

Khazei, Alan, and Michael Brown. "New Pathways to Civic Renewal." In *Shaping the Future of American Youth: Youth Policy in the 21st Century*. Washington, D.C.: American Youth Policy Forum, 2003. This book of essays contains thoughtful suggestions for a comprehensive and coordinated youth policy.

Kleeman, David W. "One Mission, Many Screens: A PBS/Markle Foundation Study on Distinctive Roles for Children's Public Service Media in the Digital Age." New York: Markle Foundation, 2002.

Kunkel, Dale, Victoria Rideout. "SEX ON TV2: A Biennial Report to the Kaiser Family Foundation." Menlo Park, Calif.: Henry J. Kaiser Family Foundation, 2001.

Levine, Arthur. "My Old Neighborhood." Teachers College, Columbia University 2002 Annual Report, 2003.

Males, Mike A. "Kids & Guns: How Politicians, Experts, and the Press Fabricate Fear of Youth." Monroe, Me: Common Courage Press, 2000.

Males, Mike A. "The Drug Abuse Warning Network." Washington D.C.: Youth Today, September 2000.

Merrow, John. *Choosing Excellence: "Good Enough" Schools Are Not Good Enough*. Lanham, Md.: Scarecrow Press, 2001.

Perlstein, Linda. *Not Much, Just Chillin': The Hidden Lives of Middle Schoolers*. New York: Farrar, Straus and Giroux, 2003.

Sizer, Theodore R., and Nancy F. Sizer. *The Students Are Watching: School and the Moral Contract*. Boston: Beacon Press, 1999.

Stepp, Laura Sessions. *Our Last Best Shot: Guiding Our Children through Early Adolescence*. Rev ed. New York: Riverhead Books, 2001.

Walsh, David. *Selling Out America's Children: How America Puts Profits before Values and What Parents Can Do*. Minneapolis: Fairview Press, 1994. A later report from the Kaiser Family Foundation report in 2003 indicates that 64 percent of all shows have some sexual content up from half (56 percent) of all shows 4 years earlier. Fourteen percent now include sexual intercourse, either depicted or strongly implied, an increase from 7 percent four years earlier; in sitcoms alone the percentage of content dealing with sex rose to 84 percent in 2000 from 56 percent in 1998.

# CITIZEN PARTICIPATION AND CIVIC ENGAGEMENT

# 9

## CIVIC CAPACITY:
## WHAT, WHY, AND FROM WHENCE

*Clarence N. Stone*

SOME OBSERVERS THINK OF A COMMUNITY'S CIVIC capacity as level of voting, volunteering, and participating in public hearings. In this essay, I put forward a different view, that of civic capacity as concerted efforts to address major community problems. By "concerted" I mean special actions to involve multiple sectors of a locality, governmental and nongovernmental. The label "civic" refers to actions built around the idea of furthering the well-being of the entire community, not just a particular segment or group.

Bringing a locality's civic capacity into play represents a deliberate attempt to move beyond business as usual. Because the community faces an out-of-the-ordinary challenge, solving the problem will require a great deal more than routine governmental action. As a concept, civic capacity rests on the assumption that government and civil society are not discrete spheres of activity. They connect and merge in myriad ways. It follows, then, that what we call public policy is in fact the joint product of governmental and nongovernmental action. Put another way, the character and effectiveness of governmental activity depends substantially on how it combines with related nongovernmental activity. The relationship is particularly important in public education, and education puts democracy in a revealing light.

Education is not so much a service delivered to the public as an aim that is served by the combined efforts of educators and members of the community. Thus, whereas many analysts treat electoral accountability as central, the democratic system allows for a wide enlistment in efforts to solve or ameliorate the major problems faced by a community. In this view of democracy, citizens are not a passive audience that approves or disapproves of the performance of public officials, but rather needed contributors to community efforts. To the extent that citizens are passive, democracy falls short of its full measure. Since public-policy results are the product of both governmental and nongovernmental action, a process such as school reform is democratic only to the extent that the community is broadly engaged.

Below I present four cases in which localities have participated in extraordinary efforts to turn school performance around. First, however, consideration is given to the nature of the education problem and why the mesh between schools and community is so important.

## The Problem of Public School Performance

Disappointing academic achievement is found primarily in areas where low-income populations are concentrated. Research has shown that the performance of individual schools is greatly influenced by the family background and community environment of the students in attendance. The education problem is thus closely linked to poverty. When the school community is affluent and the parents themselves are well educated, there is an easy fit between what public schools do routinely and the population served.

The education problem is class-based for several reasons. First, better-educated parents provide their children with greater readiness for conventional academic learning. Moreover, affluent parents provide home advantages and auxiliary resources for the schools their children attend. Children of the affluent middle class exist in an environment of high expectations, reinforced by abundant examples of realized opportunities. Support, encouragement, and aspirations are not missing from households of low and modest means, but they are harder to come by, more difficult to sustain, and face more barriers.

Schools themselves play a major role in shaping expectations. As early as the mid-1960s the psychologist Kenneth B. Clark, in the book *Dark Ghetto: Dilemmas of Social Power*, identified a pattern of low regard for poor and minority students, lax standards, and an undemanding curriculum. A destructive cycle of low expectations feeding low achievement has long been at work. Throughout much of the twentieth century, urban schools faced little pressure to change their approach.

Educator expectations and performance, along with student response, do not occur in a vacuum. They take shape in an environment of school-community relations, with social, political, and economic dimensions. Contrast the experience of schools serving the poor with an account of school-community relations in a setting of affluence. A former school board member from Houston, Texas, says this of the parents in his middle-class district:

> Most volunteered some time in their neighborhood school. Some, the school activists, were exceptional. I called them the PTO mothers. They were usually wives of professional men with excellent incomes. Some

had professional degrees themselves. They had put their careers on hold to be full-time homemakers. And as their children grew older, some became practically full-time, unpaid school employees.

The PTO mothers volunteered time to chaperone students on field trips, assisted teachers in the classroom, worked in the office, and managed events like fall concerts, show choirs, carnivals, auctions, Christmas programs, and fundraising walkathons. Some programs attracted nearly 1,000 parents. These PTO mothers (and sometimes fathers) helped raise $30,000, sometimes up to $100,000, per year for teaching materials, computers, stage curtains, or whatever the school needed. And they didn't just serve their own children. . . .

These PTO mothers made schools successful. They demanded effective teaching, high academic standards, and strong leadership. They were towers of strength to effective principals. But if principals were ineffective or the bureaucracy did not respond to programmatic or facilities needs, they took action. They called their [school board member], took him out to lunch, organized letter-writing campaigns or circulated petitions. They knew how the system worked, and they got results.[1]

In concrete and direct ways, schools and community formed an integrated system. Parents volunteered and raised money privately for extras, thereby enhancing school resources. They not only had the time and inclination to be involved, they also made demands on the schools directly and through the school board. And in some matters they were allies of principals and the school board. Parents possessed a high sense of political efficacy on school matters to go along with the fact that they were organized and had resources and connections. Almost certainly, students in these schools came from households in which academic achievement was expected and college attendance was the norm. Parental engagement was a powerful signal to children about the great importance of education. Family and friendship connections provided concrete reinforcement for aspirations that linked academic achievement with personal career goals and the promise of a satisfying life. These connections also provide detailed information about how to pursue paths of educational advancement. As the psychiatrist and education reformer James P. Comer would argue, school and community outlook and expectations were aligned around academic achievement. What Comer in his book *School Power* called "the hand of hopelessness" (p. viii) that grips many urban schools posed little threat to this affluent corner of Houston, where school and community formed a productive partnership.

Consider now the contrasting situation in many schools serving lower-income neighborhoods. Distrust is pervasive—in the words of Charles M. Payne, "The basic web of social relationships is likely to be severely damaged."[2] Instead of home and school reinforcing one another, they may be in conflict, and teacher–parent tension may run at a high level. In such circumstances, Comer argues in *School Power*, students have unfulfilled needs and become negative about their school experience. He observes: "The power of all involved is amorphous, fragmented, and tenuous. Thus nobody is able to address the school mission in a cooperative, systematic, sustained way. . . . Administrators, teachers, and parents are paralyzed" (p. 30). Instead of promoting an effective collaboration between school and neighborhood, community conditions and household vulnerabilities conspire to promote disappointment and defensiveness.

By no means do all schools in lower-income neighborhoods perform weakly, and some educators are quite skillful in mobilizing resources from the larger community and enlisting constructively the support of parents. Still, the pattern is clear; schools in poor neighborhoods face greater challenges—parents have fewer material resources, they tend to be less strongly organized, external assistance is often scarce, central offices often seem overwhelmed, union officials may be unhelpful, and the struggle to combat low expectations is unending.

When schools are predominantly middle class and affluent, public and private efforts often cohere without extraordinary mobilization. The private (that is, the nongovernmental) contribution to a joint effort is not always appreciated by the casual observer. Yet the closer one looks, the more the nongovernmental part stands out, and the private infusions include intangible matters of outlook and aspiration as well as tangible forms of assistance. In nonaffluent areas, school and community can come together, but the pull of centrifugal forces is strong and good intentions are hard to sustain.

The mesh between school and community depends on both what the households of students bring to the engagement and what schools provide. Under terms of strong fiscal constraints, traditionally public schools provide a set of standardized education practices. These are adjusted to the particular situation of the community they serve, but schools have a much more difficult time responding effectively to the circumstances of students from backgrounds scarce in privileges and opportunities. In a predominantly middle-class society, educators have no built-in propensity to reach out to and meet the needs of families at the poverty level. To do so likely means extraordinary effort. The school-community relationship often turns on the stubborn fact that much of society's investment in children and youth occurs through the household, and some households are able to invest a great deal more than others.

The American dream pictures schools as the great equalizer.[3] Yet an accompanying belief sees performance as a matter of individual effort, leaving one with little inclination to look widely for systemic forces at work. Without a larger sense of direction and purpose, individuals tend to make what they can of the immediate situation.

The impetus for big-picture reform seldom comes from professionals on the inside, operating as insiders. It almost always involves the entry of a new and more wide-ranging set of actors. Once education became a national concern, reform and reexamination of schools became matters of widening public debate. With a national movement under way, communities were in a better position to challenge the traditional position of schools as insulated from external scrutiny and establish education as a problem that could be tackled as a local issue of wide civic importance. Reform-minded educators could search for allies, and civic and political leaders could put forward their concerns without being rebuffed by claims that they were intruding into matters best left to educators. Contemporary local efforts thus operate under an umbrella of a national movement that has made it easier to identify education as a problem for community-wide action. The ongoing national movement for education reform has activated crucial state players, but even combined federal and state action has limited impact without local enlistment in the effort.

Turning the situation around involves intentional and concerted efforts to move beyond the usual state of affairs and create a new set of conditions. At the local level, it means making moves to bring a community's civic capacity into operation. The national climate is important but in itself amounts to little without local communities taking concrete action. Let us turn now to the local process of building civic capacity around school reform.

## Building Civic Capacity: Four Cases

### Kent County, Maryland

Kent County is a small, nonmetropolitan jurisdiction on Maryland's Eastern Shore. It is a place neither of great affluence nor of high poverty. Of the county's 2,795 students, 38 percent are eligible for federally assisted meals, and the racial breakdown is 30 percent African American and 70 percent white.[4]

When the state's education department first put into operation its Performance Assessment Program, Kent students scored quite low. Reflecting community concern, the elected school board moved immediately to address the problem by hiring a new school superintendent who could be a strong instructional leader. Board members decided on Dr. Lorraine Costella, who had previously served as assistant superintendent for curriculum and instruction for the state. Costella had a reputation as an innovator, and by hiring her, this rural county showed its willingness to pursue a new path to school reform. Urgency to move beyond business as usual came from the disappointing scores on the state test.

The new superintendent immediately laid the groundwork for a cross-sector coalition. Including key stakeholders from the very beginning, she started by holding an all-day strategic planning forum that included teachers, principals, school board members, and community leaders. The forum refined the school system's goals into a list of five, headed by academic achievement. The main activities were curriculum development, which included aligning curriculum with state standards and tying these aims to professional development. Superintendent Costella tackled the difficult work of building an organizational infrastructure by devising multiple ways to involve principals and teachers, relying particularly heavily on principals rather than central office staff to implement reforms. She followed through on the strategic planning forum by turning to a school board member for guidance in adopting a special management process designed for education—the Baldrige in Education approach. Involving all stakeholders in devising an implementation plan, this process was initiated by creating a Baldrige Leadership Team to begin the planning and to oversee its implementation. This team included members from the school board, the union, principals, teachers, parents, and the community. The approach involved a year's training, and led to a classroom compact through which teachers could work with students in determining goals and defining how those goals would be met. As part of the process, there were also site teams in each school.

What is striking about the Kent County experience is that the initial involvement of multiple stakeholders was followed by extensive continuing engagement. The superintendent also adopted the practice of meeting regularly with the union president, and those meetings yielded concrete results such as decentralizing professional development to the school level and shifting responsibility for it to the faculty.

Dr. Costella created a Professional Development Council, again made up of multiple stakeholders. Professional development included sending teachers and principals to other school districts to observe their practices and also putting them into special summer training programs. These extraordinary measures cost money, and the superintendent used her expertise in proposal writing to bring external funds into the district from the state, federal government, and private sources. That too became a collective enterprise as the superintendent trained staff at all levels in grant seeking.

Professional development also served to create networks of teachers to support professional growth and to link new teachers with mentors. Collaboration occurred at the top as well. The superintendent met regularly with the board chair and distributed a weekly newsletter to board members. Relationship building thus included the superintendent's high accessibility to school board members, as she sought to keep all elements closely involved.

A process of setting goals and measuring progress on those goals can be unsettling to members of an organization. Superintendent Costella's strategy for easing this transition was to create structures and informal practices to encourage collaboration and innovation. These efforts worked, and three years after Dr. Costella became superintendent Kent County moved to the top in performance on the state's tests. How did such a quick turnaround happen? Togneri and

Lazarus explain: "Only by building internal leadership capacity at the school level were district leaders able to infuse improvement throughout the district" (p. 28). Kent County provides an example of reform based on clear goals with detailed attention to creating a sense of inclusion in planning and implementation. Partnership and pursuit of shared understanding were not confined to an initial exercise, but very much a continuing part of the reform process. The superintendent took little for granted and made Kent County into a clear case of a locality that "worked on working together" (Togneri and Anderson, p. 32).

A superficial observer might take Kent County as evidence that school systems need only try harder. However, the multifaceted approach pursued in Kent was not done within the confines of the ordinary budget. Moreover, Dr. Costella developed the professionalization of her staff in such a way that they put in long hours and extra effort. They did so because they felt valued and saw themselves as respected members of a team. Teachers and principals also found themselves under a heavy workload. The superintendent's approach was to distribute leadership throughout the district, but not without making changes. During her eight years as superintendent, she replaced a majority of the school principals as she reshaped the system into one in which principals are instructional leaders.

As a small school district, Kent County is administratively simpler than large urban districts. But small rural districts are not known for being especially open to change. The superintendent managed the feat of shaping a highly innovative system by clear direction from the top, legitimized by extensive consultation not just with the school board and community leadership but also with the professional staff through multiple channels of interaction. She balanced direction from the top with dispersing leadership responsibility throughout the system. And by combining careful orchestration inside the system with added resources from outside, she engendered an ethos of professional pride that nurtured a willingness to make extra efforts.

## El Paso, Texas

El Paso, Texas is a border city, with a population of more than a half million. In Texas, school districts do not match city or county boundaries. The city is served by three districts, two of which spill outside the city limits. The three urban districts in combination contain 163 schools and enroll 135,000 students, of whom 85 percent are Hispanic. Two-thirds of the students are low income, and about half begin school with limited proficiency in English.[5]

Whereas Kent County is small enough for most exchanges to occur between individuals personally connected, El Paso's route to school reform involved significant interaction among people possessing important institutional bases. And while reform in Kent County took place primarily in a single small school system, reformers in El Paso established an education intermediary, the El Paso Collaborative for Academic Excellence, housed on the campus of and supported by the University of Texas at El Paso (UTEP). Launched in 1992, the collaborative originated in discussions around education and a changing economy.

As a border city with a low-wage economy, El Paso is highly vulnerable to the forces of globalization. In this context, a conversation opened up between the chamber of commerce and Sister Maribeth Larkin, lead organizer for the El Paso Interdenominational Sponsoring Organization (EPISO), a community-based organization and the local affiliate of the Industrial Areas Foundation. The recently inaugurated president of UTEP, Dr. Diana Natalicio, joined the discussions as someone interested in seeing the university take a larger role in the community.

President Natalicio also brought into the discussions Dr. Susana Navarro. A native of El Paso, Navarro had just returned to the city after involvement in education reform in California. From this experience Navarro had a clear vision of the need to combine standards reform with a closing of the achievement gap, and she had a firm idea of how to go about it. President Natalicio agreed to base an initiative at UTEP, and Navarro was named executive director. The collaborative thus became an autonomous unit on the UTEP campus, headed by a broadly representative board with President Natalicio as chair. Joining her on the board were Larkin of EPISO, representatives of the business sector (the presidents of the Greater El Paso and El Paso Hispanic Chambers of Commerce), major local-government officials (the mayor and the county chief executive), and key education figures (the three school superintendents, the executive director of the regional service center of the Texas Education Agency, and the president of the community college).

Larkin, Navarro, and Natalicio formed an inner core of actors with a close harmony of vision and complementary roles to play. As a highly regarded university president, Natalicio could bring key people to the table. Larkin provided an important community base of support, and Navarro gave the initiative a concrete form that had strong appeal to the three school superintendents. In bringing to fruition the collaborative, its architects made use of a network of existing organizations and specially created task forces. Taking a cue from an approach Navarro had developed in her earlier work, they used education data to highlight the problem of weak academic performance, especially its equity dimension. State testing added urgency to the picture.

The collaborative represented a response to the concerns of educators, the community, and the business sector. Heading an organization with a distinct and appealing mission, Navarro recruited a dedicated and focused staff. She also made good use of her connections to the foundation world. Although a small operation at first, the collaborative got off to a fast start and, with the backing of the superintendents, established momentum early on.

The approach of the collaborative resembles the systemic effort that Kent County followed. It included close attention to curriculum, extensive use of data, and the involvement of parents and other members of the community to foster support for standards-based schooling. The central activity, however, was teacher training and professional development for administrators, teachers, and staff. Like Kent County, El Paso's schools have experienced significant increases in test-score performance. In addition, growing percentages of students enroll in and pass demanding math and science courses.

The launching of the collaborative coincided with a state mandate for site-based management, and the initial effort of the collaborative was to encourage teachers, administrators, and parents to work together at the school level to develop a team approach. Thus a Teams Leadership Institute held a central place in the work of the collaborative from early on, and professional development for principals enjoyed high priority. Principals provide a vital link to parents and community, and they have been a key to building and maintaining school-level support for standards-based reform.

With teacher quality a critical concern, the collaborative worked closely with the College of Education to align teacher preparation with school reform. UTEP became a member of John Goodlad's National Network for Educational Renewal, and the college restructured its teacher preparation to a field-based program, working more closely with and in the area's public schools. Collaboration is by no means restricted to matters of curriculum. The university's Center for Civic Engagement seeks to help area schools foster parent involvement.

In working with the three urban school districts (and then extending some of its activities to the smaller districts in the county), the collaborative wanted the schools to be active partners. As a manifold force, the collaborative offered technical assistance in various forms, tangible resources through its success in grant seeking, an accessible fount of ideas, and a communication link to various elements of the wider community. The collaborative also has operated a series of yearlong seminars and offers follow-through sessions as part of a Parent Engagement Network. The meetings of the collaborative's board provided a way to disseminate ideas and lay groundwork for high-profile work. Because the board meets on a regular basis and deliberates about priorities, it can orient newcomers, whether they be school superintendents, the lead organizer for EPISO, the chamber of commerce president, or the new head of the community college.

The collaborative and its goal of systemic reform have been backed by major centers of institutional power in the community. Its board members are top officials in various organizations and institutions; in February 2000, the executive director of the collaborative and a leading business figure co-chaired an Education Summit to bring together more than three hundred participants—educators, parents, businesspeople, government officials, and community representatives—to discuss ongoing challenges and consider steps for the future. Several task forces were created to pursue specific aims identified in summit discussions. With the collaborative as a continuing source of ideas, activities, and outreach, educational achievement remains a focal concern in the community, and the collaborative has fostered initiatives, encompassing EPISO, UTEP, and the business sector, such as one to increase college enrollment in the community.

In a large and diverse community like El Paso, building civic capacity is no easy matter. For action to take place, someone needed to identify a crisis and frame it as a specific problem in need of urgent action. The convergent concerns of Natalicio, Navarro, and Larkin provided that framework, and data on student performance, dropouts, and low college enrollment made the problem specific and concrete. With Navarro's prior experience to draw on, the collaborative provided a proven solution to fit the problem. As in the case of Kent County, state actions provided important context. Skillful framing is thus one important step—identifying a problem broad enough to address concerns of a wide cross-section of civic and other community actors, while specific enough to show that planned actions could make a difference.

Second, the initiating actors had high civic standing. It made a difference that the president of UTEP was not only head of a major institution in the city, but also someone of stature, widely recognized for her leadership and accomplishments. That the governing board of the newly formed collaborative was both broadly representative and composed of important figures in the locality reinforced the credibility of the initiative.

Significantly, the El Paso Collaborative for Academic Excellence has enjoyed substantial corporate and foundation support that enables it to employ full-time professionals and offer high-quality and focused professional development. Local nonprofits dealing with education and other issues of children and youth are often shoestring operations in which the staff finds itself having to cut corners and raise funds just to meet the payroll. By contrast, the collaborative operated from the beginning in a secure position with ample backing. Furthermore, being housed at a university highlighted the collaborative's professionalism and expertise. Following through on initial support from Coca-Cola and Pew Charitable Trusts, funding from, among others, the National Science Foundation (NSF) has provided resources and additional credentialing.

Developing civic capacity is a dynamic process that, at any given time, can break down. Personal misunderstandings, the allure of new and different calls for action, the coming and going of central figures, or simply the erosion over time of important connections among people or between organizations can cause an initiative to lose force. It is important, therefore, to display continuing momentum. The collaborative benefited greatly from the fact that its first program effort was fully embraced by one of the area's school superintendents, who committed his entire system to taking part from the beginning. That contributed to early drive, and substantial NSF funding along with such events as the Education Summit sustained momentum to give the collaborative a recognized place in the community.

*Boston*

In the same population category as El Paso, Boston also has a sizable poverty population among its schoolchildren, with 71 percent eligible for federally assisted meals. But that figure derives partly from the fact that one-quarter of the school-age children in Boston attend private schools or schools in the suburbs. Whereas El Paso is overwhelmingly Hispanic, Boston has a diverse school population, and runs programs for a total of seven language groups. Combined with a school population made up mainly of children of color, Boston has a white-majority electorate. It also has a history of racial tension.[6]

For much of the latter half of the twentieth century, Boston, with its changing student demography, provided an example of low civic capacity with respect to education. In the post–World War II era, Boston schools were noted first for their isolation from the community they served. The school system next went through a prolonged battle over school desegregation and busing, and, as a result, a federal judge assumed control.[7] Racial and ethnic conflict, patronage and scandal, demagoguery by members of the city's elected school committee, and an inwardly focused school administration helped keep business at a distance and academic achievement levels in the background.

A mix of racial discord and public cynicism gave Boston's school system an unpromising heritage to overcome. Yet several factors converged to turn around school politics and make possible the building of civic capacity. First of all, with desegregation at an impasse in 1974, when Judge W. Arthur Garrity took charge, he formed community support structures including a Citywide Coordinating Council to monitor compliance with the desegregation order, but also district advisory councils, racial-ethnic parent councils for each school, and an extensive set of school-college and school-business partnerships.

In a second significant turn, Boston's business sector recognized its growing need for a workforce of high-tech employees. However, business needed a comfortable platform for its involvement, and that came through its participation in job training. The Boston business group the Vault had no infrastructure of staff and programs. But its involvement in the Private Industry Council (PIC), created under the federal Job Training Partnership Act, led to the development of business-school partnerships. The PIC did possess staff, and became the entity for creating and housing the Boston Compact, initially an agreement between the school system and the business sector involving a pledge by business to provide summer jobs and hire graduates in exchange for a promise by the school district to bring about educational improvement. Although the Compact has had a somewhat rocky history, it has focused attention on academic achievement and enlisted a growing number of partners—higher education, labor organizations, the local public education fund, the Boston Human Services Coalition, and the Boston Cultural Partnerships.

Business funding helped initiate the public education fund—the Boston Plan (short for the Boston Plan for Excellence in the Public Schools)—as a spin-off of the Compact. Among other activities, it was initially home to a scholarship and mentor program to boost college attendance among high school students, and that program—ACCESS—was in turn spun off as an autonomous operation.

It is not clear how much business involvement would have taken place anyway, but Judge Garrity played a key role, not only in bringing about a desegregation plan and ending that impasse, but also in helping spur the process of building civic capacity by pressuring "businesses, higher education institutions, community organizations, and parents to become more involved" (Portz, Stein, and Jones 1999, p. 89). Regardless of the initial motivation, business proved to be a willing participant and became increasingly important as the federal presence diminished.

However, even with an expansive business role, the enlistment of other partners, and the growth of the local education fund into one of the premier intermediaries in the nation, Boston's education politics still had to overcome a difficult history. Conflict centered in the elected school committee and frequent turnover in the office of superintendent. In reaction, business played a major role in the move to replace the elected body with one appointed by the mayor. The move to an appointed school committee began with Mayor Raymond Flynn and was carried forward eagerly by his successor, Thomas Menino.

Although the emergence of mayoral leadership is the most visible change to occur in Boston, it was but one of a series of moves to replace an older system of provincial politics centered in the city's Irish Catholic population. A turn to strong, professionally minded superintendents was a key factor in the transition, and creation of the Boston Plan as reform intermediary was a parallel move. It too has given focus to reform, as business began to support systemic change. The Boston Plan's leadership and the superintendent's office, backed by a sizable Annenberg grant, thus give the city a scope of professional capacity and vision, without which the mayor's leadership would amount to little. Further Mayor Menino's recruitment of Thomas Payzant in 1995 was an important step. From previous service as U.S. assistant secretary of education and before that superintendent of San Diego schools, Payzant had a reputation as eminent education administrator, and his professional standing contributed to the reform alignment.

With the mayor's office as a pivot around which change was accomplished, it is significant that the appointed school committee was overwhelmingly affirmed in a 1996 referendum. Nevertheless there is criticism that the school committee is not as attuned as it should be to the city's grassroots groups and to the African American community particularly. Be that as it may, the mayor provided political protection for the school committee and the superintendent, claiming that the mayor wanted to be judged by what happened with the city's schools.

Professional development (largely school-based) around standards-based reform and improved classroom instruction are central activities. Parent and community engagement are recognized goals and the system makes use of part-time liaisons in an effort to build a parental network. Extra resources have come through foundation and private and public sector grants. A thriving economy in the 1990s enabled the state to increase its education funding and add momentum to school reform. (A prolonged downturn in the national economy after 2000 took a toll on funding.) More than most places, Boston under mayoral leadership has linked schools with health, youth development, and other social services. The elements of mayoral leadership, business support, a top-notch education fund, and varied forms of parent and community involvement along with a respected superintendent and a teachers' union that is (for the most part) an ally of school reform provide a good base on which to build civic capacity.

Still, the legacy of the past remains and the foundation of collaboration is less than rock solid. In Boston, as in Kent County and El Paso, state testing is an important feature of the context, and time is a scarce commodity. A high level of commitment to raising academic achievement puts large demands on staff, and, as Michael Usdan and Larry Cuban have observed, "There persists the feeling that the school system is 'drowning' with all it has to do to improve instruction and student achievement."[8] High school test scores have proven stubbornly static, even as elementary scores rose, and the school system continues to receive criticism for the slow pace of reform. Despite an unpromising legacy, Boston has moved on a variety of fronts, but success remains uneven.

## Philadelphia

Although its population had declined to a million and a half by 2000, Philadelphia remains one of the nation's largest cities. As in El Paso and Boston, the school population is preponderantly children of color and poor. Like Boston, Philadelphia received an Annenberg grant; and launched school reform with backing from the business sector. From there the similarity breaks down. Whereas Boston eventually worked its way through intergroup conflict and public cynicism to get on track, Philadelphia saw its reform initiative derail. The damage may not be permanent, as a reform effort continues to be mounted, but the civic disrepair was serious.[9]

The context is important. Since 1950, Philadelphia has lost about one-third of its population and four-fifths of its manufacturing jobs. The city also has a high tax burden and receives a low level of assistance from the state, Pennsylvania being one of the weakest states in the nation in efforts to equalize expenditure on education. Suburbs around Philadelphia offer higher salaries to teachers than the city does and spend considerably more per pupil. The teachers' union is strong and not averse to strikes, and the school bureaucracy and union displayed strong resistance to a major reform initiated under

Constance Clayton, Philadelphia's superintendent of schools from 1980 to 1992.

In 1994 a city newspaper series highlighted dismal performance by the school system. Finger-pointing was commonplace. Business saw a weak school system as a major cause of the city's economic decline, but some community-based leaders, in the words of Jolley Christman and Amy Rhodes, "resented what they perceived as unrealistic expectations for public education" and "were angry that school bore the blame for deep-seated social ills." A foundation study characterized the city's civic leadership as "disengaged" and caught up in a "pervasive defeatist mentality."[10]

Yet the story is not entirely one-sided. Business and philanthropy established an important education intermediary, the Philadelphia Education Fund. Numerous other education and youth-related organizations populate the civic landscape, and business leaders have long been concerned about school performance. Moreover, under Mayor Edward G. Rendell's tenure from 1992 to 2000, the city experienced a modest economic resurgence.

Into this mix of forces came David Hornbeck, appointed superintendent of schools in 1994. That event came very shortly after a 1993 state legislative decision to freeze the funding formula for local school districts. Adjusted for inflation, state assistance to Philadelphia schools declined by 5.9 percent over the next five years, one study found.[11] In the fall of 1994 Republican Thomas Ridge was elected governor, and he quickly proved to be an unsympathetic participant.

Hornbeck was not a professional educator by background, but he had served as state school superintendent in Maryland and as a consultant to the state of Kentucky in implementing the widely touted Kentucky Education Reform Act in 1990. Drawing on his experience in Kentucky, Hornbeck initiated his reform plan, Children Achieving, in February 1995, and Philadelphia received a $50 million Annenberg Challenge grant for a five-year period, matched by $100 million from Philadelphia businesses and foundations and from federal grants.

Children Achieving was a comprehensive approach aimed at reforming the system around the twin aims of achievement and equity, very much in line with the aims identified in Kent County, El Paso, and Boston. It was standards based, embracing the principle that all children can achieve at a high level with appropriate learning opportunities. Ongoing assessment and accountability, professional development, and, at least in rhetoric, parent and community engagement were important elements, again closely similar to the three communities described above. However, a close examination of parent engagement in Philadelphia showed that pursuit of parent and community involvement was quite limited, with the superintendent preoccupied with mobilizing support behind his effort to obtain greater funding from the state. Staff development was a part of the "Action Design" of the initiative, but, given scarce resources, it also failed to get full attention. Indeed, earlier work in professional development through teacher networks was largely ignored.

Corporate and other civic leaders saw Hornbeck's initiative as an important vehicle for improving schools, and they provided not only matching funds for the Annenberg grant but a business-created entity, Greater Philadelphia First, that served to administer the grant. Initial corporate enthusiasm was high, and Philadelphia moved quickly to raise the matching funds. Early support, however, was not sustained. Five years after the launching of Children Achieving, as the Annenberg grant period was coming to a close, Superintendent Hornbeck resigned when he faced the prospect of his initiative being dismantled. How did reform get off track? An important fact is that school performance did improve initially in that five-year period. Test scores went up, and there was greater public attention to education. In the aftermath, some observers complained that test scores did not go up fast enough and far enough. Yet an analysis of test results showed that Philadelphia's performance not only went up, but city schools also made more progress than other districts. On the face of it, Philadelphia's performance was for a time stronger than Boston's in test-score improvement.

Philadelphia's coalition of business and philanthropic interests and the school superintendent was not in itself a sufficient base from which to launch and sustain comprehensive school reform. There were two main sources of conflict, one involving the city and the state. In Kentucky, where Hornbeck had promoted comprehensive reform with considerable success, the state made major increases in funding. In Pennsylvania, Governor Ridge proved totally unresponsive to city pleas for more money. A board member of Greater Philadelphia First recounted his conversation with the governor, in which he asked Ridge how they could "link arms" in reforming Philadelphia's schools. The response was that the governor saw the existing system as something that could not be fixed and that energy should go into "building an alternative system."[12] Ridge twice introduced but failed to get enacted statewide voucher plans. The funding impasse held throughout Ridge's tenure as governor.

Teachers and principals also failed to join the reform coalition and widely resisted accountability provisions. Some observers fault Hornbeck's approach. His version of systemic reform avoided incrementalism, going after everything at once. Even though this approach put everyone under pressure, a sustained effort to bring teachers and principals along did not materialize. As some saw it, the architects of change tended to fault teachers rather than working with them to gain support for reforms. For their part, school officials viewed the teachers' union, the Philadelphia Federation of Teachers (PFT), as adversarial and intransigent, often either unwilling to take part in meetings or obstructionist in those they did attend. In turn, PFT saw Children Achieving as a threat and strongly objected to its accountability provision. The researcher Ellen Foley reported that during "four years of meetings with and interviewing central office staff and

PFT representatives, we did not hear a single positive comment from either group about the other." When Hornbeck attempted to reconstitute two poorly performing high schools, school staff challenged the move and, according to Foley, an external arbitrator found the process faulty because "the District failed to engage in the necessary consultation with the PFT."[13]

Further, flawed implementation included awkward sequencing, with the accountability mechanism put in place before curriculum and professional development were established as support. Indeed, even though the Philadelphia Education Fund persuaded the central office that a capacity-building role was needed, scarce resources meant that teachers were given little time for professional development, to develop curriculum, and to build relationships with colleagues. Insufficient classroom materials aggravated the situation further. Much of the professional development effort that did take place focused on informing staff about Hornbeck's ambitious program of reform. With little input from teachers and principals, the experience came across more as mandates from the central office than as something related to classroom experience.

In a climate of friction and misunderstanding, many principals and other administrators resisted various parts of the initiative and held back support during Hornbeck's clash with the state over additional funding. The teachers' union, in particular, made relations with the state and the business sector more difficult by giving no ground on key changes sought, from a longer school day to pay for performance. Failing to gain such concessions, the school district saw its standing with the business sector nosedive.

Instead of moving toward calibration, the planets of reform stayed in serious misalignment. As the Annenberg grant approached its close, Governor Ridge proved to be ideologically unbending and Hornbeck by many accounts was undiplomatic and confrontational. When Ridge yielded nothing as state education aid continued to decline, school and city officials along with community leaders filed a lawsuit against the state (a successful suit in Kentucky had been a precipitating event in that state's embrace of school reform). The case in Pennsylvania was dismissed by the state supreme court, which held that funding decisions must be made by the legislature. The next year, Hornbeck threatened to adopt an unbalanced budget unless the state provided more money, and he and city officials filed a federal civil rights suit against the state, contending that its funding practices discriminated against school districts with large numbers of nonwhite students. As the conflict began to take an increasingly personal form, the chances of resolution faded away. For its part, the state responded by passing a takeover law aimed at Philadelphia.

Further adding to the isolation of city and school officials, business support for Children Achieving eroded badly, and the makeup of the Greater Philadelphia First board changed—by 2000 only four of the founding twenty-three CEOs remained. The days of early enthusiasm for Hornbeck's initiative gave way to a new political era; in March of 1999 board members of Greater Philadelphia First endorsed Governor Ridge's second attempt to enact a statewide voucher plan. One observer offered this comment: "David [Hornbeck] believed you could make a social contract with the business community, but he looked up and they were gone. I don't think the corporate community is playing a healthy, visible constructive role in public education. But they carry tremendous weight. It's a combination of factors. So few businesses are local now. And there are some leaders who came through the Archdiocese system. They want to keep taxes down and have vouchers."[14]

A study by the Philadelphia-based Consortium for Policy Research in Education offered a mixed assessment of Hornbeck's superintendency. He brought significant strengths to his position: "David Hornbeck was an attractive candidate for Philadelphia's superintendency. He brought star power as a national educational reform figure, and a passionate commitment to improving both urban schools and the life chances of poor students of color. He also had a strong belief that his systemic approach to school reform could turn around a poorly performing urban school system."[15] Yet the study also found contradictions in Hornbeck's approach, and the superintendent's effort to be truly comprehensive and move on all fronts at once meant that building broad support and achieving a shared understanding suffered.

Business proved to be an unreliable ally, reluctant to do battle for enhanced state funding and easily attracted to such market-like solutions as vouchers. Against a backdrop of the city's fiscal squeeze, the launching of something as ambitious as Children Achieving was, in the words of Foley, "a calculated risk that the Annenberg Challenge grant could be used to improve performance, and that improved performance would generate the political will to obtain increased funding either through the city, the courts, or the legislature."[16] The gamble failed, even with early test score gains.

Although the presence of parochial schools may have weakened the support of the city's business leadership for sustained reform of the public school system, the Boston example shows that the presence of parochial schools is not a sufficient stumbling block to account for the failure of civic capacity to be sustained behind reform. No single factor stands out as the source of the demise of Hornbeck's initiative. The superintendent's political skill can be faulted, but there is also no doubt that sustaining a coalition around school reform is particularly difficult when financial resources are lacking.

Declining assistance from the state was a major obstacle, and that has to be understood against the background of the political isolation of the city. Hornbeck may have played that isolation badly, even worsening it, but the friction between Mayor John F. Street, who took office in 2000, and Governor Mark Schweiker, who succeeded Ridge in 2001, suggests that the problem was more than a clash of personalities. It had deep partisan roots in the state-city relationship between Pennsylvania and Philadelphia. Race also played a part.[17] When Hornbeck arrived, the city's voluntary desegregation plan had already given rise to explicit concerns about equity and inadequate school finance. Yet Governor Ridge and Republican legislative leaders proved unresponsive to calls to address the city's funding situation; and they also ignored a referendum call for Mayor Street to assume a leadership role in education parallel to that of mayors in Boston and Chicago. Still, Hornbeck made significant missteps. Frustrated over an extremely difficult financial position, Hornbeck found himself consumed by conflict. Promising initiatives, such as those on parent engagement, lost priority standing as the superintendent became preoccupied with his fight over state funding.

For Philadelphia, the resignation of Superintendent Hornbeck brought an end to Children Achieving, but one community activist saw a silver lining: "I think the ability to have a running conversation about achievement for all kids for 4 years running is a huge accomplishment. I think that people on the street have something to say about the education crisis we're facing because of David's efforts. It gives us something to build on, but we have to remember that it takes a long time."[18] Yet there is no avoiding the harsh reality that, even though Hornbeck brought powerful ideas to bear, they proved not to be enough to carry the day.

The derailment of Hornbeck's Children Achieving is one part of the story, but not the final word. Immediately following Hornbeck's resignation, his program was dismantled as the state exercised its takeover option. A proposed broad-gauge privatization in school management set off another round of conflict. Subsequently the election of a Democratic governor opened a new episode in state-city relations and gave fresh footing for the challenge of building civic capacity. The story continues to unfold.

## Civic Capacity and Local Democracy

In school reform, local action is a complement to, not a substitute for, national and state action. Still, local action is necessary. Federal- and state-initiated reforms are not self-executing. Across the four jurisdictions examined here, significant actors set in motion out-of-the ordinary processes to tackle the problem of weak academic achievement. Many other places have experienced ferment around education, but the nature and scope of activity vary greatly, with some communities still largely attached to business as usual. One purpose of civic capacity as a concept is to provide a framework for assessing the degree to which business as usual has been surmounted by a wider engagement in reform of public education.

Skeptics, particularly those who believe that improved academic achievement is strictly a matter of proper classroom technique, question whether wide engagement is really a positive factor. Given that reform, particularly systemic reform of the kind promoted in the four communities covered here, is multifaceted and given that reform efforts face a certain amount of lag time, we can hardly expect an authoritative resolution of the issue to happen overnight. What we can observe is that Kent County and El Paso did show substantial test-score improvement. In addition, El Paso students have greatly increased enrollment in demanding math and science courses.[19] Philadelphia showed some short-term improvements, but, as might be expected, they tailed off as Superintendent Hornbeck and his initiative became increasingly enmeshed in conflict. Of the four considered here, Boston is the unclear case. Elementary scores went up, but high-school scores did not. Yet Boston is unquestionably a different school system from the one described in telling detail by observers in the pre-reform days.[20] Moreover, high-school improvement has now moved to center stage, and the final chapter of reform has yet to be written.

Two big questions remain: First, what is the logic behind viewing civic capacity as a useful response to school reform? Second, how does civic capacity relate to democracy?

The logic is embedded in the Houston example cited at the beginning of this essay. The basic premise is that policy results such as educational achievement derive from the dual impact of governmental and nongovernmental actions. In the case of affluent, middle-class communities, the mesh of these two forces is usually academically productive because parents and their networks furnish academic readiness and reinforcing support to students, contribute supplementary resources to their schools, and provide monitoring of school performance. In lower-income and less-educated communities, the mesh between these two forces is not as smooth. Despite individual exceptions, these communities provide weaker readiness and support to students, contribute fewer supplementary resources, and are less able to monitor school performance. This pattern has a long history, based in racial stereotyping and discrimination, multigenerational confinement to low-wage work, and a general position of marginality.

For much of the twentieth century, schools serving the nonaffluent were politically insulated enough to cope with and even foster low expectations without pressure to perform effectively on counts of academic achievement. But now a new political climate has emerged. Within a larger national context of concern and action, civic capacity focused on education problems can provide a means whereby school isolation is ended and expectations of effective academic performance are brought to bear. When conditions are favorable, civic capacity brings additional resources (tangible and intangible) into play, and it provides a broad political framework within which school performance is scrutinized.

The full civic capacity of a community is a highly complex matter, and may be only partly realized even when strong efforts are made to mobilize it, particularly in communities with large populations of lower-income and minority students. Mobilization is an effort to compensate for the consequences of the usual course of affairs in a stratified society, but those consequences have multiple aspects that are not easily overcome. Immediate matters such as curriculum and teacher preparation are most readily identified, but much more is at stake. That is why parental engagement is important, though not easily achieved. Parent involvement is itself a form of resource, but, as is often the case, it takes resources to generate resources. And it requires looking beyond the classroom.

Overall, it is important to remember that not all resources are of a material kind. The expertise of educators, the political skill of central figures, proficiency in specialized matters such as proposal writing, and legitimacy and credibility generated by reform coalition membership are also important elements. In the overall mix, the effort and insight that parents can contribute, though not easy to enlist, have a potential to deepen the impact of school reform. The observers Cuban and Usdan caution against the "shallow roots" of top-down reform, pointing out that because the aim is to enhance "classroom teaching and learning, securing teachers' endorsement and parents support for changes are essential."[21] Thus civic capacity itself is not a particular blueprint for how schooling should take place, but a way of realigning how the community supports its education effort.

Important as civic capacity may be to school reform, it is also part of a larger story about democracy. It provides an important perspective on the practice of local democracy. To be true to the ancient understanding of a form of governance in which all rule and are ruled in turn, democracy must be differentiated from majoritarianism. Democracy precludes practices by which any group is relegated to the position of permanent minority, either by the ballot box or other means.

Local democracy involves much more than holding periodic elections or town-hall-style meetings. If having a role in shaping public policy is integral to local democracy, then voting or even a chance to voice opinions falls short of what is needed. Full citizenship means contributing to major areas of public policy, particularly those that bear directly on daily life. From the Houston vignette, we can see what is missing when educators are isolated from their communities. For good reason, Joel Handler, in *Down from Bureaucracy* (1996), speaks of "service engagement" rather than service delivery.

The quality of citizenship can be affected in various ways. Some observers equate democracy with the sounding of diverse voices without regard to what follows and how talk connects to action. Yet to the extent that democracy is about problem solving, the community in its various segments needs to develop and utilize a shared framework of action. If the populace is so divided that no common framework of action can be devised, then the chance to contribute to problem solving is diminished and so is the quality of citizenship. Conciliation, not impasse, is at the heart of democratic politics. Philadelphia during the

Hornbeck era is a telling example of how deadlock constricts the practice of democracy.

Thus, building civic capacity involves developing a shared understanding, even if loose in significant details and even if coexistence is part of the understanding. With the importance of a shared understanding in mind, we can see why professional development occupied such an important place in Kent County, El Paso, and Boston, and why in Philadelphia the relative neglect of professional development left deadlock undiminished. In short, when professional development gives educators a shared understanding of their task, augments their capacity to perform that task, and opens them to greater interaction with parents and other community members, then it is an effective, indeed much needed, contributor to civic capacity.

In full measure, building civic capacity also involves enhancing the abilities and opportunities to contribute of those previously excluded. To the extent that segments of the population continue to fall into a pattern of noninvolvement, then the principle of no permanent minority is violated and democratic practice falls short.

For lower-income parents, often unaccustomed to asserting themselves with professionals in positions of authority, an unwelcoming manner by educators can end the process. Barriers of mutual mistrust and apprehension can be substantial. A twofold process may be needed—one to orient parents toward participation in broader ways and the second to direct educators along the path toward embracing new modes of practice. However, in Philadelphia, top school officials failed to incorporate into professional development the practice of working with parents and viewing them as assets in the education of children. In some cases intermediaries have at least partially filled that gap. El Paso's collaborative, for example, has included parent engagement in its agenda, and the Boston plan also works on parent-educator collaboration. Significantly, despite overall weaknesses, Philadelphia had two intermediaries, the Alliance Organizing Project (AOP) and Teachers and Parents and Students (TAPAS) working to establish new relationships between parents and schools, and these organizations had some successes. However, these were selective instances in which not only were school-site educators receptive but special external funding provided support for outreach and organizing. This scope of effort is rare, and it had no large role in any of the four communities examined here.

An analysis of one such experience in Philadelphia, that of the Watkins Elementary School (a pseudonym), is nevertheless revealing. AOP provided a community organizer to work with the school as part of a broader strategy of strengthening lower-income neighborhoods. The school was performing relatively well, but the principal, after some initial reluctance, proved open to the idea that parents might provide him, as he put it, "with another level of support."[22] With assistance from the school counselor, the organizer found a small group of parents as a starting base, and then used one-on-one meetings to expand the circle of participants. When these parents talked about their concerns, safety emerged at the top of the list. And restoring some of the crossing guards cut in recent budgetary moves became the solution they settled on and around which they worked with parent groups at other schools. A few teachers joined the "public action" as well. With success on that matter, the parents moved on to the issue of an after-school program. Initially rebuffed by a no-resources response from the principal, they turned to the idea of an after-school parent-run homework club. The aim was academic enrichment, and the principal consented to the use of school facilities. The Philadelphia Education Fund provided training and assistance in writing what proved to be a successful funding proposal. Some teachers began to cooperate by offering their classroom materials for use and by referring students with need for assistance, and soon teachers and parents were working together for the benefit of children. Parents gained skill and confidence working with the students, and teachers saw the parents in a new light. Although coming from a background of exclusion and marginality:

> parents learned how to research an issue of concern; they were trained in classroom management, instruction, and curriculum; they learned to write funding proposals; they gained the confidence to interview public officials; they led public meetings; and they created a political campaign to focus attention on their children's needs. The AOP organizing process provided parents the opportunity to learn the skills of civic participation.[23]

The example is a small and unrepresentative one in the large picture of Philadelphia schools, but it shows that participation by parents can make substantive contributions to academic achievement, not just for their own children, but in shaping the climate for learning at the schoolwide level. In addition, parent engagement brings a broader set of concerns to bear, and can contribute needed "local knowledge." Moreover, questions of societal inequities are often pushed to the surface" (Gold 2001, p. 47). Wider participation expanded the scope of concerns considered.

The promise of building civic capacity is that, when carried through thoroughly, it can both serve instrumentally to advance school reform and at the same time strengthen democratic practice. The task of school reform is formidable; it involves changing expectations, increasing commitment, and expanding efforts all around. For local democracy's part, understood as containing a contributory dimension, it is no starry-eyed luxury. Rather it is essential if school reform is to be achieved in full measure.

Although the four cases in the condensed versions provided here can give only brief illustrations of civic capacity at work, they do show something of what is possible and of the dynamics of the process. At an abstract level, key elements in building civic capacity may sound formulaic: a shared definition of a problem as an agenda for action, combined with cross-sector mobilization of a coalition, yielding a proper mix and amount of resources, and executed through an appropriate and detailed plan. However, the process is more organic than this statement conveys. A community's problem-solving capacity has to do fundamentally with relationships—with who is included and on what terms. Moreover, for education particularly, a full capacity rests on what is in reality a democratic foundation; that is to say, a full capacity includes all stakeholders, parents and frontline educators among them. Thus, building civic capacity typically involves more than employment of existing relationships. As the AOP example illustrates, it sometimes means shaping new relationships, particularly in communities with sizable lower-income and minority populations.

## Notes

1. Quoted in McAdams, *Fighting to Save Our Urban Schools*, 60-61.
2. Payne, "So Much Reform, So Little Change," 243.
3. See Hochschild and Scovronick, *The American Dream and the Public Schools*, and Chapter 13 in this volume.
4. The account of school reform in Kent County, Maryland, is based on a study for the Learning First Alliance by Wendy Togneri and Lisa Lazarus, *It Takes a System: A Districtwide Approach to Improving Teaching and Learning in Kent Count Public Schools* (Washington, D.C.: Learning First Alliance, 2003). Kent County was one of five districts studied by the Learning First Alliance, each of which had measurable success in pursuing systemic reform focused on instructional improvement. An overview of findings from all five districts is presented in Wendy Togneri and Stephen E. Anderson, *Beyond Islands of Excellence: What Districts Can Do to Improve Instruction and Achievement in All Schools* (Washington, D.C.: Learning First Alliance, 2003).
5. The account of El Paso's experience draws heavily on a case study conducted by the author for the Annenberg Institute for School Reform, *Civic Cooperation in El Paso*, 2003. More information can be found at http://www.schoolcommunities.org/Portfolio/. Other sources include M. Susan Navarro and Diana Natalicio, "Closing the Achievement Gap in El Paso," *Phi Delta Kappan* 80 (April 1999): 597–601; and Mary Alicia Parra, "A Case Study of Leadership in Systemic Education Reform: The El Paso Collaborative for Academic Excellence," Ph.D. diss., University of Texas at El Paso, 2002. I am also indebted to Professor Kathleen Staudt for her invaluable observations about El Paso.
6. The presentation of Boston's experience is based mainly on: Portz, Stein, and Jones, *City Schools and City Politics*; Gary Yee, "From Court Street to City Hall"; Usdan and Cuban, "Boston: The Stars Finally in Alignment"; Boston Plan for Excellence in the Public Schools, "Triennial Report 1998–2001," www.bpe.org/publications.aspx; and Portz, "Boston: Agenda Setting and School Reform." John Portz also kindly read a draft of the chapter and provided comments.
7. Useful accounts of the Boston busing crisis can be found in Lukas, *Common Ground*; Lupo, *Liberty's Chosen Home*; and Formisano, *Boston against Busing*.

8. Usdan and Cuban, "Boston: The Stars Finally in Alignment," 46.
9. The Philadelphia case narrative is based mainly on research reports by the Consortium for Policy Research in Education, and by Research for Action: Ellen Foley, *Contradictions and Control in Systemic Reform: The Ascendancy of the Central Office in Philadelphia Schools* (Philadelphia: Consortium for Policy Research in Education, 2001); Eva Gold et al., *Clients, Consumers, or Collaborators? Parents and Their Roles in School Reform during Children Achieving, 1995–2000* (Philadelphia: Consortium for Policy Research in Education, 2001); and Christman and Rhodes, *Civic Engagement and Urban School Improvement.* See also William Boyd and Jolley Christman, "A Tall Order for Philadelphia's New Approach to School Governance," in *Powerful Reforms with Shallow Roots: Improving America's Urban Schools,* edited by Larry Cuban and Michael Usdan, 96–124 (New York: Teachers College Press, 2003); Jolley Christman et al., "Philadelphia's Children Achieving Initiative," in *A Race against Time: The Crisis in Urban Schooling,* edited by James G. Cibulka and William L. Boyd, 23–44 (Westport, Conn.: Praeger, 2003). Personal communication with Ellen Foley, Eva Gold, Elaine Simon, and Jolley Christman also helped refine the author's understanding of Philadelphia's experience.
10. Christman and Rhodes, *Civic Engagement and Urban School Improvement,* 14–15.
11. Ibid, 11.
12. Quoted in Boyd and Christman, "A Tall Order for Philadelphia's New Approach to School Governance," 111.
13. Foley, *Contradictions and Control in Systemic Reform,* 30–31.
14. Quoted in Boyd and Christman, "A Tall Order for Philadelphia's New Approach to School Governance," 109.
15. Christman and Rhodes, *Civic Engagement and Urban School Improvement,* 57.
16. Foley, *Contradictions and Control in Systemic Reform,* 26.
17. Useful background on this issue can be found in Jon S. Birger, "Race, Reaction, and Reform: The Three R's of Philadelphia School Politics, 1965–71," *Pennsylvania Magazine of History and Biography* 120 (July 1996): 163–216.
18. Quoted in Boyd and Christman, "A Tall Order for Philadelphia's New Approach to School Governance," 114.
19. Stone, *Civic Cooperation in El Paso.*
20. Schrag, Peter, *Village School Downtown* (Boston: Beacon Press, 1967); Kozol, Jonathan, *Death at an Early Age: The Destruction of the Hearts and Minds of Negro Children in the Boston Public Schools* (Boston: Houghton Mifflin, 1967).
21. Usdan and Cuban, "Boston: The Stars Finally in Alignment," 160.
22. Gold et al., *Clients, Consumers, or Collaborators?,* 23.
23. Ibid, 30. For parallel instances, see Shirley, *Community Organizing for School Reform*; and Warren, *Dry Bones Rattling.*

## Bibliography

Christman, Jolley, and Amy Rhodes. *Civic Engagement and Urban School Improvement: Hard-to-Learn Lessons from Philadelphia.* Philadelphia: Consortium for Policy Research in Education and Research for Action, 2002.

Clark, Kenneth B. *Dark Ghetto: Dilemmas of Social Power.* New York: Harper and Row, 1965.

Comer, James P. *School Power: Implications of an Intervention Project.* Repr. New York: Free Press, 1993.

Crick, Bernard. *In Defense of Politics.* 4th ed. Chicago: University of Chicago Press, 1993.

Formisano, Ronald P. *Boston against Busing: Race, Class, and Ethnicity in the 1960s and 1970s.* Chapel Hill: University of North Carolina Press, 1991.

Handler, Joel F. *Down from Bureaucracy: The Ambiguity of Privatization and Empowerment.* Princeton, N.J.: Princeton University Press, 1996.

Hochschild, Jennifer L., and Nathan Scovronick. *The American Dream and the Public Schools.* New York: Oxford University Press, 2003.

Kozol, Jonathan. *Death at an Early Age: The Destruction of the Hearts and Minds of Negro Children in the Boston Public Schools.* Boston: Houghton Mifflin, 1967.

Lukas, J. Anthony. *Common Ground: A Turbulent Decade in the Lives of Three American Families.* New York: Vintage, 1986.

Lupo, Alan. *Liberty's Chosen Home: The Politics of Violence in Boston.* 2nd ed. Boston: Beacon Press, 1988.

McAdams, Donald R. *Fighting to Save Our Urban Schools . . . and Winning!* New York: Teachers College Press, 2000.

Metz, Mary H. "How Social Class Differences Shape Teachers' Work." In *Contexts of Teaching in Secondary Schools: Teachers' Realities*, edited by Milbrey McLaughlin, Joan E. Talbert, and Nina Bascia, pp. 40–107. New York: Teachers College Press, 1990.

Payne, Charles M. "So Much Reform, So Little Change." In *Education Policy for the 21$^{st}$ Century*, edited by Lawrence B. Joseph, pp. 239–278. Chicago: University of Chicago, 2001.

Portz, John. "Boston: Agenda Setting and School Reform in a Mayor-Centric System." In *Mayors in the Middle: Politics, Race, and Mayoral Control of Urban Schools*, edited by Jeffrey R. Henig and Wilbur C. Rich, pp. 96–119. Princeton, N.J.: Princeton University Press, 2004.

Portz, John, Lana Stein, and Robin R. Jones. *City Schools and City Politics: Institutions and Leadership in Pittsburgh, Boston, and St. Louis.* Lawrence: University Press of Kansas, 1999.

Schorr, Lisbeth B. *Common Purposes: Strengthening Families and Neighborhoods to Rebuild America.* New York: Doubleday, 1997.

Shirley, Dennis. *Community Organizing for School Reform.* Austin: University of Texas Press, 1997.

Stone, Clarence N., et al. *Building Civic Capacity: The Politics of Reforming Urban Schools.* Lawrence: University Press of Kansas, 2001.

Togneri, Wendy and Stephen Anderson. *Beyond Islands of Excellence.* Washington, D.C.: Learning First Alliance, 2003.

Togneri, Wendy and Lisa Lazarus. *It Takes a System: A Districtwide Approach to Improving Teaching and Learning in Kent County Public Schools.* Washington, D.C.: Learning First Alliance, 2003.

Usdan, Michael, and Larry Cuban. "Boston: The Stars Finally in Alignment." In *Powerful*

*Reforms with Shallow Roots: Improving America's Urban Schools*, edited by Larry Cuban and Michael Usdan, pp. 38–53. New York: Teachers College Press, 2003.

Warren, Mark R. *Dry Bones Rattling: Community Building to Revitalize American Democracy*. Princeton, N.J.: Princeton University Press, 2001.

Yee, Gary. "From Court Street to City Hall." In *A Race against Time: The Crisis in Urban Schooling*, edited by James G. Cibulka and William L. Boyd, pp. 82–105. Westport, Conn.: Praeger, 2003.

# 10

## THE EDUCATION OF DEMOCRATIC CITIZENS: CITIZEN MOBILIZATION AND PUBLIC EDUCATION

*Wendy D. Puriefoy*

*An important thing to understand about any institution or social system is that it does not move unless it is pushed.*

—John Gardner

*There is no easy way to create a world . . . where all children receive as much education as their minds can absorb. But if such a world can be created in our lifetime, it will be done in the United States . . . by people of good will.*

—Martin Luther King, Jr.

*Public education consistently ranks as a top priority for Americans. Citizens are five times more likely to cite public schools over churches, hospitals or libraries as the most important institutions in their communities.*

—PEN/*Education Week* national polls, 2000–2004

FROM THE FOUNDING OF THE REPUBLIC TO THE PRESENT day, Americans of all stripes and stations have worked to establish, define, and provide a system of public education that benefits people individually and the nation collectively. Underlying these efforts is a resolute belief in an educated citizenry as the bedrock of a democratic way of life, and in public education as the critical link between individual advancement and a citizenry loyal to the nation's democratic ideals and values.

To one degree or another, every generation of Americans has wrestled with the challenge of educating the nation's children. Today, most Americans acknowledge the need to educate all children to a high standard. Social, political, and economic pressures such as globalization, rapidly changing demographics, immigration, and the interplay between domestic and international policymaking make it clear that citizenship in the twenty-first century demands a higher level of knowledge and skills, and greater levels of civic participation.

While there are multiple challenges to creating an equitable system of quality public education in the United States, three things are clearly within the public's influence and control: demand for and expectation of excellence, accountability for the provision of quality public education by elected officials and through effective school governance, and adequate and stable financial resources for public schools. Coordinated and aligned actions in these three arenas would create a system of public education that fulfills the nation's needs and meets its aspirations.

Yet despite generations of consistent and extraordinary effort, the United States has fallen short in this endeavor—fallen short in providing a system of public education that delivers all children a quality public education, and fallen short in elevating public education to its rightful place as a preeminent public institution fundamental to a democratic, civil society.

This leads to an inescapable conclusion: Public education cannot exist as a valued public institution, and quality public education will not be provided to all children, without the vigilant, knowledgeable, and active support of the American people. What can be done to attain the goal that has eluded so many generations of Americans? How can the United States provide the kind of public education that fulfills the republican ideals espoused by the founding fathers and captured in the Declaration of Independence and in the preamble to the U.S. Constitution? How do we educate Americans to value the benefits of quality public education, and how do we inspire them to extend those benefits to every child in every community across the nation?

This essay argues that, without citizen mobilization, reform and continuous improvement in public education cannot occur, and, further, that mobilization on behalf of public education in the twenty-first century must have two goals: to ensure quality public education as a civil right for every child, and to elevate public education to an unequivocal status as a fundamental institution of democracy.

Typically, citizen action on behalf of public education has been captured in the term "public engagement." In making the case for citizen mobilization, this essay first explores the social context of public engagement and the role of public-engagement activities in stimulating and motivating citizens to improve and reform their public schools. It then goes on to examine the concept, the role, and the potential of citizen mobilization (a specific type of citizen action) in securing a system of public education that serves the evolving needs of democracy in America.

## Social Context and Implications

The right of citizens to speak out on matters of public interest is deeply embedded in the American ethos. It is this uniquely American tendency to join forces to work for the public good that prompted Alexis de Tocqueville to attribute the strength of America to its voluntary groups and associations.

By the turn of the twenty-first century, however, it is economics rather than democracy that has the strongest impact on the form and level of public engagement in the United States. Public action is being shaped by globalization and consumerism. In *Jihad vs. McWorld* (1996), Benjamin Barber notes that people in contemporary society tend to think of themselves more as consumers than as citizens—a worldview that affects why people become engaged, their attitudes toward engagement, and their expectations regarding engagement outcomes.

Social issues gain prominence based as much on their popular appeal as on their relevance. Public institutions are also reacting to economic forces, rather than fulfilling their fundamental function of championing the public interest. Barber writes that it has become necessary to resurrect the nation's sense of "public"; given that our public schools define what constitutes "public" for most Americans, public schools are the strongest association citizens have with any public institution outside of government. In this consumer-oriented environment, achieving quality public education for all children means finding a balance between self-interest and the public good. Public engagement embodies this delicate balance.

Engaging the public in public education is both a form of community building and a way of strengthening democracy. It also provides an answer to the perplexing question of how to revitalize communities raised by Robert Putnam in *Bowling Alone: The Collapse and Revival of American Community* (2000), and by Benjamin Barber and Richard Battistoni in *Education for Democracy: Citizenship, Community, Service: A Sourcebook for Students and Teachers* (1993).

Demographic shifts beginning in the late twentieth century have raised the importance of getting the public engaged in public education. Parents with children in public schools once represented more than two-thirds of the adult population. Parental action could be equated to public action, and parental involvement was a significant indicator of school and student performance. Typically, it is parents who make sure that children do their homework, go to class, and are prepared to get the most out of their educational opportunities. Parents volunteer in classrooms, organize carpools, assist teachers and administrators, and contribute to fund-raisers to support student services and extracurricular activities. Most important, they help their children succeed.

In 2004, however, parents with children in public schools comprise approximately one-third of all adults; in many communities, they comprise less than one-quarter of the adult population. The demographic shifts described by Jennifer Hochschild and Nathan Scovronick in this volume make it essential that we take to heart the maxim "It takes a village" when it comes to reforming our public schools.

The challenge, of course, is to reach out to the public in a way that makes people feel invested in the institution of public education and helps them recognize the benefits they receive from the institution as individuals and those they receive as members of a civil society. A high-quality system of public education that educates all children to their full potential has positive trickle-up effects for the entire nation. Everyone benefits from a well-educated voting populace, and everyone benefits from a well-educated, competitive workforce.

Conversely, if public education should fail, it will have a disastrous ripple effect on American democracy, on the American market economy, and on the American dream itself. Uneducated citizens are less likely to vote; unskilled workers are not valued by the marketplace; and low-income families cannot break the cycle of poverty without acquiring better-paying jobs.

## Framework for Action

Misconceptions about public engagement abound. The terms *parental involvement, community engagement, civic engagement,* and *public engagement* are used interchangeably, and often serve to confuse and obscure meaning, thus making it difficult for citizens to recognize their responsibility, accept accountability, and act collectively on behalf of their communities and their country.

It is also important to note that the various modes of public engagement are used with equal effectiveness by both ends of the political spectrum. Community activists, philanthropic entities, education reformers, the Christian Right, and neoconservatives all use the same engagement concepts and strategies, though their objectives vary dramatically.

Historical images of effective public engagement tend to be dramatic: suffragists chained to the White House gates; civil rights activists marching on Washington; war protestors burning flags and effigies. And therein lies one of the biggest challenges of public engagement—the idea that, in order to effect change, there has to be a huge turnout, a dramatic event, or a new constitutional amendment. Such misconceptions, along with the fuzzy terminology of engagement, have kept the vast majority of "ordinary" people from seeing a role for themselves in public engagement.

In reality, public engagement is a flexible concept covering a wide range of activities by which citizens can effect change. It encompasses distinct activities such as the dissemination of information, involvement in school activities and programs, and supporting causes and issues regarding public education. In short, public engagement is the best tool available for ensuring that everyone—voters, elected officials, educators, students, administrators, parents—knows about the strategies for school improvement and is held accountable for improved education performance.

To define public engagement, it is first necessary to clarify who makes up the "public," and what the mechanisms of engagement are. Public Education

Network has developed a framework for initiatives being undertaken by member local education funds to change education policy and practice at the district and state levels. The framework is based on a theory that posits that, for sustained policy change to occur, the public must be engaged in identifying and working toward specific education-reform goals. With respect to its initiatives, PEN categorizes the public as three distinct groups: the community at large, organized stakeholders, and policymakers.[1]

The community at large includes individuals not associated with or linked to formal groups, who may not have direct contact or relationships with schools, and whose voices often go unheard in local decision-making processes. These individuals include recent immigrants, the elderly, youth, and residents without children in public schools. Organized stakeholders are groups of individuals or institutions with formal mechanisms to relay demands for policy change; these include teachers' unions, parent-teacher associations, faith-based groups, professional associations, and chambers of commerce. Policymakers are defined as individuals who are either elected or appointed to public office and have the power and authority to set policy and allocate resources; these individuals include school board members, city council members, superintendents, mayors, and neighborhood commission officers.

Each sector is engaged through different tactics at varying levels of participation during the engagement process. Local nonprofits or intermediaries such as local education funds partner with community organizing experts to engage the community at large in developing an overarching vision of quality public education. A strategic planning process is used to get stakeholder groups deeply involved in translating that vision into a specific plan of action. Finally, advocacy strategies are employed to target those who can change policy and allocate resources.

## Terminology of Engagement

If we are to meet the challenges posed by citizen mobilization, we must have a greater level of clarity and precision in the engagement terminology we use. By breaking public engagement down into five distinct categories, the activities that can be undertaken by citizens individually and/or collectively then become clear. Table 1 illustrates the categories, participants, and potential impact.

### Information

Disseminating information is the most basic form of public engagement. Though largely passive, in that there is little expectation of change other than increasing public awareness, information can nonetheless be transformative, especially since most Americans have limited knowledge about what goes on inside the nation's public schools. Survey results reveal that they have little infor-

TABLE 1
Public Engagement Categories

| Category | Participants | Intended Impact |
|---|---|---|
| Information | Individuals | Increase individual awareness |
| Involvement | Individuals, stakeholder groups | Increase sense of connection, increase institutional resources |
| Collaboration | Individuals, stakeholder groups, institutions | Increase level of partnerships and shared resources at local/state level |
| Constituency Building | Individuals, stakeholder groups, institutions | Change in local or state policy, and in institutional practice |
| Mobilization | Individuals, stakeholder groups, institutions | Change in local, state, or national policy, extension of democracy, broad societal good |

mation about teacher qualifications, the quality of teaching, and school performance.[2] And this lack of information, they say, inhibits their ability to make good choices regarding public education. One obstacle to the dissemination of information is the lack of centralized data sources; the availability and content of information can vary dramatically from state to state, and from locality to locality. Data can be found through a wide variety of sources ranging from the World Wide Web to organizations such as The Education Trust, a Washington-based think tank that provides data about school performance in every state in the nation.

Reliable information, widely dispersed and effectively marketed, makes all the difference when it comes to school-reform efforts. Perhaps it is a mark of our consumer society, but Americans like to know what they are paying for and what they are getting in return. So if we want Americans to take civic action on behalf of public schools, we must begin by collecting and providing reliable information on things such as literacy rates, school safety, the availability and quality of learning tools, school budgets, and how local schools compare with others in the state.

In 1983, the National Commission on Excellence in Education shook the nation with the release of *A Nation at Risk: The Imperative for Education Reform,* a report that presented, in readily accessible terms, indicators of the deterioration in American public education, and of the poor academic performance of millions of children who went through the system. It called for improving the quality of America's public schools and outlined a set of recommendations for doing so.

The federal No Child Left Behind Act of 2001 was expected to address many information needs. As a result of this legislation, states and school districts, community groups, and the media began generating information about teacher credentials, test scores, and a host of other performance indicators. But information dissemination, as a type of public-engagement activity, has a limited impact. Its main purpose is to build public awareness and knowledge of a set of issues. For the public to use that knowledge to take action requires a more dedicated effort. As we have noted, providing data is simply a dissemination process. But when the provision of data is supported by a concerted drive toward action then it becomes part of a campaign. The approval of a 2003 bond referendum in Portland, Oregon, is a case in point. Investing time and money to inform voters is an important strategy for "solving" yearly budget crises. Through an information campaign conducted by the Portland Schools Foundation, Portland residents received extensive information on the damage that proposed cuts to the education budget would inflict on Portland's public schools. Convinced of the need for additional funding, Portland citizens voted to raise local taxes for education in May 2003, thus guaranteeing the city's public schools sufficient funds for the next three years.

## Involvement

Involvement entails direct action arising from an informed understanding of specific issues. Voting is one of the most important forms of involvement. Public action on behalf of public education must include the ballot box: If education is freedom's classroom, then voting is democracy's test. Whether it is an election for the local school board or an election for the presidency of the United States, proponents of quality education must enter the voting booth to make a difference. Project Vote, a nonprofit, nonpartisan organization with offices in Ohio, New York, Arkansas, and the District of Columbia, has registered over 2.7 million newly registered, low-income, and minority citizens. By providing voter-education training to low-income and minority citizens, Project Vote enables these individuals to become involved in the democratic process. Information is provided along with avenues for involvement such as voter registration, networks, and turn-out-the-vote campaigns.

Involvement in activities such as PTA meetings, principal-for-a-day campaigns, and adopt-a-school programs allows the public to see firsthand what is going on in the public schools. This kind of involvement allows for direct interaction with school personnel, which in turn can lead to a broader appreciation of the many challenges—budget shortfalls, teacher shortages, achievement gaps—that public schools grapple with every day. The Right Question Project (RQP), a nonprofit organization based in Massachusetts, has a strategy that has been effectively used by some federally funded parent information and resource centers to help thousands of parents become more effective in supporting, monitoring, and advocating for their children's education. RQP has been used to start parent-school collaboratives, set up family resource centers, and facilitate parent support groups and home visits, constructing parent-led violence prevention and attendance-improvement plans and helping parents choose after-school programs for their children.

Then there is a level of involvement that brings citizens directly into the classroom and allows them to make a significant difference in a localized arena. Volunteering as tutors, teacher's aids, and chaperones; participating in fundraising activities; and monitoring homework assignments are just some of the ways that parents and community members get involved with their local schools. A good example of this level of involvement is Experience Corps, a groundbreaking program that engages Americans age fifty-five-plus in vital public and community service. In 2004, more than one thousand Experience Corps members were serving as tutors and mentors to children in urban public schools in a dozen cities across the country, helping children learn to read and develop the confidence and skills they need to succeed in school and in life.[3]

National foundations and philanthropic entities have invested millions of dollars to promote parent and community involvement in the public school system. Some examples are private foundations that have set up community grants programs whose mission is to help improve the quality of life, including education, in communities where customers and employees reside. Others involve the elderly or other community members in creating safe and caring environments for children.

## Collaboration

Collaboration—the pooling of resources, expertise, and contacts in pursuit of a common goal—is the mode of engagement typically employed by established organizations and groups. Collaborations are often quite successful in producing change at a local level; however, they typically lack the resources to achieve systemic change at a national level.

Many organizations form successful collaborations to improve public education. For example, community schools—which pool school and community resources as an integral part of their design and operation—are the result of a collaborative effort by various community entities to provide students with a comprehensive array of supports, programs, and enrichment activities that extend learning beyond the classroom.

Local education funds (LEFs) are an excellent example of organizations that work collaboratively with other organizations to improve education outcomes for all students. LEFs—first launched in the 1980s with support from the Ford Foundation, community foundations, corporations, and concerned individuals—focus on building the capacity of school districts to increase student achievement, and on helping the public understand the relationship between quality public education and family, community, and national stability.

As community-based, nonprofit change agents, LEFs play a unique role in school reform by leveraging a variety of community resources. LEFs not only work to enhance school performance, they engage, inform, and mobilize communities to demand improvement and accountability. Their effectiveness lies in their ability to get a broad cross section of the community to come together and solve problems.

In Mobile, Alabama, for example, the Mobile Area Education Foundation (MAEF) collaborated with the school district and mayor's office to engage parents, educators, members of the faith community, and business leaders in ongoing discussions on academic standards. The Yes We Can initiative, launched in September 2001, is the largest community engagement campaign ever undertaken in Mobile County, with some fourteen hundred citizens taking part in forty-eight different community conversations over a fourteen-week period. A panel of demographically representative Mobile residents then reviewed the data, along with the ideas generated from the community conversations, to arrive at the "realm of the possible" for Mobile. A document of community agreement, incorporating this realm of the possible, has been vetted throughout the county, and will provide the basis for all strategic planning efforts about public education in Mobile over the next several years.[4]

## Constituency Building

Constituency building, the development of support for a specific cause or issue, requires rallying individuals and organizations to take action. Constituency building targets established groups and individuals, and usually entails educating and motivating the public—in some instances, even changing beliefs—to convince people of the benefits of a particular course of action or policy. Consequently, constituency building takes a long time and requires significant resources.

Yet, as is the case with collaboration, the broad societal impact can be limited. While the Christian Right has built a strong base to support its conservative agenda, its appeal is limited to those who share a similar worldview. The religious coalition first united over issues such as secular textbooks, sex education, and the use of what it considered inappropriate instructional materials. By 2004, it was focusing on school-reform efforts such as outcome-based education, multiculturalism, global education, and values education, finessed the issue by deleting reference to critical thinking, all of which relate to a specific religious point of view, as the educators Marilyn Grady and Jack McKay point out:

The difference between earlier groups and the current special interest groups being studied is the blending of quasi-political and religious interests that tend to be weighing heavily on the side of conservatism. This special interest group has generally been called the "New Christian Right."...The effectiveness of the New Christian Right (NCR) is net-working on the national level so they can have an influence on local level political action. Instead of focusing on a national agenda of reli-gious and political conservatism, the NCR is coordinating efforts to gain control of local and state government: e.g., school boards, city councils, county boards, and state legislatures.[5]

The nature of constituency building has been transformed by technology. The ease and speed of electronic communications has created the ability to gen-erate dialogue and formulate shared strategies across cultures and across national and ethnic boundaries. Communities are no longer defined by geography, and education activists are learning how to use the Internet to generate broad public support and to educate and guide supporters on how to make an impact on pol-icy issues.

MoveOn.org, which began in 1998 as a modest online petition drive, has burgeoned into one of the most effective constituency-building tools in America. From an initial e-mail sent to approximately three hundred individ-uals, MoveOn.org now has more than 1.5 million people in its database. The organization is a catalyst for a new kind of grassroots involvement that helps concerned citizens find a political voice. It has taken action on issues such as campaign-finance reform, the environment and energy, gun safety, and nuclear disarmament.

Other forms of online organizing also hold promise for education applica-tions. Meetup.com helps people organize local gatherings through Meetup.com's advanced technology platform and global network of local ven-ues. "Meetups" have taken place in hundreds of cities in dozens of countries at cafés, restaurants, bookstores, and other local establishments. Since education is such an intensely local matter, the creation of a national constituency for public education must incorporate ways for individuals to act locally while thinking about the global implications of their actions.

## Mobilization

As previously outlined, various modes of public engagement can produce positive change in public education. Collectively, however, the strategies employed tend to tinker with the system rather than change how it works. One reason for the limited impact is the insular, often personal interest that motivates the action. In order for broader change to occur, self-interest must give way to public interest. A good example can be found in the way Abraham Lincoln approached the issue of slavery. Although he was not an abolitionist, and although he personally believed that slavery was protected by the Constitution in states where it already existed, he came to see the abolishment of slavery as necessary for the preservation of the union.

Citizen mobilization delves deeper into the fabric of our social contract and comes into play when the benefits of democracy apply to some but not all. When the threat is external, the mobilization is known as war. When the threat is internal, the mobilization is called a movement.

Mobilization by its very nature is designed to change the values and beliefs of its adherents, redistribute social and political power, improve public institutions by changing the laws and structures that govern and shape them, and change the relationship between public institutions and the public itself. It is the deep end of public engagement—the stage where citizens are informed, involved, and convinced of the value of a specific goal; motivated to make fundamental changes in the political structure; and cognizant of both the benefits and the risks of the proposed action.

As with all other public-engagement strategies, citizen mobilization can be used for both liberal and conservative ends. Therefore, the ultimate litmus test for citizen mobilization lies in its intention to extend democracy to people within the fabric of the nation who are excluded from the full rights and privileges of democratic life. Is the goal equal rights for all? Will it extend benefits currently enjoyed by a select few? Will it ultimately change the power structures within the system? Change the status quo? Allow the democratic process to determine and serve the public interest?

The historical frame of reference for mobilization comprises social movements that extend democracy. Indeed, the most beneficial and successful social and political movements in the United States have used citizen mobilization to achieve far-reaching change. The women's suffrage movement, the fight to abolish slavery, the movement to unionize labor all shape our perceptions of citizen mobilization, often conjuring up a vision of tens of thousands of people marching and demonstrating.

One of the most powerful examples of citizen mobilization is the 1963 civil rights march on Washington, a mobilization of Americans who, by their very presence, demonstrated the magnitude of their belief. The march was a culmination of many small local efforts to desegregate voting booths, public transportation, eating establishments, department stores—places deemed legally off limits to black Americans in the South. The civil rights movement resulted in major federal legislation that conferred voting rights to disenfranchised blacks across the South.

Most citizen-mobilization efforts were not mass movements; indeed, many began with just a handful of citizens. The very intention of citizen-mobilization efforts—extending rights enjoyed by a select few to a larger group—is unlikely to attract massive support at first. Neither the civil rights movement, nor the movements for suffrage and economic and societal parity for women, involved the majority of Americans at first. While the desired outcome of these mobilization efforts was far reaching, the number of people directly involved initially was relatively modest in view of the radical change being sought. The success of these movements rested not in numbers but in the unassailable "rightness" of the causes they espoused, proving the power of Margaret Mead's maxim: "Never doubt that a small group of thoughtful, committed citizens can change the world. Indeed, it is the only thing that ever has."

## Benefits of Public Engagement

Various forms of public engagement are capable of producing broad societal benefits, and numerous positive outcomes can occur when residents take public action. As Clarence Stone makes clear in this volume, communities that take greater responsibility for public education reap benefits in the form of better schools, stronger communities, and improved prospects for the future.

SCHOOL IMPROVEMENT EFFORTS BECOME INVIGORATED. Many policymakers approach reform like a scientist holed up in a laboratory—isolated from the very people for whom the "medicine" is intended. Reform in which the public is not involved can actually widen the divide between the public and educators, and undermine any lasting impact the reforms might have. Public engagement must be a prerequisite, not an afterthought, of school reform.

SCHOOLS GAIN A MANDATE FOR SUCCESS. Schools function best when they enjoy a mandate from the communities they serve. Devising elaborate reforms without actively involving the ultimate stakeholders denies the public the opportunity to take ownership.

DIVISIONS ARE MINIMIZED AND CONSENSUS EMERGES. In *Bowling Alone,* Robert Putnam notes that the "moderate" segment of the citizenry is the one most often absent from civic life, leaving a disproportionate share of key decisions to be made by partisan forces that may have little or no connection to the community. The absence of a mainstream voice could explain the public acrimony that has stalled substantive reform, poisoned morale, and replaced consensus building with a zero-sum approach to decision making. With the public in the "convener" role, recasting issues in terms that reflect shared interests and reveal areas of agreement can minimize divisions.

THE GAP LEFT BY OVERWHELMED PARENTS IS FILLED. Parents—particularly single working parents—are under intense pressure to meet their work and family responsibilities. The broader public can fill the involvement gap left by overextended parents of school-age children. When schools aim their outreach efforts exclusively at parents, they are writing off large segments of the community that have the time and the desire to get involved. In addition, research indicates that peers and community members can have as significant an influence on young people as their parents.[6]

## Principles of Mobilization

Most education-reform efforts use engagement strategies that attempt to strengthen and enhance public education from within the system, not change the system itself. While such efforts improve the quality of education that some children receive, they do not address the fundamental flaws in an institution that should serve the needs of *all* children, nor do they extend the benefits of democracy to all children. Indeed, in asking public education to make the shift from a system that provides access *to* all into a system that guarantees a high-quality education *for* all, we are challenging more than two hundred years of American history—a history marked by discrimination based on race, gender, class, and religion—and we tamper with established economic, political, and social systems.

Mobilization strategies are designed to expand civil rights through new laws and within the framework of the Constitution. Litigation, public relations and media campaigns, grassroots get-out-the-vote campaigns, lobbying, and the Internet are just some of the current strategies employed. Coordinating these disparate strategies into a comprehensive, effective citizen-mobilization effort is *the* challenge facing education reformers. Fortunately, education reformers can draw upon the lessons learned in previous successful mobilization efforts to help them address the challenge of quality public education for all in the twenty-first century.

Effective citizen mobilization is guided by three key principles. First, it is *intentional,* and based on a structured theory that embodies a clear vision of success that includes targets and outcomes. A movement needs to have clarity in direction and articulation of its goals and outcomes from its leaders and proponents.

A second key principle of citizen mobilization is that it is *systemic,* which means the mobilization effort exposes the problem, addresses the fundamental and structural issues of the system that created the problem, and rearranges the structures of authority, power, and culture to support the proposed change. The civil rights and women's movements were very clear in identifying the fundamental issue of inequality in American society.

Citizen mobilization requires stewardship. Independent intermediary organizations are well positioned to be stewards of both the clarity of intention and the systemic approach. Intermediary organizations perform a variety of functions vital to mobilization efforts: first and foremost, they provide the necessary infrastructure—communications, outreach, and fund-raising, to name just a few—to sustain the mobilization over time. Understanding the infrastructure that supports mobilization is vital to success, since transparency in the mechanics of the movement is essential for attracting adherents. The civil rights movement would not have succeeded without the support of entities such as the National Association for the Advancement of Colored People, nor the women's movement without the support of groups such as the National Organization for Women. The independent status of intermediaries becomes particularly important when it comes to school-reform efforts, since the traditional players in the public education structure—schools, school districts, state agencies, and state legislatures—are set up to maintain the system, not reform it.

The third key principle of citizen mobilization is that is must be *sustainable* and able to hold citizen attention and interest for a long period of time. Very few citizen-mobilization movements achieve their goals quickly: The fight for civil rights for blacks took more than two centuries; indeed, many would say the battle still continues. Public ("common") schools, developed in the nineteenth century, did not become available to all children until the twentieth century. The women's suffrage movement took over seventy years to achieve its goals. The movement for equal rights for gays and lesbians has been going on since the Stonewall riots in 1969.

Paradoxically, mobilization can become more difficult as the movement gains traction, especially if initial goals are met with relative ease, in which case victory can be declared prematurely. Despite progress in affirmative action, the achievements to date are being challenged by public perceptions that the battle for equity has been won and affirmative action protections are no longer needed. A case in point is the continuing efforts to eliminate university admission policies that benefit racial minorities. It took a Supreme Court decision to uphold the right of universities to consider race in admissions procedures in order to achieve a diverse student body.

Sustainable movements use key messages and themes to embed the movement's vision into people's daily lives and conversation. Successful mobilization efforts are fueled by a powerful commitment to an inspirational ideal, an ideal that finds voice in the songs and language of popular culture. Stirring anthems ("America, America, God shed his grace on thee"), popular songs ("I am woman, hear me roar"), moving speeches ("Free at last, free at last. Thank God Almighty we're free at last"), and symbolic poetry ("I know why the caged bird sings") have inspired generations of Americans to take action and change history.

Sustainable movements also monitor change on an ongoing basis. Wendell Berry in his *Citizenship Papers* (2003) defines sustainability as "a way . . . that can be continued indefinitely because it conforms to the terms imposed upon it [by the change]"(p. 130). When a community mobilizes on behalf of its children and its public schools, a social contract is created: the public provides the means and resources to ensure that all children receive a quality public education; school district officials and others in public office ensure that the policies and practices necessary to maintain and sustain quality public education are implemented.

The fact that all children in the United States do not have access to a quality public education is deeply detrimental to the American way of life. Just as slavery threatened the existence of the Union, so, too, does inequity in public education threaten the survival of our democratic way of life. Wide gaps in student achievement ensure that, unless the system is changed, generations of Americans will not have the capacity to compete in the global economic marketplace or the ability to deal with the challenges of everyday life. This gross inequity in our system of public education, along with decades of reforms that have had minimal scaleable impact, has eroded public trust in this vital public institution, and has opened a door for those who would dismantle the system by diverting public funds.

The standards-based reform movement has revealed what it takes to educate children at high levels: starting school ready to learn, a rich curriculum aligned with standards, quality instruction, a school environment conducive to learning, and nonacademic supports that enhance learning. In addition, research has led to significant breakthroughs in how human potential is viewed, and in how learning and schools should be organized—thus helping to forge agreement on the attributes that constitute a quality education: quality teachers and teaching, fair and helpful assessments, small classes, and safe, well-equipped facilities.

The idea that all children can learn and learn at high levels represents a marker in how we as a civilized society view and value human potential. By stating that all children can learn at high levels, we acknowledge that human potential is fluid, that all children can participate in society, and that all children can develop the capacity to influence and shape the world around them.

At the core of standards-based reform is student work and learning. It requires a school culture and an orientation set in the belief that children can achieve at high levels given the appropriate teaching, curriculum, and support. In the words of Anne Wheelock, "It is the vision of better quality student work overall that inspires . . . and to this end, they are putting new routines, beliefs about learning, and relationships into practice to develop a 'culture of high standards.'"

If we assume that the American people are in agreement with the problem, aligned with the strategies, and aspire to the vision, then why haven't we been able to achieve the goal of quality public education for all children? The answer lies in citizen mobilization. And the use of the term "mobilization" in the context of citizens and public education is deliberate and intentional. For it is only through citizen mobilization that we will be able to generate a mandate for excellence in our public schools, accountability for the quality of education delivered by those schools, and funding for adequate and stable resources needed by those schools. In pursuing this mandate, we increase citizen trust in public institutions, strengthen the social relationships between and among institutions, and fulfill the American ideals of democracy and a civil society.

## Conclusion

The founding fathers saw education as an essential tool for the formation of citizens able to understand and obey the law. Ultimately, public education evolved into a more fundamental instrument for building and sustaining democracy and civil society. Public education paved the way for blacks, women, immigrants, and the poor to become active participants in the political life of the nation and constructive contributors to the social and economic development of American society.

In a time of globalization and marketplace economics, it is imperative that all children have access to quality public education. Education is the only assurance our children have of acquiring the skills and capacities they will need to compete in the global marketplace, to have the ability to process large amounts of information, and to participate in the democratic process.

We know what quality public education looks like: high expectations for teachers and students; standards aligned with curriculum, instruction and assessment; qualified teachers; safe and healthy learning environments; comprehensive academic and social supports for students; and high levels of parent and community involvement. Attaining this goal calls for a movement of national proportions. The American public needs to be mobilized to demand, support, and ensure that all children—irrespective of class or race or gender or creed or family income—have access to a quality public education. History shows that this nation can provide various segments of society with equal rights under the law, and technology makes it easier for private concerns to become public action. Modern technology allows us to gather and share information; look at past, current, and future trends; and create mechanisms to move large numbers of people to action.

While we know many things about citizen mobilization activities, there is much that we do not know. We need more research on exactly how a strong civic infrastructure within and for schools leads to more effective education, and how different communities build public responsibility for their schools, demonstrate strong parental and business involvement, use information about schools more effectively, and work with intermediary organizations.

The ultimate aim of citizen mobilization in the context of school reform is to reshape the relationships people have with one another, with their community, their neighborhood, their state, and their country. Eleanor Roosevelt echoed this sentiment when she said that the work for human rights begins "in small places, close to home." Unless each man, woman, and child experiences justice in their neighborhood, their school, and their workplace, human rights, dignity, and democracy are diminished everywhere.

The use of citizen mobilization to exert and sustain public pressure on law-makers to act on issues of public concern has characterized important milestones in U.S. history. But public education has not enjoyed the benefit of such activism. Despite a deeply held belief in the value of public education in this country, parents have been the primary shapers of local public schools, while the role of the general public has remained limited in time, scope, and breadth.

This, then, is our challenge: to inform the public about the value and benefits of quality public education, and to build a broad base of people who know what takes place in our public schools and know how to transform concern about education into effective action. The time to bring the awesome force of an organized citizenry to advance the quality of public education for every child in America has arrived. When our democracy reaches *all* citizens, especially the smallest ones, only then, in the words of the educator Horace Mann, will we have achieved a "victory for humanity."

## Notes

1. More information about PEN's framework for action can be found on the organization's Web site at www.publiceducation.org.
2. Public Education Network/*Education Week, Accountability for All: What Voters Want from Education Candidates*, national survey of public opinion, 2003, available from Public Education Network, www.publiceducation.org.
3. More information on the involvement initiatives mentioned in this section can be found at the Web sites ww.projectvote.org; www.rightquestion.org; and www. experiencecorps.org.
4. Mobile Area Education Foundation, www.maef.net/pages.
5. Marilyn Grady and Jack McKay, *Perceptions of the New Christian Right: A Survey of the Membership of the Horace Mann League*, 1994, available at www.unocoe.unomaha.edu/mckay/hmlpercepts.html#horace.
6. National Research Council, *Community Programs to Promote Youth Development* (Washington, D.C.: National Academy Press, 2002).

## Bibliography

Barber, Benjamin R., and Richard M. Battistoni, eds. *Education for Democracy: Citizenship, Community, Service: A Sourcebook for Students and Teachers.* Dubuque, Iowa: Kendall/Hunt, 1993.

Barber, Benjamin R. *Jihad vs. McWorld.* Repr. New York: Ballantine, 1996.

Berry, Wendell. *Citizenship Papers.* Washington, D.C.: Shoemaker and Hoard, 2003.

Putnam, Robert. *Bowling Alone: The Collapse and Revival of American Community.* New York: Simon and Schuster, 2000.

Wheelock, Anne. *Safe to Be Smart: Building a Culture for Standards-Based Reform in the Middle Grades.* Columbus, Ohio: National Middle School Association, 1998.

# 11

# THE ELUSIVE IDEAL: CIVIC LEARNING AND HIGHER EDUCATION

*Matthew Hartley and Elizabeth L. Hollander*

THROUGHOUT AMERICAN HISTORY, COLLEGES AND universities have espoused various conceptions of civic responsibility, adapting them to meet the contingencies of the times. The colonial colleges of the 1700s trained the children of the elite in order to perpetuate the religious and civic leadership of their communities. Over the next two centuries, as higher education expanded from a select group of private academies into a broad national system, other notions concerning the purpose of the university began to vie for dominance. Nevertheless, a higher purpose for higher learning—to foster citizenship and to serve a democratic society—has remained an enduring, if contested, ideal.

Today there is in place a multiplicity of efforts aimed at promoting civic engagement at colleges and universities. Since the 1970s these activities have evolved from individual acts of student volunteerism to comprehensive institutional efforts. Many colleges and universities now embrace the notion that they have a responsibility as "institutional citizens" within their communities and have cultivated sophisticated, sustained, and reciprocal community partnerships. Some have attempted to embed service into the curriculum and to encourage scholarly work that addresses local concerns.

Although these efforts have become more prevalent, they are not universally accepted or supported. The very structure and culture of the system of higher education are often at cross-purposes with civic engagement. Nonetheless, the movement toward greater campus engagement continues to gather momentum on campuses across the country.

In this essay we examine how the democratic purposes of colleges and universities have been expressed historically and are being pursued in the twenty-first century on numerous campuses, despite powerful forces acting against such efforts. First we offer a historical perspective on the evolving conception of higher education's civic purposes. We next examine how the organizational qualities of colleges and universities tend to push civic education to the margins. Finally, we describe the ways in which many institutions have begun to actively engage in meaningful civic work. We contend that these institutions are participating in the reinvention of American higher education and are continuing the long-contested dialogue about what it means to educate in a democracy.

## Changing Conceptions of Democratic Education: A Brief History

The earliest colonial colleges trained the sons of wealthy patrons of a particular locale. Yale was conceived as an institution "wherein youth may be instructed in the arts and sciences, who through the blessing of Almighty God, may be fitted for public employment, both in Church and civil State." Rutgers University (then Queen's College) was created "for the education of youth in the learned languages, liberal and useful arts and sciences, and especially in divinity, preparing them for the ministry and other good offices" (Brubacher, p. 8).

This rather elitist rationale was mirrored in the constrained reach of these institutions. Historians estimate that no more than one in a thousand students attended college before the American Revolution. In *The American College and University: A History,* the educational historian Frederick Rudolph wryly observes that "[Although] some middle- and lower-class families sent their sons to the colonial colleges . . . it should not be forgotten that the overwhelming majority of their sons stayed home, farmed, went West, or became—without the benefit of a college education—Benjamin Franklin or Patrick Henry" (p. 22).

### Serving the Republic

The purpose of higher education began to shift in the aftermath of the Revolution as it became explicitly linked to the fortunes of the fledgling democracy. No longer was higher education the sole purview of the rich. In the two decades following the Revolution, nineteen colleges were chartered, tripling the number of institutions of higher learning. At the same time, the idea of a civic purpose for higher education began to grow. As Rudolph notes, "A commitment to the republic became a guiding obligation of the American college" (p. 61).

Religious movements also played an important role in shaping the civic purposes of colleges. The Second Great Awakening, a religious revival that swept the country in the early nineteenth century, spurred the founding of many small denominational colleges. Although these institutions educated only a fraction of the population, in their founding, higher education took its first halting steps toward democratization. Expressing the populist ideals championed by President Andrew Jackson, these institutions saw themselves as serving the democracy by providing higher education to a wide range of students, especially the poor. In 1847 the Reverend John Todd, in an appeal to philan-thropists, proclaimed: "Our colleges are chiefly and mainly institutions designed for the poor and those in moderate circumstances, and not for the rich. . . . We have no institutions in the land more truly republican than our colleges" (Lucas, p. 121).

Up to this point, the civic purpose of higher education was largely limited to shaping the minds and hearts of future civic leaders. However, the industrial revolution brought with it a new imperative—vocational training and the expansion and proliferation of practical knowledge on industry and farming. The Morrill Acts (1862 and 1890) gave large tracts of federal land to the states to create public universities. These acts came after the Agricultural College of the State of Michigan (now Michigan State University), founded in 1855, served as a successful prototype. The acts emphasized the teaching of trades as well as the application of scholarship to the practical needs of the community. In attempting to resolve the problems of the farmer down the street, the land-grant universities expanded knowledge about agriculture to the benefit of all. They exemplified an ideal of the institution of higher learning as a solver of local problems and a servant of the people.

## The Research Paradigm

In the latter half of the nineteenth century the German university model, with its focus on research and specialization, began to establish dominance. This change profoundly influenced American higher education. The search for new knowledge through research presented a powerful purpose that began to eclipse others. With specialization came the creation of academic departments and the rise of disciplines whose narrow focus created fissures in the university community. The new university model and its ethos of pure, or "value-free," research heavily influenced academic norms and helped to de-emphasize higher education's role in shaping students' values. The civic purposes that had been central to many institutions were now competing with an increasingly crowded field of other institutional imperatives and goals.

The twentieth century witnessed the creation of a mass system of higher education, and with it new imperatives regarding institutional purpose. The first three-quarters of the century brought unprecedented growth in both numbers and types of students. The proportion of graduating American students attending college tripled from about 4 percent in 1900 to 15 percent in 1940. The government invested heavily in higher education through the Servicemen's Readjustment Act of 1944 (more commonly known as the GI Bill), which provided financial assistance to 2.25 million World War II veterans, swelling the enrollments of colleges and universities across the country. In 1954 the landmark legal decision *Brown v. Board of Education* fractured the wall of segregation and made it possible for men and women of color to attend previously all-white colleges. The percentage of American students attending college tripled again between 1940 and 1970 to reach 45 percent. The range of institutional types increased dramatically as well, most notably in the rise of community colleges (Geiger, p. 61).

Even while these dramatic shifts were broadening the mission of higher education to encompass vocational training, economic development, and other new imperatives, the research paradigm still largely reigned supreme. During the postwar period, the engines of scientific research were stoked by federal funds during the technological race against the Soviet Union. While such efforts were no doubt viewed as "serving" the nation, they were tied to nationalistic ambitions. Research on local problems received no concomitant financial support.

## The Business Paradigm

In the last quarter of the twentieth century, higher education experienced another major shift. The late 1970s were a difficult time for American colleges and universities. A stagnant economy and rampant inflation drained state coffers and decreased state funding for public education, which by that point covered 80 percent of all college students. Tremendous fears of a demographic slump caused some experts to predict that within one to two decades, nearly a third of all colleges and universities would merge or close.

In response to these pressures, institutions began to pursue a business model. Increasingly, students were viewed as "customers" whose interests needed to be accommodated. Surveys at the time made clear that what these "customers" wanted most was jobs. During the 1980s and 1990s, when Wall Street traders became national heroes, there was a dramatic shift toward careerism. Professional education elbowed past the liberal arts and quickly dominated the curriculum, leading some to wonder whether higher education was more of a private than a public good.[1]

## Development of Campus-based Civic Engagement

The shifts that were occurring in the academic enterprise were so profound that many within higher education began to call for reform. They contended that higher education could best serve students—and the public good—by providing educational experiences that combined real-world and academic knowledge through civic engagement.

Since the 1980s, the move toward civic education and community engagement among higher education has grown tremendously. This change has come only with great effort. The barriers to any kind of institutional change, particularly change that requires a coordinated effort among parties with divergent interests, are high. The following sections examine the challenges to civic engagement and the ways that higher education institutions and associations are working to overcome those challenges.

## Systemic Challenges

ORGANIZATIONAL FACTORS. The very structure of American postsecondary institutions works against broad-based change efforts. Each college or university is divided into schools, which are further divided into divisions and again into departments. Coordination of this complex structure is complicated by the fact that colleges and universities are institutions with diffuse power. Although the regents or boards of trustees hold ultimate authority, they cannot implement broad-based change unilaterally. They depend both on the insight of administrators who are closer to the institution's inner workings and on the curricular expertise and cooperation of the faculty. On the other hand, the faculty cannot advance an institutional initiative without the financial support of the administration and the board. In essence, each constituency has sufficient power to block any new initiative. As Clark Kerr, former chancellor of the University of California system, once observed, universities often end up maintaining the status quo because it is the only option that cannot be vetoed.[2]

Curricular change is particularly difficult because it requires the cooperation of many academic departments. Such cooperation requires faculty members to look beyond the confines of their departments, where most of their work is centered, in order to serve a larger institutional purpose. In addition to this hurdle, comprehensive change necessarily creates winners and losers. For example, the English department may be reluctant to allow a course on business writing to fulfill a distribution requirement for fear that such a change will drain freshmen from introductory English classes and result in a decline in humanities majors. In addition, there are ideological differences about what collection of courses constitutes a meaningful core set of knowledge for students.

FACULTY NORMS AND THE ROLE OF DISCIPLINES. A second factor that inhibits civic engagement is the set of beliefs, values, and customs that guide the work of the professoriate. In the late 1950s Alvin Gouldner observed that many professors feel a greater affinity for members of their disciplinary community at other institutions than for the faculty members down the hall. Certainly more are inclined to participate in disciplinary activities than they are to serve, say, on the parking subcommittee of the faculty senate. In short, the discipline tends to draw faculty members away from institutional matters, particularly at research universities.[3] Further, academic disciplines have tended to denigrate academic work aimed at addressing local problems. The system of peer review, though a useful means of evaluating research, tends to reward scholarship in its familiar forms. Ernest Boyer's idea of a "scholarship of application," in which disciplinary knowledge is put to use in addressing community concerns (outlined in the highly influential book *Scholarship Reconsidered: Priorities of the Professoriate,* 1990), is only just beginning to gain legitimacy at some institutions.

Another factor that impedes faculty engagement is lack of time. Faculty members are pulled in a multitude of directions. They teach, research, advise, write letters of recommendation, mentor young scholars, participate in peer review for academic journals, and much more. They have precious little time to pursue any activity whose purpose may be construed as tangential to their core duties. The dramatic increase in the number of part-time teaching positions has exacerbated this problem. The sentence now beginning "In 2000" should read, "In 1999, 43 percent of faculty members worked part-time, up from 34 percent in 1980 and 22 percent in 1970. Adjuncts whose terms of employment are uncertain and who must cobble together positions at several institutions to earn a decent living are understandably less likely to invest time and energy supporting broad-based change at any one institution.[4]

EXTERNAL FACTORS. The instability of financial resources experienced since 2000 has given external constituents (state legislators, boards of higher education, donors) unprecedented influence over the agendas of colleges and universities. Legislators increasingly are pushing the "useful" aspects of education (e.g., job training) and greater efficiency. A preeminent American scholar of higher education, Richard Chait, points to this shift in the governance of American institutions of higher learning as a serious threat.

> The "enemy," if one chooses to apply that term to the marketplace and to external constituencies, is much stronger than any of these three groups alone, and perhaps stronger than all three together. If the board, the administration and the faculty do not coalesce, and maybe even if they do, the "market revolution" will supplant the "academic revolution."[5]

CONTESTED PURPOSES. Finally, many scholars question the validity of promoting civic engagement. They argue that the primary purpose of higher education is to encourage the development of analytical skills, facility in written and oral communication, and knowledge of a particular field of inquiry. What students choose to do with this knowledge (or whether they do anything at all) is beyond the scope of higher learning. The idea of value neutrality remains a potent inhibiting force.

## The Civic Education Counterrevolution

Despite the forces standing in opposition to the civic mission of higher education, the last two decades of the twentieth century witnessed a resurgence of efforts to foster community action and civic engagement. It is striking that such activities were achieved with a minimum of government involvement. Instead, they arose from a confluence of grassroots factors.

Some proponents of community and civic engagement have felt that scholarship has been overly attentive to the theoretical interests of disciplinary communities. Some have grown anxious over the commercialization of higher education and fear that the pursuit of financial stability has compromised the nonprofit mission. (This became particularly evident with the increasing corporate sponsorship of research.) Community-based learning has also proved to be a useful means of accommodating the emerging emphasis on preprofessional training and job preparation, while remaining consonant with the ideals of liberal arts learning. Many campuses located in low-income communities have been spurred by enlightened self-interest, hoping to improve their communities and in the process become more attractive to prospective students. Finally, there are deepening concerns about the state of America's civil society, particularly low levels of democratic participation among young people and doubts as to whether the next generation of adults is prepared to take up their democratic responsibilities. Taken together, these factors have refocused attention on civic education.

Concerns about an increasingly self-centered society have been building since the 1970s, as expressed by the social critics Tom Wolfe, who coined the term the "Me Decade," and Christopher Lasch, who condemned a growing "culture of narcissism." By the 1980s such concerns focused on America's youth. Surveys of college students showed a rise in the percentage of students who saw making money as a primary personal goal and a corresponding decrease in students who wanted to develop a meaningful philosophy of life. Fewer students indicated that they were interested in participating in community affairs, protecting the environment, or working to promote racial understanding.[6]

Such concerns galvanized college students and college presidents alike. In 1984 a recent Harvard graduate, Wayne Meisel, walked from Maine to Washington, D.C., and visited seventy campuses in order to find and motivate other students who were deeply committed to social issues and willing to go "into the streets" and give their time to help others. His journey led to the founding of the Campus Outreach Opportunity League (COOL), whose primary function was to mobilize college students in the service of their local communities. COOL also forcefully demonstrated that the negative stereotypes of students as entitled and self-indulgent did not reflect the values of many young people.

The following year, Frank Newman, former president of the University of Rhode Island and then-director of the Education Commission of the States, wrote a report that highlighted the need to reassert civic education in college.[7] Newman's missive caught the attention of a group of prominent university presidents, including those of Stanford, Georgetown, and Brown, who met with Newman in 1985. This group agreed that college students were being mischaracterized and that if students were given a chance to serve their communities, they would hasten to do so.

Out of this small gathering and several subsequent larger ones was born a presidential organization called Campus Compact. Its mission was to create public service opportunities for college students and to develop an expectation of service as an integral part of the student experience. The dream of its founders was to gather one hundred like-minded presidents to further this work. (In 2004 Campus Compact had more than nine hundred member colleges and universities supported by a network of national and state offices that provided training and technical assistance to students, faculty, and administrators in support of the civic mission of higher education.

The focus of these early efforts was to encourage and demonstrate the capacity of young people to act on behalf of those less fortunate than themselves. Through such activities as tutoring a child, volunteering in a soup kitchen, or cleaning up a park, young people could "give back" to society while gaining active learning experiences to prepare them for civic responsibility.

Soon, however, college educators who supported the idea of encouraging student volunteerism began to question whether students were learning the "skills and habits" of citizenship. There is value in recognizing societal problems and serving others. But students also needed to develop the skills to analyze the causes of social ills and to craft policies to address them. From these concerns the broader concepts of service-learning and civic engagement emerged.

### From Service to Service-Learning

During the early 1990s, service-learning became the preeminent vehicle for promoting civic education at colleges and universities. Service-learning—the embedding of student service into the curriculum—proved to be an excellent way of promoting deeper understanding of complex societal problems. Service-learning also met other pedagogical aims by marrying disciplinary theory with practice in the context of active learning. In other words, the experience of putting their academic knowledge to work in the community bolstered students' understanding of classroom material.

It also became clear that incorporating service into coursework offered the best hope of sustaining these efforts long term and ensuring that they did not become marginalized in the academy. A number of important efforts on the part of individual campuses as well as education associations were aimed at accomplishing that goal. In the late 1980s Campus Compact organized the Invisible College, a group of faculty committed to service-learning. This group recognized that many faculty members were reluctant to try service-learning because they could not envision how such work would help promote learning within their disciplines. It therefore proposed developing a series of books on service-learning in specific academic disciplines. By 2004 this series, published by the American Association for Higher Education (AAHE) in conjunction with Campus Compact, included nearly twenty volumes. In addition, the peer-reviewed *Michigan Journal of Community Service Learning* emerged to further the advancement of knowledge about service-learning.[8]

In 1998 Campus Compact received a major grant from the Pew Charitable Trusts to spread the practice of service-learning across higher education. This grant resulted in the creation of a series of practical publications, such as the *Introduction to Service-Learning Toolkit* and *Fundamentals of Service-Learning Course Construction*. Training sessions across the country involved nearly fourteen hundred faculty and administrators. An extensive Web site and a journal compiling published articles about civic engagement and service-learning from around the country (the Campus Compact *Reader*) exposed the practice to tens of thousands of others. Campus Compact also gave grants to seventeen disciplinary associations to encourage service-learning through their Web site, special editions of disciplinary journals, and conference sessions.[9]

The impact that such activities have had in promoting service-learning nationwide is reflected in data gathered from Campus Compact member institutions. Between 1998 and 2002, the average number of service-learning courses on member campuses grew from sixteen to thirty and the proportion of faculty undertaking service-learning grew from 13 percent to 22 percent. Other evidence that all of this activity took service-learning from the margins to the mainstream of higher education is found in *U.S. News & World Report*'s annual rankings of colleges, which in 2002 began including "active pedagogical practice" in its calculation.[10]

## Development of the "Engaged Campus"

An early goal of service-learning was encouraging students to grapple with societal problems. At the same time, many also began to question the role of colleges and universities as institutional citizens.[11] In 1999 Campus Compact and the American Council on Education (ACE), arguably the most influential higher education association in America, organized a meeting of sixty college presidents that resulted in the issuance of the "Presidents' Declaration on the Civic Responsibility of Higher Education," which stressed the need to educate the next generation of active citizens and for campuses to be good citizens in their own communities. The document featured a civic self-assessment guide that included such questions as: Do our students have an opportunity to practice the arts of democracy on campus? Is our faculty actively engaged in addressing community problems? Is our staff valued for what they can bring to civic engagement? (More than 535 college and university presidents have since signed this declaration.)[12]

In the early twenty-first century there was an outpouring of writing on civic education.[13] Many education associations, including the American Association of State Colleges and Universities, the National Association of Independent Colleges and Universities, and the National Organization of State Universities and Land-Grant Colleges, have published works or begun initiatives focusing on civic engagement in higher education.

These efforts evolved from a shift in focus from student community service to a comprehensive idea of the "engaged campus"—the concept that colleges and universities have a responsibility both to educate students for citizenship and to act as good institutional citizens in their own communities. These efforts also evolved from an understanding of active citizenship that moved beyond simple acts of compassion expressed through volunteer activities to active engagement in social, political, and policy issues. Two driving forces for this change were concern about democratic participation among young people and new thinking about the relationship between civic education, liberal arts, and issues such as diversity.

DEMOCRATIC PARTICIPATION. In 1998 an influential study by Arthur Levine and Jeanette Cureton, *When Hope and Fear Collide*, found that students felt disenfranchised from the political process: "Undergraduates reserve their strongest criticisms for government and the American political system. They don't believe either works" (p. 28). Levine and Cureton noted a "new localism"—a shift toward small, pragmatic, manageable agendas for change. As one student in their study observed, "I can't do anything about the theft of nuclear-grade weapons materials in Azerbaijan, but I can clean up the pond, help tutor a troubled kid, or work at the homeless shelter" (p. 36). Students were not entirely apolitical; in fact, Levine and Cureton's analysis showed a substantial jump in student demonstrations between 1976 and 1993, a finding supported by Robert Rhoads's 1998 text *Freedom's Web*, an investigation of student activism in the 1990s. However, students had lost interest in voting and saw no connection between the ballot box and the societal problems they were seeking to alleviate.

During the same time period, a series of highly publicized surveys highlighted this disengagement. In 1998 Public Allies published a poll by Peter Hart Research Associates revealing the distaste of young people for politics, including their reluctance to vote. In 1999 a poll for the National Association of Secretaries of State reaffirmed these findings. Regular polling by the Institute of Politics at Harvard University continues to chronicle the preference for service over politics. In 2002 a study by Scott Keeter et al. found that 40 percent of fifteen- to twenty-five-year-olds volunteered, but only 3 percent volunteered for a political group. These studies have raised the question of what role higher education might play in reconnecting students' societal concerns to active democratic participation through politics and policy making.[14]

CIVIC EDUCATION, LIBERAL EDUCATION, AND DIVERSITY. As the broader framework for civic education in higher education gained traction, there was increasing examination of the intersection between civic education, liberal education (referring to the liberal arts, not a political viewpoint), and diversity initiatives. The most fully developed of these explorations is the intersection of civic and liberal education. The Association of American Colleges and

Universities (AAC&U) has been the most influential higher education association espousing the importance of a liberal education. In 2002, consciously echoing Campus Compact's "Presidents' Declaration on the Civic Responsibilities of Higher Education," the group issued a call for a Presidents' Campaign for the Advancement of Liberal Learning. This initiative stresses the intersection between higher education and the needs of the democracy and posits that a liberal education is the best way to achieve education for global democracy, including developing "intellectual and ethical judgment; expanding cultural, societal and scientific horizons; cultivating democratic and global knowledge and engagement; and preparing for work in a dynamic and rapidly evolving economy."[15]

In 2003 Campus Compact and the AAC&U joined together to establish the Center for Liberal Education and Civic Engagement. The center's guiding principle is that "education for democratic engagement in the face of differences both embodies the best of a liberal education and sharpens its purposes." The initial purpose of the center is to encourage on-campus dialogue about liberal education and civic engagement.

At the opening of the twenty-first century the relationship between civic engagement and efforts to grapple with inequality and diversity was just beginning to be explored. During the debates over the legal future of affirmative action, which was decided in 2003 by the Supreme Court, campuses began to think about alternative strategies for attracting and retaining a diverse population. Many minority faculty members have expressed a desire to do more engaged scholarship. Legitimizing this form of scholarship is therefore important to retaining faculty of color in the academy. In addition, students have articulated a connection between their community work and their deeper understanding of diversity. A number of the studies cited earlier indicate that students place high value on understanding diverse peoples. The service work that students carry out in diverse communities is an important experience for building that understanding.

## Civic Engagement on Campus

Despite the internal and external hurdles to incorporating civic engagement into institutional priorities, many colleges and universities have made a significant commitment to doing so. The following sections examine campus practices designed to educate the next generation of active citizens and offer a few of the many examples of campuses that act as engaged citizens in their own communities.

To describe the progress that has been made thus far, we turn to a set of thirteen indicators of campus engagement first outlined by Elizabeth Hollander, John Saltmarsh, and Edward Zlotkowski in 2002.[16] Each indicator addresses a particular constituent whose participation is required to achieve full institutional commitment to the civic mission: administrators, faculty, staff (in particular community service or service-learning directors), students, and community partners. The indicators also address structures needed on the campus to achieve full engagement:

mission and purpose
administrative and academic leadership
external resource allocation
disciplines, departments, and interdisciplinary work
faculty roles and rewards
internal resource allocation
community voice
enabling mechanisms
faculty development
integrated and complementary community service activities
pedagogy and epistemology
forums for fostering public dialogue
student voice

No campus has every indicator of engagement, and some campuses are stronger in certain realms than others. However, each indicator represents an important element in achieving comprehensive and long-term change.

How can an institution traverse the distance between an ideal and realization of that ideal? One description of this process is provided by Paul S. Goodman and James W. Dean (1982), who delineate five stages in the spread of a particular behavior throughout an institution:[17]

1. Knowledge of the behavior: People within the organization become aware of a new activity or behavior.
2. Performance of the behavior: Certain individuals (though often a tiny minority initially) begin to perform the activity. Over time, the behavior becomes more pervasive.
3. Preference for the behavior: Individuals express a preference for the new activity. Institutional recognition and rewards for the activity may follow.
4. Normative consensus: As more people become aware of the new activity, a consensus emerges that it is appropriate.
5. Values: The institution states its commitment to the activity, which comes to represent an expression of the core purpose of the institution.

This framework is a useful yardstick for measuring progress toward institutionalized civic engagement efforts.

## Knowledge of the Behavior

DEFINING CIVIC EDUCATION. Typically, civic engagement begins with a person (or small group of persons) and an idea. In the 1980s faculty who pioneered community-based work were often iconoclasts and mavericks who received little support and less encouragement. More recently, a number of civic engagement efforts have been advanced by senior administrators or multiple constituent groups. In each case people within the institution must define civic education in ways that best fit their institutional circumstances.

At the University of Minnesota in Minneapolis this was accomplished by a civic engagement task force that was supported by the president, charged by the provost, and convened by a number of prestigious faculty members. The task force spent a year organizing conversations on the campus in every dorm, in roundtables with community leaders, state legislators, and foundation directors, and even in a local drugstore known for political discussion groups. These conversations led to a broad understanding of the public role of the university.

Rockford College in Illinois entered into a discussion of civic engagement by revisiting its historic legacy. This small, private college was the alma mater of Jane Addams, the social innovator who founded the settlement-house movement in Chicago in the early twentieth century. Rockford's president is promoting a college-wide conversation about the values held by Addams and how these values can be reflected in the college's mission, vision, and student life.

FACULTY SOCIALIZATION. To lay the groundwork for the future involvement of other faculty members, it is imperative that faculty members establish for themselves the legitimacy of any new pedagogy or scholarly activity. Since few faculty encounter purposeful civic education in graduate school, they must learn what it is in its particulars and assess its efficacy as a tool for teaching and learning. To that end, professional-development opportunities have been a useful step toward introducing specifics to a campus.

## Performance of the Behavior

ENABLING MECHANISMS. Translating knowledge into behavior requires both administrative and academic leadership as well as an investment of resources in new structures necessary to sustain the contact between faculty and students and the larger community. Not every faculty member needs to adopt engaged pedagogies for these pedagogies to be institutionalized on campus. Instead, the aim is to legitimize this form of teaching and give it equal status on campus.

Both Eastern Michigan University and Montclair State University in New Jersey offer a series of workshops to faculty members interested in experimenting with civic engagement. These workshops provide examples of civic engagement from other campuses and introduce faculty to available institutional and community resources. These schools and others also provide minigrants to faculty to develop new courses and incorporate democratic education into their work as teachers and as scholars. Some campuses (e.g., Brown University, the University of Wisconsin-Madison) even make grants available to students wishing to do community-based research projects as part of their coursework.

Perhaps the most visible means by which institutions are encouraging the practice of civic education is the growth in the number of community service and service-learning offices on campus. Hundreds of colleges and universities now have such offices. Their resources, especially their knowledgeable staff, make it easier for interested faculty members to become involved. Such offices identify a wide range of community projects and can match them to the goals of particular courses. They often provide training to students to prepare them for community work. At Brevard Community College in Florida, the Center for Service-Learning offers a full range of services, including faculty development workshops and minigrants. It is a model that is becoming increasingly popular.

At James Madison University in Virginia, the Center for Leadership, Service, and Transitions introduces students to individual community involvement in their first year; the goal is to equip students by their fourth year to analyze or even influence policies that affect the community. Students themselves attest to the success of this approach. One such student, Kymber Lovett, worked in the community as part of a freshman social work course; as she noted in a 2002 speech at the launch of Virginia Campus Compact, "I had never thought to ask why so many children that I worked with . . . were not reading at their grade levels or why they did not have health care service. But once I started asking, I realized that there were opportunities that I had as a member of the community to work to make changes." By her senior year, she was taking a health policy course and lobbying for health legislation for children.

RESOURCE ALLOCATION AND LEADERSHIP. Enabling mechanisms such as service-learning offices can succeed only if the administrative and academic leadership of the institution support them. Obviously this means adequate funding. Increasingly, campuses are seeking to endow this function by finding donors to support the college's civic mission. However, it is also important for the chief academic officer to discuss the civic mission with deans and department chairs and to invite them to foster department-specific initiatives or interdepartmental projects.

At American University in Washington, D.C., the president challenged each department to put on an event as part of a yearlong celebration of the civic purpose of the university, and he provided funding to assist them. At California State University at Northridge and at Miami Dade College, the provost and president sponsored Engaged Department Institutes in which thirty-five departments participated in a three-day discussion of the theory and practice of civic education.

Such action by top administrators is an effective means of overcoming the perception that civic engagement does not warrant institutional attention.

INTEGRATING ENGAGEMENT ACTIVITIES. As discussed earlier, departments have an organizational tendency to operate in relative isolation. This necessitates bringing together the academic and cocurricular staff, as well as providing "bridging" mechanisms between the campus and the community. Such mechanisms vary considerably depending upon the size and complexity of the institution. Coordination is particularly challenging at large comprehensive universities, where each school (e.g., law, medicine, etc.) may have its own outreach activities. One way this is handled is to start with an inventory of all the activities on campus and post it on a Web site where additions can easily be made. Harvard University, among others, has such an inventory. To sustain coordination and collaboration, some campuses assign responsibility to an academic leader; others create centers for engagement.

Some campuses have adopted a strategy of focusing on particular neighborhoods to maximize their impact. Trinity College in Connecticut created a learning corridor adjacent to its campus that included a Boys and Girls Club as well as elementary and high schools. Students from the campus regularly volunteer in this corridor as part of a comprehensive effort to improve the quality of Hartford public schools. These activities have led to a major effort to integrate community learning courses, student volunteer activities, and community outreach through regular meetings and a new Web site.

## Preference for the Behavior

Faculty who use engaged pedagogies point to numerous benefits. Community-based work enriches students' understanding of the theories to which they are being introduced and enlivens class discussions. The inherent messiness of resolving problems in a community setting disabuses students of the notion that "textbook" answers exist. Many faculty also point to the intrinsic rewards of applying their expertise to help others. Further, given the brief shelf life of disciplinary content, community-based learning is seen as a way to instill certain habits of mind and a sense of agency that students can carry with them.

However, no activity can last long if it is outside of the existing formal reward structure of the institution. In order to draw a larger cadre of faculty to the practice, it is essential to adjust both the internal and the external reward systems. Currently, faculty in the most elite American research universities are rewarded primarily for their research, second for the quality of their teaching, and last for their "service," which in most institutions means membership on faculty committees rather than service to the larger community. Of course, many institutions place a higher priority on teaching than on research (e.g., small liberal arts colleges, community colleges, urban comprehensive universities), but even at these institutions the standard of the research university is influential.

Creating alternative reward systems that rigorously assess and honor community-based scholarship and teaching is one of the most difficult aspects of achieving an engaged campus. A few leading campuses, such as Indiana University and Michigan State, have added community engagement as one basis on which a faculty member might seek tenure, along with research and teaching. Some campuses use a portfolio approach for tenure review. The contents of the portfolio (e.g., unpublished research conducted on behalf of a particular community-based organization) are reviewed and critiqued by academic peers across the country. On campuses where the practice has taken hold, such as Montclair State, job descriptions for faculty positions include requirements for experience in service-learning and are a part of the review process for faculty hiring.

Because the faculty is generally self-governing, it is essential that the disciplines and academic leadership of departments support engaged teaching practices and help create rigorous review systems. In the meantime, as the slow process of winning over departments and disciplines takes place, administrators have sought to support these practices through alternative reward systems such as institutional teaching and engagement awards, course design grants, and administrative support.

## Normative Consensus

PUBLIC DIALOGUE. Maintaining institutional commitment to civic engagement requires on-campus dialogue and debate. At the University of Minnesota, conversations with state legislators and others brought into focus the extent to which the public purpose of the institution was under challenge. The American Council on Education, as part of its civic initiative in 1999, helped a dozen campuses host "Listening to Communities" sessions, designed to help campuses understand how they could work with community organizations.

The college campus has traditionally been a space for debating public issues with rigor, not rancor. Public forums that involve a wide range of constituencies can be an important vehicle for both applying academic knowledge to community problems and modeling democratic debate for students. The University of California, San Diego, sponsors the San Diego Dialogue, which addresses the economic future of the San Diego/Tijuana metropolitan area. The dialogue involves community leaders of all kinds and is informed by academic research on such topics as the role of historic associations in building social capital, and U.S./Mexico border crossings. The campuses of North Shore Community College in Massachusetts and Gulf Coast Community College in Florida are known as important places for everyone in the community to learn about and debate public policies. To achieve this aim, the campuses regularly invite public leaders to open events.

STUDENT VOICE.  Schools that want to encourage civic engagement need to create meaningful mechanisms for students to participate in democratic decision making on their own campuses. This can range from student participation in faculty hiring to serving on the board of trustees. Many public universities include a nonvoting member on the board. In Oklahoma, the board of regents for the public university system has very active student participants. Under their leadership, Campus Compact set up a state office in Oklahoma to help create more volunteer options on campus. Some campuses, such as Antioch College in Ohio, have a long tradition of student involvement in all aspects of campus life. Students serve as full voting members on every tenure and hiring committee, as well as on budget and administrative committees. Every week the entire campus community is invited to a meeting at which issues can be raised and discussed and action taken. At Hampshire College in Massachusetts, the president has an open breakfast every Monday at which students may discuss special concerns. These are rare practices, however, and many campuses find that there is little student interest even in the more traditional student governments.

Much more common are issue-oriented student groups. At Stanford University, students counted more than four hundred such groups in an undergraduate student population of fourteen thousand. Student groups undertake direct service, advocacy, and politics. Generally they are not in regular touch with one another, even though they may be addressing similar issues. A few campuses are consciously bringing these student groups together to learn from one another and deepen their engagement practices. At the University of Pennsylvania's Civic House, the center that supports student volunteerism, students are encouraged to root their advocacy work in local service and to understand advocacy issues in their service work.

In a broader effort to coordinate student activity, Campus Compact has launched a national initiative entitled Raise Your Voice: Student Action for Change. The purpose of this initiative is to encourage more students to become involved in all kinds of civic activities, and to help them see the connection between service work and public policy. This campaign has led to reforms on dozens of campuses. For example, Stanford students have initiated a dialogue between student service and political groups on campus to achieve greater impact. Students have also advocated for their own civic engagement with state legislators' and governors' offices. These initiatives to nurture the policy and political engagement of students beyond community service can be found across the country, but they are not yet as widespread as either volunteer service or service-learning initiatives.

COMMUNITY PARTNERSHIPS.  Truly engaged campuses have also found ways to honor the input and knowledge of the communities with which they are partnering and are deploying their resources strategically for maximum community impact. Many campuses have created community advisory boards. Some, like Clark University, the University of Pennsylvania, and Spelman College, were instrumental in forming nonprofit community development agencies in which they participate without dominating. Others have added their resources and expertise to existing municipal redevelopment efforts, such as Bates College's role in the larger community of Lewiston/Auburn, Maine, through the community-based alliance LA Excels. Some institutions, including Yale University, have well-supported centers that work to ensure that campus resources are effectively deployed to meet the community's needs. Visible enabling mechanisms like these help the community know how to approach the campus for assistance. Such centers can also leverage campus resources such as hiring, purchasing, and construction contracting on behalf of local residents.

At the curricular level, well-developed community partnerships may involve bringing in compensated community instructors to co-teach. For example, at Providence College in Rhode Island, one history professor co-taught a course called Community Service in American Culture with the codirector of Amos House, a multiservice agency focusing on peace and justice. At San Francisco State University, a political science professor co-teaches a course called San Francisco Political Issues: Housing and Economic Development with the city's former deputy mayor and staff from several local agencies.

These kinds of deep community connections can have a powerful influence on both students and faculty, and even the institution itself. Faculty at Goucher College in Maryland note that a subtle institutional transformation occurs when faculty meet regularly with community partners and weave their perspective into the classroom. As one professor put it, "Instead of experiencing a 'split' between the mandates of the curriculum and 'extra-curricular commitments' that render one or the other marginal, students, faculty, and ultimately the institution itself re-envision academic expertise as a way to leverage our capacity to create change."[18]

## Values

Finally, a fully realized change in an institution, according to Goodman and Dean, is reflected in the values that the institution holds and in the institution's willingness to measure its success in accordance with these values. In higher education, this stage is reflected in serious attention to the institution's mission and in assessment procedures designed to make the civic mission "count" in meaningful ways such as allocation of funds.

The mission statement of many (indeed, most) colleges includes a civic purpose. On most campuses, however, few staff, students, or faculty can cite the institutional mission. Campuses that are serious about realizing their civic mission undertake a conscious process to reexamine their mission and have widespread discussions about it on campus. One example is DePaul University, a large

Catholic institution in Chicago that has a strong commitment to its namesake's mission of serving the poor. (Saint Vincent de Paul was a French priest known for his work among the poor in the 1600s.) This commitment is evident in many ways. It is discussed in new staff and faculty orientations and posted prominently on the university's Web site. Most significantly, the mission is built into the university's strategic plans. These plans are widely discussed with the campus community and reported upon after implementation.

Another example is Portland State University, which has its mission—"Let Knowledge Serve the City"—carved into a bridge crossing a major downtown thoroughfare. Beyond this symbolic gesture, Portland State has evaluation systems for both faculty and students to help measure the extent of civic engagement on campus. Such measurements are important because one of the ways to determine whether the mission statement is actually a driving force is to examine whether a college assesses its own success on the basis of its values and mission.

Increasingly, engaged campuses are realizing this aim by identifying student outcomes that they hope to achieve. Hocking College, a two-year school in Ohio, requires eight "Success Skills" of all students who complete an associate's degree. The college measures these skills with pre- and post-testing, course evaluations, and other means. One of these skills is "community, cultural, and global awareness," including knowledge of social and political processes, civic rights and responsibilities, community needs, and other indicators.

As the engaged-campus movement has gained momentum, so has the practice of assessing campus engagement.[19] The effort to measure civic outcomes for students and the campuses is taking place in a context in which American higher education is being urged to focus more attention on student outcomes rather than simply measuring inputs such as credit hours. Campuses are increasingly using a national survey of student engagement to assess how well the campus is actually achieving student learning.

## Conclusion

American campuses offer a wealth of activities whose purpose is explicitly linked to building a democratic society. And despite prodigious resistance, evidence suggests that these activities are beginning to move from the margins toward the mainstream. In 1998, when Campus Compact first began using its Service-Learning Pyramid—a tool to measure the extent to which individual colleges and universities have institutionalized civic engagement—these activities were marginal on most campuses. More than two-thirds (68 percent) of the 578 Campus Compact member schools surveyed reported that they were at the bottom of the pyramid, with less than 10 percent of their faculty using service-learning. By 2002, the strata of the pyramid had begun to shift. Only 52 percent of member schools (then 868, approximately one-quarter of all colleges and universities nationwide) remained at the bottom level of the pyramid, while those at the most advanced level (25 percent or more of faculty using service-learning) increased from 4 percent to 12 percent. The average number of service-learning courses per campus continues to climb, reaching thirty-seven in 2003.

Faculty engagement in service-learning is, of course, only one measure of civic engagement (although it may be the most difficult to achieve). The number of signatories of the "Presidents' Declaration" suggests that civic responsibility is being embraced by senior administration as well. Further, these activities are not occurring only at small colleges or religiously affiliated institutions. There is increasing activity from many of the most influential research-oriented campuses. In 1998 30 percent of research-intensive institutions (based on the Carnegie classification system) were Campus Compact members; by 2002, this number had risen to 61 percent.[20]

Despite a waxing of interest in civic education, campuses have a long way to go before such activities become mainstream for most faculty members. Civic engagement remains a contested ideal. In 2003 Stanley Fish, dean of the College of Liberal Arts and Sciences at the University of Illinois at Chicago, called into question the development of civic capacity in principle and in practice: "My main objection to moral and civic education in our colleges and universities is not that it is a bad idea (which it surely is), but that it's an unworkable idea."[21]

Fish's first assertion reflects the continued dominance of disciplinary aims over all other concerns, including societal ones. To the world beyond the ivied walls, however, academics who want students to breathe only the rarified air of disciplinary theory sound a bit like the two sociologists who came upon a man who had been set upon by thieves, beaten, and left unconscious at the side of the road. Turning to one another they exclaimed: "The man who did this needs our help!" The point of this old joke is not that efforts to understand the root causes of social ills are not valuable, but that we need to consider ways to address the community needs that are immediately before us.

The perceived distance between the work of the academy and the exigencies of daily life has, since the 1980s, spawned a veritable cottage industry of higher education critics. Misperceptions about the work of the academy have caused the traditional appeals for public support of higher education—which focused on its contribution to the public good—to lose their resonance. The fruits of this misunderstanding are visible in the unprecedented cuts now being made in public higher education. A number of states have even attempted to privatize the flagship public research universities, allowing them to raise their tuitions to reflect the value of their education if they will forgo or accept reduced public support.

Part of the problem is that members of the academy have done a poor job of informing external constituents (e.g., legislators, leaders in the corporate world, taxpayers, the public at large) of the civic role they play, the knowledge they can bring to pressing issues of the day, and the impact of civic education on their students. Too much effort is put into trying to secure public funds without making a clear case about the public benefits of higher education beyond obtaining a job. Sustaining the future of the civic engagement movement in higher education will require giving it a much more public face.

Fish's second assertion, that civic education is "unworkable," points up the difficulty of measuring the impact of engagement efforts. The nascent research on service-learning and civic engagement clearly indicates that institutions can influence students' knowledge of politics and the systemic nature of social problems. Studies have shown that students who participate in service activities (even if it is required) grow to be more concerned about social issues, enjoy learning, and do at least as well in their nonservice courses as their nonparticipating peers. (That is, service work as an extracurricular activity is not a drain on their academic work.)[22] Researchers are developing tools to measure the civic behaviors of college students. Longitudinal studies are needed to determine the impact on behavior after graduation.

What is clear is that students value civic work. Volunteerism by college students is increasing; one-third of all undergraduates are estimated to have participated in volunteer work in 2002-2003. In addition, a 2002 study shows that linking volunteerism to class discussion leads to deeper civic engagement by students:

> Student volunteers who are encouraged to talk about their volunteer work in class are much more likely to stick with it. . . . This group is twice as likely to volunteer regularly as those who don't get the chance to talk about their experiences (64% vs. 30%, respectively). They are also much more likely than those without such discussions to work on a community problem (47% vs. 32%), to participate in a run, walk, or bike ride for charity (27% vs. 15%), or to influence someone's vote (50% vs. 34%). These findings remain valid even when a lot of other factors are taken into consideration.[23]

Of course the decades of cynicism (including faculty cynicism), government bashing, and "dirty" politics have taken a large toll. Students are not, in the main, naturally sympathetic to the benefits of political participation. However, helping them understand that their action in the community is an expression of their political will may be a means of encouraging greater involvement.

Robert Maynard Hutchins, president of the University of Chicago during the 1930s, once observed: "The death of democracy is not likely to be an assassination from ambush. It will be a slow extinction from apathy, indifference and undernourishment." Higher education has a responsibility to help nourish civically engaged students. The work will be contested, the outcome may be uncertain, but the imperative is clear. John Dewey, the great educator of the early twentieth century, sums it up best: "Democracy has to be born anew every generation, and education is its midwife."

## *Notes*

1. The most prominent surveys were conducted by UCLA's Higher Education Research Institute. For a synopsis of trend data, see Astin, Alexander. "The Changing American College Student: Thirty-Year Trends, 1966-1996," *The Review of Higher Education,* 21(2), 1998, 115-135.

2. Clark Kerr, "Postscript 1982: The Uses of the University Two Decades Later," *Change* 14 (September/October 1982), 23–31.

3. Alvin W. Gouldner, "Cosmopolitan and Locals: Toward an Analysis of Latent Social Roles," *Administrative Science Quarterly* 2 (December 1957), 281–307.

4. U.S. Department of Education, National Center for Education Statistics. "Digest of Education Statistics, 2002." Available at http://nces.ed.gov/programs/digest/d02/tables/dt227.asp.

5. Chait, "The 'Academic Revolution' Revisited," 273.

6. Tom Wolfe, "The Me Decade and the Third Awakening," in *Mauve Gloves & Madmen, Clutter & Vine* (New York: Farrar, Straus and Giroux, 1976); Christopher Lasch, *Culture of Narcissism: American Life in an Age of Diminishing Expectations* (New York: Norton, 1978).

7. Frank Newman, *Higher Education and the American Resurgence* (Princeton, N.J.: Carnegie Foundation for the Advancement of Teaching, 1985).

8. Joseph Galura and Jeffrey Howard were the series editors for volumes 1–3 of PRAXIS (Ann Arbor, Mich.: OCSL Press, 1993–1995); these volumes on service-learning led to the establishment of the influential *Michigan Journal of Community Service Learning.*

9. Campus Compact, *Fundamentals of Service-Learning Course Construction* (Providence, R.I.: 2001) and *Introduction to Service-Learning Toolkit: Readings and Resources for Faculty,* 2nd ed. (Providence, R.I., 2003). More information can be found on Campus Compact's Web site at www.compact.org/.

10. Campus Compact, *2002 Annual Service Statistics* (Providence, R.I., 2003); "Programs That Really Work," *U.S. News & World Report,* America's Best Colleges 2003, September 23, 2002, 114.

11. See Bringle, Games, and Mallory, *Colleges and Universities as Citizens,* and Harry Boyte and Elizabeth Hollander, *Wingspread Declaration on the Civic Responsibilities of Research Universities* (Providence, R.I.: Campus Compact, 1999).

12. Campus Compact, "Presidents' Declaration on the Civic Responsibility of Higher Education" (Providence, R.I., 2000), www.compact.org/presidential/declaration.html.

13. See for example Ehrlich, *Civic Responsibility and Higher Education;* Rosovsky, "No Ivory Tower"; and Robert Zemsky, "Have We Lost the 'Public' in Higher Education?" *Chronicle of Higher Education,* Chronicle Review, May 30, 2003, B7.

14. Peter D. Hart Research Associates, *New Leadership for a New Century: Key Findings from a Study on Youth, Leadership, and Community Service* (Milwaukee: Public Allies, 1998); National Association of Secretaries of State, *New Millennium Survey: American Youth Attitudes on Politics, Citizenship, Government and Voting* (Washington, D.C., 1999), www.stateofthevote.org/survey/index.htm; Scott Keeter et al., *The Civic and Political Health of the Nation: A Generational Portrait* (College Park, Md.: Center for Information and Research on Civic Learning and Engagement, 2002).

15. Association of American Colleges and Universities. "Presidents' Campaign for the Advancement of Liberal Learning." Available at www.aacu-edu.org/CALL/CALLtext.cfm

16. Elizabeth Hollander, John Saltmarsh, and Edward Zlotkowski, "Indicators of Engagement," in *Learning to Serve: Promoting Civil Society through Service Learning,* edited by Maureen E. Kenny et al. (Boston: Kluwer, 2002).

17. Paul S. Goodman and James W. Dean, "Creating Long-term Organizational Change," in *Change in Organizations: New Perspectives on Theory, Research, and Practice,* edited by Paul S. Goodman (San Francisco: Jossey-Bass, 1982).

18. Quoted in Burton et al., "Liberal Arts College Faculty Reflect on Service Learning," 162.

19. A seminal assessment tool is Gelmon et al., "Assessing Service-Learning and Civic Engagement."

20. Campus Compact, *2002 Annual Service Statistics.*

21. Stanley Fish, "Aim Low," *Chronicle of Higher Education,* May 16, 2003, A10.

22. Alexander W. Astin and Linda J. Sax, "How Undergraduates Are Affected by Service Participation," *Journal of College Student Development* 39, no. 3 (1998), 251–263.

23. Keeter et al., *The Civic and Political Health of the Nation, 33.*

## Bibliography

American Association of State Colleges and Universities. *Stepping Forward as Stewards of Place: A Guide for Leading Public Engagement at State Colleges and Universities.* Washington, D.C., 2002. Outlines the place of state institutions as stewards in their regions.

Battistoni, Richard M. "Service Learning and Civic Education." In *Education for Civic Engagement in Democracy: Service Learning and Other Promising Practices,* edited by Sheila Mann and John J. Patrick, pp. 29–44. Bloomington, Ind.: Educational Resources Information Center, 2000. Addresses the move from volunteer service to civic engagement.

Bonnen, James T. "The Land-Grant Idea and the Evolving Outreach University." In *University-Community Collaborations for the Twenty-First Century: Outreach Scholarship for Youth and Families,* edited by Richard M. Lerner and Lou Anna K. Simon. New York: Garland, 1998.

Boyer, Ernest L. *Scholarship Reconsidered: Priorities of the Professoriate.* San Francisco: Jossey-Bass, 1990. A seminal work validating teaching and service as scholarly pursuits.

Bringle, Robert G., Richard Games, and Edward A. Malloy. *Colleges and Universities as Citizens.* Boston: Allyn and Bacon, 1999. A thorough discussion of institutional citizenship.

Bringle, Robert G., Mindy A. Phillips, and Michael Hudson. *The Measure of Service-Learning: Research Scales to Assess Student Experiences.* Washington, D.C.: American Psychological Association, 2004. An extensive compilation of scales for use in studying student behavior and attitudes.

Brubacher, John S., and Willis Rudy. *Higher Education in Transition: A History of American Colleges and Universities, 1636–1968.* New York: Harper and Row, 1968. A look at shifting priorities and paradigms in higher education.

Burtchaell, James Tunstead. *The Dying of the Light: The Disengagement of Colleges and Universities from Their Christian Churches.* Grand Rapids, Mich.: W. B. Eerdmans, 1998. Documents the loss of religious identity in America's Christian colleges and universities since the 1960s.

Burton, Joan, et al. "Liberal Arts College Faculty Reflect on Service Learning: Steps on a Transformative Journey." In *Learning to Serve: Promoting Civil Society through Service-Learning,* edited by Maureen E. Kenny et al. Boston: Kluwer, 2002. Documents the experiences of service-learning faculty, in their own words.

Campus Compact. *Introduction to Service-Learning Toolkit: Readings and Resources for Faculty* (second ed.). Providence, RI: Campus Compact, 2003. A compendium of writing on the theory and practice of service-learning.

Carnegie Corporation of New York and the Center for Information and Research on Civic Learning and Engagement (CIRCLE). *The Civic Mission of Schools.* New York: Carnegie, 2003.

Chait, Richard. "The 'Academic Revolution' Revisited." In *The Future of the City of Intellect: The Changing American University,* edited by Steven Brint, pp. 293–321. Stanford, Calif.: Stanford University Press, 2002.

Civian, Jan T., et al. "Implementing Change." In *Handbook of the Undergraduate Curriculum: A Comprehensive Guide to Purposes, Structures, Practices, and Change,* edited by Jerry G. Gaff and James L. Ratcliff, pp. 647–660. San Francisco: Jossey-Bass, 1996.

Ehrlich, Thomas, ed. *Civic Responsibility and Higher Education.* Phoenix, Ariz.: Oryx, 2000.

Furco, Andrew. *Institutionalizing Service-Learning in Higher Education.* Bolton, Mass.: Anker Publishing, 2005. Includes a comprehensive self-assessment rubric.

Geiger, Roger. "The Ten Generations of American Higher Education." In *American Higher Education in the Twenty-first Century: Social, Political, and Economic Challenges,* edited by Philip G. Altbach, Robert O. Berdahl and Patricia J. Gumport, pp. 38–69. Baltimore, Md.: Johns Hopkins University Press, 1999.

Gelmon, Sherril, et al. *Assessing Service-Learning and Civic Engagement: Principles and Techniques.* Providence, R.I.: Campus Compact, 2001. A guide to assessing service-learning, including assessment tools for use with students, faculty, and community partners.

Jencks, Christopher, and David Reisman. *The Academic Revolution.* Garden City, N.Y.: Doubleday, 1968. Discusses the shift in academic focus to the research-oriented German model.

Kellogg Commission on the Future of State and Land-Grant Universities. *Returning to Our Roots: The Engaged Institution.* New York: National Organization of State Universities and Land-Grant Colleges, 1999.

Levine, Arthur, and Jeanette S. Cureton. *When Hope and Fear Collide: A Portrait of Today's College Student*. San Francisco: Jossey-Bass, 1998. A study of college students focusing on how campus faculty, administrators, and staff can help students achieve their potential.

Lucas, Christopher J. *American Higher Education: A History*. New York: St. Martin's, 1994.

Maurrasse, David J. *Beyond the Campus: How Colleges and Universities Form Partnerships with Their Communities*. New York: Routledge, 2001.

National Commission on Civic Renewal. *A Nation of Spectators: How Civic Disengagement Weakens America and What We Can Do About It*. College Park, Md., 1998.

National Survey of Student Engagement. *From Promise to Progress: How Colleges and Universities Are Using Student Engagement Results to Improve Collegiate Quality/2002 Annual Report*. Bloomington, Ind., 2002.

Putnam, Robert D. *Bowling Alone: The Collapse and Revival of American Community*. New York: Simon and Schuster, 2000. Data-driven look at how Americans have become increasingly disconnected from family, friends, neighbors, and democratic structures, and a discussion of ways to reconnect.

Reuben, Julie A. *The Making of the Modern University: Intellectual Transformation and the Marginalization of Morality*. Chicago: University of Chicago Press, 1996. A thorough discussion of the underpinnings of "values-free" education.

Rhoads, Robert A. *Freedom's Web: Student Activism in an Age of Cultural Diversity*. Baltimore, Md.: Johns Hopkins University Press, 1998.

Roper Starch Worldwide. *Public Attitudes toward Education and Service-Learning*. Battle Creek, Mich.: W. K. Kellogg Foundation, 2002. Results of a national opinion poll showing that the public wants colleges to teach social skills, tolerance, and good citizenship, as well as academics.

Rosovsky, Henry. "No Ivory Tower: University and Society in the Twenty-First Century." In *As the Walls of Academia Are Tumbling Down*, edited by Werner Z. Hirsch and Luc E. Weber. London: Economica, 2002.

Rudolph, Frederick. *The American College and University: A History*. New York: Knopf, 1962.

Stanton, Timothy K., Dwight E. Giles Jr., and Nadine I. Cruz. *Service-Learning: A Movement's Pioneers Reflect on Its Origins, Practice, and Future*. San Francisco: Jossey-Bass, 1999. Insight into the development of the service-learning movement.

# VISIONS AND POSSIBILITIES

# 12

## AGENCY, RECIPROCITY, AND ACCOUNTABILITY IN DEMOCRATIC EDUCATION

*Richard F. Elmore*

THE POLICY DEBATE CONCERNING ACCOUNTABILITY has triggered fundamental questions about democracy and schooling. Since the 1980s, local, state, and federal policies have come increasingly to focus on holding schools accountable for student learning. Advocates of performance-based accountability argue that schools should answer to public authorities for the value they produce for students. Opponents argue that focusing on measurable student performance narrows the purpose of schooling and demeans and trivializes the work of educators. Debaters on both sides of the issue wrap themselves in the rhetoric of democratic education. Advocates argue that performance-based accountability delivers on the promise of democratic schooling by assuring that all students have the opportunity to learn to a high standard. Opponents argue that performance-based accountability undermines the democratic standard of local control by substituting state and federal determinations of what students should know for local ones, and it undermines the preparation of students for democratic life by narrowing the purposes of schooling to purely cognitive ends.

Education policy debates in the United States are always about democratic schooling in one way or another. In fact, one could argue that policy debates are the main way through which Americans express what they mean by democratic schooling. The debate about accountability contains a fundamental problem of democratic education: The problem of agency, or control, over learning. How do we model what it means to be a well-educated person by the way we control, manage, and govern schools?

Is it possible to square the theory of performance-based accountability with "democratic" conceptions of schooling? "Democratic" schooling in this sense

277

refers to two things: schools that nurture high levels of knowledge, skill, and competence in students in order to prepare them for participation in democratic life, and schools in which students, parents, and educators have a role in determining the conditions of their own work. This essay begins with the classroom, examining conceptions of powerful instructional practice and learning that link to competence in democratic participation, and the conditions that promote such practice. At the school level, it looks at powerful instructional practice nested in schools, and the organizational conditions that promote and nurture this practice. Moving to the system level, it analyzes the kinds of policies that correspond with effective instructional practice at the classroom level and of organizational success at the school level. The essay concludes with a theory that connects the classroom, the school, and the system using the central ideas of agency, reciprocity, and accountability. The thrust of the argument here is that the conditions for success of democratic schooling are powerfully parallel at the classroom, the school, and the system levels, and that these conditions are not necessarily inconsistent with strong performance-based accountability.

## *The Socratic Paradox: Agency and Reciprocity in the Classroom*

A truism of education is "I can teach you, but I cannot 'learn' you," a phrase that is meant to convey the importance of the learner's active consent in the instructional process. Teachers require from learners their participation as active agents in order for learning to take place. Conversely, the learner's success depends on the teacher's ability to engage him or her in an activity that leads to learning. There are two fundamental principles at work here: One is the principle of *agency,* which requires the learner's active consent and engagement with the teacher in the social activity of learning, and the teacher's active engagement in eliciting that consent and engagement. In order for teaching and learning to occur, both teacher and student must actively consent to be engaged. The second principle is *reciprocity,* which requires both teacher and student to agree to be influenced in their common work by the other's needs and interests; the teacher's interest and need to be effective depends on the student's interest and need to gain something of value from the student/teacher relationship.

These principles of agency and reciprocity are also at the center of democratic theory. Democracies operate through implicit or explicit mechanisms of consent—voting, coalition building, persuasion, logrolling. These mechanisms depend on fundamental processes of reciprocity, by which individuals agree to orchestrate their actions in common because collective action has greater benefits, individual and collective, than individual action.

Teaching and learning, then, form one way of negotiating individual needs and interests. In this way, it is a quintessentially political act, a microcosm of democracy.

There is, however, buried in this relationship of "teacher" and "learner" a noble lie, or more politely, a paradox. In order for learners to exercise agency, they must believe that, in some sense, they control the conditions of their learning—at least to the degree that they can claim their portion of the reciprocity in the relationship. But the whole purpose of being in relation to someone called a teacher is that the teacher is understood to know more than the student. If it is true that the teacher knows what the student doesn't know, then how is it possible for the student to exercise agency or assert reciprocity in the relationship?

A significant piece of Western philosophy—and Eastern philosophy, for that matter—revolves around this central paradox in the relationship between teacher and student. It can be labeled the Socratic paradox because it is clearly presented in the role that Socrates plays in the Platonic dialogues, and by extension in the role of the teacher in the practice of "Socratic pedagogy." Plato's Socrates claims, in the key dialogues that focus on the problems of knowledge and virtue, not to know the answers to the questions he poses, to be interested only in exposing the defects and shortcomings of other philosophers' ideas rather than in elaborating his own views, and only to be revealing knowledge that already exists in the mind of the student with whom he is engaged rather than in any way actively "teaching" that student. In the Socratic dialogue, it is nearly always the student, not Socrates himself, who displays the knowledge or learning that emerges from the discourse.

But how is it possible to get such a result without Socrates actually knowing more than the student with whom he is engaged? Does he "pretend" not to know, skillfully steering the dialogue in the direction of what he already knows and what he wants the student to learn? Or is he genuinely only asking questions that cause the student to reveal the knowledge that is already present, but undisclosed, in the student's mind? If the knowledge that the student reveals exists apart from both Socrates and the student, then isn't Socrates also a student, and if he is, who is the teacher? If Socrates were to confess to manipulative intent and simply tell the student what he was thinking, would the student actually "know" it in the same way that he would if he and his teacher were to "discover" it through the process of dialogue? If one believes that the teacher always knows more than the student, then one resolves the Socratic paradox by calling it a noble lie. The teacher pretends not to know what she knows in order to engage the student in a line of questioning that leads the student to a predetermined destination described by the teacher's knowledge. On the other hand, if one believes that, while the teacher may have some advantage in knowledge relative to the student, the good teacher is always "ignorant" or "innocent" in certain important respects, then one treats the Socratic paradox as a genuine paradox. By taking this posture, teachers learn things that they did not know about the content itself, and they come to know how their students think about the content in ways that are central to the teacher's competence as a teacher.

At relatively low levels of cognitive demand, the Socratic paradox is less visible than at high levels, but no less present. That is, when teachers and students are engaging around factual knowledge ("What did Laura say when she confronted Fred in chapter three?") or procedural knowledge ("Change this adjective to an adverb"), it often looks as though there is no ambiguity in the relationship between teacher and student. It is the student's job to find the place in the text where Laura speaks to Fred and to report to the teacher what Laura said; it is the student's job to add an "*ly*" to "swift" and thereby create "swiftly" ("Now use this word in a sentence"). It is when teachers try to get students to reproduce and extend this factual and procedural knowledge that the Socratic paradox becomes more visible. Why is it important to pay attention to instances in fiction where one character confronts another? How is "the swift river" different, in the diction of a poem, from "the river ran swiftly"? Can a teacher engage a student in these latter questions without, in some sense, being genuinely innocent about what the students' answers might reveal? About the students' interpretation, perception, understanding? About the teacher's interpretation, perception, understanding of the questions? Of the students' responses to the questions? Could the teacher actually be sure that the students "knew" anything at all about how to read, interpret, and produce written text if they could answer the first set of questions but not the second? So the Socratic paradox is embedded in learning at all levels of cognitive demand, though it might be more visible at some levels than at others.

Let us now revisit the problems of agency and reciprocity in teaching and learning in light of the Socratic paradox. Reciprocity is not just about the problem of how to engage the student in the teacher's agenda. It is also about what the teacher learns from the student by putting herself in the position of ignorance and innocence about that which she is alleged to know. Agency is not just about the student's active consent to be taught. It is about the teacher's active *transfer of agency* over learning from herself to the student. Living inside the Socratic paradox means that the roles of teacher and student are complex, reversible, and reciprocal. If the teacher is doing her job, she is actively engaged in learning the content in greater depth as a consequence of teaching it, and actively engaged in understanding what students' responses say about the nature of the knowledge she is alleged to know. If the student is doing her job, she is actively teaching the teacher the puzzles that the knowledge presents by the form of the questions she asks. And the questioning means that, over time, in specific domains of knowledge, agency or control over learning passes from teacher to student and back again.

In a widely shown videotape of an eighth-grade Japanese math lesson, created as part of the Trends in International Mathematics and Science Study (TIMSS, formerly known as the Third International Mathematics and Science Study), a teacher of a class of thirty-eight students asks how to straighten a crooked boundary between two pieces of land while at the same time preserving the landowners' respective shares. As the lesson progresses, students work individually, then in pairs, drawing on the teacher and his assistant circulating through the room and on "hint cards" available to anyone who needs them. Then individual students, selected by the teacher, present their work on the blackboard, each taking a somewhat different approach, some leading directly to the correct answer, some not. Students model with some confidence and pride what they think of as "good" teaching practice in presenting their work, even satirizing their teachers' penchant for keeping order in the classroom by chastising their fellow students in a good-natured way. The teacher asks questions about the students' solutions. The students question and challenge each other's solutions. Students posing difficult questions come to the blackboard to present their own alternatives. The teacher at one point struggles to find the exact example of student work on the blackboard that demonstrates a particular idea, in effect modeling his own uncertainty. At the end of the class, the blackboard is covered with student work. The teacher calls the students' attention to the various approaches they have taken to solving the problem, and poses a more complex version of the same problem for the next day. In this lesson, there is no question who is the teacher and who are the students. There is, however, a great deal of action and ambiguity at any given point in the lesson about who is teaching whom, and about who is authorized to say what a good solution is. The classroom is a complex anthropological study in reciprocity and agency. The cognitive demand is high. The evidence of learning is abundant, clear, and visible.[1]

Walter Doyle, in his classic 1983 article "Academic Work," argues that the tasks that teachers and students engage in are, among other things, discrete microclimates of accountability.[2] That is, each task embodies an activity of some kind, a more or less explicit purpose for that activity, a product of some kind, and a set of expectations between teacher and student about what constitutes successful accomplishment of that work. Notice the repetition of the qualifier "of some kind." A classroom task does not have to be well designed and taught in order to convey powerful ideas about accountability. In fact, all academic tasks convey powerful ideas about accountability. A badly designed and taught task—one in which the activity, its purpose, product, and criteria of success—communicates powerfully that the teacher lacks knowledge and authority in the classroom and therefore that the students' role is either to adjust to the teacher's incompetence through compliant behavior, or to resist. In other words, a task does not have to be successful in order to communicate powerful ideas about accountability. One could think of the culture of the classroom as the accumulated residue of the beliefs and expectations about academic work that are conveyed in hundreds, probably thousands, of academic tasks. Later, we will see that the culture of a school can be understood, among other things, as the accumulated residue of thousands, perhaps tens of thousands, of academic tasks across classrooms.

Under the best of circumstances, there is a discipline inherent in academic tasks that is external to both the teacher and the student. In *The Informed Vision: Essays on Learning and Human Nature,* David Hawkins's formulation of this dynamic takes the form of a triangular relationship among the "I" (teacher), the "Thou" (student), and the "It" (content). There are many ways, Hawkins argues, for adults to relate to children in society. These relationships take many forms. What distinguishes the role of teacher, Hawkins continues, is that it is disciplined by the presence of content; without content, the relationship of teachers and children is essentially indistinguishable from other possible relationships among adults and children—and, one can argue, therefore lacks the social authority of education.

Accountability, here, is a positive, rather than a normative, concept. That is, accountability occurs whether we are conscious of it or not, and its precise enactment is a consequence of the nature of academic work. Teachers and students internalize their notions of accountability as a consequence of the work they do, whether that work embodies powerful normative ideas about accountability or not.

So, for example, low-level academic tasks—filling out worksheets, looking up words in the dictionary and writing out definitions, learning vocabulary words outside the context of written text, extracting historical facts from textbooks—communicate not just a view of knowledge and what it consists of, but also a view of the nature of accountability in academic work: My relationship, as a student, with the teacher consists of following instructions embedded in well-defined tasks and producing discrete responses to well-defined questions. My relationship, as a teacher, with the student consists of defining tasks that I am certain students will respond to in predictable ways so that we, jointly, minimize the level of ambiguity and uncertainty—and cognitive demand—in our relationship. Notice that in this formulation the teacher "solves" the Socratic paradox by limiting the knowledge that is available to both teacher and student to that which the teacher can control. Reciprocity, in this accountability system, approaches zero, because there is little in the task for the student to teach the teacher, and knowledge is defined in a way that puts the teacher in the role of transmitter. The transfer of agency from teacher to student is minimal because the nature of the task locates the knowledge with the teacher and the obligation to learn with the student—knowledge is transferred, agency over learning is not.

Higher-level academic tasks increase the level of complexity of accountability considerably. Giving students the responsibility for forming their own solutions to mathematics problems, based on prior knowledge, inference, and estimation, requires students essentially to teach the teacher and their fellow students the logic behind their solutions. This kind of teaching also requires teachers to know, and anticipate in their practice, the range of solutions that students will produce, the knowledge of mathematics embodied in those solutions, and the possible misconceptions represented by different solutions. One cannot understand the nature of accountability embedded in this type of task without a detailed knowledge of academic content and of the dynamics of reciprocity and agency between teacher and student. Putting students in charge of initiating solutions to complex problems, for example, sends a very strong signal about the transfer of agency from teacher to student. But it also raises complex issues of what happens when student work reveals "buggy algorithms" and mathematical misconceptions. Tactically, the teacher is then faced squarely with the Socratic paradox: Should she "take control" of the students' learning and rectify errors, or should she lead the students, through skillful questioning, to diagnose these problems themselves? Who is accountable to whom in this transaction? The student is clearly accountable to the teacher and her fellow students for both forming and arguing a solution. The teacher is accountable to students and possibly also to external authorities for setting the task within which the student initiates a solution, and for engaging students in the diagnosis of their work. But the effectiveness of the teacher depends heavily on the level and range of students' responses; the effectiveness of the students depends heavily on the teacher's diagnostic ability and her command of the content. There is no way to define the accountability in this task without resorting to ideas of reciprocity and agency. High levels of cognitive demand require attention to the shifting locus of accountability in the task, and to the transfer of agency for learning within the task.

Notice that, in this formulation, accountability in academic work is coterminous with learning. But it is learning of a particular kind—what Chris Argyris and Donald Schön have called "double-loop learning": it is about developing increased fluency both in the *processes of learning* academic content and in reflecting on and improving the *conditions under which the learning occurs.* Higher-level thinking about instruction is about learning both how to teach and how to learn about teaching. In order to be accountable in a learning relationship, as teacher to student or as student to teacher, an individual must accept responsibility for his or her own learning. Learning requires agency over learning.

These transactions between students and teachers are a microcosm of political relations in the larger society. Students, in effect, learn about authority, consent, agency, and reciprocity through their dealings with one another and with significant adults in their world. Not the least of these dealings is with teachers. The more demanding the work, the more complex the political relations underpinning it, and the more likely the work is to develop strong understandings of agency and reciprocity among students and teachers. The less demanding the work, the more learning becomes the transmission of knowledge from the teacher to the student, and the less either learns about the underlying problems of agency and reciprocity in their relationship.

## Individual Actions, Collective Results: Agency and Reciprocity in Schools

The learning that occurs in schools is a composite of the thousands—indeed, tens of thousands—of microdecisions involving academic work among teachers and students in classrooms. Likewise, since each academic task is its own micro-climate of accountability, accountability in schools is constructed from these microdecisions. Accountability in the aggregate is about accountability in the smallest unit—the teacher and student in relation to each other in the presence of the content. Schools in which students and teachers do low-level work, requiring neither to exercise much agency over their learning, create powerful accountability environments—powerful in reinforcing low levels of learning, agency, and accountability. Schools in which students and teachers work together on higher-level tasks requiring higher levels of learning and agency over learn-ing construct equally powerful accountability environments at higher levels of learning, agency, and accountability.

The problem of learning and accountability in schools is a problem of col-lective action, similar to that of classrooms, but at a higher level of organizational complexity. The fact that learning is supposed to occur in schools is no guarantee that it actually does occur, nor does the existence of the school as an organization assure that the learning that occurs in one classroom bears any necessary rela-tionship to that which occurs in any other classroom. If schools tend toward being "loosely coupled" organizations, as many sociologists argue, then one should expect a high degree of variability among classrooms in the tasks that teachers and students construct for learning. This variability in practice would produce variability in student learning. But accountability applied to schools, as opposed to teachers and students working in classrooms, presumes that schools are able to act as collectivities, not just as collections of teachers and students in classrooms.[3]

Whether they are aware of it or not, schools construct powerful accountabil-ity environments out of the way that they envision academic work. The school environment can operate toward higher levels of collective action and higher levels of student learning, or toward highly variable individual behaviors and weak learning outcomes.

There are essentially two solutions to the problem of collective action in organizations—control and coordination. In the first instance, someone—a prin-cipal, for example—assumes responsibility for telling students and teachers what to do, in order that the efforts of individuals and of individual classrooms aggre-gate to produce a coherent result at the level of the school. In the second instance, individuals agree on their own to coordinate their behavior in such a way that it produces a coherent result. Most strategies for making schools act as if they were organizations involve combinations of both control and coordination. But accountability systems, and enduring American views of leadership, tend to treat school leaders or principals as the primary agents of accountability in schools. The mythology of American education is heavily tilted in the direction of the view that "strong leaders make good schools."[4]

Our interest here is not in determining which solution to the problem of collective action is more promising, however, but in showing how the problems of control and coordination at the organizational level are similar to the problems of the Socratic paradox at the classroom level. In fact, control and coordination present problems at the school level that are nearly identical to those presented by the Socratic paradox inside classrooms. If I, as a leader, induce collective action through control, I have in effect taken responsibility for telling you what to do, which is the equivalent of the teacher assuming full responsibility for imparting to the student what he or she needs to know. Notice that when control falls apart as a strategy of collective action, it does so for exactly the same reasons that "telling" falls apart as a strategy of teaching. For the "teller" to tell you what to do requires (a) that the teller knows what to tell you to do; (b) that you are willing to consent to what the teller tells you to do; and (c) that you actually know how to do what the teller tells you to do. If any of these conditions is not present, the power to produce collective action is lost. If a principal, for example, tells a teacher to teach reading and writing at a higher level, there is no guarantee that the principal knows how this is to be done, or that, if the principal knew, he or she would be able to effectively communicate that to teachers. Since the principal is not him- or herself doing the teaching, the teacher can chose, within limits, whether and how to consent to the principal's request; if the teacher chooses to resist, he or she substantially decreases the principal's ability to be an effective manager and leader. Suddenly, the teacher becomes a very costly part of the principal's organization. Finally, the principal's directive assumes that the teacher actually knows what to do, and implies that at the present time the teacher is not doing it. It is likely that the teacher is not doing what the principal wants him or her to do because the teacher doesn't know how to do it; the fact that the principal tells the teacher to do something doesn't mean that the teacher is able to learn. This conundrum sounds suspiciously like the "I can teach you, but I can't 'learn' you" issue discussed earlier. It sounds the same because, in a fundamental way, it *is* the same.

Leaders are to those they lead as teachers are to students. The ability of teachers to respond to leaders depends on the teachers' capacity to learn new practices, but in order for teachers to learn, they must, in some sense, take responsibility for their learning; in order for this to occur, the leader must transfer agency for learning from the leader to the teacher. As with the relationship between teachers and students, the more demanding and complex the task that a leader asks a teacher to do, the more the leader/teacher relationship hinges on agency and reciprocity.

When leadership and accountability become synonymous with learning in schools, reciprocity governs relations between leaders and teachers. Teachers can only do what they know how to do. The leader's responsibility is to set the conditions in place that allow him or her access to the work that teachers do. The leader's effectiveness depends in large part on his or her capacity to learn how to function at higher levels as an enabler of teacher learning, and the leader does this in part by examining his or her own knowledge and skills as a leader based on an understanding of individual teachers' practice. Hence, control succeeds as a strategy of collective action to the degree that it evolves toward the transfer of agency and reciprocity. To the degree that control evolves toward the transfer of agency and reciprocity, it ceases to look like control and begins to look like coordination.[5]

Below the level of formal structures and mechanisms of control, there is the "real game," the continuous play of individuals in real time. And out of this play develops the informal structures and routines by which things get done. One level of knowledge about the play involves the work itself; another level involves interaction with others around the work. One can be good at the work and lousy at interacting with others around the work, or vice versa. Being good at one does not guarantee being good at the other, although being good at the work collectively requires that everyone be good at interacting with others in some degree.

Formal and informal structures can enable the work or they can constrain it. Learning how to create structures that support the work of instruction is a domain of knowledge in itself. It is also a domain that entails individual and collective learning. It does a leader no good to have knowledge about how structure influences work, or vice versa, if that knowledge is not shared by people who work in the structure, because they have to act on the knowledge in order to make the structure work. Notice the parallel here between how people in schools learn about the relationship between structure and practice and the idea of double-loop learning around instructional practice in classrooms. Just as the learning around practice in classrooms is both about the practice itself and the conditions under which the practice can be improved, so learning at the school level involves learning both about how to cooperate around practice and how to make the structures within which people work operate instrumentally to enable cooperation around practice.

When we say that schools are "accountable" in everyday discourse we usually mean that schools are acting in socially approved ways toward certain external publics—parents, communities, policymakers, and so on. This use of the term suggests that some schools are accountable and others are not. In a positive, as opposed to a normative, sense, however, *all* schools are accountable in some ways for some things to someone. That is, schools that appear to be atomized and purposeless in their approach to academic work—apparently accountable to no one—have chosen, either actively or by default, to construct accountability in a certain way. The people in these schools have, in effect, decided that they are primarily accountable to one another to maintain and protect a work environment that they perceive to be beneficial to themselves. If members of the organization violate this fundamental understanding of accountability, they will likely face sanctions from their colleagues. Likewise, when schools form tight and corrupt relationships with their communities—when they serve as employment agencies and conduits for political patronage, for example—they are in powerful accountability relationships with external actors. Failure to provide the benefits that the community expects brings sanctions. Similarly, schools in high-socioeconomic-status communities often form implicit contracts with their communities in which the school agrees to provide access to privilege in the attainment structure—university admissions, for example—in return for social support in the community. Community members have strong incentives to participate in this bargain because their property values and property taxes reflect the implicit price that they have paid for access. These schools are, in a sense, highly accountable, but they are accountable primarily for attainment, not for academic learning or for performance. If members of these schools violate the implicit attainment contract by, for example, calling attention to grade inflation or the low quality of academic work done by teachers and students, they will be sanctioned both by their peers and their communities.[6]

In each of these cases, and in many more we could describe, schools are highly "accountable" to their own constructions of accountability and/or to the constructions of accountability that are hardwired into the logic of confidence by which they maintain relations with their communities. Performance-based accountability policies embody a particular normative view that is just one of many possible versions of accountability vying for the attention of schools and their communities, and not necessarily the most powerful one at that. Accountability policies do not operate in a vacuum. Accountability was not simply "discovered" with the advent of performance-based policies in the latest era of educational reform. Various forms of accountability are already embedded in schools, and the current form of accountability that is sanctioned by policy is one among many forms abroad in schools.

To say that schools are, or should be, accountable for students' academic learning, then, is to take a particular normative view of what accountability means. When this view of accountability is embodied in policy and set in motion in the world, it refracts through many different accountability microenvironments at the school and community levels. If this situation sounds similar to the problem of adapting teaching to the multiple demands of students' prior knowledge in the classroom, it is. Just as teachers face students with multiple points of access to learning, so do policymakers and administrators face schools, and school systems, with widely divergent points of departure. Some of these points of departure entail fundamental conflicts over the meaning and purpose of accountability itself.

Schools differ not just in their constructions of accountability but also in their organizational attributes, capacities, and cultures. Probably the most robust finding to come out of research on accountability policies is that the strongest initial predictors of the impact of policy on student performance are the attributes of schools rather than the attributes of the policies themselves.[7] That is, policies send a signal about the type and level of performance expected of schools; this signal is refracted through a multitude of schools, and what emerges is a highly variable response depending on the specific characteristics of the schools. There is also a high degree of convergence on which aspects of schools seem to be most influential in determining their responses to external pressure for performance. The basic finding here is that schools that have high levels of agreement on the nature of the work, coupled with powerful normative cultures for making those agreements binding, are more successful in responding to external pressure for academic performance than schools that do not have these attributes.

One construction of what these powerful normative cultures are about is "internal accountability." Internal accountability is constructed as a deliberate contrast to external accountability.[8] That is, internal accountability describes the conditions in a school that precede and shape the responses of schools to pressure that originates in policies outside the organization. The level or degree of internal accountability is measured by the degree of convergence among what individuals say they are responsible for (responsibility), what people say the organization is responsible for (expectations), and the internal norms and processes by which people literally account for their work (accountability structures). Weak internal accountability occurs when there is little convergence between what individuals think they are responsible for, what people express as the collective aims of the organization, and the structures by which work is monitored. So, for example, a school with weak internal accountability might have high variability among teachers in classroom practice, low agreement on whether the school can actually affect student learning in the face of community influences, and limited ways of finding out what is actually happening in classrooms. Conversely, strong internal accountability might manifest itself in high agreement among teachers on what good instructional practice looks like, high agreement on the aims of the school in influencing student learning, and visible norms and practices for monitoring the work of teachers and students. It is, however, possible to have high internal accountability and low expectations for student learning. These schools meet the conditions of coherence and alignment of individual responsibility, collective expectations, and accountability structures, and they are therefore more tightly aligned internally, but they may also have achieved this agreement by reducing their expectations for their own and their students' learning. Nonetheless, the theory predicts, and the evidence suggests, that schools with higher internal accountability are more likely to be responsive to external pressure for performance than those with low internal accountability.[9]

Another parallel construction of what powerful normative cultures look like in schools is the idea of trust. In this formulation, the level of trust in schools is a compound of respect, listening to and valuing the views of others; personal regard, intimate and sustained personal relationships that undergird professional relationships; competence, the capacity to produce desired results in relationships with others; and personal integrity, truthfulness and honesty in relationships. These "discernments" that individuals in and around schools make of one anothers' behavior and intentions develop into networks of social exchange among key actors—teachers with principals, teachers with other teachers, professionals with parents, teachers with students, and so on. At the aggregate or organizational level, high levels of trust occur when there are high levels of agreement—or synchrony—concerning the specific norms that shape interpersonal exchanges. Higher levels of relational trust, not surprisingly, is a predictor of higher levels of individual and organizational agency, which in turn is a predictor of higher levels of student performance.[10]

Both of these theories stress convergence, alignment, or agreement among individuals (students, teachers, administrators, parents) that lead to powerful, binding collective norms that govern the organization as a whole. Norms of internal accountability or trust are evident in the work of people in the organization and their behavior vis-à-vis one another, not just in the purposes to which people subscribe. More importantly, both theories portray strong normative cultures in schools as the result of active construction—purposeful, explicit work, work that stresses strong interpersonal connections and skills, and work that pushes in powerful ways against the prevailing culture of isolation and autonomy in teaching. In this sense, then, both theories are countercultural. These theories also lead to a particular normative view of accountability that a strong normative culture precedes and shapes a school's response to external pressures for performance, that there is no necessary contradiction between the presence of a strong normative culture internal to a school and that school's responsiveness to external pressure for performance, and that accountability can be an occasion for powerful learning about what makes schools successful in promoting students' learning.

Running parallel with these ideas of internal accountability and trust in schools is the idea of trust in public institutions generally. This discussion centers on such questions as how are issues of trust resolved in interactions among individuals in everyday life, how are they resolved in political relationships, and how does trust or distrust in public or governmental institutions arise?

In general, issues of trust in political life are complicated by the need to reconcile self-interested behavior with the necessity for cooperation in order to secure the benefits of collective action. One solution to the problem of trust at both the individual and institutional level is the idea that trust is "encapsulated self-interest."[11] In this view, one does not have to posit that humans are altruistic in some way in order to think them capable of trust or of inspiring trustworthiness. At the individual level, trust can occur when I conclude that you will take my interests into account in your own behavior because you have an interest in maintaining our relationship. Hence, "my trust in you is . . . encapsulated in your interest in fulfilling my trust."[12] At the institutional level, organizations create incentives for people to act in concert with one another; they direct and moderate individual interests for collective ends. If encapsulated self-interest is possible in relations among individuals, it is possible among individuals within organizations. And, to the degree that individuals internalize the interests of others (teachers of students, students of students, teachers of teachers) in the interest of maintaining stable and predictable relations with one another, the institution itself becomes trustworthy. Trustworthiness is defined as being stable, predictable, and transparent in the degree to which the organization encapsulates the interests of members and clients.

Another key idea that links individual interests to trust in public institutions is "contingent consent," a corollary of encapsulated self-interest. Individuals will trust a public institution "to the extent that they believe it will act in their interests, that its procedures are fair, and that their trust of the [institution] and of others is reciprocated."[13] The important principles here are those of fairness and reciprocity. Fairness matters because it allows individuals to sustain their commitment to an institution, and to others in the institution, even in those instances when the institution operates against the self-interest of the individual. That is, individuals are willing to suspend their self-interest in some instances if they are assured that norms of procedural fairness have been followed in reaching decisions, and that, over the long run, the institution encapsulates their interests. In addition, individuals calculate whether the trust that they put in the institution is reciprocated, that is, whether their interests are encapsulated in the behavior of others and in the norms, rules, and procedures of institutional life.

Hence, the principle of reciprocity, so powerful in instructional relations between teachers and students, is also present, in a more complex form, at the next level of aggregation in relations among individuals and institutions. So too is the principle of transfer of agency. Life in organizations involves a series of negotiations between the individual and the collective over the degree to which the individual agrees to adjust her interests to the expectations of others. This is a peculiarly modern problem. According to Adam Seligman, "Trust. . ., which emerges as a function of negotiation. . ., is also predicated on human agency. Without the idea of agency, any notion of negotiation would itself be severely limited." "The idea of the individual . . . emerges as a locus of moral value in the same period that the idea of trust begins to take on its very modern characteristics."[14] In order for trust to work, in other words, individuals must see themselves as capable of exercising human agency over the expectations of others. In order for my interest to be encapsulated in yours, I must assume agency and responsibility for acting on my interest in relation to you.

Trust is a fragile commodity, hard to construct, easy to destroy.[15] For a variety of reasons, public schools have not been exemplars of trust in action. The fact that we can identify trust as an exceptional variable in determining school performance means that it is in short supply.[16] The very processes by which trust, or internal accountability, are created in schools—building up the connective tissue of relationships around instructional work—are easily reversible.

Issues of reciprocity and agency in classrooms and schools are similar in at least one respect: they can be worked out through face-to-face relationships. A classroom can become a highly functioning democratic community through the development of strong interactions among teachers and students involving demanding content. Likewise, a school can become a powerful democratic community by developing strong norms of agency and reciprocity in collaborative work. In both instances, the micropolitics of agency and reciprocity are present every day in the work of adults and students. When the issue is the accountability of schools, or school systems, to the larger polity, face-to-face relations are often not—are usually not—the primary means of working out issues of agency and reciprocity, but the dynamics of the process are similar to those at the classroom and school level.

### Moving the Herd Roughly Northeast: Agency and Reciprocity in Systems

At a certain scale, accountability becomes impersonal. The force of law and regulation begins to displace the force of interpersonal influence and consent as a determinant of collective action. Agency and reciprocity recur as fundamental issues of accountability, but in different forms.

Accountability in large-scale systems can be constructed as a simple problem of regulatory control. A principal (not the kind who runs a school, but someone in a general position of authority) finds it necessary to form a relationship with an agent (someone with knowledge and skill that the principal needs) in order to accomplish something that the principal desires. The problem the principal faces is how to control the agent, where the agent has interests of his own and possesses information or knowledge that the principal may not have. These "information asymmetries" require the principal to create incentives that structure and direct the agent's behavior in the desired direction, and they also require the principal to assume the costs of oversight and enforcement in order to make the incentives work.[17] In educational accountability, the principal-agent problem boils down to finding the right combination of standards, performance measures, rewards, and sanctions that will induce schools to improve. The underlying bet in accountability systems is that schools, and the people in them, will respond to these incentive structures by using their knowledge and skill in the service of the principals, in this case policymakers.

Notice how the central problem in principal-agent theory is essentially the same as the problem of consent at the classroom and school level. My success as an agent—especially if the task I have been asked to perform is complex—depends on my taking control of the task. Your success as a principal depends on setting the conditions of our relationship in a way that allows you to rely on my knowledge, skill, and agency to make us both more productive.

Skeptics argue that the accumulated residue of school culture, the limited competence of people in the system, the limits of measurement, and the unreliability of rewards and sanctions make it difficult to imagine that accountability systems could actually accomplish their intended purposes.[18] In addition, principals or policymakers face daunting strategic problems of oversight and enforcement. If they set standards too high, they produce extremely high monitoring and enforcement costs. Rewards and sanctions are only as effective as the probability that they will be enforced; high standards with low enforcement are, in effect, low standards. But high standards carry high enforcement costs. So regulatory theory suggests that principals will "optimize"; that is, they will set standards to match the resources they have available for enforcement, thereby creating the maximum level of compliance possible within a given level of resources.[19] An optimal regulatory system is one in which a rational agent will meet the principal's expectations based on his calculation that the costs of noncompliance exceed the benefits.

This model of accountability has a few advantages and many disadvantages. Its main advantages are that it focuses attention on the likelihood, within a given level of resources for oversight and compliance, that schools will actually act in accordance with the aims of accountability policies, and it suggests that the interests of people who work in schools will drive the results of accountability systems unless there are countervailing forces that move schools in another direction.

Among the disadvantages of the simple principal-agent model are the following: The model is static with regard to the knowledge and expertise that the principal requires of the agent. It assumes that the agent knows what he needs to know in order to meet the expectations of the principal. Accountability problems, especially those in education, require changes in knowledge and expertise that in turn require investments in human knowledge and skill in order for the systems to work. These investments in knowledge and skill can act as rewards, in and of themselves, and can alter the relationship between the principal and the agent. Educators may value the additional knowledge and skill they acquire as a consequence of having to meet higher expectations, and this value may act as a positive incentive in meeting those expectations. The model is also quite schematic in its assumptions about how organizations, as opposed to individuals, respond to incentives. The theory extrapolates from the individual to the organizational level and assumes that bureaucratic organizations maximize the interests of those who work in them. In the absence of external controls, public institutions cannot be trusted to take account of broader societal interests. What this view ignores is that public institutions operate under mixed incentives. In addition to acting on their own interests, they must encapsulate the interests of their clients, and they have to be responsive to the broader society in order to sustain their legitimacy. So while institutional self-interest may be the default mode for public institutions—and may, in fact, be a sign of institutional failure—it is certainly not the only factor that explains institutional behavior.

The model describes the relationship as a simple problem of contractual compliance. I agree to do something for you in return for some reward, and you set up the incentive structure that assures that I will do what you desire. In fact, most relationships that involve high levels of knowledge and skill are much more complex than this. The agent often has to teach the principal what to ask for, or what it is reasonable to ask for. Think of an architect trying to convince a client that a cantilevered structure perched precariously over a river is not a good idea, but that a desirable result could be achieved by redefining the roofline. In addition, the principal and the agent often have to acknowledge that neither of them knows what to do, but they nonetheless have to proceed on the assumption that they will learn. What actually *is* a reasonable rate for reading and mathematics performance to improve, and how long will it actually take? No one really knows the answer to these questions, but accountability systems require a tentative answer that can be revised over time. In these situations, principals and agents are heavily dependent on each other in ways that a simple contractual relationship does not describe.

We should not lose sight of the fact that, as the simple principal-agent model would have it, individuals and institutions act in self-interested ways and their behavior can be influenced by external incentive structures. But like most simple insights, this one crosses the boundary between simple and simplistic.

A key strategic issue in the construction of accountability systems is whether they are designed to produce compliance or improvement. Compliance-based systems assume that the individual or organization that is being held accountable has the knowledge, skill, and capacity to do what the principal requires, and the essential problem is how to direct the agent's resource toward the principal's ends. Improvement-based systems assume that accomplishing the principal's ends requires a change in the knowledge, skill, and capacity of the agent in order to meet the principal's ends. The difference between these two models, as we shall see, is huge in practice. Virtually all state accountability systems and the system embedded in the No Child Left Behind Act of 2001, which largely determines the structure of state accountability systems, are intended to foster improvement. Their basic design is to set a standard against which the performance of all schools will be measured, to measure a school's initial performance relative to that standard, and to judge a school's performance on an annual or biennial basis by the increment of performance of the school in reaching the standard. Schools are required to produce increments of performance not only in the aggregate, but for specified groups of students—low-income students, students of different racial and ethnic groups, English-language learners, and so on. States vary in the degree to which they allocate stakes or sanctions among schools and students, but the underlying principle is that stakes reinforce the improvement targets that are embedded in the performance standards. But while state and federal accountability systems may be improvement-oriented in intent, they are often compliance-oriented in practice.

In order for an accountability system to be based on improvement, it has to embody an underlying theory of how schools improve their performance. Simply constructing an incentive structure of standards and testing around the expectation of steady improvements in performance is not a theory of improvement. A theory of improvement actually has to account for how people in schools learn what they need to know in order to meet the expectations of the accountability system. By this standard, no existing state or federal accountability system is improvement-oriented. That is, there is no existing accountability system that allocates or scales investments in capacity at the school level according to a theory, however primitive, of how schools improve teaching and learning to produce performance. There are, to be sure, assistance programs for low-performing schools and there are, in some jurisdictions, investments in curriculum, professional development, and teacher recruitment that are intended to foster higher capacity in schools. But these measures are not directly related to what schools are expected to do in order to improve their performance. In the absence of explicit theories of improvement connected to standards and testing, all accountability systems degrade in the direction of compliance, away from improvement.

The politics of this process are relatively straightforward. For policymakers the political rewards attached to increased school accountability accrue mostly at the initiation stage, rather than the implementation stage. Most policymakers are elected officials. Most electoral cycles run in two- and four-year terms. Any process or event that takes longer than an electoral cycle is of dubious value in generating electoral credit. Accountability systems, if they are to work, require complex institutional processes; these processes are distant from and largely inscrutable to policymakers. But accountability systems do produce one thing that has value—positive or negative—for policymakers: test scores. They produce some kind of evidence on a recurring basis of how well the system is performing at an aggregate level. To the extent that accountability systems have any value at all for public officials it is to the degree that they produce evidence that can be used for political advantage. Hence, over time, other things being equal, one would expect accountability systems to evolve toward increased reliance on testing and away from the more complex, inscrutable, and longer-term processes of improvement that produce increases in performance. The job of people in schools, then, increasingly becomes to produce gains in performance from their existing base of knowledge and skill rather than to improve performance by improving knowledge and skill. The job of school people becomes compliance.

As accountability systems degrade from improvement to compliance, so too does their authority to influence the behavior of people in schools and, hence, their capacity to produce benefits for elected officials. People who are being asked to do things they do not know how to do, and being rewarded and punished on the basis of what they do not know, rather than what they are learning, become skilled at subverting the purposes and authority of the systems in which they work. Bad policies produce bad behavior. Bad behavior produces value for no one.

Notice here the similarities between compliance-oriented accountability systems and low-level teaching in the problems of agency and reciprocity they raise. Just as low-level teaching puts the teacher in charge of determining what counts as knowledge, and in the (inherently impossible) position of taking full responsibility for what the student learns, so too does compliance, in its extreme form, put the policymaker in the position of having to predict, anticipate, and determine his or her constituents' every action—again inherently impossible.

It is in no one's interest for accountability systems to degrade in this way. But as with most interesting and powerful problems of political behavior, this one requires an acknowledgement that actors with different incentives and interests have to learn to orchestrate their behavior for mutual benefit.

What would a theory of improvement look like and how might it be used to alter the political incentives that surround accountability structures? Not surprisingly, the answers to these questions look very similar to the solutions to the puzzle of accountability at the classroom and school levels. A theory of improvement would, first and foremost, take into account the incentives that drive performance in classrooms and schools. As we have seen, these incentives derive their force from agency and reciprocity. Students and teachers derive personal agency from success in the accomplishment of higher-level tasks. These tasks construct microclimates of accountability that model the transfer of agency for learning from teacher to student. In order for these incentives to work, there must be a high degree of reciprocity between teacher and student. That is, the student must be able to teach the teacher how to teach more effectively by providing visible evidence of performance at the same time that the teacher is teaching the student how to take control of his or her own learning. A theory of improvement would posit that these skills around agency and reciprocity can be learned, that they are probably best learned in the context of practice in real time, and that, once learned, they become self-reinforcing. A theory of improvement would also posit that informed, collective judgments can be made about which teachers are capable of learning practice at this level and which are not, as well as which teachers are capable of practice at higher levels than others. It becomes the job of policy both to assure that the capacity exists in schools to construct powerful microclimates of instructional practice and provide administrators with the capacity to reward and deselect teachers on the basis of whether they are capable of learning these skills.

Schools work as accountable organizations to the degree that they nurture and demand from their participants—teachers, students, parents, administrators—high levels of agreement, convergence, or alignment around the conditions of powerful practice in classrooms. Powerful organizational environments require trust, embodied in the norms of respect, personal regard, competence, and integrity. People within and outside public organizations form trusting relationships with those organizations to the degree that they feel that their own interests are encapsulated in the interests of the institution. This process of forming trusting relationships requires constant attention and reinforcement of the kind that occurs in powerful teaching relationships within classrooms and powerful normative environments in the organization that surrounds the classroom. The formation of trust, in other words, requires high levels of reciprocity among key actors in the organization. It is the job of leaders to provide the normative and social structure within which reciprocity takes place. These qualities of human interaction and skills of organization can be learned. People who work in schools can be expected to learn them as a condition of their employment, and we can select and deselect people based on their mastery of these skills. It becomes the job of policy both to set the expectation that schools will become powerful normative environments and to reinforce the expectation that success should be visible both in classroom practice and in student performance, and to assure access to learning for adults in acquiring the skills necessary to meet these expectations.

At the system level improvement works to the degree that it explicitly acknowledges agency and reciprocity in relations among policymakers, system-level leaders, and people who work in classrooms and schools. Compliance is not reciprocity; as accountability systems degrade toward compliance, they lose their capacity to generate improvement and they create impossible problems of enforcement. The first principle of system-level design of accountability systems should be that they are fundamentally about the transfer of agency from the system level to the school level to the classroom level. An accountability system that is working well is one in which people in schools and classrooms are doing most of the work and people at the system level are busy meeting their commitments to provide capacity and access to learning for people in schools. An efficient accountability system is one in which the enforcement costs associated with monitoring compliance are effectively zero, and the money that would have been used for enforcement is used instead for the improvement of human skill and knowledge in schools and classrooms. One approaches this optimum through the transfer of agency from system-level monitoring and compliance to school-level capacity-building.

Since schools come into the process of improvement at a variety of levels, system-level accountability systems that embody the principle of transfer of agency need well-developed strategies of differential treatment for individual schools. That is, schools should be treated as organizations that are at a particular position on an improvement path, characterized by classroom and organizational competencies, and the job of system-level people is to do whatever is necessary to move that particular school to the next level. If performance and quality are on the vertical, and time is on the horizontal, improvement means moving the herd—the entire distribution of schools in a system—roughly northeast. The other part of this bargain is that as the quality of instructional practice and organizational coherence improves, system-level administrators provide less guidance and control in return for higher levels of performance. Transfer of agency consists of moving as many schools as possible out of the category of heavy supervision and control as fast as possible. Reciprocity consists of an explicit contractual agreement between system-level and school-level people that every unit of increased performance that the system demands carries with it an equal and reciprocal obligation on the part of the system to provide access to an additional unit of individual or organizational capacity, in the form of additional knowledge and skill. The job of system-level people is to add value to instructional practice and organizational coherence or to get out of the way.

The nature of the contractual relationship between system- and school-level practitioners and policymakers is equally clear. In order to keep improvement from degrading into compliance, practitioners must produce short-term results that are useful as electoral credit. The reciprocity bargain here is easy to state, but more difficult to actualize. Schools have to produce visible evidence of improvements in practice and performance in the short term in order to bind policymakers to longer-term commitments to increasing the knowledge and skill that will produce improvements in individual and organizational capacity. These bargains must be explicit, and the parties must understand the stakes involved for each of them. Policymakers have to understand that their short-term behavior creates potentially destructive incentives for people in schools. School people have to understand that they must produce short-term evidence of improvement in order to gain the discretion and control to engage in longer-term investments in knowledge and skill. These bargains will probably involve much less reliance on annual standardized test scores as evidence of improvement and greater reliance on more proximate measures of the improvement of instructional practice and curriculum-based measures of student learning. It is the job of educators to "fill in" the measures that provide evidence of improvement over and above the standardized measures of external accountability systems. That is, accountability at the system level requires active engagement of school- and system-level people in inventing the measures on which their performance will be judged—another manifestation of the principle of reciprocity.

While the problems of agency and reciprocity are similar in most respects from the classroom to the school to the system level, they are different at the system level in at least one important respect: Since the relationships that determine agency and reciprocity are more impersonal, and the scale of those relationships is too broad for face-to-face interactions, the means of creating and directing agency and reciprocity must, of necessity, be more formal—hence, the language of contractual relationships.

The cultural divide that educators and policymakers must cross in order for a more powerful type of accountability to occur involves moving from treating schools as passive receptacles of ideas about what good education is toward treating schools as active agents in the learning of children and adults. Neither educators nor policymakers are particularly well prepared for this passage. Schools and school systems have avoided in the past the kind of explicit bargains around transfer of agency and reciprocity that would be required of them if they were to become active agents in an accountability system. Policymakers have often treated schools as ready receptacles for any random idea that an influential constituent proposes. The move toward performance-based accountability signals the possibility of a shift away from traditional patterns of interaction between policy and practice. The issue is whether the actors can find a way to orchestrate their behavior for mutual benefit.

## Conclusion: Accountability and Democratic Education

Accountability begins in the classroom, with relations among teachers and students in the presence of content; it is this fundamental relationship that communicates to young people whether and to what degree "democratic" relationships exist in school and in the broader society. To the degree that these relationships model reciprocity and the transfer of agency, schools will become "democratic." But they will not become democratic unless the organization of schools and the systems that govern them operate by the same principles of agency and reciprocity. In this sense, the problems of agency and reciprocity are parallel and complementary from the classroom to the school to the system level.

Performance-based accountability systems open up the opportunity for a fresh look at the social contract between schools and the public. The discipline of accountability can open up more powerful ideas about practice, school organization, and policy, or it can close down and narrow purposes of schools. If accountability in the classroom means teachers and students engaged in complex and demanding work that requires teachers to think of teaching as the transfer of agency for learning from themselves to their students, then issues of reciprocity will come to the fore, and with them, issues of accountability. What is it that I, as a teacher, must provide by way of challenge and support in order to make this student a powerful agent in his or her own learning? How do we negotiate our relationship so as to make more explicit our reciprocal accountability to each other for our mutual learning?

Likewise, at the school level the discipline of internal accountability, based on strong relations around learning in the classroom and a strong normative environment about adult and student relationships at the school level, can strengthen the authority and legitimacy of schools, as well as the trust invested in them as public institutions, or it can degrade and undermine their authority, legitimacy, and trust. If accountability at the school level means the creation of strong norms of reciprocity and trust, based on clear understandings of mutual benefit, then the strength of schools as agents in their own work will be reinforced. And schools will also become more active in demanding the resources, knowledge, and skills that they require to do the work that governments demand of them.

Finally, at the system level the stakes of agency and reciprocity are especially high. If accountability systems are allowed to degrade in the direction of compliance, away from the more challenging work of agency and reciprocity between schools and their governing agencies, then policymakers will be entering a quagmire in which, as the old saying from the Prussian Empire notes, "that which is not prohibited is required." Avoiding the trap of compliance requires more or less explicit contractual agreements that emphasize the reciprocity of performance and investments in knowledge and skill. People in schools cannot be expected to do things that they do not know how to do, but they can be expected to learn how to do what is necessary if they operate in an environment in which demands for performance are coupled with reciprocal support for learning. In this sense, we come full circle in the relationship between accountability and democracy: "I can teach you, but I cannot learn you." Your learning is a prerequisite for my success.

## Notes

1. *Teaching Mathematics in Seven Countries: TIMSS Video Study* (2003), available from Research for Better Schools, www.rbs.org. See also James Hiebert et al., *Teaching Mathematics in Seven Countries: Results from the TIMSS 1999 Video Study* (Washington, D.C.: National Center for Education Statistics, 2003).
2. Walter Doyle, "Academic Work," *Review of Educational Research* 53, no. 2 (1983): 159–99.
3. See Elmore, *Building a New Structure for School Leadership.*

4. Brian Rowan, "Commitment and Control: Alternative Strategies for the Organizational Design of Schools," in *Review of Research in Education*, vol. 16, edited by Courtney Cazden (Washington, D.C.: American Educational Research Association, 1990).
5. See Elmore, *Building a New Structure for School Leadership.*
6. These conceptions of accountability are drawn from Charles Abelmann et al., *When Accountability Knocks Will Anyone Answer?*
7. See Carnoy, Elmore, and Siskin, *The New Accountability.*
8. Abelmann et al., *When Accountability Knocks Will Anyone Answer?*
9. Ibid.
10. See Bryk and Schneider, *Trust in Schools,* 122–44.
11. Hardin, "Trust in Government."
12. Ibid, 12.
13. Levi, "A State of Trust," 88.
14. Seligman, *The Problem of Trust,* 55.
15. Levi, "A State of Trust," 81, quoting Dasgupta, "Trust as a Commodity," 50.
16. See Bryk and Schneider, *Trust in Schools.*
17. See Terry Moe, "Politics, Control, and the Future of School Accountability," paper presented at the conference Taking Account of Accountability, Kennedy School of Government, Harvard University, Cambridge, Mass., June 10–11, 2002; Pratt and Zeckhauser, *Principals and Agents;* Jonathan Bendor, "Formal Models of Bureaucracy: A Review," *British Journal of Political Science* 18 (1988): 353–95; and Canice Prendergast, "The Provision of Incentives in Firms," *Journal of Economic Literature* 37, no. 1 (1999): 7–63.
18. Moe, "Politics, Control, and the Future of School Accountability."
19. Viscusi and Zeckhauser, *Optimal Standards with Incomplete Enforcement.*

## Bibliography

Ablemann, Charles, Elmore, Richard, et al. 1998. *When Accountability Knocks Will Anyone Answer?* Philadelphia: Consortium for Policy Research in Education. Reprinted in Richard Elmore, *School Reform from the Inside Out: Policy, Practice, and Performance.* Cambridge, Mass.: Harvard Education Press, 2004.

Anderson, Lorin W., and David Krathwohl. *A Taxonomy for Learning, Teaching, and Assessing: A Revision of Bloom's Taxonomy of Educational Objectives.* New York: Longman, 2001.

Argyris, Chris, and Donald Schön. *Organizational Learning.* Reading, Mass.: Addison-Wesley, 1978.

Bryk, Anthony S., and Barbara Schneider. *Trust in Schools: A Core Resource for Improvement.* New York: Russell Sage Foundation, 2002.

Carnoy, Martin, Richard Elmore, and Leslie S. Siskin. *The New Accountability: High Schools and High Stakes Testing.* New York: Routledge, 2003.

Dasgupta, Partha. "Trust as a Commodity." In *Trust: Making and Breaking Cooperative Relations,* edited by Diego Gambetta, pp. 49–72. Cambridge, Mass.: Blackwell, 1988.

Elmore, Richard. *School Reform from the Inside Out: Policy, Practice, and Performance.* Cambridge, Mass.: Harvard Education Press, 2004.

Hardin, Russell. "Trust in Government." In *Trust and Governance,* edited by Valerie Braithwaite and Margaret Levi, pp. 9–27. New York: Russell Sage Foundation, 1998.

Hawkins, David. "I, Thou, and It," in his *The Informed Vision: Essays on Learning and Human Nature,* pp. 49–62. New York: Agathon, 1974.

Levi, Margaret. "A State of Trust." In *Trust and Governance,* edited by Valerie Braithwaite and Margaret Levi, pp. 77–102. New York: Russell Sage Foundation, 1998.

Pratt, John W., and Richard J. Zeckhauser, eds. *Principals and Agents: The Structure of Business.* Boston: Harvard Business School Press, 1985.

Seligman, Adam B. *The Problem of Trust.* Princeton, N.J.: Princeton University Press, 1997.

Viscusi, W. Kip, and Richard Zeckhauser. *Optimal Standards with Incomplete Enforcement.* Cambridge, Mass.: John F. Kennedy School of Government, 1979.

# 13

## DEMOGRAPHIC CHANGE AND DEMOCRATIC EDUCATION

### Jennifer Hochschild and Nathan Scovronick

*The American Dream will succeed or fail in the twenty-first century in direct proportion to our commitment to educate every person in the United States of America.*

—President Bill Clinton, 1995

*Both parties have been talking about education for quite a while. It's time to come together to get it done, so that we can truthfully say in America: No child will be left behind.*

—President George W. Bush, 2001

THE PROFILE OF AMERICANS IS CHANGING. IN THE FIRST few decades of the twenty-first century, the most dramatic demographic impact will come from the aging of the baby boomers and, absent major changes in immigration laws and birth rates, from increased racial and ethnic diversity in the population. The most diverse segment of the U.S. population will be school-aged children. While the new demography creates the potential for serious disagreements about public education, it also provides an opportunity for Americans to strengthen their commitment to the public schools.

The demographic change facing the United States increases the chances for polarization between young and old, wealthy and poor, immigrants and native-born Americans, cities and suburbs, and among ethnic and racial communities. School funding could become more contentious as a result, governance issues more difficult, testing more divisive, and multicultural policies more controversial. Groups that feel excluded from the American dream could become more likely to reject it rather than seek to participate in it. The privileged could become even more protective of their insulation and resources.

In the new demographic context, however, the essential role of public education will also be clear. The American dream will continue to require an institution to teach and sustain it, and to provide the tools children need to pursue it. The public school system is *the* only American institution that reaches across all citizens for a large portion of their lives; no other institution plays such a central role in promoting the American dream. While much must be done to improve the schools, public education will remain the best lever Americans have to create a society in which the ideology of the American dream has a chance to thrive.

With the new demography, it should be possible to build a solid coalition in support of public education, one that includes immigrants who see public schooling as the vehicle for success in their new country as well as native-born Americans who see it as a way to incorporate immigrant children into the wider society. It should also be possible to build broad support for the kind of inclusive, fair-minded, and effective educational policies that are right for the new situation. Politically, in the long run, the large number of new Americans might appeal more to political actors as members of a forward-looking coalition than as targets of old-fashioned demagoguery.

This essay describes the demographic changes occurring in the American population in the early years of the twenty-first century, briefly comparing this period with the last great era of immigration. We then propose a framework for avoiding the worst problems and promoting the best results from rapid demographic change. That framework revolves around the ideology of the American dream.

## Ideology of the American Dream

Underlying many of the tasks of public schools in the United States is the often-unstated goal of creating the conditions needed for people to believe in the American dream and to pursue its promise. Former president Bill Clinton described the conventional understanding of the dream in 1993: "The American dream that we were all raised on is a simple but powerful one—if you work hard and play by the rules you should be given a chance to go as far as your God-given ability will take you." The dream is the unwritten promise that all residents of the United States have a reasonable chance to achieve success through their own efforts, talents, and hard work. Success is most often defined in material terms, but individuals can define success for themselves in any terms they choose.

This promise of opportunity also requires that residents of the United States acquire the habits and values needed to maintain democratic institutions and sustain the ideology of the American dream. Those values include belief in the rule of law, respect for people different from themselves, majority rule, minority rights, and the nonviolent, constitutional resolution of disputed national issues. Finally, the dream requires that public institutions pro-

vide the structures and resources that make it possible for everyone to succeed. In short, the American dream asks the public schools both to teach democratic values and to provide the tools for individual success. As President
Clinton went on to say, "Most of all, we believe in individual responsibility
*and* mutual obligation; that government must offer opportunity to all and
expect something from all, and that whether we like it or not, we are all in
this battle for the future together."[1]

Most Americans accept the framework that President Clinton laid out.
When a 1995 *Washington Post* survey asked, "Do you believe in the American
dream?" at least three-fourths of the population said yes. Slightly fewer blacks
and Hispanics than whites and Asians endorsed the ideology, but just as many
poor as wealthy Americans did. In other surveys, 90 percent of Americans
agree that "our society should do what is necessary to make sure that everyone has an equal opportunity to succeed."[2] Just as many young as old stated
their belief in the American dream, and those under fifty agreed slightly more
than those over fifty that American society should ensure equal opportunity
to succeed.

Most important, Americans want the educational system to help move the
American dream from vision to reality. Campaign rhetoric, results from public
opinion polls, and advertisements constantly make the connection. As President
George W. Bush put it in 2000, "The quality of our public schools directly affects
us all—as parents, as students, and as citizens. . . . If our country fails in its responsibility to educate every child, we're likely to fail in many other areas. But if we
succeed in educating our youth, many other successes will follow throughout
our country and in the lives of our citizens." In surveys during the 1990s,
Americans ranked "prepar[ing] people to become responsible citizens" and
"help[ing] people to become economically self-sufficient" highest among various possible purposes of public schooling.[3]

The American dream is a brilliant ideological invention, but in practice it
leaves much to be desired. It depends on the government to create the conditions in which it can work, but at the same time it makes failure seem personal
even when that failure results from public policies, structural constraints, or inadequate resources. Through no fault of their own, for much of American history, a
majority of the population—those without property, women, African
Americans, Asian immigrants, and the disabled—have all been denied participation in the dream and its benefits. In the early years of the twenty-first century
too many poor people, including many recent immigrants, still lacked an equal
chance to fulfill their promise, partly because of policies that determined the
structure, content, and financing of public education. The American dream is
thus a good yardstick for evaluating educational policies at a time of demographic transformation, and for suggesting ways that the United States can promote democratic citizenship as well as individual success.

## Changing Demography of the United States

The first of the baby boomers will reach age sixty-five shortly after 2010. In 2000, about 13 percent of the American population was over sixty-five; by 2030, the aged will comprise roughly 20 percent, more than 70 million people. Only Florida had an elderly population approaching 20 percent at the turn of the twenty-first century, but a majority of states are expected to exceed that figure by 2030. At the same time, the Anglo population of the country will become a smaller proportion of the total, decreasing from 70 percent in 2000 to about 60 percent in 2020 and 50 percent in 2050. Forecasters expect the black population, about 13 percent of the total in 2000, to grow slowly, but the percentages of Hispanics (also 13 percent) and Asian Americans (4 percent) are both projected to almost double by 2050.[4]

These trends will be felt most powerfully in California; by 2000 non-Anglos made up more than half of the state's population, and the number of Latinos could exceed the number of whites by 2020. Other states will see major changes as well; in at least fifteen states, more than 40 percent of the school-aged population will be non-Anglo by 2015. In 2000 Latino children outnumbered black children by several million. Large cities will be especially affected; about 40 percent of the residents of New York City in 2000 were born outside of the United States, and over half of its children were immigrants or children of immigrants. They came from close to two hundred countries, and there were no indications that the influx was slowing. Los Angeles and Miami had even higher proportions of immigrants of the first or second generation than New York.

Because of the growth in the elderly population and the size of the school-aged population, the dependency ratio—the ratio of those of working age to the young and old—is likely to become much higher. The Census Bureau predicted in 2000, for example, that the dependency ratio in the United States will increase from about 63:100 in 1992 to about 83:100 in 2030. In addition, children will be more racially and ethnically diverse, while the aged will be disproportionately Anglo. In 2003 the Census Bureau reported that only 5 percent of Latinos in the nation were over sixty-five, compared with three times that number of Anglos; conversely, over one-third of Latinos were under age eighteen, compared with fewer than one-quarter of Anglos. In Los Angeles County, as the demographer William Frey has noted, the "elderly population is still majority white, its working-aged population is only about one-third white, and its child population is predominantly Hispanic and other racial and ethnic groups." As these changes spread across the country, they "are going to have enormous implications. We're looking down the road at a huge racial generation gap between the old, white baby boomers and these young, multiracial people."[5] This racial and ethnic generation gap could create considerable policy dilemmas. The need for schooling for the young will be great at the same time that the demand for health care and social services for the elderly will peak; at the least, we can expect severe competition for scarce public resources. In California, according to a survey by the Field Institute in 2002, the older the survey respondents, the more they reported being extremely concerned about health care costs and the less they were concerned about public schools or higher education. As the school finance expert James Poterba pointed out in the late 1990s, "an increase in the fraction of a jurisdiction's population over the age of 65 tends to reduce per-child school spending." The effect is strongest "when the elderly residents are from a different ethnic group than the school-age population."[6]

The potential for social division is very high. Polarization by generation, by wealth, or by race or ethnicity could mean greater divisions with respect to how much should be spent on public education, how students should be placed in classrooms, and what they should be taught when they get there. It could lead to increased attempts by identity groups to attain separate education, and a greater movement toward education that denies the validity of democratic values or rejects the American dream entirely.

The key question is whether political leaders will enflame the social divisions or seek to ameliorate them, practice the politics of educational exclusion or inclusion, try to preserve the old social order of the schools or ease the entry of the new one. Of course, many policymakers, particularly elected officials, think little about the long run; the horizon until the next election is too short and the rewards for small symbolic actions too great. In the face of the new demography, some will no doubt yield to the temptation for demagoguery, especially in situations of volatile transition. Other political activists will concentrate on securing benefits for their group rather than on broader policy considerations.

But others might take a different stance. As the demographic and political situation changes, some ethnic group leaders will seek coalitions rather than focus on competition. And most importantly, some candidates for public office will decide it is best to try to lead all Americans by placing a priority on the democratic, collective values of participation, respect, inclusion, and opportunity. With the potential for political and social chaos so great, it is possible that more Americans will want their leaders on the high road rather than in the swamp.

## Politics of Demographic Transformation

Political developments in California provide evidence that this is more than wishful thinking. Early in the 1990s, political debate in the state revolved around the conflict between native-born residents and undocumented immigrants, which blurred into a conflict between white and nonwhite Americans. In 1994 Governor Pete Wilson and the Republican Party sponsored Proposition 187 (initially known as "Save Our State"). It proposed that illegal immigrants be denied public services such as schools and hospitals, and it would have required public employees to report service-seekers presumed to be illegal. The proposition distinguished legal from illegal immigrants, but supporters and opponents alike frequently saw it as a signal of general opposition to immigration; as one coauthor claimed, "Those who care at all about our country will support this [proposition] to save our country from the immigration invasion."[7] The Mexican ambassador to the United States complained that "there is an equation now in California that goes: Illegal immigrants equal to Mexicans, equal to criminals, equal to someone who wants social services."[8] Proposition 187 passed overwhelmingly, supported by more than 60 percent of Anglo voters, almost 60 percent of Asian American voters, and over half of black voters. Latino voters opposed it two to one.

Proposition 187 was followed two years later by Proposition 209, which abolished affirmative action programs in public institutions in California. Opponents interpreted this measure also as an effort to protect white domination. It too passed, by a narrower but still persuasive margin of eight points. Whites again were most favorable (over 60 percent support), followed by Asian Americans (about 45 percent); again, few Latinos (about 30 percent) concurred. Three-quarters of African Americans opposed it.

In short, racial and ethnic tensions worsened during the early 1990s as the proportion of non-Anglos in California rose. In a 1993 *Los Angeles Times* poll, one-third of non-Hispanic whites agreed that Hispanics had a "negative impact" on life in southern California. A year later, a quarter of whites in Los Angeles County in another *Times* poll thought the influx of nonwhites had made their quality of life worse, and over one-third agreed that the government "paid too much attention" to minority groups.

By 1999, however, the politics of division no longer worked so well in California. The proportion of Anglos agreeing in a *Times* survey that Hispanics had a negative impact on life in Los Angeles declined by one-third, and the proportion saying the same about African Americans declined by over one-half. Only half as many whites in 1999 as in 1994 felt that the influx of immigrants had harmed their quality of life; one and a half times as many whites in 1999 as in 1994 felt that the new groups had improved it. A solid majority in a 1998 survey by the Public Policy Institute of California supported "outreach programs" and "special educational programs" to help minorities get jobs and a college education. In a follow-up survey a year later, almost three-fourths of non-Latino Californians agreed that illegal immigrants should not "be prevented from attending public schools." In the three years ending in December 2001, again in a poll by the Public Policy Institute of California, the proportion of Californians who perceived immigrants to be a "benefit" to their state increased substantially while the proportion who saw them as a "burden" decreased.[9]

There remains plenty of prejudice and discrimination in California. And an economic downturn could weaken the fragile acceptance of demographic change in evidence at the turn of the twenty-first century. Nevertheless, overall public opinion has moved toward a greater accommodation of diversity.

Electoral politics moved in the same direction during this period. A November 5, 1998 *Los Angeles Times* headline proclaimed, "In contests big and small, Latinos take [a] historic leap." Hispanic candidates won the positions of lieutenant governor, sheriff of Los Angeles County, additional seats in the legislature, and the first major city mayoralty since statehood. The Democratic candidate for governor in 1998 ran on a platform of tolerance and accommodation, won, and was reelected four years later. In 2003 a Republican replaced him after a recall, but the new governor was an immigrant himself and at least during the first months of his tenure gave no sign of launching broad attacks on immigrants. In the mid-1990s, said a Latino assemblyman, "[Hispanics] were scapegoated and used as political fodder. Now that era is over. Thank God." Many factors led to this change, but what matters most over the long run is that demographic transition was followed by political recalibration. In 1994 non-Anglos comprised about one-seventh of California's registered voters; by 2001, that percentage had increased to almost one-third. Their proportions will continue to increase. Roughly one-third of the 35 million Hispanics in the United States are registered to vote; perhaps another one-quarter are eligible, and more will become so as Latinos become naturalized citizens or their children reach adulthood. As the director of the National Immigration Forum pointed out, "How they [immigrants] break to one party or another may well determine which party dominates in the next few decades. It's a high-stakes battle."[10]

California is not the only state that has begun to accommodate rather than resist demographic change. Texas, in which 40 percent of public school students are Latino and 15 percent are black, pioneered the effort to call attention to the performance of low-achieving children. During the 1990s, educators there required that test scores be reported for groups of students defined by poverty, race, ethnicity, disability, and limited English proficiency so that the achievements of high-scoring students in a school would no longer mask the low scores of others. An expert on testing from Texas made clear the virtues of this approach: "Prior to ... the accountability system, for many groups of kids no teaching had been going on.... [Now there are] fewer kids who fall through the cracks, fewer kids who are ignored, and fewer kids whose education is considered irrelevant."[11] The tests were controversial and their implementation faulty; excessive pressure for good results apparently has led many schools to focus predominantly on test preparation, and some to push low-achieving students out altogether. But at least in principle, leaders in Texas were trying to include immigrants in the pursuit of the American dream rather than to leave them out of the schools and society.

Between them, California and Texas were home to roughly half of all Hispanic Americans in 2000, making these states potential bellwethers for others in their treatment of immigrants and their children. Furthermore, at the national level, both major political parties made at least gestures toward inclusion. In a policy initiative widely interpreted as an attempt to win the crucial Hispanic vote in the 2004 national election (as well as the vote of Anglos repelled by xenophobic politics), a conservative Republican president proposed a program to improve the status of many illegal immigrants. "As a nation that values immigration and depends on immigration," said President Bush, "we should have immigration laws that work and make us proud. . . . Our nation needs an immigration system that serves the American economy and reflects the American dream." Leading Democratic politicians concurred with the sentiment, while contesting the details.

## Threshold Issue: Bilingual Education

Disputes about bilingual education are one of the clearest indicators of how immigrant children are being incorporated into American schools and society. These disputes were very sharp during the 1990s but have quieted down somewhat since then.

The extraordinarily rapid increase in the number of young English-language learners fueled the controversy. Roughly 4 million school-aged children in 2000 did not speak English well; this number represents more than 7 percent of all students and an increase of more than 200 percent since the early 1980s. About three-quarters of English learners spoke Spanish, followed by Vietnamese, Hmong, and up to 150 other languages spoken by no more than a few percent of children with limited English proficiency (LEP). In the early 1990s, a substantial majority of these individuals lived in just six states (California, Texas, New York, Florida, Illinois, and New Jersey, in descending order) and were concentrated in a few school districts within them. Although the immigrant population has spread to many more states and districts, it remains the case that 40 percent of English learners live in California, comprising roughly one-quarter of the state's students. Districts vary widely; among the fifteen largest school districts in the country, according to the National Center for Education Statistics, 43 percent of the students in Los Angeles but only 7 percent in the state of Hawaii (all one school district), were being served in programs for English learners in 2000.[12] By the end of the 1990s, due to a combination of federal and state laws and court rulings, eight states mandated bilingual education—that is, programs that included teaching substantive courses in the native language of the LEP students. Twenty-six states required help for English learners but did not specify programmatic content; they therefore permitted everything from "immersion" programs, which typically have bilingual teachers providing instruction in English, to extended bilingual programs designed to maintain the native culture of the immigrants. Five states forbade all but short-term transitional programs; and eleven had no laws on the subject. The quality of these programs also varied enormously, from successful dual-immersion schools (in which English-speakers and non-English-speakers jointly learned one another's language) to classrooms that were little more than warehouses for poor children whose parents had not yet learned how to navigate the educational bureaucracy.

Evidence on the effectiveness of different forms of bilingual education was equally varied. So far as can be determined from the voluminous literature on evaluation, measurable outcomes of bilingual education depend more on the quality of teaching in any given program, or on the fit between the details of the program and the particular children in it, than on its form or duration. Programs help students if they are carefully designed, enthusiastically and knowledgeably supported by parents and teachers, based on high expectations for achievement, balanced in curriculum, open to student participation, and appropriately assessed and revised. In other words (and not surprisingly), good programs work and bad programs do not. Dual immersion seems to have the best results, but its application is limited because of the difficulty of finding enough students whose first language is English in schools where immigrant children are concentrated.[13]

After a period of intense, polarized, and sometimes racially offensive debate over bilingual education through the early 1990s, Californians in 1998 voted on Proposition 227, which proposed to restrict special programs for most English learners to one year. Over 60 percent of Hispanic voters opposed it, while half of black, two-thirds of white, and almost three-fifths of Asian American voters supported it. The proposition passed overwhelmingly, as did a similar one in Arizona in 2000 and in Massachusetts in 2002. In Colorado, however, the equivalent proposition lost in 2002. Although anti-immigrant sentiment contributed to support for these referenda, they were also favored by those who thought it generally best for immigrants and the nation to bring English learners into mainstream classes more quickly. In the words of Wilfredo Laboy, the superintendent of the Lawrence, Massachusetts, school district, "What we know from the evidence is that even though there are pockets of success, children in bilingual education fall further and further behind. That painful experience has moved me to say that after 29 years [of supporting such a program], we have to change it."[14] Many supported the propositions only because they were appalled at the poor quality of so many bilingual programs; even the California Association of Bilingual Educators (CABE) conceded that "perhaps 10 percent or fewer of the state's bilingual programs are well implemented."[15] By the beginning of the twenty-first century, even in California disputes over bilingual education focused more on pedagogy than on identity politics or hostility to immigrants. In the 2000 electoral campaign the presidential candidates pursued a bland middle ground; as candidate George W. Bush put it, "If a good immersion program works, I say fine. If a good bilingual program works to teach children English, we should applaud it." Then-vice president Al Gore supported bilingual education more strongly and urged more funding, but he focused mainly on improving the quality of teachers' training to help children learn English quickly. Finally, the No Child Left Behind Act of 2001 gave parents greater influence and more information about their children's assignment to bilingual classes, and changed the financial and regulatory incentives that had favored the bilingual approach during the Clinton administration. Democratic as well as Republican members of Congress strongly supported the new law. By this time, concern about public schooling had largely shifted to issues of class size, teacher quality, overcrowding, and test scores. These issues are not easy to resolve, but they need not divide Americans by identity group.

Despite the fact that nativist sentiment sometimes underlies support for eliminating bilingual-education programs, the inclusionary position on this issue is the right general policy. Bilingual education can be an effective academic approach, but as actually practiced it too often creates obstacles to the achievement of the American dream. Immigrant children in bilingual classes frequently suffer from overidentification and stigmatization, as well as from adjustment problems when they move into conventional classes. They are too often victims of poor teaching, and there are no grounds for believing that the federal government will ever provide funds to generate the additional training and higher salaries needed to improve teaching in the field. States show little inclination to fill the gap; if they did not do so during the booming 1990s, they are unlikely to do so in more stringent times. In this case, as in others, separate education too easily turns into second-class education.

In addition, if bilingual programs are of extended duration they do little to promote training for democratic citizenship. By the late 1990s, most white and African American students attended schools in which fewer than 5 percent of their peers were English learners; conversely, nearly half of LEP students were in schools in which one-third or more of their schoolmates did not speak English fluently.[16] Separating students with limited English proficiency for extended periods reduces diversity in classrooms and creates an obstacle to the acquisition by all students of democratic values through direct, daily contact. Mixing students from different backgrounds does not always lead to real integration—but not mixing students guarantees that integration will not occur.

## Central Issue: Inequalities in Public Schooling

Beyond bilingual education, the ideology of the American dream provides a particularly effective framework for evaluating issues of inequality in American education. While the ideology is widely shared, the context for pursuing one's dreams is not. Some schools provide a first-rate education; some "are terrible." Some schools are blessed with well-fed children; others struggle to teach children who lack basic amenities. Some districts have their pick of the best teachers; others count themselves lucky to have any warm body in front of the classrooms come September. Huge disparities in education spending persist, and some states or districts spend twice as much as others. Well-off parents usually manage to ensure that their children are in decent if not excellent schools; poor parents have a much harder time doing so.

Class disparities among schoolchildren and their parents are closely linked with, although not identical to, differences in immigration status and in race or ethnicity. According to the Census Bureau, 17 percent of foreign-born Americans lived below the poverty line in 2002, compared with only 12 percent of native-born Americans. Among the foreign born, those from Europe and most nations in Asia have poverty rates similar to Anglo Americans, but up to twice as many immigrants from Latin America are poor (and Latin Americans have represented over half of new immigrants since the 1970s). From a different angle, only 8 percent of non-Hispanic white and 10 percent of Asian and Pacific Islander families lived below the poverty line in 2002; that compares with fully 22 percent of Hispanics and 24 percent of African Americans.[17] Problems in schools that are associated with student poverty are therefore also disproportionately associated with the nation's rapid demographic change (along with the persistent problem of black inequality).

Not surprisingly, the worst problems occur in schools in large, poor central cities (and in some small rural schools as well). According to the Department of Education, in the one hundred largest school districts in 2000, almost 70 percent of the students were non-Anglo, compared with 40 percent of students nationally; over half were poor or near poor, compared with about 40 percent nationally. There were more Hispanic than African American students in seven of the ten largest school districts.[18] Poor, non-Anglo students were concentrated; more than six in ten black and Latino students, compared with fewer than three in ten Asian and Anglo students, attended schools in which at least half of their peers were poor. Three-quarters of Hispanics, almost as many blacks, and more than half of Asian Americans attended schools in which at least half of the students were non-Anglo.

Although their students are needier, cities often have fewer resources to help them than do wealthier suburbs. Cities have larger schools and larger classes, as well as less adequate buildings, classrooms, and technology. Compared with suburban districts, teachers in urban schools are less likely to be certified or to have studied in the areas that they teach, and they have less experience; they are also more likely to leave before the end of the school year. These schools suffer from much more administrative and behavioral turmoil and have higher levels of disruption, violence, and anxiety about safety. All of the districts with high dropout rates are in large cities. Urban children have much lower test scores than others, and they perform less well on measures of civic training.[19]

Urban or not, schools with many non-Anglo students also typically offer education of a poorer quality. For example, the Center for the Future of Teaching and Learning reports that throughout the late 1990s and early 2000s, in schools in California with more than 90 percent minority students, as in those with high proportions of poor or low-achieving children or English learners, one in four teachers lacked teaching credentials; in schools with the most Anglo, affluent, or high-achieving students, only one in twenty teachers lacked the proper credentials. Formal certification is not sufficient to ensure a good teacher, but if schools with many resources desire credentialed teachers, schools with few resources would presumably also benefit from their presence.

In short, the worst-off students and schools have a completely different educational experience from the best off, and the outcomes are predictably very different. The National Center for Education Statistics reported in 2003 that among adults, almost 30 percent of Hispanics, compared with 11 percent of blacks, 7 percent of Anglos, and 4 percent of Asian/Pacific Islanders, had not completed high school by age twenty-four. The problem is most acute among Latino immigrants, of whom 43 percent leave high school without finishing. (Only 6 percent of non-Hispanic immigrants drop out.) In all three grades (four, eight, and twelve) tested in math, science, and reading by the National Assessment of Educational Progress (NAEP), Hispanic and black students score notably lower than Anglo and Asian students. Black and Hispanic students are much less likely than Anglos and Asians to take advanced mathematics and science courses—at least partly because poor inner-city schools offer many fewer such courses, can accommodate fewer students in them, and have insufficient equipment.[20]

Given this background, it is no surprise that fewer immigrants, fewer students of color (with the exception of Asians), and fewer poor students attend or complete college compared with well-off, native, or Anglo students. Fully 60 percent of young adults in the wealthiest quartile of the population had a bachelor's or higher degree in 2000, compared with only 24 percent of the middle two quartiles and a shockingly low 7 percent of the poorest quartile.

The pattern is clear. Those segments of the population that are growing most rapidly—Latinos, and immigrants and their children—are likely to live in school districts that can offer them only the poorest quality of education. Usually excepting Asian Americans, who comprise less than 5 percent of the American population, non-Anglos from these districts have poor test scores and low levels of attainment.[21]

Americans generally understand all of this, and residents of states that faced the demographic transition earliest, such as California and Texas, began to change their practices to confront it. They are moving, even if haltingly, from policies based on fear and antagonism to those that seek accommodation, incorporation, and the amelioration of educational disadvantage. But there is a long way to go in these states and elsewhere, and the demographic changes are continuing.

## Education in the New America

If leaders really believe that no child should or need be left behind, or even if they think that it is in their best interests to act as though they believed it, the huge demographic and political changes shaping the United States presents an opportunity to create education policies that can make the American dream work for more people. As in the early decades of the twentieth century, a large group of immigrants combine an experience of exclusion with a strong desire to realize the American dream.

Poor and non-Anglo residents of the United States are especially likely to see schools as the route to achieving their dreams. In a survey conducted for the Center for the Future of Teaching and Learning in 2002, a plurality of Californians agreed that improving education is the highest priority for their state government, and that the state should spend "a lot more" on K–12 education—but blacks and Hispanics were most likely to hold those views. Latinos and African Americans appropriately expressed the most criticism of the quality of teaching in the public schools, but more people in all three minority groups, compared with Anglos, agreed that all students should be held to the same standards of achievement. Also in this survey, low-income respondents were more enthusiastic than those with higher incomes when asked to evaluate a wide range of proposed reforms to improve educational quality; Latinos and blacks always showed the highest level of support. In a California referendum in 2002, non-Anglo voters, especially Hispanics, strongly endorsed before- and after-school programs; Anglo voters were less enthusiastic. In short, the most disadvantaged residents of the most demographically transformed state are committed to schooling as the route to success, recognize schooling inequities, and support measures to improve its quality.

National surveys show the same pattern. In a 2002 national survey by the Pew Hispanic Center, more Hispanic and African American than Anglo parents reported that it was "very" important to them that their child receive a college education. In another 2002 Pew survey, more registered voters said that a political candidate's views on education would affect their vote more than any other issue—and support was strongest among African Americans and (especially) Latinos.[22] Such sentiments provide a strong platform from which to move the nation toward adaptation to demographic change rather than polarization.

Americans should begin by reaffirming their commitment to public education. Many new immigrants will be interested in parochial education and some will want to separate themselves by identity group (as some native-born Americans may want to further separate themselves from immigrants). But that does not mean that vouchers will be a sufficient or appropriate policy for the new context. Publicly and privately financed programs to provide private education through vouchers together involve only a tiny fraction of students—fewer than 1 percent in 2004. There is disagreement on whether voucher programs improve schooling outcomes for African Americans, and general agreement that they do not help Latino and Anglo children. Some analysts also fear that if such programs were expanded they could harm the quality of schooling of the many remaining behind.[23]

The public has consistently favored the idea of more options, especially for children in underperforming schools; a majority of Latinos, African Americans, poor people, and urban residents frequently support the idea of vouchers in surveys. Nevertheless, when confronted with a direct choice, a larger majority prefers investment in school reform to spending on vouchers for private schools. When asked in 1999 what the next president should do to improve education in the United States, for example, almost two-fifths of respondents endorsed increases in public school funding, and only 2 percent chose vouchers. By 2004, proposals for public support of private schooling had suffered definitive losses ten times that they had been put to a popular vote in various states. Two-thirds of voters opposed the propositions for vouchers in California and Michigan in 2000, and no demographic group came close to giving vouchers majority support in either state. Two states had approved pilot programs, although both encountered legal and implementation problems.

Voucher programs challenge the very *publicness* of education. They undermine the only U.S. institution in which people of different groups and classes at least have the chance of coming together for an important part of their lives, and they threaten the central democratic institution for promoting the American dream. In a new demographic context where finding common ground will be more important than ever, vouchers could lead to a high level of educational fragmentation by affinity and ethnic group.

More generally, immigrant students were separated from others in the public schools for too long in too many places in American history, and public policies should not begin once again to encourage separation. "Guard well the doors of our public schools that they do not enter," said the San Francisco Board of Examiners in an 1885 report on Chinese immigration. "For however stern it may sound, it is but the enforcement of the law of self preservation, the inculcation of the doctrine of true humanity, an integral part of the iron rule of right by which we hope presently to prove that we can justly and practically defend ourselves from this invasion of Mongolian barbarism."[24] (By 1906, Asians in San Francisco received public education, but only at the segregated Oriental Public School.) Similarly, immigrants from Mexico were often given a separate and generally inferior education; in 1931, a survey by California's state government found that a large majority of Mexicans were relegated to separate classes or schools.[25]

Separated or not, immigrant children also faced a particularly narrow form of Americanization in the early twentieth century. "In their demands for total assimilation, for Anglo-conformity," wrote the historian David Tyack,

Nothing less would satisfy [many educators] than assaulting all forms of cultural difference. There is no reason to suppose that the Americanizers were being hypocritical in talking of opportunity or in preaching Anglo-conformity and middle class standards. They were mostly true believers and perhaps were accurate in believing that in an opportunity structure dominated by WASPS, the immigrant youth would find success easier [through assimilation].[26]

Regardless of good intentions, this approach could take a toll. "Too often," wrote the American social reformer Jane Addams in 1897, "the teacher's conception of her duty is to transform him [the student] into an American of a somewhat smug and comfortable type. . . . She fails . . . not only in knowledge of, but also in respect for, the child and his parents." In a 1904 article titled "How It Feels to Be a Problem," Gino Speranza echoed Addams, pointing out that "too often . . . does the American of common schooling interpret differences from his own standards and habits of life as necessarily signs of inferiority."[27]

Attitudes have changed since the early decades of the twentieth century, along with institutions and laws. In 1994 and again in 2000, for example, only one-third of respondents to the national General Social Survey (GSS) agreed that "groups should change so that they blend into the larger society," rather than being neutral on the point (another one-third) or agreeing that "racial and ethnic groups should maintain their distinct cultures" (the final one-third). Over three-quarters agreed that increased immigration will "make the country more open to new ideas and cultures." Americans are more aware, even if grudgingly, that immigrants come to a nation powerfully shaped by the groups that came before and continually shaped by new values, cultures, and desires. Although current residents in the United States seldom support increased levels of immigration and fear a loss of jobs to newcomers, half of the GSS respondents agreed in 2000 that more immigrants to the United States would lead to "higher economic growth," up from one-third in 1994. Pluralities see immigrants as "hard-working"; large majorities see Hispanics and Asian Americans as "committed to strong families." More respondents agree than disagree that changes in American demography over the next twenty-five years "will be a good thing for the country."[28]

Furthermore, in the 2000 GSS, a large majority concurred that American children should learn a second language fluently before finishing high school. Three-quarters of respondents in a national survey in 1997 endorsed teaching "the diverse cultural traditions of the different population groups in America" along with the "common, predominant cultural tradition," rather than the common tradition alone. In the same year in a different survey, half even reported willingness to support reductions in "the amount of information [taught] on traditional subjects in U.S. . . . history" in favor of increasing "information on non-Western cultures and on women and minorities in the U.S."[29]

In this new demographic and social context, public schools not only should but also have a broad mandate to refine their efforts to inculcate appreciation for the culture and history of a wide spectrum of groups without trivializing the curriculum. Students should learn that different cultures have different norms, that cultural differences are legitimate, and that most such differences occur within a common framework of values.

At the same time, although not in the same way as at the turn of the twentieth century, public schools should transmit a common American culture, rooted in the history of the United States and based on English. English will remain the shared language of public discourse in the United States as well as the language required for individual economic success. But it need not be the only language children learn, or learn to respect. *How well* children are taught English and other languages, not how they are taught a language, should be the focus of attention for parents and educators; various methods may be appropriate so long as they aim to bring children together and do not separate them into first- and second-class citizens. Most immigrant children are eager to succeed in American society, and immigrant parents, like all others, want the best for their children. In the long run, this kind of motivation should help schools to overcome inevitable disagreements about the best means to a shared end, and should help reduce the volatility of these issues.

This approach to the issues raised by diversity will displease members of racial, ethnic, or religious groups who want a longer or different exposure in the public schools to their particular views, values, or culture. Since opposition to these preferences can be taken for discrimination or at the very least insensitivity, it can become political dynamite.[30] Opposition need not, however, imply a failure to recognize persistent discrimination or a rejection of distinctive cultures. American society has many arenas in which groups can legitimately work to maintain their language, culture, values, and distinctive perspectives. Americans have always done that in their homes, churches, and community organizations; a liberal democracy permits and even encourages group self-definition, and the nation is richer for it. Private and parochial schools can help fulfill this function as well.

But it should not be part of the mission of public schools to help groups define themselves separately from the rest of American society. Public schools certainly have an obligation to teach critical thinking, so that students can assist the society in adjusting to new conditions (including a changing population), preserve what is best about American institutions, and attend to what must be changed. That must include questioning the ideology and practice of the American dream. Public schools cannot, however, take on the responsibility of maintaining the culture of any particular ethnic group; they simply would not be able to deal with the hundreds of legitimate claims that would result.

As a matter of practicality, then, as well as purpose in a diverse country, public education must focus on what residents have in common. As the law professor Alexander Aleinikoff puts it, "What the *unum* has a right to ask of the *pluribus*, . . . is that groups identify themselves as American. To be sure, there may be significant disagreement over what it means to see oneself as an 'American.' But the central idea is that a person be committed to this country's continued flourishing and see himself or herself as part of that ongoing project."[31] Democratic debate also requires some level of identification with others in the conversation; as Alan Patten contends, "Fellow citizens must be willing to tolerate and trust, defer to the requirements of public reason, and accept certain burdens and sacrifices for the sake of the common good."[32] Identification of this kind can only happen if well-off Anglos abandon their complacency and sense of entitlement, *and* if new immigrants accept the challenges of moving into a new society. Both groups must change, and each will do so in part because the other does.

As the twenty-first century proceeds, education will be more costly, more important for success, and more central to the national well-being than ever before. To make the American dream work as it should and to avoid wasting human resources that the country will need, communities with a large number of poor or immigrant children will require extra help. They will, at a minimum, need as much financial support per student as districts with a concentration of affluent or native-born families. For both political and substantive reasons, this is best done through state-financed increases to poor and non-Anglo districts rather than decreases in expenditures in wealthy or white ones. Beyond equality of resources and for the same reasons, all students should be funded well enough to receive an education adequate to their particular educational needs. This new understanding of adequacy provides more flexibility than does financial equity alone and keeps the focus where it ought to be, on the quality of education that is provided.

It will be hard to pay for all needed reforms, but it can be done. To build support, it will be essential to invest resources in programs with demonstrated success, such as quality preschool, small classes in the early grades for poor or minority students, and professional development for teachers. Americans in fact have endorsed a wide range of school reforms and provided substantial increases in funding for them since the 1970s; they claim in a multitude of surveys to be willing to provide funds for even more.[33] The votes of younger Americans can help offset the resistance of some senior citizens. And advocates can continue to push the courts to maintain pressure on state legislatures for financial reform.

For all the difficulties involved in school finance reform and in the wise use of the money it generates, it will remain necessary to equalize educational opportunities and to promote policies that give poor and non-Anglo children a chance to achieve their dreams. It is easier to move money than to move state borders, district boundaries, or people. Inequalities among states, districts, schools, and classrooms will not disappear, and people will often sort themselves by race or ethnicity and class. Racial desegregation has met its limits, and privileged parents have shown that they are no more enthusiastic about bringing low-income children of any race into their schools than white parents have been about mixing races.[34] This reluctance is part of the reason that choice programs will probably not do much to break down racial and class barriers. The United States will have to rely on more funding, and its more effective use, if poor Americans and new immigrants are to have a better chance of participating in the American dream.

Even with greater and more wisely used resources, however, first-class schooling will always be more available on the right side of the tracks. Because the education of children depends to a large extent on the social class and origins of their peers, it remains important to do whatever possible to educate poor and immigrant children; not only *like* middle class or Anglo children, but *with* them (Kahlenberg 2001). Even though such programs are likely to remain too limited to have a dramatic impact on the structure of education, public officials should do what they can to promote magnet schools and interdistrict plans that permit disadvantaged children to leave their neighborhoods to find a better education; they should also promote dual-immersion programs. These actions will not solve the problems of the worst urban schools, but they will give some children a greater chance for success and more contact with students from different backgrounds. The residential separation embedded in the current structure of education will continue to severely limit the amount of interaction across racial or ethnic, and class, lines. But within those limitations it will be increasingly important to take steps for students to be educated together as much as possible.

Class issues will remain the most difficult, and ethnic and racial issues will not go away. But for all of its flaws, public education remains America's most accessible and democratic political institution with national scope. Public action around schooling will provide the best chance for the liberating side of the American dream to take effect; schools can help to meet the challenges of a new economy and to realize the opportunities of the new demography. But if poor and non-Anglo children continue to lack sufficient resources, good teachers, decent facilities, and real connections with other Americans, the ideology of the American dream will be just a cover for systematic injustice, and the promise that "no child will be left behind" will be just another lie. Public education *can* help make the American dream work for everyone, and that will be more important than ever in the new America.

# *Notes*

1.  See Jennifer L. Hochschild, *Facing Up to the American Dream: Race, Class, and the Soul of the Nation* (Princeton University Press, 1995), chapter 1, for more on the virtues and defects of the ideology.
2.  In the decade from 1994 to 2004, six national surveys asked questions using that wording, with the same results in each. The surveys included *Times Mirror,* July 1994; American National Election Study, November 1994; Pew Research Center, November 1997 (2 surveys), October 1999, and July 2003.
3.  Survey results come from Phi Delta Kappa, 1996 and 2000. They vary little according to race and ethnicity, levels of education, or income.
4.  These figures assume that the racial and ethnic categories in use in 2000 will remain meaningful over the twenty-first century. If intermarriage continues to grow at the rate that it has since the 1970s, adjustment in the categories will be necessary. Nationally, at least 8 percent of children had parents of two races or ethnicities in 2000.

    At the same time, almost twice that proportion of births in California were multiracial or multiethnic. (California: Sonya Tafoya, *Mixed Race and Ethnicity in California.* San Francisco: Public Policy Institute of California, 2000).
5.  William H. Frey, "The New Urban Demographics: Race, Space, and Boomer Aging," *Brookings Review* 18 (summer 2000), 21.
6.  James Poterba, "Demographic Structure and the Political Economy of Public Education," *Journal of Policy Analysis and Management* 16, no. 1 (1997), 60–61. Field Poll, "California Opinion Index: How Concerned Californians Are about Major Issues Facing the State," San Francisco: Field Institute, 2002. Another study has shown that older African Americans and Latinos continue to support high levels of school funding: Kent L. Tedin, Richard E. Matland, and Gregory R. Weiher, "Age, Race, Self-Interest, and Financing Public Schools through Referenda," *Journal of Politics* 63, no. 1 (2001), 270–94.
7.  Quoted in Martin Wisckol, "GOP Distances Itself from 'Son of 187,'" *Orange County Register,* December 12, 1999.
8.  Quoted in Karen Rosenblum, "Rights at Risk: California's Proposition 187," in *Illegal Immigration in America: A Reference Handbook,* edited by David W. Haines and Karen E. Rosenblum (Westport, Conn.: Greenwood, 1999).
9.  In 1999 almost half of Anglos and almost three-fifths of African Americans living in Los Angeles still saw "too many immigrants in Los Angeles today." More than two-fifths of Anglos, more than one-third of blacks, and even one-quarter of Latinos in the same survey agreed that immigrants have had a negative impact on the public schools of their city. (Both proportions had declined since 1993, substantially for Anglos.) About 40 percent of Latinos concurred that Los Angeles had too many immigrants; in 1993, almost two-thirds had done so. All of these results come from polls by the *Los Angeles Times* in 1993 and 1999.
10. "As GOP Reaches Out to Immigrants, Some Find It a Stretch," Associated Press, June 26, 2000.
11. Quoted in Debra Viadero, "Testing System in Texas Yet to Get Final Grade," *Education Week* 19, no. 38 (2000), 20.

12. National Center for Education Statistics, *Characteristics of the 100 Largest Public Elementary and Secondary School Districts in the United States: 2000-2001* (Washington D.C.: U.S. Department of Education, 2002), table 15.

13. For more on bilingual education, see Diane August and Kenji Hakuta, eds., *Improving Schooling for Language-Minority Children* (Washington D.C.: National Academy Press, 1997); and Jennifer L. Hochschild and Nathan Scovronick, *The American Dream and the Public Schools* (New York: Oxford University Press, 2003), 148–159 and 176–181.

14. Quoted in Scott S. Greenberger, "Bilingual Ed Loses Favor with Some Educators," *Boston Globe*, August 5, 2001, A1.

15. Quoted in Gregory Rodriguez, "English Lesson in California," *The Nation* (April 20, 1998), 16.

16. Jorge Ruiz-de-Velasco and Michael Fix, *Overlooked and Underserved: Immigrant Students in U.S. Secondary School* (Washington D.C.: Urban Institute), 2000.

17. Current Population Reports, *Poverty in the United States: 2002* (Washington D.C.: U.S. Bureau of the Census, 2003), tables 1–2.

18. National Center for Education Statistics, *Characteristics of the 100 Largest Public Elementary and Secondary School Districts in the United States: 2000-2001,* tables C, 9.

19. Evidence on these points comes from "Quality Counts '98: The Urban Challenge" (Washington, D.C.: *Education Week* and Pew Charitable Trusts, 1998), the National Center for Education Statistics, the General Accounting Office, and the Department of Housing and Urban Development. See also Hochschild and Scovronick, *The American Dream and the Public Schools,* chapters 1 and 4.

20. National Center for Education Statistics, *The Condition of Education 2003* (Washington D.C.: U.S. Department of Education, 2003).

21. Jorge Ruiz-de-Velasco and Michael Fix, with Beatrice Chu Clewell, "Overlooked and Underserved: Immigrant Students in U.S. Secondary Schools" (Washington, D.C.: Urban Institute, 2000).

22. Pew Hispanic Center/Kaiser Family Foundation. "National Survey of Latinos: The Latino Electorate" (Washington, D.C.: Pew Hispanic Center, 2002).

23. Hochschild and Scovronick 2003: chap. 5; Gill et al. 2001; Howell and Peterson 2002; Krueger and Zhu 2003.

24. Quoted in Charles Wollenberg, "Yellow Peril in the Schools (1)," in *The Asian American Educational Experience: A Source Book for Teachers and Students,* edited by Don T. Nakanishi and Tina Yamano Nishida (New York: Routledge, 1995), 3.

25. Rubén Donato, Martha Menchaca, and Richard R. Valencia, "Segregation, Desegregation, and Integration of Chicano Students: Problems and Prospects," in *Chicano School Failure and Success: Past, Present, and Future,* edited by Richard R. Valencia, 2nd ed. (London and New York: Routledge/Falmer, 2002), 35.

26. David Tyack, *The One Best System* (Cambridge MA: Harvard University Press, 1974). 235–36.

27. Addams and Speranzo essays can be found in *The Ordeal of Assimilation: A Documentary History of the White Working Class,* edited by Stanley Feldstein and Lawrence Costello (Garden City, N.Y.: Anchor, 1974), 251–55 and 187–94.

28. Survey data are from the General Social Survey for 1994 and 2000, by the National Opinion Research Center (NORC) at the University of Chicago.

29. Phi Delta Kappa, *Attitudes toward the Public Schools, 1994* (Bloomington, Ind.: Phi Delta Kappa); *Time*, CNN, survey, June 12, 1997.

30. See L. Delpit, "Education in a Multicultural Society: Our Future's Greatest Challenge," *Journal of Negro Education* 61, no. 3 (1992), 237–49.

31. T. Alexander Aleinikoff, "A Multicultural Nationalism?" *American Prospect* 9, no. 36 (1998), 85.

32. Alan Patten, "Political Theory and Language Policy," *Political Theory* 29, no. 5 (2001), 701.

33. See Jennifer Hochschild and Bridget Scott, "The Poll Trends: Governance and Reform of Public Education in the United States," *Public Opinion Quarterly* 62, no. 1 (1998), 79–120.

34. See David Rusk, "Trends in School Segregation."

## Bibliography

August, Diane, and Kenji Hakuta, eds. *Improving Schooling for Language-Minority Children: A Research Agenda.* Washington, D.C.: National Academy, 1997.

Burtless, Gary, ed. *Does Money Matter?: The Effect of School Resources on Student Achievement and Adult Success.* Washington, D.C.: Brookings Institution Press, 1996.

Gill, Brian P., et al. *Rhetoric versus Reality: What We Know and What We Need to Know about Vouchers and Charter Schools.* Santa Monica, Calif.: Rand Education, 2001.

Henig, Jeffrey R. *Rethinking School Choice: Limits of the Market Metaphor.* Princeton, N.J.: Princeton University Press, 1994.

Hochschild, Jennifer L. *Facing Up to the American Dream: Race, Class, and the Soul of the Nation.* Princeton, N.J.: Princeton University Press, 1995.

Hochschild, Jennifer L., and Nathan Scovronick. *The American Dream and the Public Schools.* New York: Oxford University Press, 2003.

Howell, William G., and Paul E. Peterson. *The Education Gap: Vouchers and Urban Schools.* Washington, D.C.: Brookings Institution Press, 2002.

Kahlenberg, Richard D. *All Together Now: Creating Middle-Class Schools through Public School Choice.* Washington, D.C.: Brookings Institution Press, 2001.

Ladd, Helen F., Rosemary Chalk, and Janet S. Hansen. *Equity and Adequacy in Education Finance: Issues and Perspectives.* Washington D.C.: National Academy Press, 1999.

Levin, Henry M., ed. *Privatizing Education: Can the Marketplace Deliver Choice, Efficiency, Equity, and Social Cohesion?* Boulder, Colo.: Westview, 2001.

Orfield, Gary, and Nora Gordon, *Schools More Separate: Consequences of a Decade of Resegregation.* Cambridge, Mass.: Harvard University: Civil Rights Project, 2001.

Rusk, David. "Trends in School Segregation." In *Divided We Fail: Coming Together through Public School Choice,* pp. 61–85. Report of the Century Foundation Task Force on the Common School. New York: Century Foundation Press, 2002.

Tyack, David B. *The One Best System: A History of American Urban Education.* Cambridge, Mass.: Harvard University Press, 1974.

# 14

## SCHOOL CHOICE AND THE DEMOCRATIC IDEAL OF FREE COMMON SCHOOLS

*Paul R. Dimond*

I N THE MID-NINETEENTH CENTURY AN ODDLY AMERICAN
notion of education financed by the public emerged in a few states—the
democratic ideal of tuition-free schools open to all regardless of family
income. Thereafter, individual states established local school districts and led the
world in offering free common schools. Only at the end of the nineteenth century, however, before Jim Crow laws rigidly segregated schools by race, did most
schoolchildren in the United States attend even primary schools approaching
this ideal: in 1900 three out of four families lived in rural areas and small towns
with only a single public school, the "little red schoolhouse" at the rural cross-
roads or town center that served all families equally.

By 1950 56 percent of the U.S. population lived in metropolitan areas.
Families with the economic wherewithal to choose the particular local school
they wanted their children to attend either paid tuition at a private school (12.1
percent of all pupils) or bought homes in exclusive neighborhoods served by a
desirable public school (another 25 percent). Attendance in such schools, private
or public, depended on a child's family income; these schools were, therefore,
neither free nor common.

Around this time, economists began touting family choice of school by
choice of residence in the burgeoning metropolitan areas as comprising a
responsive market that efficiently matched the quality of local public services
with the amount of local taxes that families were willing to pay. For example, by
thus "voting with their feet" in a market of competing local school districts, families could choose low tax rates and low-cost schools, high tax rates and high-
cost schools, or some mix in between. But the theory of numerous local school
districts competing through the private housing market to better serve the

diverse tax rate/school cost preferences of American families foundered on two harsh facts: First, the rigid racial segregation of schools throughout the country relegated minority children to unequal as well as separate schools. Second, since public schools were funded predominantly by means of local property taxes, disparities in the private taxable wealth of local districts led to gross spending inequities between local schools. As a result, this "free market" of school choice by place of residence completely frustrated the democratic ideal of free common schools open to all.

Over the next three decades judicial decrees and legislative actions struck down official school segregation and limited many local-school funding disparities resulting from systematic inequalities in local district tax wealth. By 2000 the local share of school funding had declined to less than 44 percent, as the state share increased to 49 percent and the federal share to 7 percent; and the disparities in amounts spent per pupil between local districts were both smaller and less related to local school tax rates than in the 1950s or 1960s. As a result, there was no longer even a *theoretical* economic rationale for the theory that competing school districts and tax-rate preferences among families create a legitimate market for school choice.

In 2000 eight out of ten American families lived in metropolitan areas, most in the geographically expanding suburbs and exurbs. A growing plurality of American families had the economic means to exercise their choice of school for their children through their choice of residence, many by paying the high cost of a house in an exclusive suburban neighborhood. The public schools serving these areas remained as out of reach to millions of ordinary working families and the poor as high-tuition private schools. They were not common, because they were not open to all families regardless of income; and they were not free, because admission was limited to those families that could afford to buy and maintain a home in the area served by the school. It is hard to imagine a more undemocratic system of public schooling than one that effectively limits to the affluent the opportunity to choose the best school for one's children.

This essay explores whether there is a more equitable approach to extending the opportunity of school choice to all families, not only to those with the economic means to buy a home in an exclusive neighborhood but to ordinary working and lower-income families. The issue is not whether families should have the opportunity to choose the best publicly funded school for their own children: that is a given in any free, democratic, largely urban, and increasingly mobile society in the twenty-first century. After all, on average, more than one family in six moves to a new home every year. The burden of this essay is to explore whether there is a way to extend the opportunity of publicly supported school choice to all families through a market more equitable than the real estate market. To this end the following democratic school choice proposition is offered:

Every family deserves an equal opportunity to choose the publicly supported, tuition-free common school that will best serve their children.

The goal of this proposition is to achieve, at long last, the democratic ideal of free common schools open to all families, regardless of income. Too often education policy analysis and discourse about school reform decline into an academic debate about whether the particular proposal improves student learning, for which class of students, and by how much. "Evidence" is demanded from social science research on one preliminary "natural experiment" or another to determine whether the reform increases, decreases, or has no material impact on student achievement or other student outputs. No one opposes such inquiry, but its import is limited by its narrow frame of reference: it fails to take account of the more powerful dynamics in the rest of the society outside the schools. These changing factors overwhelm the research on school inputs and student outputs and obscure causes and effects. For example, as discussed above, Jim Crow segregation, systematic inequalities in school funding based on local tax wealth rather than family tax effort, and the growing urbanization and upward mobility of American families all may have had more enduring impact on schools and children than can be measured by studies of changes in student outcomes at any set of schools that adopt any particular education reform or other input change.

The first part of this essay, therefore, will examine another powerful dynamic in American schooling—the changes in the national economy over the twentieth century, with a focus on the century's last three decades, during the difficult transition from the industrial era to the information age. Understanding this larger economic context offers a more insightful lens than narrow empirical studies of school inputs and outputs. It provides a better tool for evaluating whether a policy principle such as that offered in the proposition above holds real promise to achieve the democratic ideal of free common schools open to all.

The second part of the essay elaborates suggestions for implementing the democratic school-choice proposition. Three principles are laid out showing how universal family choice can be designed to create an equitable and dynamic market among competing, free common schools regardless of family income. The essay concludes in the third part by exploring how extending the opportunity of such informed choice of school to all families fits within the democratic traditions and decentralized nature of the American republic.

## American Economic Transitions and School Response

At the dawn of the twentieth century, the U.S. economy was still in the early stages of a transition from farming to manufacturing. It would be more than ten years before Henry Ford transformed the landscape with the factory assembly line and mass-produced goods that every worker could afford to buy. In 1900 40 percent of the workforce still toiled at manual labor on farms spread across the countryside. The owners of these small farms closed the barn door and the gates around the fields to protect their most valuable assets—feed, tools, machinery, livestock, and crops.

Most schools had only a single teacher, and this individual guided the learning of all her students from ages five through thirteen in primary school. Only 10 percent of children ages fourteen to seventeen then enrolled in high school. Of the smaller fraction of those who graduated from high school, only a more elite few sought to enter college. In an economy in which most opportunities were still limited to manual labor on the farm or in town, college for most was irrelevant.

## Manufacturing and the Assembly Line

In the mid-twentieth century, mass-production manufacturing dominated the U.S. economy. More than 40 percent of workers labored at relatively low-skill manufacturing jobs. Giant industrial concerns employed machines, hierarchical command-and-control structures, and highly segmented and routinized tasks to leverage human muscle-power. The salaried managers locked the plant gates at night after the workers left to protect the shareholders' most valuable assets—the factory, machines, goods in progress, and inventory. These big employers were confident that their workers, who were hired for life at the highest wages and benefits in the world, would return the next day to man the machines in the factory.

From 1946 through 1973, overall U.S. productivity grew at a rapid clip, averaging about 3 percent per year. American workers and firms thereby generated the first upwardly mobile, continuously growing middle-class majority of any nation in the history of the world; and median family income doubled during this generation. The resulting purchasing power fueled the demand of most Americans to own their own single-family homes on a quarter acre. Coupled with new investment in more efficient single-story, long-line factories, this spurred continuing suburban and exurban expansion throughout this period.

By 1950 most schools reflected the prevailing mass-production model of the industrial economy, with a local school board hiring a superintendent and central administrative staff to run each district and a principal (analogous to a foreman) to manage each school. Teachers (analogous to plant workers on the floor) took a batch of students into separate classrooms. By passing the children on grade by grade along this production line, schools sought to train most boys to man the factories in the mass-manufacturing economy and most girls to serve as homemakers.

Unlike her counterparts on the factory assembly line, each teacher could isolate herself by closing her door and thereby largely determine what would go on in her classroom. Overall, however, school organization mirrored the increasing specialization and scale in industrial organizations and factories. Big "comprehensive" high schools grew to sort out the relatively elite few boys who would be educated to go on to college as white-collar managers and professionals in the industrial economy, as they prepared a relatively elite corps of women to go on to teacher colleges to be trained as schoolteachers. The public address system, the clock, and the hourly bell kept this mass school production line moving.

Like their industrial counterparts, each state created its own defined-benefit pensions for school employees, which were not portable among employers across state lines. Each state also created separate licensing requirements, often by grade level and subject matter, without reciprocity between states. As a result, there was little regional or national competition among schools to hire accomplished teachers. Like factory workers, teachers once hired in a local district were stuck there unless they wished to give up their pension to start over elsewhere.

## Information and Services Economy

At the dawn of the twenty-first century, 75 percent of American workers were employed in service jobs—management, professions, marketing, sales, office, transportation, retail, communication, tourism, health care, and education. In 2000 less than 1 percent of American workers toiled on farms and less than 14 percent in manufacturing. Continuing developments in agriculture and manufacturing productivity throughout the twentieth century enabled a small and declining proportion of workers to produce an amount, variety, and quality of food and goods unimaginable in 1900 or 1950.

To be sure, the office managers of the diverse service enterprises, large and small, still locked the doors at night in 2000. In contrast to 1950 or 1900, however, the most valuable employees of most service firms had their own keys to the office. These workers were networked to one another and to a growing web of rapidly growing, ever more user-friendly sources of information, communication, and software in the office, on the road, and at home. They worked in teams that changed whenever needed to provide or to invent more customized value-added services to meet increasingly diverse consumer demand. These networks also empowered workers to leverage human mind power and information very efficiently, whether to serve millions of customers with common needs or a single user with a unique demand. In such knowledge work, workers learn every day on the job and apply that new learning to add more value to their services.

The biggest fear of the owners of the new service firms, big and small, was that their workers would decide to go to work for a competitor or start their own business. In this more competitive and diverse information age, the workers, consumers, and families with the greatest personal stake in the outcome all have much greater opportunity to choose than ever before. Not surprisingly, the personal returns to higher education in the rise of this information age continue to increase. On average, annual personal earnings increase more than 10 percent for each year of higher education attained.

Make no mistake, however: the transition from the industrial era to the information age proved very difficult: From 1974 through 1995 average annual growth in national productivity in the United States declined substantially—to little more than 1 percent per year, despite the continuing strong productivity growth of more than 2.5 percent per year in manufacturing and farming. Moreover, median family income adjusted for inflation remained flat over this generation. Viewing this relative stagnation compared with the much stronger growth in the prior generation, many economists posited that the inevitable course of mature industrial nations was to evolve into slow-growth service economies: as increasing proportions of the labor force worked in the service sector where there was little growth in productivity through 1995, the overall rate of productivity growth would continue to decline and wages and incomes would stagnate. Some economists even argued that the labor-intensive, personal nature of most service work would operate forever to prevent any significant, sustained growth in productivity in the expanding service sector.

In the 1970s and 1980s a cadre of industrial policy pundits emerged to challenge this dour advice to settle for slow growth. These reformers argued that national industrial policies to better manage domestic education, training, labor, capital, consumer, industrial, and foreign trade markets could generate faster growth. They touted the greater central planning and coordination of big government, big business, big labor, and more national school systems in Germany and Japan as the way to spur growth in the mature industrial economy.

For the most part, Americans resisted the calls to embrace such top-down, industrial policies or to settle for slower economic growth. An odd thing happened. Beginning in 1996, America's service workers and firms finally contributed to increasing the average rate of productivity growth in the overall U.S. economy to 2.6 percent per year; and this strong increase continued during the mild recession that began in 2001 and appeared to be gaining momentum during the expansion beginning in November of 2002. Precisely what caused this structural rise in productivity growth in the United States is a subject of debate. Those portions of the service sector in which competition among providers was most robust led the way. They succeeded in integrating computer systems, software, and the World Wide Web into efficient networks that added more value: the rate of productivity growth throughout the entire service sector averaged 2.5 percent per year. In contrast, the once vaunted top-down industrial policies of Japan and Germany withered in the 1990s: they generated no such growth in productivity, and in 2000 Japan and Germany were being forced toward greater flexibility and market competition in their domestic economies in order to spur growth. By 2000, there were already four times as many knowledge workers in good-paying jobs as factory workers; and their rising productivity helped fuel sustained growth in family income for the first time in a generation and the longest economic expansion this century.

Unlike the more competitive portions of the service sector, schools saw no increase in productivity in the 1990s. In 2000 the median local K–12 school still looked and operated much the same as it did fifty years before, in the industrial era. Unlike knowledge workers in other high-value services, a majority of teachers had not yet come out from behind the closed doors of their separate classrooms to form teams with their peers, let alone leverage the power of interactive networks with students and their parents in school and at home to transform student learning. Unlike other professions, even the market for most school textbooks was still being driven by the lowest common denominator of supply and demand: a few large publishing firms supplied standard texts to meet top-down, bureaucratic adoptions by a few large states. The considered judgments of millions of accomplished teachers and the diverse demands of tens of millions of informed parents and their school-age children were not considered, let alone met.

The primary economic change in schools since the 1950s has been to try harder to do the same thing better: cut pupil/teacher ratios by more than 40 percent (from 27:1 in 1955 to 15:1 in 2001) and average class size by more than 25 percent; spend in total more than four times more per pupil in attendance (from $2,132 in 1951 to $9,354 in 2001 in inflation-adjusted dollars); and continue to decrease the proportion of school operating budgets spent on teachers and student learning (from 57.2 percent in 1970 to 52.8 percent in 2000).

From 1955 through 1990 average annual salaries for teachers did rise—from less than $30,000 per year in inflation-adjusted dollars to almost $45,000. In the 1990s, however, due to the lack of competition among school employers for accomplished teachers and the lack of portable pensions enabling teachers to accept higher-paying teaching jobs anywhere in the country, average teacher pay did not increase at all in inflation-adjusted dollars. While most other knowledge workers (including more mobile higher education faculty) earned substantially more during the rise of the information age, the ratio of teacher pay to average worker pay *fell* over the decade—from 1.28 of an average worker's pay in 1990 to 1.16 in 2000.

Given the lack of growth in productivity in the rest of the more competitive service sector for decades prior to 1996, it would be surprising if schools had been able to increase their capacity to produce better outcomes, including student achievement. Moreover, given the lack of direct competition between local school providers, the absence of reliable market signals to inform schools and families as to relative value added in school and student performance, and the inequity and unresponsiveness of a school market based primarily on place of residence, it should be expected that K–12 schools would not reflect the structural increase in productivity evidenced in many other parts of the service sector since 1995. In this context the hard but unsurprising fact for defenders and critics alike of local public schools in the United States is clear: overall student attainment and achievement remained fairly constant over the several decades leading up to 2000.

For example, the percentage of seventeen-year-olds graduating from high school has remained about the same since the mid-1960s, declining from 75 percent to 70 percent. The percent of high school dropouts among the population ages sixteen to twenty-four has also remained much the same, falling from about 14 percent in 1970 to 12 percent in 2000. Similarly, average SAT scores also stay in a narrow range, declining slightly over the entire period.

The National Assessment of Education Progress (NAEP) suggests that average student proficiency of students in reading, writing, math, and science at ages nine, thirteen, and seventeen continued in a narrow range from 1970 through 1999. The average across the full range of tests for younger-age groups rose modestly over the entire period, while seventeen-year-olds scored on average lower in 1999 on the NAEP science exam than in 1970 and only slightly higher in math. Similar international tests of samples of students from developed countries in the 1990s offer no evidence to contradict the basic finding from NAEP studies and SAT scores—small gains in achievement for younger students in the United States since the 1970s and little if any gains in achievement for high schoolers through 2000.

With respect to student achievement and attainment, it is time to end the "blame game." Despite adult nostalgia about school days of yore, or growing fears about a decline in the quality of schooling in America, students in 2000 achieved about the same as schoolchildren did ten, twenty, thirty, or forty years ago.

Schools have responded better to some of the other demands arising during the transition to the information age. For example, most schools have dropped the mid-century industrial notion that college is only for the elite few or that schools are the appropriate place to slot and to specially train young persons for different lifetime vocations. Instead, since 1980, the average high school graduate has increased the number of Carnegie college-prep units taken from 21.5 to 25.1, with most of the increase in additional science and math courses. The percentage of high school graduates going on to college has grown even more dramatically—from 48 percent in 1980 to 63 percent in 2000, the highest in the world.

Similarly, there is no question that the racism and sexism that divided the nation throughout most of the twentieth century is waning. Although most schools do remain substantially racially and ethnically isolated, state-mandated segregation has been outlawed; racial segregation in housing finally began a slow decline after 1980; and ghettoization of poor and minority families in high-poverty tracts in inner cities declined substantially in the 1990s. Whether predominantly black, white, brown, yellow, red, tan, or any mix of color and national origin in between, just a decade or two into the twenty-first century, all U.S. schools will have much greater difficulty figuring out who is the majority and who is the minority. Within this generation, minorities and mixed-race students will make up a majority of students in American schools.

Finally, as explored more fully below, there are signs that K–12 schools are beginning to take advantage of new opportunities in the information age—by increasing relevant information on school and student performance and by expanding opportunities for school choice.

## Expansion of Information on School and Student Performance

In April 1983 the Commission on Education Excellence issued its final report, *A Nation at Risk: The Imperative for Educational Reform.* The report included the following dire warning:

> Our nation is at risk. . . . The educational foundations of our society are presently being eroded by a rising tide of mediocrity that threatens our very future as a Nation and a people. . . . If an unfriendly foreign power had attempted to impose on America the mediocre educational per-formance that exists today, we might well have viewed it as an act of war. As it stands, we have allowed this to happen to ourselves.

The report declared in just as apocalyptic terms that the United States was falling behind its international competitors and was "at risk" of becoming a second-class power in the increasingly competitive global economy.

Both of these claims were false. As discussed above, if student achievement in U.S. schools was mediocre in 1983, it was just as bad—or good—in 1950 and was only modestly, if anything, better in 2000. If there was an interna-tional economic war in 1983, within a decade America's workers and firms had won it hands down. This report was of the same ilk as all of the other wrong calls in the 1980s for top-down, industrial policies to better manage all sectors of the U.S. economy.

Nevertheless, *A Nation at Risk* did catalyze an education-reform movement all across the country led by a bipartisan coalition of governors, presidents, and business leaders. National education goals were adopted. Each state developed standards for what students should know and be able to do. Each state developed assessments of student achievement to measure individual student and school progress against each subject matter standard by student age or grade level. States required local districts to test every eight-, twelve-, and sixteen-year-old student in every school. By commanding teachers to teach to these tests, states hoped to align curriculum and student learning in local public schools and thereby improve achievement among students in all schools over time. Twenty years after *A Nation at Risk*, thoughtful proponents of the standards and testing movement suggested that such concerted reform may finally have begun to contribute to budging both overall and lagging minority student achievement upward in several states since 2000.

There is, of course, an alternative explanation for the increase in student achievement in schools in some states since 2000: the substantial increase in the rate of productivity growth generated in most of the service sector since 1996 may also be creeping into schools, albeit belatedly. In this context, it is likely that state standards and test results are beginning to form a useful common currency or language to better inform the actions and choices of parents and children, teachers and students, and schools in some places. Whatever their curious origin, the evolving state standards and assessments may over time provide a key element to enable the market for schools to become more democratic and dynamic—by enabling families to make a more informed choice of school, teachers to make more informed judgments to guide student learning, and elected representatives to make more informed decisions about how to hold schools accountable.

## Expansion of School Choice

From 1993 through 1999 there was a stunning increase in the number of children whose parents chose to enroll them in schools of choice by means other than place of residence. One-third more students enrolled in such schools of choice in 1999 than just six years earlier, including a 45 percent increase in the number of students in public schools of choice. By 1999 parents chose to enroll more than 25 percent of school-age children in schools of choice: public (14.2 percent), private (9.5 percent), or at home (1.6 percent).

Although a disproportionately higher number of public schools of choice serve inner cities, minorities, and the poor, a majority of the children who enroll in such schools are white, non-poor, and live outside central cities. Parents with the wherewithal are also free to vote with their feet by moving in order to choose the local public school at which they will enroll their children. Today, in our increasingly mobile society, a growing plurality of American families can afford to choose the school in which they want their children to be educated. They pay the cost of moving to a new home; they choose among the increasing number and range of available public school choice options; they homeschool; or they pay the cost of tuition at a private school.

Four major impediments still restrict families in choosing the best school at which to educate their children. First, the transaction costs of moving to a favored public school district are very high, more than the cost of tuition at most private schools. As a result, millions of young working families do not have much chance—let alone an equal opportunity—to choose a local public school that will do best for their own children.

Second, millions of minority families with the financial capacity are prevented from moving to a new home in a preferred school district due to racial or ethnic discrimination in the local regional housing markets. Although pervasive racial segregation by residence has begun a slow decline in most metropolitan areas, the customs of racial steering in home-buying and apartment rentals still mark many local housing markets.

Third, the supply of alternative school choices is artificially constrained. The linkage of public school and private residence provides no effective market signal to local school providers about how to respond to the more diverse demands of families for their children's education. Instead, local public schools are controlled by the more narrow commands of their local bureaucracies and local school boards elected by only a small minority of the eligible resident voters, a substantial majority of whom have no children in school; and none of these local officials have any incentive to enroll students whose families do not live within "their" local district.

Fourth, although the range and number of public schools of choice are increasing rapidly, choice is still very limited. Many local districts resist chartering or running public schools of choice to compete within let alone among local school districts. Many local districts also resist efforts by community colleges, universities, and intermediate school districts—much less private schools—to operate, organize, or charter schools to compete with their local public schools. Most local districts still operate as if they were monopoly providers of private schooling for gated clubs that exclude students whose families are not dues-paying, resident members.

## Choice and Inner-City Schools

In 2003, there were a number of inner-city school districts in which a significant number of schools were failing students by any measure. For example, in some urban districts 50 percent of ninth-graders never even made it through the twelfth grade. In other inner-city districts statewide tests revealed that most schools fell below the level of annual yearly progress toward minimum proficiency set by each state.

One response has been to help parents residing in such districts enroll their children in a school that they believe will do better. For example, the sprawling Los Angeles district has chartered over fifty schools since 2000; in response to resident parent demand leading to the chartering two of Los Angeles' largest and highest-performing high schools, School Superintendent Roy Roemer proposed citywide reorganization for all high schools into open-enrollment magnets. Similarly, U.S. Secretary of Education Rod Paige embraced a major magnet program to expand school choice for all families in Houston, while New York City Schools Chancellor Joel Klein nurtured dozens of small alternative schools of choice.

As another example, the State of Ohio established a program to fund expanded school choice for families stuck in poor urban schools. In Cleveland in the 1999–2000 school year, thirty-seven hundred pupils chose to enroll in fifty-six private schools (92 percent in parochial schools); nineteen hundred pupils enrolled in ten charter schools; and nineteen thousand pupils enrolled in twenty-three magnet schools. Despite being invited to participate at no cost in this school choice program, no suburban school district allowed a single Cleveland child to enroll.

Upon review of a claim that this program established religion in violation of the First Amendment, the Supreme Court ruled:

> The Ohio program is entirely neutral with respect to religion. It provides benefits directly to a wide spectrum of individuals, defined only by financial need and residence in a particular school district. It permits such individual [families] to exercise genuine choice among options, public and private, secular and religious. The program is therefore a program of true private choice. We hold that the program does not offend the Establishment Clause.

Similarly diverse programs of school choice have been implemented in other cities in Ohio, and in Wisconsin, Florida, and Colorado.

In 2002, at President George W. Bush's urging, a large bipartisan congressional majority enacted the No Child Left Behind Act to put teeth into the previously mandated standards and assessments adopted by each state for its local districts and schools. The act empowers families of students in schools with poor progress in student achievement to send their children to better-achieving schools in the local district. This act offers another signal that expanding family choice of school beyond choice of residence is an integral part of national education reform; and the Congress appropriated funds for greater school choice, including in private schools, for families in the nation's federal enclave, Washington, D.C.

Publicly supported, universal family choice among competing schools, whether nominally public or private, is already the norm in many democratic nations throughout much of Europe and the Pacific Rim, including under Labor Party leadership in the United Kingdom, New Zealand, and Australia. The particular designs for financing school choice in some of these countries perpetuate significant inequities, for example, by encouraging substantial tuition differentials that disadvantage mot young working families of moderate income and the poor. There is no evidence, however, that any have an adverse impact on the average distribution of student achievement, civic attitudes, voting, or other outputs compared with the United States. Moreover, in none of these other democracies is the choice of a publicly financed school limited to those families with the means to reside in an exclusive neighborhood. Instead, consistent with the United Nations Universal Declaration of Human Rights, these countries are striving to recognize that "parents have a prior right to choose the kind of education that shall be given to their children."

## Democratic School Choice

The decentralized system of local schools in the United States was in substantial flux in the opening years of the twenty-first century. The system was evolving to develop more school choice to respond to the rising demand of parents to choose a quality school for their children. What principles can best guide expansion of school choice in the United States? The school-choice proposition presented above offers a democratic answer: Every family deserves an equal opportunity to choose the publicly supported, tuition-free common school that will best serve their children.

Three sets of subsidiary principles serve to implement this proposition.

Principle 1: Expand family choice of schools, and increase competition among schools for students.

- *Demand:* Family choice of school. A family's opportunity to choose the school that will be best for their own children should not depend on their color, creed, or place of residence, nor on their ability to pay the cost of tuition at a private school or the greater cost of moving to a new home.
- *Supply:* Public support for school choice. Where a state has undertaken to provide the opportunity of an education, it should fund publicly supported schools that are open to students regardless of their color, creed, or place of residence and without their parents having to pay (a) tuition or transportation costs and (b) the greater cost of moving to a home in a different neighborhood.

These twin ideas should not be misunderstood as the supply and demand sides of a simple economic market for a commodity or good. To the contrary, together they create a social market by eliminating from family choice of school two financial variables: (1) differential pricing in the cost of tuition or the costs required for moving to a new home; and (2) the widely varying ability of families to pay for the complex service of learning in school. As a result, all publicly supported K–12 schools must operate as if tuition-free for all families and children.

Nor is the last portion of the demand principle intended as a call to provide low- and moderate-income families with housing vouchers to pay the cost of buying or renting a home in a different neighborhood. Rather, it assures that family choice of publicly supported schools does not *require* a family to move. Under the democratic school-choice proposition presented above, the geographic boundaries of local districts and their school "attendance zones" may not be used to limit enrollment exclusively to residents.

This principle implements the democractic school-choice proposition by engaging all parents directly in exercising their responsibility for choosing the free common school that will do best for their own children. As a result, the proposition is much more about the visible hand of parents than the invisible hand of Adam Smith.

Over time, this principle will also promote much more direct competition between publicly supported schools, including a growing and increasingly diverse supply of publicly supported school providers. Schools governed by local districts will continue to have advantages over other publicly supported schools in competing for students. Such local public schools can continue to compete for nearby residents based on the convenience of location and such affinity as may be generated among residents by the local school board election process.

Some may argue that local school districts are irrelevant in any thoroughly decentralized system of universal family choice. Local districts, however, can enter this social market for school choice as by far the largest current supplier of free common schools open to all. Whether and which local districts will thereafter thrive or wither depends only on each district's ability to continue to supply schools that families choose.

In addition, states should continue to expand the supply of publicly supported choices available to families by encouraging new schools chartered or operated by local districts, intermediate school districts, municipalities, community colleges, universities, and other cultural institutions. States should also consider establishing an independent agency to charter additional schools.

Finally, states must also enable families to choose private schools that agree to participate within the equitable social market established democratically by each state. For example, no private school should participate if it discriminates in its admissions based on a family's wealth, income, race, creed, or place of residence. In addition, admission to private schools must be based solely on need-blind criteria so that no child is excluded because of their parent's inability to pay tuition or any other fee. One means of enforcing this requirement is that any private school tuition-price-per-student higher than the public-support-per-pupil could be met by the private school itself, whether from charitable sources or offering additional scholarship aid to those in need.

In contrast, several "school choice" state ballot initiatives touted by conservative think tanks propose a small "voucher" or "tuition tax credit" to help a few more parents pay whatever admission fee private schools charge. Such proposals utterly fail to empower ordinary, young working families and the poor with a meaningful opportunity to choose any school, public or private, that the parents determine will do better for their children.

Of course, many private schools, both parochial and secular, may decide not to participate in a publicly funded, equitable social market. For example, some religious schools may decide that they wish to serve only members of their faith. Other private schools may decide that they wish to charge parents higher tuition rather than receive public support. Such private schools remain free to choose to rely exclusively on private financing, including tuition, without any public funding.

Whether and how each state may choose to build a dynamic social market of free common schools will no doubt vary. It is difficult to imagine, however, such programs benefiting only inner-city or poor families. In fact, most young working families with children are in the early stages of their earnings careers; these families of modest income also want, and as responsible citizens, deserve, the opportunity to choose the school that they believe will best educate their children.

With the opportunity of school choice comes a reciprocal obligation: Each family must take greater responsibility for assuring that their children succeed in the hard but rewarding work of student learning, in school and at home. Parents, as well as children, will no longer be able to blame "school" or "teacher" for failure to learn. As the opportunity of school choice is extended to all families, parents and children must accept personal responsibility for student learning.

Principle 2: Expand teacher choice of schools, and increase competition among school employers for teachers.

- *Demand:* Teacher choice of school and learning materials. A teacher's opportunity to practice her craft and to be rewarded for her accomplished teaching should not be limited by government-imposed restrictions, either (1) on her primary responsibility for guiding student learning and learning materials in school, or (2) on the mobility of her pension, experience, and credentials.
- *Supply:* Public support of teacher choice of school. States and local school employers should (1) recognize the primary responsibility of teachers for guiding student learning and for learning materials in school, (2) assure that teacher pensions and credentials are fully portable within and between states, and (3) compete for accomplished teachers in national and regional labor markets.

The only way for schools to compete effectively for teachers in the much more open and competitive labor markets of the information age is to respect teachers as responsible professionals. College-educated women are no longer limited by discrimination to "female" jobs. Employers and entrepreneurs throughout the economy value their skills, knowledge, and experience: non-school employers will compete with schools for talented teachers, both male and female. To attract, employ, retain, and reward accomplished teachers, school employers must therefore expand the opportunity for teachers to take primary responsibility for guiding their students' learning in school.

Research suggests that the quality of teachers and their teaching—good or bad—can powerfully impact student learning. There is less evidence that such insights into the fundamental nature of teaching and learning have yet swept through the K–12 schools with any significant impact on student achievement. If an understanding of how individual teachers can inspire students to learn better had truly penetrated education policy, top-down command of schools would be put aside in favor of bottom-up operation of informed choice by families and teachers in a more open social market of competing providers. Lessons learned during the transition to the information age in the rest of the service sector testify to the more powerful impact of continuous reform driven by informed consumers and workers choosing among providers and employers in a competitive market.

A second priority is to make the skills, experience, and accomplishment of teachers—and their pensions—portable between local school employers throughout the country. A voluntary national exchange association made up of the fifty separate state teacher pension systems could be organized to permit trading of pension credits and debits whenever experienced teachers take teaching jobs in another state. In the alternative, new teachers could be afforded the opportunity of a fully portable pension, as college teachers and federal employees were decades ago. The states should also accord reciprocity in credentials to the teachers of any other state with comparable standards for entry into the teaching profession, including alternative avenues available to knowledge workers who wish to switch to teaching in midcareer. Given the increasingly competitive regional and national labor markets for all educated workers, states can no longer afford to wall off teachers into fifty separate schoolteacher-only markets.

With this greater mobility, teachers should gain the confidence to emerge from behind the closed doors of their separate classrooms to take greater personal responsibility with their peers to guide each student's learning. By working together in teams, networking with students and parents at home as well as at school, using the resources of the World Wide Web, and creating and sharing their own learning materials with their peers, teachers can become much more productive professionals in the information age. Teachers may also be aided by the greater personal responsibility that every parent and child must accept for learning in their schools of choice. As a result, teachers may be better able to help guide student learning at home in cooperation with parents who are fully engaged in assuring that their own children seize the opportunity to learn.

By empowering both teachers and families to choose in a dynamic social market for schools, new forms and organization of student learning will emerge. "School" may look much different when students, teachers, and parents can not only choose one another but can network together and learn interactively in school and at home. Smaller schools and longer-term relationships between teachers as professionals and families as clients may replace the old industrial model of big school factories and students being passed in lockstep to different teachers from hour to hour and grade to grade. Groups of teachers may form professional partnerships to own and operate school enterprises to compete with their former school district employers. School may also begin to encompass resources and internships available throughout the community and on the World Wide Web rather than within a single building. New small, fully networked "little red schoolhouses" may emerge. Or schools may continue to look much the same from the outside but will evolve inside by reorganizing the work of teaching and student learning in the classroom and fully integrating interactive networks to connect students, parents, and students with learning opportunities at home.

Principle 3: Expand information on school and student progress and require minimum school progress.

- *Demand:* Reliable information for families. Every school receiving public funds should provide reliable information both (1) confidentially, to parents, of their child's progress throughout the school year, and (2) publicly, to parents, taxpayers, and all other citizens, of overall student achievement and progress, rates of graduation, and year-by-year performance.
- *Supply:* Minimum accountability for all publicly supported schools. Any school receiving public funds that fails in any year to meet minimum levels of overall student-achievement progress set by each state should become ineligible to receive further public support after three years unless the achievement levels at the school rise to meet the minimum progress standards.

The demand factor here can help provide all families, students, teachers, and administrators with better, more reliable information on which to act. As each of the fifty states grapples with implementing state tests and higher education explores changes to national college entrance exams, more meaningful measures of student learning—and the value added by teachers and schools—can emerge. More insightful reporting of student progress and development can then build an ever more useful common currency or language on which parents, children, and teachers may act. Parents can then make not only a more informed choice of school, but with their chosen teachers can also better monitor and encourage their children's learning at the chosen school and at home.

The supply aspect of this principle provides each state with the oversight power to stop all public support for schools that fail, over any four-year period, to enable their students to meet minimum levels of achievement progress set by each state. This form of school accountability supplements the direct market impact of student enrollments changing over time as a result of informed family choice among competing schools. By setting and enforcing a minimum floor of student-achievement progress, states can identify poor schools and deny them public support. In a dynamic social market, failing schools would close to make way for potentially better schools.

Together, these three principles can guide the expansion of universal school choice into a more equitable and dynamic social market of free common schools open to all. What are the potential benefits of such a transition over the next generation?

First, while it can be debated whether and how much the learning of all students—including the disadvantaged and children of ordinary working families previously denied school choice—may improve, the direct engagement of parents and children, students and teachers, in choosing their own school holds potential for improving student achievement over time. At the very least, such engagement of parents in choosing in which school to educate their own children and invest their own time and energy provides a *potential* lever to better enable teachers to engage students in learning in school and at home.

Second, such a social market for elementary and secondary schooling promises to be at least as dynamic and responsive over the next generation as the other competitive parts of the service sector. In fact, the much more equitable social market of tuition-free K–12 education may prove even more responsive over time because all families will have good information and substantial and roughly equal purchasing power in choosing among school providers. At a minimum, such a social market provides schools, teachers, parents, and students with a solid platform for generating the continuous improvement in student learning now possible in the information age.

Finally, there should be no dispute that millions of ordinary working families and the poor deserve an equal opportunity in choosing a good, publicly supported school they determine is best for their children. For too long the system of financing public schooling has limited this opportunity to families with higher incomes in metropolitan areas who can afford the admission price of purchasing a home in an exclusive neighborhood served by a high-performing local school. Again, it is hard to imagine anything in the American democracy more corrosive to students learning to become free, full, and loyal citizens than tens of millions of children experiencing the second-class citizenship of a forced inferior education.

## *School Choice and America's Federal Democracy*

This brings us to a final question: How does a publicly financed social market of common schools fit with the democratic tradition of decentralized local public schools? The short answer is that any social market for publicly supported school choice will evolve in any state *only* if it grows out of and continues to operate, in fact, within the democratic traditions of the American federal republic. Several reasons support this conclusion.

First, the decentralized system has already evolved substantially in this direction. School choice based on factors other than place of residence is expanding rapidly. As of 1999 more than 25 percent of all families exercised the option of choosing a school, and from 1993 to 1999 the number of families exercising this option increased by 33 percent. The momentum for expanding school choice has since picked up substantially, as evidenced by the 80 percent increase in the number of charter schools since 1999 and the national expressions of support for expanding school choice by the U.S. Congress, president, and Supreme Court. A large majority of Americans—of every color, creed, income level, and residential area—now favor the simple proposition that every family should have the opportunity to choose the publicly supported school the parents deem best for their children. In addition, the 2002 *Phi Delta Kappan* annual poll showed for the first time that a majority of Americans would favor a proposal in their state to allow parents to send their children to any public, private, or church-related school and for the state to pay the tuition; and 69 percent of prime childrearing-age families favored such a proposal. Today, the continuing expansion of family choice of school is reaching the tipping point where extending school choice to all families may be inevitable.

Second, a mix of federal, state, and local financing will continue to support schools in such a social market. Along with these funds will come the power of democratic oversight by the voters and their elected representatives at each level of the federal system. The nature and extent to which this power should be exercised to command particular regulations across a broad range of school functions can be debated. But the democratic power of majority rule will remain intact at all levels of government, subject to the restraints imposed by the U.S. Constitution and the traditions of the American federal system. For example, any state or local district surely can deny all public funding to any school—public, charter, or private—that preaches violence against any person, race, national origin, or creed or teaches the overthrow of representative democracy in the United States: no breeding grounds for intolerance or terrorism need apply.

Third, states have long permitted, encouraged, or funded a wide range of private and public service providers to compete with local government providers, including school districts. Similarly, state and federal legislatures and courts have long imposed a variety of restrictions on local government financing, exclusivity or monopoly provision of services, including on local school districts. From this perspective, increasing the competition faced by each local district provider of schools would amount to no more than another aspect of the ever evolving interplay in the United States between democracy, decentralization, and competition among local jurisdictions and alternative public and private providers of service.

To be sure, there is vigorous opposition in some quarters to extending school choice to all families regardless of income, race, religion or residence. First, some individuals residing in exclusive neighborhoods served by high-performing schools fear that the value of their homes or the quality of their schools may be adversely impacted if school choice is extended to families of lesser means. Second, some teachers fear that their job security or bargaining power with their local district employers will be threatened in a climate of enhanced choice. Third, some communitarians and other community activists contend that particular schools should serve particular communities, with attendance limited to children residing in the community. Such opponents of school choice ignore the idea that in a democracy—and in neighborhoods throughout the United States' expanding metropolitan regions—the glue that holds civil societies together and provides vitality to communities is voluntary association.

There are many voters who fear—and many partisan politicians who claim—that the only available educational policy choice is saving local public schools as now financed, organized, governed, and chosen, or funding parochial schools at the expense of public education. Inequitable proposals to fund small vouchers or tax credits, which do not extend any meaningful opportunity of school choice to low- and moderate-income families, offer easy fodder for opponents of more equitable, fully funded school choice.

There are also education policy researchers who oppose expanding school choice—even if fully and equitably funded and offering accountability and democratic control—because there is not sufficient empirical evidence available to prove that this reform will lead to better student learning or better citizens. Finally, there are some who oppose any public financing of a social market for family choice of school because, they argue, schooling is too important in a democracy to give individual parents the power to choose which institution will serve their children. Of course, both sets of opponents ignore the systematic inequity of the market for public school choice that has long been tolerated—families choosing among local public schools as best they can afford, depending on their widely varying incomes, by their choice of private residence.

Given the intensity of this continuing opposition, it is impossible to predict with any certainty whether and how the expansion of school choice will evolve in any state into a more dynamic social market of free common schools open to all. Any such evolution will result only from the voting power of the people and decisions and rules set by elected and appointed officials at all levels and branches of government. Over time, these diverse representative decisions, no doubt varying from state to state, will interact with the choices of tens of millions of families, millions of teachers, and thousands of schools. Any dynamic social market of universal family choice among free common schools that emerges will thereby be squarely embedded in the democratic traditions of the American federal republic.

It is time to build on the United States' increasingly diverse, decentralized system of K–12 education by enabling all families, regardless of income, to choose the publicly supported school that is best for their children. By empowering all families with this equal opportunity, states and their local districts can once again lead the United States and the world in achieving the democratic ideal of free common schools open to all.

## *Bibliography*

For discussion of racial segregation in schools and housing, ghettoization by race and socioeconomic status, and restrictions on residential choice in metropolitan areas:

Cashin, Sheryll. *The Failures of Integration: How Race and Class Are Undermining the American Dream.* New York: Public Affairs, 2004.

Dimond, Paul R. *Beyond Busing: Inside the Challenge to Urban Segregation.* Ann Arbor: University of Michigan Press, 1985.

Dimond, Paul R. "Empowering Families to Vote with Their Feet." In *Reflections on Regionalism,* edited by Bruce Katz, pp. 249–271. Washington, D.C.: Brookings Institution Press, 2000.

Jargowsky, Paul A. *Poverty and Place: Ghettos, Barrios and the American City.* New York: Russell Sage, 1996.

Kluger, Richard. *Simple Justice: The History of Brown v. Board of Education and Black America's Struggle for Equality.* New York: Knopf, 1976.

For discussion of the market theory of school choice based on preferred levels of local taxation and inequities in local school financing based on local tax wealth:

Buchanan, James M. *Public Finance in Democratic Process: Fiscal Institutions and Individual Choice.* Chapel Hill: University of North Carolina Press, 1967.

Coons, John E., William H. Clune III, and Stephen D. Sugarman. *Private Wealth and Public Education.* Cambridge, Mass.: Belknap Press of Harvard University Press, 1970.

Coons, John E. *Education by Choice: The Case for Family Control.* Berkeley: University of California Press, 1978.

Tiebout, Charles M. "A Pure Theory of Local Expenditures," *Journal of Political Economy* 64 (October 1956): 416–424.

For statistics and discussion of rates of productivity growth in the U.S. economy:

Bosworth, Barry P. and Jack E. Triplett. "Productivity Measurement Issues in Service Industries: 'Baumol's Disease' Has Been Cured" (Washington, D.C.: Brookings Institution, 2003), http://www.brook.edu/views/articles/bosworth/200309.htm.

Gordon, Robert. "Five Puzzles in the Behavior of Productivity, Investment and Innovation," September 10, 2003, http://faculty-web.at.northwestern.edu/economics/gordon/researchhome.html.

Greenspan, Alan. Remarks on productivity at the U.S. Department of Labor and American Enterprise Institute Conference, Washington, D.C., October 23, 2002, http://www.federalreserve.gov/BOARDDOCS/SPEECHES/2002/20021023/default.htm

U.S. Department of Labor Bureau of Labor Statistics. "Major Sector Productivity and Cost Index, 1947–2002," http://data.bls.gov.

For statistics on and discussion of historic data relating to schools, academic performance, school choice, and international comparisons: See the various periodic and special reports with statistical appendices available from the National Center for Education Statistics, http://nces.ed.gov., including "The Digest of Education Statistics"; "The Condition of Education"; "Trends in the Use of School Choice, 1993–1999"; and "Trends in Academic Performance."

For discussion of conflicting views of public opinion and preliminary empirical evidence on the potential impact and limits of various accountability systems, including standards, information, and extending family choice of school beyond residence:

Barnard, John, et al. "Principal Stratification Approach to Broken Randomized Experiments: A Case Study of School Choice," *Journal of the American Statistical Association*, 462 (June 2003).

Caldwell, Brian and John Roskam. "Australia's Education Choices" (Canberra: Menzies Research Centre, 2002), www.mrcltd.org.au.

Coleman, James S. and Thomas Hoeffer. *Public and Private High Schools: The Impact of Communities.* New York: Basic Books, 1987.

Fiske, Edward B., and Helen F. Ladd. *When Schools Compete: A Cautionary Tale.* Washington, D.C.: Brookings Institution Press, 2000.

Gill, Brian P., et al. *Rhetoric versus Reality: What We Know and What We Need to Know about Vouchers and Charter Schools.* Santa Monica, Calif.: Rand, 2001.

Gorard, Stephen, John Fitz, and Chris Taylor, "School Choice Impacts: What Do We Know?" *Educational Researcher* 30, no. 7 (2001).

Hoxby, Caroline ed., *The Economics of Education.* Chicago: University of Chicago Press, 2003.

Krueger, Alan B., and Pei Zhu. "Another Look at the New York City School Voucher Experiment," December 2002, http://www.irs.princeton.edu/krueger/working_papers.html

Moe, Terry M. *Schools, Vouchers and the American Public.* Washington, D.C.: Brookings Institution Press, 2001.

Smith, Marshall, "Standards-Based Reform." Philadelphia: Consortium for Policy Research in Education, 2003.

For more detailed discussion of ways to extend equal opportunity school choice to all families, including young working families and other families with low and moderate incomes, within the United States:

Coons, John E. "Dodging Democracy: The Educator's Flight from the Specter of Choice," *American Journal of Education* (forthcoming 2005).

Coons, John E., and Stephen D. Sugarman. *Making School Choice Work for All Families: A Template for Legislative and Policy Reform*. San Francisco: Pacific Research Institute for Public Policy, 1999.

Gorman, Siobhan. "Pro Choice: How Democrats Can Make Vouchers Their Secret Weapon" (*Washington Monthly,* September 2003), http://washingtonmonthly.com/features/2003/o309.gorman.html.

National Commission on Choice in K–12 Education. *School Choice: Doing It the Right Way Makes a Difference* (Washington, D.C.: Brown Center on Education Policy, Brookings Institution, 2003), http://www.brook.edu/gs/brown/20031117school-choicereport.htm.

Reid, Alan. "Reconciling Choice and the Public Good: Towards an Education Commons," U.S.-Australia Education Policy Discussion Forum, August 4, 2007.

Rottherhan, Andrew J. "Putting Vouchers in Perspective," July 2002, Progressive Policy Institute report, www.ppionline.org/ppi_ci.cfm?contentid=250627&knlgAreaID=110&subsecid=134.

# AFTERWORD:
## DEMOCRATIC DISAGREEMENT AND CIVIC EDUCATION

## *Amy Gutmann*

THIS BOOK ADDRESSES A WIDE RANGE OF THE CHAL-
lenges that are faced in educating future generations of democratic citizens. Some pressing challenges stem from demographic processes that
are creating an aging population, which may siphon away economic support for
education of the young toward caring for the old. Other challenges arise from
growing social and economic inequalities, making the work of schools in providing an education of both high quality and equal opportunity for all children
increasingly difficult.

There are limits to what is educationally possible at any given time, but it is
essential to recognize that democratic societies have significant choices to make
among competing educational ends and means. Even if we never achieve a complete societal consensus, the search for ways of living together with our disagreements as fellow citizens has profound educational implications. Whether
consciously or not, democracies rely on educational systems to shape the way in
which diverse individuals learn from one another—or fail to do so—both within
and across generations. That is what education—for better and for worse—is
about.

This book is in large part concerned with how educational systems of various sorts can support the betterment of a democratic society. I will suggest here
how we might orient our search for an answer by way of a democratic perspective—which takes disagreement seriously while benefiting from alternative
approaches to problems.

Moral disagreement—disagreement about the desirable way to address
issues that pertain to individuals' moral positions (gay marriage, stem cell
research, and abortion are possible examples) is a persistent feature of an open

democratic society. Free and equal citizens can be expected to have different ideas about how to address these matters politically.

What is the capacity of a democratic society to cope in a morally reasonable way with political disagreements among citizens? The first part of my answer highlights three major ways that a democracy deals with disagreement: procedurally, constitutionally, and deliberatively. Each of these approaches is emphasized by a major conception of American democracy. Yet when push comes to shove, proceduralists, constitutionalists, and deliberative democrats alike recognize that fair procedures, constitutional rights, and moral deliberation are *all necessary, none sufficient* in engaging the wide range of disagreements that are unavoidable in a morally pluralistic society. The second part of my answer connects these three ways of dealing with disagreement with corresponding skills and virtues of democratic citizenship. The third part connects these skills and virtues with a rationale for the public schools' embrace of civic education.

## Democratic Approaches to Disagreement

How can democracy best respond to moral disagreements?[1] Procedures are necessary for the fair and peaceful resolution of moral conflicts, and no one has yet proposed a decision-making procedure that is generally more justified than majority rule. If political equals disagree on moral matters, then the greater rather than the lesser number should normally rule. The alternative imposes the claims of the minority on the majority. The alternative may sometimes be preferable, but it calls for a justification of why some citizens' moral convictions count for more than those of others.

When majority rule is justified, the decision of a majority at any particular time is provisional. Subsequent majorities may enact revisions. Members of the losing minority can accept majoritarianism as a fair practice even when it yields incorrect results, as long as the minority's status as political equals is respected. The results of majority rule are legitimate as long as the procedure is fair. The results are not necessarily right. Numerical might does not make a decision morally right. When majority rule is not the fairest procedure, then another procedure needs to be justified with a rationale that is compatible with democratic values.

Fair procedures are essential to a healthy democratic society. But for procedures to be fair, citizens must appreciate the value of fairness as well as the value of majority rule (or its cousin, plurality rule). Majority rule is not always fair in and of itself. It typically must be accompanied by a concern for fairness so that majority decisions do not infringe upon the legitimate claims of individuals who find themselves in the minority. Fundamental constitutional values—including free speech, a free press, free association, the rule of law, universal adult suffrage, and religious freedom—serve therefore as constraints on majority rule in

American constitutional democracy. Some of these values are justified on procedurally democratic grounds; some are necessary to preserve the integrity of the democratic process over time. If a majority votes to disenfranchise women, for example, then it will be destroying an important precondition of a fair democratic procedure: universal adult suffrage. Something similar can be said if majorities take it upon themselves to restrict political speech, which is necessary to ensure that the considered opinions of citizens as free and equal beings are allowed public expression.

But it is not only as a condition of a fair democratic process that constitutional constraints on majority rule can be justified. Freedom of religion and conscience, and equal protection under the law, for example, are valuable independently of any contribution they make to the democratic nature of the political process. Religious freedom is widely recognized as a basic liberty of individuals, and deserves protection as an important value in its own right, not only as a precondition of a fair democratic process. Equal protection under the law is necessary to protect the basic opportunities of all individuals. As these examples suggest, American constitutional democracy recognizes certain substantive values not only as preconditions to a fair democratic process but as fundamental values independently of that process, and as such, they represent a second basis for resolving political disagreements.

The Bill of Rights is the primary (although not the only) collective reference point for these substantive values in American democracy. Not only the judiciary, but legislatures, bureaucracies, private associations, and individual citizens are responsible for respecting and protecting individual rights, to the extent that it is within their legitimate power. Constitutional rights need to be protected against both majorities and minorities who threaten the basic liberties or basic opportunities of individuals.

The basic liberties and opportunities of individuals are not always easily discernible. In the past, American constitutional democracy did not recognize or respect many of the basic liberties and opportunities that are routinely recognized and respected today, most conspicuously those of women and black Americans, but also of many other Americans. It would be hubris on the part of American citizens today to assume that American political institutions are now recognizing every basic liberty and opportunity, and not only those now considered "worthy" of protection.

It is also obvious (although too easily overlooked) that Americans disagree on how to interpret even constitutional protections—including freedom of speech, religious freedom, equal protection, and due process of law—that most Americans would affirm in the abstract. The "we" who disagree, often reasonably, include Supreme Court justices, legislators, public officials in charge of interpreting statutes, and private citizens to whom public officials are accountable.

We cannot realistically expect to resolve all of our politically relevant disagreements, nor would it be desirable for us to do so unless we resolved them on terms that were clearly justifiable. But who among us can demonstrate that controversies over abortion, affirmative action, capital punishment, pornography, school reform, health care reform, welfare reform, foreign interventions, and terms of trade with foreign countries are resolvable, either for now or once and for all, on clearly justifiable terms?

The third way that democracies can deal with disagreements is by citizens and public officials deliberating over the moral disagreements that proceduralism and constitutionalism, taken alone, leave unresolved. Deliberation is public discussion and decision making that aims to reach a justifiable resolution, where possible, and that fosters respect among individuals with regard to those reasonable disagreements that remain irresolvable. James Madison emphasized the importance of deliberation to American democracy, or what he and the other founders called republican government.[2] Voting is a far more valuable act if preceded by open-minded argument in which different sides not only represent their own views, but also listen to others and try to reach an economy of moral disagreement—avoiding unnecessary conflict by searching significant points of convergence—which minimizes rejection of those opposing positions that are worthy of respect.[3]

Defenders of proceduralism, constitutionalism, and deliberative democracy agree that the fundamental values of democratic institutions—such as equal political liberty—must be justified by moral arguments that are in principle acceptable to citizens who are bound by them. All seek to show that democratic institutions protect the equal right of citizens to participate in political processes and to enjoy basic liberties and opportunities. They also agree that individual citizens should be regarded as moral agents who deserve equal respect in any justifications of basic procedures and constitutional rights.

Deliberation, rather than being an alternative to procedures or constitutional rights, adds to both proceduralism and constitutionalism a way of explicitly respecting individuals as moral agents in a context of continual disagreement about important issues in everyday democratic discussion and decision making. Deliberation calls upon citizens and public officials to try to justify their political positions to one another, and in so doing to take into account the viewpoints of others who reasonably disagree. We can sum up the relationship between proceduralism, constitutionalism, and deliberation: Democratic procedures require that individuals are counted as one, and no more than one, among equals in political decision making. Constitutional rights require that the basic liberties and opportunities of all individuals are respected and protected even against a majority's decision to override those rights. Democratic deliberation requires that individuals discuss their political disagreements with one another, including disagreements over fair procedures and constitutional rights, in an attempt to economize on moral disagreements and respect those that invariably remain.

If fair procedures, constitutional constraints, and moral deliberation could resolve political disagreements once and for all, then a sophisticated democratic form of government would not be necessary. But an end to political disagreement in any modern democracy would reflect the rise of repression, not the success of proceduralism, constitutionalism, and deliberation.

## Skills and Virtues for Dealing with Disagreement

For its effectiveness in dealing with disagreements, American constitutional democracy has been designed to depend partly on institutions such as an electoral system that secures one person, one vote, a judiciary empowered to protect constitutional rights, and a legislature that deliberates before it votes. But people with certain skills and virtues—not those of saints, but those of citizens—are needed to realize the moral promise of the methods of proceduralism, constitutionalism, and deliberation. These methods do not work automatically. They depend for their success on citizens and accountable public officials acting in a spirit of cooperation and mutual understanding. One need only think of a citizenry voting to disenfranchise women and a judiciary deferring to the majority on this decision. Or one might imagine voting on any and all public matters by means of a personal computer terminal without any deliberation among citizens or their representatives. Considering these possibilities serves to indicate the considerable extent to which American democracy depends on the willingness and ability of individuals to support institutions that try to resolve disagreements consistently with fair procedures, constitutional rights, and public reasoning.

The procedural, constitutional, and deliberative practices that exist in American democracy depend on the ongoing support of citizens and their representatives. But this is only half of the story. Those practices that *could improve* the capacity of American democracy to resolve disagreements also depend on citizens and their representatives to collectively identify and create them. And those that present obstacles to improving American democracy similarly depend on citizens to reject them.

There is no reason to believe that either every existing practice and policy or none well serves the purposes of proceduralism, constitutionalism, and deliberation as modes of resolving disagreements on moral terms in American democracy. In light of the reasonable disagreements that exist, citizens and representatives should try to justify controversial political practices to one another.

Mutual justification is often an effective means to better outcomes, and it is also in itself a manifestation of mutual respect. Deliberation is the greatest political promise of American democracy. It is also one of the greatest challenges, especially as the United States continues to grow in diversity.

Proceduralism, constitutionalism, and deliberation depend on individuals in ways that therefore call for certain civic skills and virtues that would otherwise be less important. To the extent that these skills and virtues are closely connected to democracy's ways of dealing with disagreement, publicly funded schools should be called upon to cultivate them. Various skills and virtues are needed to support proceduralism, constitutionalism, and deliberation, and there are a number of ways in which schools can be called upon to foster them.

Each way of resolving disagreements calls upon citizens to exercise certain civic skills and virtues more than others. Proceduralism requires law-abidingness, respect for fair rules, and reasonable expectations of winning and losing. Fair political procedures cannot possibly guarantee that any person's opinion will carry the day, even when that person's opinion is correct. Proceduralism therefore also requires a capacity to delay gratification of one's desires, to tolerate dissent, and to persist in pursuing an outcome that one believes is just.

Proceduralism cannot assume that established procedures are fair, so it also calls for the ability of citizens to discern the difference between fair and unfair procedures. Citizens should try to change unfair procedures, in the way that some Americans opposed the discriminatory poll tax in 1964. Citizens also need to discern the difference between procedural outcomes that lie within the bounds of constitutional legitimacy and those that do not. From the perspective of procedural democracy, for example, a majority vote to decrease (or even end) public support of the arts is a qualitatively different outcome from a majority vote to fine or disenfranchise artists whose work offends the moral sensibilities of the majority. The former is within the legitimate power of the majority to legislate, while the latter is not.

People are likely to disagree about where the legitimate power of the majority ends and illegitimate power begins (where individual rights are violated). Others may disagree about fair democratic procedures in today's political context. Thoughtful citizens are bound to disagree over a wide range of procedural matters, since a wide range is subject to reasonable disagreement. Any procedure that is in place for resolving such disagreements over process is itself likely to be subject to reasonable disagreement. There is no morally certain escape from the possibility of such ongoing disagreement. Proceduralism looks to procedures for resolving disagreements. But it must look beyond procedures in any narrow sense of the term for dealing with moral disagreements about those procedures, such as which are fair and what outcomes are illegitimate, even if they followed from established procedures.

This limitation of proceduralism in dealing with disagreement points to the need for citizens to possess another important set of skills and virtues, without which proceduralism would be far less likely to distinguish fair from unfair or legitimate from illegitimate. These skills and virtues are closely tied to constitutionalism and deliberation. Constitutionalism calls for the capacity of citizens to distinguish between legitimate and illegitimate outcomes of political procedures, as well as between fair and unfair procedures. Citizens must not only discern their own rights but also respect the rights of others. Restraint is often required to respect the rights of others, as when someone publicly speaks in terms that are morally offensive. Constitutionalism also calls on citizens to have the courage to stand up for those rights that are being violated, whether by a minority or majority.[4]

Several important constitutional rights—such as free speech and freedom of religion—require citizens to possess the virtue of tolerance. Other constitutional rights—such as equal protection and due process—require citizens to possess and practice the virtue of nondiscrimination in their everyday associations with one another. Americans must not discriminate against one another on the basis of color, gender, religion, and sexual orientation in any business, commercial endeavor, or other public association. And they must be able to discern what kind of behavior nondiscrimination entails: more than just a prohibition on charging more or paying people less but also a prohibition on decreasing (or increasing) their opportunities because of irrelevant characteristics such as skin color.

Because deliberation entails trying to reason together about public policy in an effort to reach mutually acceptable decisions, it explicitly calls upon citizens who disagree on many moral and political issues not only to tolerate one another but also to develop mutual respect. Mutual respect entails the capacity to discern and respectfully discuss disagreements over what constitute fair procedures and defensible constitutional rights. Both the procedural and constitutional aspects of democracy have more potential for self-improvement to the extent that citizens and their accountable representatives are willing to deliberate about fairness and legitimacy of outcomes.

Although the civic skills associated with democracy also include the ability to negotiate and bargain, the deliberative capacity of citizens is needed to distinguish between those times when bargaining and negotiation are more and less appropriate. Bargaining and negotiation, we might think, are important skills to enlist in situations where agreement on moral terms is unnecessary (because nothing morally important is at stake) or undesirable (because one or another side in the controversy is unwilling to assume a moral perspective and therefore likely to take advantage of anyone who did). It is the willingness and ability to deliberate that enables citizens to discern when these situations arise. Without the capacity to deliberate, there would be no escaping from power politics—which give power priority over both justice and deliberation— which all moral conceptions of democracy are intent on avoiding.

Why do American citizens need to deliberate about constitutional rights when a written constitution enumerates those rights, and a judiciary is authorized to interpret and enforce them? Any extended discussion of the practical implications of free speech, religious freedom, and nondiscrimination would demonstrate that interpretations of constitutional rights are open to reasonable disagreement.

Does the constitutional protection of free speech also protect all forms of pornography? Does the constitutional protection of religious freedom permit parents to exempt their children from any parts of a public school curriculum that offend their religious beliefs? Does the constitutional prohibition on racial discrimination also extend to a prohibition on taking race into account as one factor among many in employment or college admissions?

For these and many other disagreements to be resolved on moral terms, rather than by self-interested or group-interested bargaining, citizens and their accountable representatives must be willing to engage in a politics of reasoning and persuasion rather than a politics of manipulation and coercion. Individuals also must be willing to engage in public discourse with one another that is empirically informed and morally reasonable. They must recognize and treat other citizens as equals in democratic discourse and decision making on the condition that they themselves are extended the same recognition and treatment. This capacity is sometimes called civility. But it should not be confused with etiquette or politeness. Civility is a moral (not an aesthetic) attitude, which depends on reciprocity. You treat me as an equal, provided I treat you as such.

We earn each other's respect as equal citizens in some very basic ways. We show ourselves capable of abiding by the results of fair procedures, honoring the rights of others, and supporting the passage of laws and public policies that we can justify to one another. We develop and defend our political positions by addressing the reasonable concerns of others, and we have similar expectations of others. Without the civic skills and virtues that allow individuals to earn one another's respect as equal citizens, a democracy cannot resolve the disagreements that arise among its citizens on moral grounds or expect its citizens to live well with those disagreements that invariably remain.

## Fostering Civic Skills and Virtues in Schools

What role should schools play in cultivating the civic skills and virtues of a democratic society? A citizenry without the tools that support proceduralism, constitutionalism, and deliberation does not bode well for a democratic society. There is a great deal of concern today that families, schools, and other social institutions are not cultivating the skills and virtues of democratic deliberation. There is also a great deal of cynicism about whether any single person or institution has the will or the means to make a moral difference. In contemporary political discourse, communicating by sound bite, competing by character assassination, and resolving conflicts through self-seeking bargaining, logrolling, and pork barreling too often substitute for moral deliberation on the merits of issues.

354

Recommitting primary and secondary education in the United States to the value of democratic citizenship would be one important way of reducing this democratic deficit. Although the need for American political life to rely less on sound bites and more on substantive interchange is ever more widely appreciated, the need to improve education in a more democratic direction is still sorely neglected, to the detriment of both education and democracy. Unless American citizens, educators, and public officials alike increase their appreciation of educating all children, not merely for literacy, numeracy, and economic productivity but for the more inclusive goal of democratic citizenship, they forsake the promise of American democracy. Emphasizing the civic responsibilities of the American educational system is certainly not the only way to improve either the educational system or American democracy, neither is it sufficient by itself. Nonetheless, the public justification offered for a publicly funded system of primary and secondary education has long been that of providing educational opportunity for all and educating all to the skills and virtues of democratic citizenship. There is no single realm more distinctively connected to these two purposes. Moreover, there is a greater social need than ever for schools to focus on civic purposes in light of the decline in other civic associations and the increasing demands placed on parents outside the family. Parents undoubtedly can have more influence over children than schools, but they also have far broader responsibilities for children than that of education for opportunity and citizenship.

Schools are the major realm in which every nonadult member of society should, if possible, be taught the skills and virtues that are necessary for effective citizenship in an increasingly complex and interdependent society. Well-run schools model some of the most basic skills and virtues of a democratic society: they institutionalize fair procedures, honor individual rights, and expect all individuals to demonstrate mutual respect by doing their share to contribute to an overriding mission.

There is also evidence, outlined in several excellent studies, that the curriculum of schools can make a difference in teaching some of the more demanding virtues of democratic citizenship, such as toleration and mutual respect.[5] Some of these studies show that diverse groups of students, working together on a project over an extended period of time, effectively increase toleration, a result that demonstrates some staying power over time.

A skeptic might still challenge the idea that teaching toleration can be publicly defended in light of the differing perspectives about right and wrong, good and bad, decent and indecent, worthy and unworthy, that are present in a pluralistic, multicultural democracy. But the skeptical challenge either proves too much or too little. It proves too much if it doubts that publicly subsidized schools can defend the teaching of *any* values. Schools cannot help but teach values, even if they do so unconsciously, in the way that they decide who teaches and who is taught, what is included and excluded from the curriculum, and how students are taught inside and outside of the classroom. The claim that teaching toleration is controversial proves too little if it simply calls attention to the lack of universal agreement on almost any basic value. The fact that toleration and other fundamental values of American democracy are controversial offers no reason not to defend their teaching. Quite the contrary, were the fundamental values of democracy uncontroversial, there would be far less reason for schools to concern themselves with teaching civic values.

Publicly subsidized schools, like democratic governments more generally, are public trusts. Democratic societies have no better alternative than to educate future citizens to those civic values, such as toleration, that are procedurally, constitutionally, and deliberatively defensible. Schools in the United States can teach toleration—probably not under all circumstances and against all odds, but in enough situations that the call for civic education in schools is not an idle one. Schools can also teach deliberation. Diane Ravitch has cited an excellent example of the way in which a public school in Brooklyn, New York, taught students to deliberate in a history class. The students in the class were discussing whether it was moral for the United States to drop the atomic bomb on Japan:

> The lesson was taught in a Socratic manner. [Mr.] Bruckner [the teacher] did not lecture. He asked questions and kept up a rapid-fire dialogue among the students. "Why?" "How do you know?" "What does this mean?" . . . By the time the class was finished, the students had covered a great deal of material about American foreign and domestic politics during World War II; they had argued heatedly; most of them had tried out different points of view, seeing the problem from different angles.[6]

This kind of teaching makes students exercise and thereby develop their capacities to reason collectively about politics—an ability that is no less essential to democratic citizenship because it is difficult to measure by survey research. Some surveys show that different kinds of teaching do make a difference in terms of how effective civic education is in the classroom.[7]

Education is not only a public good. The parental prerogative must also be given its due in a constitutional and deliberative democracy. Parents are a child's primary educators, except in desperately unfortunate situations. But just as democratic governments in the United States are constitutionally bound to recognize the rights of parents, parents have a constitutional responsibility as American citizens to recognize that their children are future citizens of a democratic society, with their own rights and responsibilities.

Should schools go beyond teaching the most basic virtue of toleration and also teach mutual respect? Toleration—an attitude of live and let live that entails no positive regard among citizens—is an essential value of American constitutional democracy, and one of its great historical accomplishments. Toleration makes possible peace—a precondition for all other democratic accomplishments. But toleration is not enough to create a democratic society with liberty and justice for all, where "all" includes people of differing religions, ethnicities, colors, and cultures. Absent mutual respect, people discriminate against one another on the basis of a host of cultural differences; we fail to take one another's political perspectives seriously; and we therefore treat one another in ways that are not conducive to constructive collective action. If educators do not try to teach future citizens the importance of mutual respect among people whose ideas and perspectives on life differ from their own, then who will?

Educators can teach mutual respect by encouraging their students to engage in the give and take of argument, as did Mr. Bruckner in the Brooklyn public school example given above. In the process of arguing vigorously but respectfully about a political issue, students learn to reflect, individually and collectively, on both the reasonable differences and commonalties that constitute a pluralistic democracy.

Toleration and recognition of cultural differences are both desirable parts of multicultural education. As part of their democratic and civic education, students should learn not only how to accept differences among groups that constitute society, but also to recognize the role that cultural differences have played in shaping society and the world in which children live. To teach and to learn in this way requires open-mindedness and engagement on the part of both teachers and students with perspectives different from one's own. It does not entail either moral relativism or skepticism.

Mutual respect can be cultivated by learning from diverse people and perspectives, not by giving up one's own beliefs, but by acknowledging that one's beliefs are informed by those of others. Learning to learn from others does not promise resolution of all the differences that divide a pluralistic democracy. Such comprehensive unity is surely impossible in a free society, and in all likelihood undesirable. Learning to learn from others is part of the virtue of mutual respect among citizens, and mutual respect expresses the democratic ideal of equal citizenship.

Mutual respect is also an instrumental value: it enables a democracy to resolve provisionally as many differences as possible in a mutually acceptable way. Bringing more mutual respect into education addresses the challenge of moral pluralism on democratic terms, rather than trying to dissolve differences by either philosophical or political fiat.

A study of perspectives on citizenship education suggests that despite varying views among social studies teachers of what citizenship education ideally should be, self-identified conservatives, moderates, and liberals all share a core set of convictions about citizenship education that include the following: encouraging tolerance and open-mindedness, addressing controversial issues, and developing an understanding of different cultures.[8] These are also among the civic virtues recommended by procedural, constitutional, and deliberative ways of resolving disagreements in democracy. I have suggested some ways that schools can teach these virtues and cited some studies that provide an "existence proof" that some ways of teaching make a positive difference in teaching some of these virtues. Were there a will among schools to teach the virtues and skills of democratic citizenship, the evidence suggests that there would be more than one way to do so.

Democratically justifiable schools are ones that work toward a democratic ideal of civic equality: individuals should be treated and treat one another as equal citizens, regardless of their gender, race, ethnicity, race, or religion. More or less civic equality distinguishes more from less democratic societies. Democratic education—publicly supported education that is defensible according to a democratic ideal—should educate children so that they are capable of assuming the rights and correlative responsibilities of equal citizenship, which include respecting other people's equal rights. In short, democratic education should both express and develop the capacity of all children to become equal citizens.

There is no simple substitute for judging schools—however they are chosen—on their educational merits, where those merits include civic education. Civic education—the aims of which include the ability to argue and appreciate, understand and criticize, persuade and collectively decide in a way that is mutually respectable even if not universally acceptable—is a central merit of schools in a constitutional democracy. The fairness of our political processes, the protection of our constitutional rights, and the quality of our collective deliberations are all the more important in this context. Schools that cultivate the capacity of citizens to deliberate on moral terms about their ongoing disagreements are our best hope for the future of American democracy.[9]

## Notes

1. The author relies in this essay on arguments and evidence presented in Amy Gutmann and Dennis Thompson, *Democracy and Disagreement* (Cambridge, Mass.: Harvard University Press, 1996).
2. See especially "Jared Sparks: Journal," in *The Records of the Federal Convention of 1787*, edited by Max Farrand, rev. ed. (New Haven, Conn.: Yale University Press, 1966), vol. 3, 479.
3. A discussion and defense of the democratic virtue of economizing on moral disagreement can be found in Gutmann and Thompson, *Democracy and Disagreement,* esp. 82–94.
4. This description and an excellent discussion of virtues attached to constitutional democracy can be found in William Galston, *Liberal Purposes: Goods, Virtues, and Diversity in the Liberal State* (Cambridge, U.K., and New York: Cambridge University Press, 1991), esp. 224–27.
5. For evidence on the effectiveness of teaching tolerance, see: Patricia G. Avery et al., "Exploring Political Tolerance with Adolescents," Theory and Research in Social

Education 20, no. 4 (fall 1992): 386–420. The pedagogical techniques that are detailed in this study include important aspects of teaching mutual respect as well as toleration.

6. Diane Ravitch, The Schools We Deserve: Reflections on the Educational Crises of Our Times (New York: Basic Books, 1985), 288.

7. Morris Janowitz discusses some surveys that "indicate that students in classrooms exposed to moderate-to-frequent amounts of classroom discussion about politics did better than those without such discussion." Students exposed to political discussion in the classroom demonstrated both better reasoning capacities and more factual knowledge. See Janowitz, The Reconstruction of Patriotism: Education for Civic Consciousness (Chicago: University of Chicago Press, 1983), 154. For another discussion of the desirability and possibility of teaching deliberation in schools, see Amy Gutmann, Democratic Education (Princeton, N.J.: Princeton University Press, 1987).

8. Christopher Anderson et al., "Perspectives on Citizenship Education," paper presented at the Annual Meeting of the American Educational Research Association, San Francisco, April 22, 1995.

9. Special thanks to the Spencer Foundation for the Senior Scholar Grant that supported work on this article.

# INDEX

# Index

# Index

Index

# Index